This second edition was researched and written by **HENRY STEDMAN**. He's been writing guidebooks for over 20 years now and is the author of Trailblazer's guides to *Kilimanjaro, Coast to Coast Path, Hadrian's Wall Path, Cleveland Way, Dales Way* and the co-author of their three titles to the *South West Coast Path*. With him on this trek, as with every walk he does in the UK, was **DAISY**, his (mostly) faithful dog. An experienced long-distance walker, Daisy has already completed all the trails above with Henry and her ambition is to walk all 15 National Trails.

JOEL NEWTON discovered a passion for walking national trails in 2007 when he tackled the 630-mile South-West Coast Path. Despite ill-fitting shoes that caused blisters and a bag that was far too heavy, that journey was the inspiration for many more on the long-distance paths of Britain. He has since completed Offa's Dyke Path, West Highland Way, Great Glen Way, Hadrian's Wall Path, Cotswold Way and sections of the Pennine Way. He is co-author of Trailblazer's *South West Coast Path* series of guides and this is his fourth book.

Authors

914.2
N

The Thames Path First edition 2015; this second edition June 2018

Publisher: Trailblazer Publications
The Old Manse, Tower Rd, Hindhead, Surrey, GU26 6SU, UK
www.trailblazer-guides.com

British Library Cataloguing in Publication Data
A catalogue record for this book is available from the British Library

ISBN 978-1-905864-97-3

© **Trailblazer** 2015, 2018; Text and maps

Editor: Anna Jacomb-Hood; **Layout & Index**: Anna Jacomb-Hood
Proofreading: Jane Thomas; **Cartography**: Nick Hill
Photographs (flora and fauna): © Bryn Thomas (unless otherwise indicated)
Cover and main photographs: © Henry Stedman (unless otherwise indicated)

Dedication

FROM HENRY – FOR ZOE: We did it! A whole summer of swan counting, pram pushing and
puncture repairing. Thank you, sweetheart, for sticking with it throughout – and for making it so much fun, too.

Acknowledgements

FROM HENRY: Firstly, thank you to Joel for writing the first edition of this guide. At
Trailblazer, thanks to Anna Jacomb-Hood for her usual forensic approach to editing the text
and also for the extra London research, Meena Storey for the distance charts, Nick Hill for
the maps, Jane Thomas for the proofreading and to Bryn Thomas, as always, for keeping me
busy. I'd also like to thank all those readers who wrote in with comments and suggestions,
in particular, Stuart Blackburne, Paul Chapman, David Schache and Janine Watson.

A request

The authors and publisher have tried to ensure that this guide is as accurate and up to date
as possible. However, things change even on these well-worn routes. If you notice any
changes or omissions that should be included in the next edition of this guide, please email
or write to Trailblazer (address above). You can also contact us via the Trailblazer website
(🖥 www.trailblazer-guides.com). Those persons making a significant contribution will be
rewarded with a free copy of the next edition.

Warning – walking beside water can be dangerous

Please read the notes on when to go (pp12-15) and health and safety (pp74-6). Every effort
has been made by the authors and publisher to ensure that the information contained here-
in is as accurate and up to date as possible. However, they are unable to accept responsibility for any inconvenience, loss or injury sustained by anyone as a result of the advice and
information given in this guide.

Updated information will shortly be available on: 🖥 **www.trailblazer-guides.com**

Photos – Front cover: London's iconic crossing point: Tower Bridge.
Previous page: Swans are among the most common form of wildlife on this walk.
This page: Westminster Bridge leads over the Thames to the Houses of Parliament and the
Elizabeth Tower (Big Ben). Refurbishment of the tower will not be complete until 2021.
Overleaf: Sheep enjoying the rich Thames-side pastures near Radcot.

Printed in China; print production by D'Print (☎ +65-6581 3832), Singapore

trailblazer

Thames Path

PLANNING – PLACES TO STAY – PLACES TO EAT
99 large-scale walking maps and
98 guides to villages, towns and London districts

THAMES HEAD TO THE THAMES BARRIER

JOEL NEWTON &
HENRY STEDMAN

TRAILBLAZER PUBLICATIONS

INTRODUCTION

History of the path 9 – How difficult is the path? 11 – How long do you need? 11 – When to go 12 – Best day and weekend walks 16

PART 1: PLANNING YOUR WALK

Practical information for the walker

Route-finding 17 – Accommodation 18 – Rates 22 – Food & drink 22 Money 24 – Other services 24 – Walking companies 25 – Information for foreign visitors 26 – Walking with a dog 28 – Disabled access 28

Budgeting 28

Itineraries

Village and town facilities 30 – Suggested itineraries 36 – Which direction? 38 – Festivals and events 38

What to take

Keep your luggage light 40 – Footwear 40 – Clothing 41 First-aid kit 42 – General items 42 – Camping gear 43 – Money 43 Maps 44 – Facts & figures about the Thames 44 – The cultural Thames 46 – Recommended reading 46 – Sources of further information 48

Getting to and from the Thames Path

Getting to Britain 50 – National transport 51 – Local transport 55 Public transport map 56 – Public transport table 58

PART 2: THE ENVIRONMENT & NATURE

Flora and fauna

Insects 61 – Butterflies 61 –Wild flowers & shrubs 62 – Trees 63 Birds 64 – Mammals 66 – Reptiles & amphibians 68 – Fish 68

PART 3: MINIMUM IMPACT & SAFETY

Minimum impact walking 69   **Outdoor health and safety** 73

PART 4: ROUTE GUIDE AND MAPS

Using the guide 77

Kemble 79

Thames Head to Cricklade 81 (Ewen 82, Somerford Keynes 82, Ashton Keynes 82, Cricklade 86)

Cricklade to Lechlade 88 (Castle Eaton 90, Lechlade 90)

Lechlade to Newbridge 95 (St John's Lock 98, Kelmscott 100, Radcot 100, Rushey Lock 104, Tadpole Bridge 104, Shifford Lock 104, Newbridge 104, Standlake 107)

Newbridge to Oxford 107 (Northmoor Lock 107, Bablock Hythe 110, Pinkhill Lock 110, Eynsham Lock 110, King's Lock 112, Lower Wolvercote 112, Binsey 112, Oxford 112)

Oxford to Abingdon 123 (Iffley Lock 123, Sandford-on-Thames 125, Radley 126, Abingdon 126)

Abingdon to Wallingford 130 (Clifton Hampden 133, Day's Lock 134, Dorchester-on-Thames 134, Shillingford 136, Benson 137, Crowmarsh Gifford 137, Wallingford 139)

Wallingford to Pangbourne 142 (Moulsford 142, Goring & Streatley 142, Whitchurch-on-Thames 147, Pangbourne 147)

Pangbourne to Henley-on-Thames 149 (Mapledurham Lock 151, Caversham 151, Sonning 157, Lower Shiplake 159, Henley-on-Thames 160)

Henley-on-Thames to Marlow 164 (Aston 166, Hurley/Hurley Lock 166, Marlow 168)

Marlow to Windsor 170 (Bourne End 172, Cookham 172, Maidenhead 174, Dorney Reach 176, Eton 180, Windsor 181)

Windsor to Chertsey Bridge 184 (Datchet 184, Old Windsor 186, Runnymede 186, Bell Weir Lock 187, Egham 187, Staines 190, Laleham 190, Chertsey 190)

Chertsey Bridge to Kingston upon Thames 192 (Shepperton Lock 194, Shepperton 194, Walton-on-Thames 194, East Molesey/Hampton Court 194, Hampton Wick 200, Kingston upon Thames 201)

Kingston to Putney Bridge 204 (**Southern bank**: Richmond 208, Mortlake 209, Barnes 214, Putney 214; **Northern bank**: Teddington Lock 216, Twickenham 216, Isleworth 217, Brentford 218, Strand on the Green 218, Hammersmith 219, Fulham 220)

Putney Bridge to Tower Bridge 220 (**Southern bank**: Wandsworth 221, Battersea 223, Lambeth 224, Southwark 224, Tower Bridge 226; **Northern bank**: Chelsea 230, Pimlico 230, Westminster 231, City of London 231, Tower Bridge 232)

Tower Bridge to Greenwich/Thames Barrier 233 (**Northern bank**: Wapping 234, Limehouse 234, Canary Wharf 236, Isle of Dogs 237); **Southern bank**: Bermondsey 237, Rotherhithe 238, Greenwich 238); **Greenwich to the Thames Barrier** (Charlton 242)

APPENDICES

A: Walking with a dog 244   **B**: GPS waypoints 246
C: Map key 249   **D**: Distance charts 250

INDEX 254

OVERVIEW MAPS 261

Contents

ABOUT THIS BOOK

This guidebook contains all the information you need to walk the Thames Path. It includes:

- All standards of accommodation from camp-sites to luxurious guesthouses and hotels
- Walking companies if you'd like an organised tour
- Suggested itineraries for all types of walkers
- Answers to all your questions: when to go, degree of difficulty, what to pack and the approximate cost of the whole walking holiday

When you're all packed and ready to go, there's detailed information to get you to and from the Thames Path and, in the route guide, detailed maps (1:20,000) and town plans to help you find your way along it. The route guide section also includes:

- Walking times in both directions on the route maps
- Reviews of accommodation including campsites, hostels, B&Bs, guesthouses and hotels
- Cafés, pubs, tea-shops, restaurants, and shops for buying supplies
- Rail, bus and taxi information for towns and villages near the path
- Street maps of the main towns on or near the path
- Historical, cultural and geographical background information

---

❏ MINIMUM IMPACT FOR MAXIMUM INSIGHT

Man has suffered in his separation from the soil and from other living creatures ... and as yet he must still, for security, look long at some portion of the earth as it was before he tampered with it.

Gavin Maxwell, *Ring of Bright Water*, **1960**

Why is walking in wild and solitary places so satisfying? Partly it is the sheer physical pleasure: sometimes pitting one's strength against the elements and the lie of the land. The beauty and wonder of the natural world and the fresh air restore our sense of proportion and the stresses and strains of everyday life slip away. Whatever the character of the countryside, walking in it benefits us mentally and physically, inducing a sense of well-being, an enrichment of life and an enhanced awareness of what lies around us.

All this the countryside gives us and the least we can do is to safeguard it by supporting rural economies, local businesses, and low-impact methods of farming and land-management, and by using environmentally sensitive forms of transport – walking being pre-eminent.

In this book there is a detailed and illustrated chapter on the wildlife and conservation of the region and a chapter on minimum-impact walking, with ideas on how to tread lightly in this fragile environment; by following its principles we can help to preserve our natural heritage for future generations.

INTRODUCTION

This book follows the Thames Path National Trail from the river's source in Gloucestershire to the Thames Barrier in London. Officially 184 miles/294km in length (although it can be anywhere between 183¼ and 188½ miles, the actual distance you walk depending on which of several alternative paths you opt to take on the way), the path meanders, accompanied by its watery muse, through pristine and tranquil countryside, past historic sites and buildings, via pub, lock, weir and the occasional scattering of waterfowl to a city, once the fulcrum of an empire and now the heart of modern-day England. The river, responsible for the metropolis's very existence, inspires artists and authors, provides a home for swans, geese, and water voles, reflects the silhouettes of red kites and

> **The path begins, as the river does, in a meadow in the Cotswolds**

kingfishers, provides employment, entices adventurers and allows time for carefree pilgrims to meditate and think. And walking alongside it is a grand way to go for a ramble!

The path begins, as the river does, in a meadow in the Cotswolds. These early stages are lonely and wild, with the meadows and banks the domain of waterfowl and willow, while the riverbanks them-

Houseboats are a common sight along certain stretches of the river although you won't see many as spectacular as this one at Streatley.

INTRODUCTION

An inscribed stone (see p79) marks the source of the Thames and the start of the walk. With the river to follow it's hard to get lost.

selves are a collage of flowers, fishermen and farmers. As the waters deepen and spread, the settlements alongside begin to grow in both size and grandeur until, reaching Oxford, the solitude of the river slowly subsides and the trail becomes less about nature and more about history. There are venerable towns such as Lechlade, Abingdon, Wallingford and Henley as well as numerous ancient churches, abbeys and castles. Going through the ancient Goring Gap, dominated by the Chiltern Hills, you pass Runnymede – the site of the signing of the Magna Carta 800 years ago – and continue to Windsor Castle, where the constant rumble of the planes overhead hint at the ominous size of the city to come.

Yet walking in London is not as blighted by sound, fury and concrete as many may imagine, as the river – and especially the route along the southern bank – remains relatively verdant, at least as far as Putney. From here as you continue eastwards the views of Westminster and Tower Bridge are as fine as any along the Thames's green and scenic upper reaches. After central London the regenerated dockland areas of East London lure you to your journey's end

and the conclusion of a most enjoyable and varied riparian ramble, quite unlike any other in Britain.

HISTORY OF THE PATH

The Thames Path is one of the 15 National Trails of England and Wales (there are another four in Scotland where they are known as Long Distance Routes). Much of the trail follows the original towpaths along the river. Where there wasn't a towpath (because, for example, that portion of the river-

The trail officially ends at the Thames Barrier (see p241), just past Greenwich.

(see p241)

bank was privately owned), either access has been negotiated with local landowners to allow you to continue along the banks, or bridges have been built to connect the trail with the opposite bank, so walkers can continue following the river wherever possible. Occasionally, where neither of these is feasible, there are diversions leading the trail temporarily away from the Thames. Indeed, the path owes its very existence to some protracted negotiations and long, hard campaigning by the River Thames Society, the Ramblers Association (now Ramblers) and Countryside Commission (now Natural England).

Below: Blackfriars Bridge, with the dome of St Paul's Cathedral rising above it on the left.

The story began in 1984 when the then Countryside Commission published a study proving that the concept of a long-distance trail along the river was viable. This led to the official declaration of the Thames Path as a National Trail in 1987 though there was still much to do before it was officially opened – complete with the iconic National Trail acorns – in 1996.

Responsible for the preservation of the Thames Path (amongst others) are Natural England, the Environment Agency, and the 22 highway authorities through whose territory the river runs. Much of the maintenance work, however, is carried out by National Trail staff and volunteers (🖳 nationaltrail.co.uk /thames-path/volunteers).

HOW DIFFICULT IS THE PATH?

Of all the great walks you could choose to do in the UK the Thames Path is perhaps the easiest. Indeed, the only aspect which makes it any sort of challenge at all is its sheer length.

Of all the great walks you could choose to do in the UK the Thames Path is perhaps the easiest.

Investing a decent amount of time in the organisation of your trip and accepting that your body may need a day's rest occasionally will make the thought of trekking 184 miles far less daunting: indeed, you'll be surprised how quickly

your mile-count adds up. With no need for any climbing equipment (there is only one gradient of note) all you will need is some suitable clothing, a bit of money and a rucksack packed with determination. With the path well signposted (although see p220) and the river as your guide you're unlikely to get lost, either.

As with any walk, you can minimise what risks there are by preparing properly. Your greatest danger on the walk is likely to be from the weather – which can be so unpredictable in England – so it is vital that you dress for inclement conditions and always carry a set of dry clothes with you.

HOW LONG DO YOU NEED?

The Thames Path can be walked with relative ease in a little over two weeks. I advise you not to do so, however, for whilst walking long distances across successive days is a great accomplishment, doing it so quickly allows little time to relax and fully appreciate many of the magnificent sights along the path. Instead, I think it's better to plan for a couple of rest days (Oxford and Windsor being two spots where you may consider relaxing for a day). Add a day's travel to get to the start of the trail and another to get home again and 18-20 days in total should see you complete the trail.

Although the Thames Path can be walked with relative ease in 15 days it's best to allow 18-20 days in total.

Left: On the Thames Path you'll stroll past the grand houses of many people from movie stars to TV chefs – not forgetting the grandest of them all: the Queen's residence, Windsor Castle.

That's one way to avoid the rush-hour traffic: a paddle-boarder enjoys the scenic commute to work at Lechlade.

Yes, you'll be weary but you'll also have a soul that's been soothed by the flowing waters of the river and a body far fitter (and lighter) than when you left home. There's nothing wrong with attempting to complete the path as quickly as possible, of course, if that's what you prefer – but what you mustn't do is try to push yourself too fast, or too far. That road leads only to exhaustion, injury or, at the absolute least, an unpleasant time.

When considering how long to allow for the walk, those planning to camp and carry their own luggage shouldn't underestimate just how much a heavy pack can slow them down.

If you have only a few days or one week don't try and walk too far; concentrate on one section such as the stretch between the source and Oxford or the approach to London. The river, after all, will still be there for you when you want to return and complete your adventure.

When to go

SEASONS

Britain is a notoriously wet country and any Thames-side adventure is unlikely to do anything to alter this reputation in your mind. Few walkers manage to complete the walk without suffering at least one downpour; two or three per walk are more likely, even in summer. That said, it's equally unlikely that you'll spend a week in the area and not see any sun at all and even the most cynical of trekkers will have to admit that, during the summer walking season at least, there are more sunny days than showery ones. The unofficial season, by the way, starts at Easter and builds to a crescendo in August before steadily tailing off in October. Few people attempt the entire path after the end of October and the opening hours of many places will be more limited in winter – though there are still plenty of people using the path on day walks.

There is one further point to consider when planning your trip. Most people set off on the trail at a weekend. This means that you'll find the trail quieter during the week and as a consequence you may find it easier to book accommodation.

Spring

Find a dry fortnight in springtime (around the end of March to mid-June) and you're in for a treat. The wild flowers are coming into bloom, lambs are skipping in the meadows and the grass is green and lush. Of course, finding a dry week in spring is not easy but occasionally there's a mini-heatwave at this time of year. Another advantage with walking earlier in the year is that there will be fewer walkers and finding accommodation is relatively easy, though do check that the hostels/B&Bs/campsites have opened. Easter – the first major holiday in the year – is the exception, for it can be very busy at this time too.

Summer

Summer, on the other hand, can be a bit *too* busy, at least in the towns and tourist centres, and over a weekend in August can be both suffocating and insufferable. Still, the chances of a prolonged period of sunshine are of course higher at this time of year than any other, the days are much longer, and all the facilities are operating. My advice is this: if you're flexible and want to avoid seeing too many people on

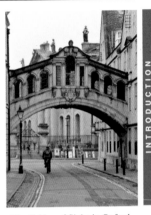

The Bridge of Sighs in Oxford, one of the most famous bridges near the Thames Path but one that doesn't actually cross the river.

the trail, avoid the school holidays, which basically means ruling out the tail end of July, all of August and the first few days of September. Alternatively, if you crave the company of other walkers, summer will provide you with the

Below: One of the many brightly-painted narrowboats that cruise up and down the Thames; this one moored near Kelmscott Manor.

In a few places along the path some people who live right by the river put out their produce and snacks for sale. You put the money in the honesty box.

opportunity of meeting plenty of them, though do remember that you must book your accommodation in advance at this time, especially if staying in B&Bs or similar accommodation. Despite the higher than average chance of sunshine, take clothes for any eventuality – it will probably still rain at some point.

Autumn

September is a wonderful time to walk; many tourists have returned home and the path is clear. The weather is usually reliably sunny too, at least at the beginning of September. The first signs of winter will be felt in October but there's nothing really to deter the walker. In fact there's still much to entice you, such as the fine, unimpeded views of the river (that are otherwise hidden by the foliage in summer) and the arrival of flotillas of migrating waterfowl on their way to warmer climes further south. By the end of October, however, the weather will

Particularly at the weekend and on summer evenings you'll see rowers out enjoying the river (**below**, © Joel Newton). Rowing's most famous event, the University Boat Race (see p209), takes place around Easter each year. The mosaic (**above**) is set into the path near Putney Bridge.

begin to get a little wilder and the nights will start to draw in. The walking season is almost at an end and most campsites and some B&Bs may close.

Winter

November can bring crisp clear days which are ideal for walking, although you'll definitely feel the chill when you stop for a break. Winter temperatures rarely fall below freezing but the incidence of gales and storms increases. You need to be fairly hardy to walk in

December and January and you may have to alter your plans because of the weather. By February the daffodils and primroses are already appearing but even into March it can still be decidedly chilly if the sun is not out.

While winter is definitely the low season, this can be more of an advantage than a disadvantage. Very few people walk at this time of year, giving you long stretches of the trail to yourself. If and when you do stumble across other walkers they will probably be as happy as you to stop and chat. Finding B&B accommodation is easier as you will rarely have to book more than a night ahead (though it is still worth checking in advance as some B&Bs close out of season). Remember, however, if you are planning to camp, or are on a small budget, you will find the choice of places to stay much more limited.

WEATHER

Before departing, tell yourself this: at some point on the walk it is going to rain. That's not to say it will, but at least if it does you will have come prepared. Besides, walking in the rain can be fun, at least for a while: the gentle drumming of rain on hood can be quite relaxing, the path is usually quiet and if it really does chuck it down at least it provides an excuse to linger in tearooms longer and have that extra scone. As long as you dress accordingly and take note of the safety advice given on pp74-6, walking in moderate rain is no more dangerous than walking at any other time; though do be careful, particularly on exposed sections, if the path becomes slippery or the wind picks up.

DAYLIGHT HOURS

If walking in winter, autumn or even early spring, you must take account of how far you can walk in the available light; it won't be pos-

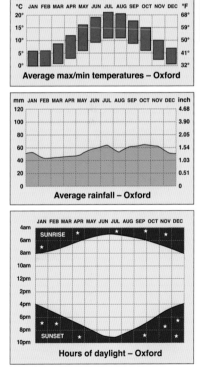

Average max/min temperatures – Oxford

Average rainfall – Oxford

Hours of daylight – Oxford

sible to cover as many miles as you would in summer. Conversely, in the summer months there is enough available light until at least 9pm. Remember, too, that you will get a further 30-45 minutes of usable light before sunrise and after sunset depending on the weather.

See pp38-9 for a list of **annual events and festivals** taking place in the area.

THE BEST DAY AND WEEKEND WALKS

There's nothing quite like the satisfaction of having walked an entire long-distance footpath from beginning to end. However, some people just don't have the time so the following offers you a 'smörgåsbord' of the best walks along the Thames, each with good public transport (see pp51-60) at the start and finish.

Day walks

● **Newbridge to Oxford**   As lonely as the Thames Path gets, this is 14 miles (22.5km) of sheer solitude, passing isolated locks and friendly riverside pubs as the Thames weaves its way to historic and magnificent Oxford; see pp107-12.

● **Abingdon to Wallingford**   Laid out between two of the most attractive Thames-side towns, this 13½-mile (21.7km) stretch visits a number of other places of note including ancient Dorchester (quarter of a mile off the trail), picturesque Clifton Hampden and several locks; see pp130-9.

● **Bourne End to Windsor**   This easy 11-mile (17.7km) stroll allows time to admire the village of Cookham as well as peer up at Windsor Castle at the day's end; see pp172-81.

● **Windsor to Staines**   An 8½-mile (13.7km) amble from the base of the Queen's favoured weekend retreat at Windsor Castle via historic Runnymede and the impressive Bell Weir Lock to Staines; see pp184-90.

● **Putney Bridge to Tower Bridge**   Follow the northern or southern bank (9¼-10 miles /14.9-16.1km) – or maybe a mixture of the two – through the heart of London where historic sites (and tourists!) abound; see pp220-32.

Weekend walks: 2-4 days

● **Thames Head to Oxford**   The perfect introduction to the river. You'll need four days to complete this 54-mile (86.9km) stretch of splendid isolation but you'll find yourself relishing every step. Frequent train services to and from both Kemble and Oxford make it easily accessible; see pp81-112.

● **Wallingford to Henley-on-Thames**   This thoroughly enjoyable 27-mile (43.5km) hike can be accomplished easily over two days. Incorporating the oft-photographed Goring Gap, a flirtation with the Chiltern Hills and the magical village of Sonning, both Wallingford and Henley-on-Thames can be reached with relative ease via public transport; see pp142-60.

● **Bourne End to Kingston upon Thames**   This 3-day, 34¼-mile (55.1km) stretch of the river mixes the historic (Runnymede, see p186) and majestic (Windsor Castle, see p182, Hampton Court Palace, see p198) with the ever-scenic river as the Thames eddies and flows into London; see pp172-201.

Colour photos (following pages)

● **Opposite, clockwise from top**: **1**. A tall ship passes the Thames Barrier. **2**. The Emirates Airlines Cable Car (see p241) near the end of the path certainly provides a unique view of the river. **3**. You'll find numerous welcoming pubs right beside the path. **4**. Cows grazing below Richmond Hill. **5**. Paddlesteamer between Hampton Court and Richmond.
● **Overleaf, top**: A tranquil stretch of the river between Lechlade and Newbridge.
Bottom left to right: **1**. WW2 pillbox, just outside Lechlade. **2**. Boathouse between Wallingford and Pangbourne. **3**. The Magna Carta monument, Runnymede (p186, © Joel Newton). **4**. Hampton Court Palace (p198, © Joel Newton).

PLANNING YOUR WALK

Practical information for the walker

ROUTE FINDING

Your chances of getting lost on the Thames Path are slim. Following the river for most of its duration, even this author – often lost in his thoughts – didn't stray from the trail throughout its entire course. Along the length of the path, gates and wooden signposts are marked with the iconic **acorn symbols** of a National Trail; on the odd occasion the path strays from the river these will ensure you stay on the path.

In London, the route may be slightly less easy to follow but the maps in this book should help you keep to the trail. The endless development in London does mean you may come across some new 'temporary' diversions.

Using GPS with this book

Given the above a GPS is clearly unnecessary in helping you stick to the correct trail. Nevertheless, it is a well-established navigational aid. In no time at all a GPS receiver with a clear view of the sky will establish your position and altitude in a variety of formats, including the British OS grid system, to within a few metres.

The maps in the route guide include numbered waypoints; these correlate to the list on pp246-8, which gives the latitude/longitude position in a decimal/minute format as well as a description. Where the path is vague, or there are several options, you will find more waypoints. You can download the complete list of these waypoints for free as a GPS-readable file (that doesn't include the text descriptions) from the Trailblazer website: 🖳 trailblazer-guides .com. It's also possible to buy state-of-the-art digital mapping to

---

(Opposite) Once past Lechlade, you'll see numerous barges and other boats moored along the banks of the Thames. Their owners are a welcome source of both information and humour.

import into your GPS unit, assuming that you have sufficient memory capacity, but it's not the most reliable way of navigating and the small screen on your pocket-sized unit will invariably fail to put places into context or give you the 'big picture'.

Bear in mind that the vast majority of people who tackle this trail do so perfectly well without a GPS unit. Instead of rushing out to invest in one, consider putting the money towards good-quality waterproofs or footwear instead.

ACCOMMODATION

There are plenty of places to stay all along the Thames Path. It is always a good idea to book your accommodation in advance (see box p20) especially as places tend to fill up quickly on national holidays and during any major festivals and events; see pp38-9 for details about what is taking place when you visit.

Camping

Camping is a glorious way to experience the Thames. Two places near the river's source at Kemble offer the chance to sleep under canvas and if you can walk the 16½ miles to Castle Eaton on your first day you can camp pretty much all the way to London; Chertsey, 139 miles from the source, is the last location of a campsite along the trail. That said, such a journey will take some organisation as you will need to use public transport (see pp55-60) on occasion. Alternatively, you can save yourself the hassle and spend the odd night in a hostel, pub, or B&B.

Booking is recommended for all campsites in school holidays and at other peak times but is otherwise usually not necessary.

The Itineraries section of this book suggests routes for campers to follow (see box p36). If planning to walk with a **dog** see p28 and pp244-5.

Campsites The campsites along the Thames Path can be split into four types. Undoubtedly the best situated are those **run by the Environment Agency** (🖥 gov.uk/river-thames-bridges-locks-and-facilities-for-boaters). Pitches (usually for up to two people and one tent) cost £7.50-11. Most of the sites are actually hidden away on islands that are separated from the riverbanks by locks. In other words, you couldn't possibly stay any closer to the river without being in it! These sites are generally open between April and September and they are quite basic with just a toilet and water supply, though a few also have showers which either operate with a token (£3.10) or will be included in the price. Most require you to arrive within the lock-keeper's hours (approximately 9am-5/6pm) so you can pay and pick up a key which will give you access to the site; Part 4 of this book provides the relevant details for each site.

Camping at one of the many **pubs** en route is also an option and sometimes a cheap one, typically cost from £8 per pitch (as charged by the Swan Inn at Radcot) though can be as much as £20 (as charged by Thames Head at the start of the walk), the exact amount depending to a large degree on the facilities. On the plus side you'll be as close to the pub as it's possible to be!

However, the most prevalent sites along the path are **privately run camp-sites**. These can vary drastically, from the serenity of small family-run sites, such as lovely Bridge House at Shillingford, to the huge family-orientated sites at Laleham and Hurley. Generally, the facilities are marvellous and most have small shops; indeed, some of them – such as Swiss Farm Touring and Camping at Henley-on-Thames – even have their own cafés and bars. Some prices are per person and some per pitch.

Then there are those sites run by **The Camping and Caravanning Club** (bookings ☎ 024-7647 5426, 🖳 campingandcaravanningclub.co.uk), who operate the sites at Oxford and Chertsey. Both are friendly, efficiently run and great sources of information though they can be crowded and aren't to everyone's taste. They can also be rather dear – we paid £32 per night for our two-man tent with a dog and a toddler. Annual membership costs £38-44, meaning that it's probably not worth joining just for the Thames Path. Wi-fi is often available (£3/day).

Finally, there is the website 🖳 **campinmygarden.com**, where homeowners offer, for a small consideration, a space in their back garden where you can pitch a tent. This site really comes into its own in London, where there are no other campsites to be found. A quick glance at the website at the time of research showed pitches advertised in Chiswick, Clapham and Greenwich, all of which may be of use to the Thames Path walker, though the situation is quite changeable and others may be available by the time you read this.

Wild camping The Thames Path is not really suited to wild camping. If you want to camp wild you should ask permission from whoever owns the land. Finding which farmhouse owns the field you want to camp in is no easy feat and you may find yourself trudging along miles of country lanes – only to be refused when you get there! Having said that, there will always be independent-minded souls who put up their tent as their spirit moves them. By pitching late in the day, leaving before anyone else is up and making sure you leave no trace of your ever having been there, it's unlikely you'll upset anyone.

Hostels
The Thames Path is not well served by hostels. Indeed, outside London – where there are two well-situated hostels – there are only four and three of these are in Oxford. All but two – Oxford Backpackers and Central Backpackers in Oxford – are run by the Youth Hostels Association (see box below).

❑ Youth Hostels Association (YHA)
You can join the YHA (☎ 0800-019 1700, or ☎ 01629-592700, 🖳 yha.org.uk) directly or at any hostel. You don't need to be a youth to stay in a YHA hostel, nor do you need to be a member, though there are several benefits if you join, including the YHA handbook which is issued annually to members and which contains full details of all their properties. Another advantage with joining is that non members pay £3 a night more than members (the rates quoted on the YHA's website are for YHA members). The annual fee is £15/20 if paid by direct debit/credit card (£5/10 for under 26s) or £25/30 for family membership.

PLANNING YOUR WALK

One of the big advantages of staying in a hostel, aside from a cheap bed, is being able to cook your own food. Most hostels provide well-equipped kitchens and all they ask is that you clean up after yourself. YHA hostels always provide bedding and don't allow you to use a sleeping bag. Most independent hostels have bedding, although sometimes you have to pay an extra few quid for its hire. Towels are hardly ever provided, however, so it's worth remembering to pack one in your rucksack. If not, you can rent one at all YHAs. Wi-fi is available at all the hostels.

Accommodation offering bed and breakfast

This accommodation is available along the length of the Thames Path in either B&Bs, guesthouses, pubs or hotels. In some places, particularly the chain hotels, the rate does not actually include breakfast though it is usually available.

The general concept of all these types of accommodation is the same: you book a room – a **single** with one bed for one person; a **double/twin** (one double/two single beds sleeping up to two people); or a **triple** or **quad** (sleeping up to three/four people with either a double and a single, or two double beds, or sometimes bunk beds or three/four single beds) for the night – and the next morning, often at a pre-arranged time if staying in a B&B, breakfast (see p22) is served to set you up for the day.

Wi-fi is available (usually free) in most accommodation though sometimes in the public areas only. If planning to walk with a **dog** see p28 and pp244-5.

B&Bs and guesthouses B&Bs are a great British institution; they give you the opportunity to stay in a room in a family's home and you will often get a very friendly welcome. These days most rooms in B&Bs and guesthouses have **en suite** facilities, though staying in accommodation with shared facilities will save you a few quid. The shared facilities in many places are usually only a few steps from your room.

❏ **Booking accommodation in advance**

Booking ahead is a good idea for all types of accommodation as it guarantees a bed for the night, but also may mean you get a better rate. If you are walking alone it also means somebody is expecting you, which could prove a lifesaver if you go missing en route for some reason.

During the high season (July and August) you may need to book a few months ahead but note that many places do not accept single-night bookings in advance at peak times or, if they do, they charge more. In the winter booking a few days or even the night before should suffice. If you are walking in the low season check that the proprietors provide an evening meal or that a local pub serves food. You may like to book through an online agency but do be aware that this may not be cheaper than booking direct; also sometimes agencies exclude breakfast from their rates. Note that however you book you may have to pay a deposit.

If the idea of booking all your accommodation fills you with dread, you may want to consider booking a self-guided holiday (see pp25-8).

If you can't fulfil the booking do telephone your hosts; it will save a lot of worry and allow them to provide a bed for somebody else.

The main difference between a B&B and a guesthouse is that the latter offers evening meals and also has a sitting room (lounge) where you can go in the evenings and meet other guests.

Pubs The initial stages of the trail are not blessed with many traditional B&Bs. Fortunately numerous fantastic pubs make up for this peculiar anomaly by offering both decent accommodation and protein-replenishing breakfasts. Many are right on the river, and thus the path too. One advantage of staying in a pub is that most offer evening meals (see p23). However, they aren't always the most peaceful of places to stay, especially if your room is above the bar.

Hotels Apart from chain establishments (see below), many of the hotels you'll come across en route tend to be upmarket, partly because they are in a wonderful location, and a few may not welcome muddy trekkers darkening both their doors and their towels. Most, however, particularly in the quieter towns and villages, are used to seeing trekkers and make a good living from them. The service they provide is similar to a B&B, though breakfast may be extra – and room rates are usually a bit pricier too. Rooms are virtually always en suite and many more services, such as in-house restaurants, are available.

In Caversham (Reading), Marlow, and the London area, apart from hostels, your best options for cheap accommodation (as long as you book well in advance) near to the Thames Path are at the **hotel chains**, particularly Premier Inn and Travelodge, though there are some branches of (the more expensive) Holiday Inn/Holiday Inn Express. These chain hotels have room rates only; generally there is a Saver rate, which must be paid at the time of booking and is non refundable and a Flexible rate which mean bookings can be changed and cancelled up to 1pm on the day you are booked to stay. All rooms are en suite and it is generally possible for up to two children to stay in a room with one/two adults, but not more than two adults.

Rooms at **Premier Inn** hotels (🖳 premierinn.com, central reservations ☎ 0871-527 8000), which are all en suite, typically cost from £35 per night but can go up to £150 or more per night in the peak season or if an event is on nearby. Booking online and well in advance is the best way to get a good deal. **Premier Inn hotels do not allow dogs** though they do now offer **free wi-fi access**. Breakfast is not included in the price and will cost at least an extra £6.99 (or from £8.99 for the full English). You'll find Premier Inns near to the trail at Reading, Marlow, Slough and Kingston upon Thames as well as several in London; for the full list of those in London see: 🖳 premierinn.com/gb/en/hotels/england/greater-london.html. Premier Inn has a new brand, **Hub by Premier Inn** (🖳 hubhotels.co.uk) which provides a few more options but expect the rooms to be compact.

The accommodation offered by their rivals **Travelodge** (🖳 travelodge.co.uk, central reservations ☎ 0871-984 8484) is very similar – Saver rates start from £29 per room (£49 in London) per night but expect to pay double that in the summer months and up to £199 in London. **Dogs are allowed** in a Travelodge, though they charge £20 per stay. Wi-fi is free for 30 minutes but if you want more than that you will have to pay. Breakfast may be available at an added cost but this depends on each lodge.

With both of these chains it is possible to book over the phone though it will cost at least 10 pence per minute; you will find better deals by booking online.

Holiday Inn (🖳 ihg.com/holidayinn/hotels) also have branches in London with reasonable rates if you book early. Some of Holiday Inn's accommodation is **apartment style** which would be a good option for the London stage of the walk as it is geared for long stays.

Airbnb

The rise and rise of Airbnb (🖳 airbnb.co.uk) has seen private homes and apartments opened up to overnight travellers on an informal basis. While accommodation is primarily based in cities, the concept is spreading to tourist hotspots in more rural areas, but do check thoroughly what you are getting and the precise location. While the first couple of options listed may be in the area you're after, others may be far too far afield for walkers. At its best, this is a great way to meet local people in a relatively unstructured environment, but do be aware that these places are not registered B&Bs, so standards may vary, yet prices may not necessarily be any lower than the norm.

RATES

Because of the sheer variety of accommodation on offer along the river you'll find drastic differences in price. A cheap hotel in Oxford can cost less than staying above a pub in Henley; a night at a hostel in London can cost a similar amount per person to a double room in a B&B in Abingdon or Goring.

You should generally be able to source a double or twin room with breakfast for £30-50pp per night based on two people sharing, sometimes less, though sometimes significantly more. Single rooms and single occupancy of double rooms can be found for as little as £35 per night but will most likely cost between £50 and £80.

Many places offer a '**room-only**' rate, typically £5-10 less per person than the full B&B price; this is worth considering if you've had your fill of the 'full English' or if the café round the corner takes your fancy. Note as well that prices at certain times of the year, especially at times of festivals and events (see pp38-9) in the local area, can soar.

FOOD AND DRINK

Breakfast, lunch and evening meals

The traditional **breakfast** is the celebrated 'full-English'. This consists of a choice of cereals and/or fruit juice followed by a plate of eggs, bacon, sausages, mushrooms, beans, fried bread and tomatoes, with toast and marmalade or jams to finish and all washed down with tea or coffee. This is good for a day's walking but, after a week or two, not so good for your cholesterol level. Some places offer a continental breakfast option or will charge less if all you want is a bowl of muesli or some toast.

For **lunch** there are several options. The cheapest and easiest, if staying in a B&B, guesthouse or pub, is asking if they would substitute a packed lunch in place of the breakfast – particularly useful if you want to make an early start – or make you a packed lunch as well as breakfast. Most of these places will also fill your flask with tea or coffee, often without charge. Alternatively, buy a picnic lunch at one of the many shops or bakeries you'll pass. Otherwise you could eat out but you need to plan ahead to make sure the pub or café is open and that you'll reach it in time. In recent times it has become quite the norm for walkers to travel very light, taking only water and a snack lunch of a muesli/energy bar and piece of fruit, eating properly only in the evening.

For an **evening meal** the local pub is often the best place. Most on the Thames Path have large beer gardens which roll down to the water's edge and have their own place in the Thames's history, with many of them being centuries old. Hearty menus are usually on offer: most pubs have a relatively standard bar 'pub grub' menu featuring such regulars as scampi, steak & ale pie or steak – all usually served with chips – supplemented by one or two 'specials' such as fresh fish; many establishments also have an attached *à la carte* restaurant with more

---

❏ Beer and breweries

The process of brewing beer is believed to have been in existence in Britain since the Neolithic period and is an art the natives have been perfecting ever since. Real ale is beer that has been brewed using traditional methods. **Real ales** are not filtered or pasteurised, a process which removes and kills all the yeast cells, but instead undergo a secondary fermentation at the pub which enhances the natural flavours and brings out the individual characteristics of the beer. It's served at cellar temperature with no artificial fizz added – unlike keg beer which is pasteurised and has the fizz added by injecting nitrogen dioxide.

There are plenty of pubs along the Thames Path serving an excellent range of real ales from around the country. The strength of beer is denoted by the initials ABV which means 'alcohol by volume' and is followed by a percentage figure. Any beer above 5% is considered strong by most drinkers.

The two most common pub chains you'll come across on the Thames Path are those run by the **Young's** (🖳 youngs.co.uk) and **Fuller's** (🖳 fullers.co.uk) breweries. Real ales commonly available include **Bombardier** (4.1%) and **Young's London Gold** (4%). At Fuller's pubs, beers to sup from their core range include **London Pride** (4.1%) and the darker **London Porter** (5.4%).

The cheapest pubs you'll come across along the Thames Path are typically those run by **Wetherspoon** (🖳 jdwetherspoon.co.uk) or **Samuel Smith Brewery** (🖳 samuel smithsbrewery.co.uk). There's generally a great range of organic lagers, ciders and ales; the lack of any TV or music keeps the price of both food and drink to a minimum.

Other pubs which you will wander by if walking the entire path include those run by **Arkells** (🖳 arkells.com), **Greene King** (🖳 greeneking.co.uk), **Adnams** (🖳 adnams .co.uk) and **Brakspear** (🖳 brakspear.co.uk). A smaller brewer you may encounter is **Rebellion Beer Company/Marlow Brewery** (🖳 rebellionbeer.co.uk), whose Rebellion range of beers are particularly popular along certain stretches of the trail.

A few pubs have their own microbreweries, such as *The Red Lion* in Cricklade (Hop Kettle Brewery; see p88).

elaborate meals. Most menus include at least two vegetarian options. A large number of the pubs en route offer real ales (see box p23) too.

All the towns along the river have restaurants and takeaways offering fish & chips, Indian, Chinese and Italian/pizza. At the other end of the scale, if you want to splash out on fine dining there are lots of very nice restaurants along the Thames Path, and one or two even bask under the radiance of a Michelin star or two; you'll have to plan and book well in advance if you want to eat at these places on your trip – and it would be wise to pack a smart set of clothes too.

Buying camping supplies

There are enough supermarkets/convenience stores and shops along the Thames Path to allow self-catering campers to buy **food** regularly along the way. All the shops are listed in Part 4. The longest you should need to carry food is for two days on the stretch between Lechlade and Oxford.

Drinking water

Filling your water bottle or pouch from the river is not recommended. Meandering its way through agricultural fields, the Thames collects heavy metals, pesticides and other chemical contaminants from the surrounding land. **Tap water** will be safe to drink unless a sign specifies otherwise; carry a two- or three-litre bottle or pouch and fill it up at night where you're staying. During the day you could refill it in public toilets although not all meet the requisite standards of cleanliness and the taps are often awkwardly placed. Cafés and pubs will often fill water bottles for you, especially if you have bought something. A three-litre 'platypus'-style bag (such as those made by Camelbak) should be sufficient for all but the hottest days.

MONEY

Many of the hotels, guesthouses, pubs and YHA hostels along the Thames Path accept payment by debit/credit card but it is still worth having a sufficient amount of **cash** on you. When booking B&Bs you should enquire whether they take cards, to save any last-minute dashes to the cash machine. Campers would be wise to always anticipate having to pay with cash.

You don't need to carry large amounts of money with you as all the towns have **banks** with **ATMs (cash machines)**; the latter are also often found in post offices, convenience stores, pubs and supermarkets though they'll often charge (£1.50-1.85) for withdrawals; there are clear signs warning you if this is the case. Alternatively, many shops and pubs will advance cash against a card ('**cashback**') often asking if you require cash when you make your purchase.

Use the Village and Town Facilities table (see pp30-5) to see where there is no ATM, or post office, and therefore where you may need to withdraw enough cash to last several days.

Getting cash from a post office

Several banks in Britain have agreements with the post office allowing customers using their debit card and PIN to make cash withdrawals at post office counters throughout the country. For a full list of banks that are part of this scheme contact the Post Office (🖳 www.postoffice.co.uk/branch-banking-ser vices). Alternatively, several of the post offices along the Thames Path have an ATM; the Post Office website can also be used to search for these.

OTHER SERVICES

Most of the main settlements along the Thames Path have shops that will provide all you need as well as tourist information centres/points (see box p48). **Wi-fi** is commonplace: you can even get online at many of the campsites along the route although they may well charge

WALKING COMPANIES

It is, of course, possible to simply rock up at the river's source wearing your boots and carrying your backpack and set off seaward, with little planned apart from your first night's accommodation. The following companies, however, are in the business of making your holiday as stress-free and enjoyable as possible.

Baggage transfer

Move My Bags (🖳 movemybags.com) can arrange luggage transfer for walkers on the entire Thames Path. Bags must not weigh more than 20kg and must not have any daypack or other bag attached. Move My Bags will not book accommodation for you so you will have to do that yourself and then book the transfer. The cost of each transfer varies so you need to complete the enquiry form on the website.

If you would prefer not to commit to anything in advance, your B&B, or a local taxi company, may be willing to transfer luggage for you (for a fee) to your next destination. If your B&B can't help they, or a local tourist information centre, should be able to provide contact details for local taxi companies.

Self-guided/guided holidays

The following companies provide packages which usually include detailed advice and notes on itineraries and routes, maps, accommodation booking, daily baggage transfer and transport arrangements at the start and end of your walk. Most companies offer a range of itineraries (taking 3-13 days) and offer the walk from west to east, though some also have east to west walks. However, **all will tailor-make your holiday** in either direction, and for however long or short you would like it to be.

Self-guided holidays can be started when you want to go but guided holidays (see HF Holidays) are only operated on specific dates.

● **British and Irish Walks** (☎ 01242-254353, USA toll-free ☎ 1-800-671-9863, 🖳 britishandirishwalks.com; Cheltenham) Offer an itinerary from the source to Pangbourne in 9 days/8 nights.
● **Celtic Trails** (☎ 01291-689774, 🖳 celtictrailswalkingholidays.co.uk; Chepstow) Offer the whole trail and also sections.

PLANNING YOUR WALK

- **Contours Walking Holidays** (☎ 01629-821900, 🖳 contours.co.uk; Derbyshire) Offer the entire path from Kemble to the Thames Barrier in 12-15 nights, as well as the east and west sections separately.
- **Explore Britain** (☎ 01740-650900, 🖳 explorebritain.com; Co Durham) Offer the full route (17 nights) as well as a number of shorter options including Oxford to Goring/Windsor/Reading (4/6/7 nights).
- **Footpath Holidays** (☎ 01985-840049, 🖳 footpath-holidays.com; Wiltshire) Can arrange the whole of the trail; they also offer some centre-based holidays beside the Thames.

❏ **Information for foreign visitors**

- **Currency/money** The British pound (£) comes in notes of £100, £50, £20, £10 and £5, and coins of £2 and £1. The pound is divided into 100 pence (usually referred to as 'p', pronounced 'pee') which comes in silver coins of 50p, 20p, 10p and 5p, and copper coins of 2p and 1p. Cash is the most useful form of payment but debit/credit cards are accepted in many places.

  Up-to-date **rates of exchange** can be found on 🖳 xe.com/currencyconverter, at some post offices, or at any bank or travel agent.
- **Business hours** Most **shops and supermarkets** are open Monday to Saturday 8am-8pm (and sometimes 7am-11pm) and on Sunday from about 10/11am to 5/6pm, though again sometimes longer. Occasionally, especially in rural areas, you'll come across a local shop that closes at lunchtime on one day during the week, usually a Wednesday or Thursday, a throwback to the days when all towns and villages had an 'early closing day'.

  Main **post offices** are open at least from Monday to Friday 9am-5pm and Saturday 9am-12.30pm. **Banks** typically open at 9.30am Monday to Friday and close at 3.30pm or 4pm though in some places they may open only two or three days a week and/or in the morning only; **ATMs (cash machines)** though are open all the time as long as they are outside; any inside a shop or pub will only be accessible when that place is open. However, ones that charge, such as Link machines, may not accept foreign-issued cards.

  Pub hours are less predictable; although many open daily 11am-11pm; often in rural areas opening hours are Monday to Saturday 11am-3pm & 5 or 6-11pm, Sunday 11am/noon-3pm & 7-10.30pm. Last entry to most **museums and galleries** is half an hour, or an hour, before the official closing time.
- **National (Bank) holidays** Most businesses in the UK are shut on 1 January, Good Friday and Easter Monday (March/April), the first and last Monday in May, the last Monday in August, 25 December and 26 December.
- **School holidays** State-school holidays in England are generally as follows: a one-week break late October, two weeks over Christmas and the New Year, a week mid February, two weeks around Easter, one week at the end of May/early June (to coincide with the bank holiday at the end of May) and five to six weeks from late July to early September. Private-school holidays fall at the same time, but tend to be slightly longer.
- **Documents** If you are a member of a National Trust organisation in your country bring your membership card as you should be entitled to free entry to National Trust properties and sites in the UK (see box p70).
- **Travel/medical insurance** Although Britain's National Health Service (NHS) is free at the point of use, that is only the case for residents. All visitors to Britain should be properly insured, including comprehensive health coverage. The **European Health Insurance Card (EHIC)** entitles EU nationals (on production of the EHIC

● **Freedom Walking Holidays** (☎ 07733 885390, 🖳 freedomwalkingholidays
.co.uk; Goring-on-Thames) The whole path and in sections (5-14 nights). Can
include boat trips and horse riding.

● **HF Holidays** (☎ 0345-470 8558, from outside the UK ☎ +44-20-8732 1250,
🖳 hfholidays.co.uk; Herts) Offer a 7-night **guided holiday** from Oxford to the
source based at their property in Bourton-on-the-Water.

● **Let's Go Walking** (☎ 01837-880075, USA ☎ 646-233-1541, AUS ☎ 02-8006
0182, CAN ☎ 647-478-6251, 🖳 letsgowalking.com; Devon) Offer the whole
walk in 15 days, or parts in 6-11 days, all in either direction.

card so ensure you bring it with you) to necessary medical treatment under the NHS
while on a temporary visit here (probably until Brexit is complete, that is). For
details, contact your national social security institution. However, this is not a substitute for proper medical cover on your travel insurance for unforeseen bills and for
getting you home should that be necessary.

Also consider cover for loss and theft of personal belongings, especially if you
are camping or staying in hostels, as there may be times when you'll have to leave
your luggage unattended.

● **Weights and measures** In Britain milk is sold in pints (1 pint = 568ml), as is beer
in pubs, though most other liquid including petrol (gasoline) and diesel is sold in
litres. Distances on road and path signs are given in miles (1 mile = 1.6km) rather
than kilometres, and yards (1yd = 0.9m) rather than metres.

The population remains divided between those who still use inches (1 inch =
2.5cm), feet (1ft = 0.3m) and yards (3ft = one yard) and those who are happy with
millimetres, centimetres and metres; you'll often be told that 'it's only a hundred
yards or so' to somewhere, rather than a hundred metres or so.

Most food is sold in metric weights (g and kg) but the imperial weights of
pounds (lb: 1lb = 453g) and ounces (oz: 1oz = 28g) are frequently displayed too. The
weather – a frequent topic of conversation – is also an issue: while most forecasts pre-
dict temperatures in Celsius (C), many people continue to think in terms of
Fahrenheit (F; see the temperature chart on p15 for conversions).

● **Time** During the winter the whole of Britain is on Greenwich Mean Time (GMT).
The clocks move one hour forward on the last Sunday in March, remaining on British
Summer Time (BST) until the last Sunday in October.

● **Smoking** Smoking in enclosed public places is banned. The ban relates not only
to pubs and restaurants, but also to B&Bs, hostels and hotels. These latter have the
right to designate one or more bedrooms where the occupants can smoke, but the ban
is in force in all enclosed areas open to the public – even in a private home such as a
B&B. Should you be foolhardy enough to light up in a no-smoking area, which
includes pretty well any indoor public place, you could be fined, but it's the owners
of the premises who suffer most if they fail to stop you, with a potential fine of £2500.

● **Telephones** From outside Britain the international country access code for Britain
is ☎ 44 followed by the area code minus the first 0, and then the number you require.

If you're using a **mobile (cell) phone** that is registered overseas, consider buying
a local SIM card to keep costs down. The Thames Path is pretty comprehensively
covered by mobile phone reception.

● **Internet access** and wi-fi See p25.

● **Emergency services** For police, ambulance, fire brigade and coastguard dial ☎
999 (or the EU standard number ☎ 112).

PLANNING YOUR WALK

● **Macs Adventure** (☎ 0141-530 8886, US toll-free ☎ 1-(720)-487-9898, ⌨ macsadventure.com; Glasgow) Offer the whole path as well as in sections.
● **Nearwater Walking Holidays** (☎ 01326-279278, ⌨ nearwaterwalkinghol idays.co.uk; Truro) Offer the whole path and sections over a range of days.
● **Responsible Travel** (☎ 01273-823700, ⌨ responsibletravel.com; Brighton) Have 3 trips: the whole path in 15 days, the Cotswolds to London in 8 days, and Oxford to London over a range of days (7-14).
● **The Carter Company** (☎ 01296-631671, ⌨ the-carter-company.com; Bucks) Offer the whole trail and also in parts.
● **Walk the Landscape** (☎ 07507 374925, ⌨ walkthelandscape.co.uk; The Cotswolds) Offer the whole path as well as sections.

WALKING WITH A DOG

Dogs are allowed on the Thames Path but should be kept on a lead whenever there are sheep or waterfowl in the vicinity. Considering much of the upper Thames is farmland it is well worth remembering that farmers are perfectly within their rights to shoot any dog they believe to be pestering their livestock.

Note that the currents in the tidal part of the river (after Teddington Lock) are very strong and therefore likely to be dangerous for a dog that goes for a swim. See pp244-5 for further advice on taking a dog.

DISABLED ACCESS

The Thames Path is relatively accessible for people with reduced mobility and the National Trail team are actively replacing stiles and poor gates to make the path as accessible as possible for all. They have also designed 12 walks suitable for anyone using a wheelchair; these cover from near Thames Head to Hampton Court (for details see the National Trail website in the box on p40). Thames Landscape Strategy (⌨ thames-landscape-strategy.org.uk/publications) have also created 10 Accessible Thames walks (between East Molesey and Kew) and the details are available on their website. Parts of London are accessible but some bridges have step access so a walk needs to be planned in advance.

Budgeting

The UK is not a cheap place to go travelling in and the accommodation providers on the Thames Path are more than accustomed to seeing tourists and charge accordingly. You may think before you set out that you are going to keep your budget to a minimum by camping every night and cooking your own food but it's a rare walker who sticks strictly to this rule. Besides, the pubs on the route are amongst the path's major attractions and it would be a pity not to sample the hospitality in at least some of them.

If the only expenses of this walk were accommodation and food, budgeting for the trip would be a piece of cake. Unfortunately, in addition there are all the little extras that push up the cost of your trip: getting to and from the path, beer, snacks, stamps and postcards, museums, buses and trains, laundry, souvenirs ... it's surprising how much all of these things add up.

Camping

You can survive on less than £20 per person (pp) if you use the cheapest campsites, never visit a pub, avoid all museums and tourist attractions in the towns, cook all of your own food from staple ingredients and generally have a pretty miserable time of it. Even then, unforeseen circumstances will probably nudge your daily budget above this figure. Include the occasional pint and perhaps a pub meal every now and then and the figure will be nearer to £25-30pp a day. And remember that once in London you'll need to allow for the extra cost of a hostel (see below) on at least two nights as there are no official campsites (though do check 🖳 campinmygarden.com; see p19).

Hostels

A dorm bed costs between £13pp (in winter) and £35pp (peak times in London) per night, although a bed usually costs £17-25pp. Some hostels offer private rooms, a few of which are en suite, but they do cost a little more; 2-bed rooms typically cost £28-70 per night depending on the location and time of year. Non-members of the YHA pay £3 per night more. Rates do not include breakfast so an allowance for this as well as for other meals, unless you are self-catering, and also for the extras mentioned above, will need to be included in your budget.

B&Bs, guesthouses and hotels

On average, a night in a B&B will cost £30-50pp based on two people sharing a room (£50-80 for a single or single occupancy) per night.

Adding the cost of food and drink for both lunch and dinner as well as an allowance for the standard expenses mentioned above, you should reckon on an average of about £65-70pp per day, although other unexpected costs will likely mean you may need to budget slightly more. See also p22.

Itineraries

To help you plan your walk see the **colour maps and gradient profiles** (at the end of the book); these show the walk divided into stages as in the route guide. The **Village and Town Facilities table** (pp30-5) provides a summary of the services en route. See p16 for a list of **day and weekend walks** which may be better if you don't have time to do the whole walk in one go. *(cont'd on p36)*

VILLAGE AND

Place name (Places in brackets are a short walk off the path)	Distance from previous place		Bank/ ATM (cash machine)	Post office	Tourist Information Centre/Point (TIC/TIP)/Visitor Info Centre (VIC)
	approx				
	miles	km			
Kemble	0			✔	
Ewen	2¾	4.4			
(Somerford Keynes)	2¼	3.6			
Ashton Keynes	2	3.2			
Cricklade	5¼	8.4	✔	✔	TIP
Castle Eaton	4¼	6.8			
Lechlade	6½	10.5	✔	✔	VIC
St John's Lock	¾	1.2			
Kelmscott	3¼	5.2			
Radcot	2¾	4.4			
Rushey Lock	2¾	4.4			
Tadpole Bridge	1¼	2			
Shifford Lock	3	4.8			
Newbridge	3	4.8			
(Standlake)				✔	
Northmoor Lock	2	3.2			
(Appleton)					
Bablock Hythe	2	3.2			
Pinkhill Lock	2½	4			
Eynsham Lock	1	1.6			
King's Lock	2¾	4.4			
(Lower Wolvercote)					
(Binsey)					
Oxford (Osney Bridge)	3¾	6	✔	✔	TIC
Iffley Lock	2½	4			
Sandford-on-Thames	1¾	2.8			
(Radley)					
Abingdon	5½	9	✔	✔	VIC
Culham	2¼	3.6			
Clifton Hampden	3	4.8	✔	✔	
Day's Lock	2¾	4.4			
(Dorchester-on-Thames)					
Shillingford	2¼	3.6			
Benson	2	3.2			
(Crowmarsh Gifford)					
Wallingford	1¼	2	✔	✔	TIC
Moulsford	4	6.4			
Goring & Streatley	3	4.8	✔	✔	
Whitchurch-on-Thames	3½	5.6			
Pangbourne	½	0.8	✔	✔	

Note: where there is no ATM shops/supermarkets may offer **cashback** as long as you spend some money
(cont'd on p32)

TOWN FACILITIES

Eating place ✔ = one ✔✔ = a few ✔✔✔ = three + (✔✔) = seasonal	Food store	Campsite (✔)=no official campsite but a tent can be pitched	Hostels YHA hostel/ H=Ind Hostel	B&B-style accommodation ✔ = one ✔✔ = two ✔✔✔ = three+	Place name (Places in brackets are a short walk off the path)
✔✔	✔	✔		✔✔	**Kemble**
✔				✔✔	**Ewen**
✔					**(Somerford Keynes)**
✔	✔			✔	**Ashton Keynes**
✔✔✔	✔			✔✔✔	**Cricklade**
✔		✔		✔	**Castle Eaton**
✔✔✔	✔	✔		✔✔✔	**Lechlade**
✔					**St John's Lock**
✔				✔✔	**Kelmscott**
✔		✔		✔	**Radcot**
		✔			**Rushey Lock**
✔				✔	**Tadpole Bridge**
		✔			**Shifford Lock**
✔✔				✔	**Newbridge**
✔	✔	✔			**(Standlake)**
		✔			**Northmoor Lock**
✔					**(Appleton)**
✔		✔		✔	**Bablock Hythe**
		✔			**Pinkhill Lock**
✔		✔		✔	**Eynsham Lock**
		(✔)			**King's Lock**
✔					**(Lower Wolvercote)**
✔					**(Binsey)**
✔✔✔	✔	✔	H/YHA	✔✔✔	**Oxford (Osney Bridge)**
(✔)					**Iffley Lock**
✔					**Sandford-on-Thames**
✔					**(Radley)**
✔✔✔	✔			✔✔✔	**Abingdon**
					Culham
✔	✔	✔		✔	**Clifton Hampden**
		✔			**Day's Lock**
✔✔✔	✔			✔✔✔	**(Dorchester-on-Thames)**
✔		✔		✔✔✔	**Shillingford**
✔		✔			**Benson**
	✔	✔		✔	**(Crowmarsh Gifford)**
✔✔✔	✔			✔✔✔	**Wallingford**
✔				✔	**Moulsford**
✔✔✔	✔		YHA	✔✔✔	**Goring & Streatley**
✔✔					**Whitchurch-on-Thames**
✔✔✔	✔			✔✔	**Pangbourne**

(cont'd on p33)

VILLAGE AND

(cont'd from p30)

Place name (Places in brackets are a short walk off the path)	Distance from previous place approx miles	km	Bank/ ATM (cash machine)	Post office	Tourist Information Centre/Point (TIC/TIP)/Visitor Info Centre (VIC)
Mapledurham Lock	2¼	3.6			
Caversham (Reading)	4¾	3.2	✔		
Sonning	3¼	5.2			
Lower Shiplake	3½	5.6		✔	
Henley-on-Thames	2¼	3.6	✔	✔	VIC
Aston	3¼	5.2			
Hurley	3	1.2			
Marlow	2¼	3.6	✔	✔	VIC
Bourne End	3¼	5.2	✔		
Cookham	1¼	2			
Maidenhead	3¼	5.2	✔		
Dorney Reach (Bray)	1½	2.4			
Eton/					
Windsor	5	8	✔	✔	TIC
Datchet	2	3.2	✔		
Old Windsor	3	4.8			
Runnymede	½	0.8			
Bell Weir Lock	2	3.2			
Egham					
Staines	1	1.6			
Laleham	2½	4			
Chertsey (Bridge)	1	1.6			
Shepperton Lock	2	3.2			
Shepperton	½	0.8			
Walton-on-Thames	1½	2.4 (or 1¼/2 by ferry)	✔		
Molesey Lock	4¼	6.8			
Hampton Crt/E Molesey	½	0.8	✔		
Hampton Wick/			✔	✔	
Kingston-u-Thames	3¼	5.2	✔	✔	

Southern bank (Kingston Bridge to Putney Bridge)

Place name	miles	km	Bank/ATM	Post office	TIC
Richmond	4¾	7.6	✔	✔	
Mortlake	4¾	7.6			
Barnes	¾	1.2			
Putney (Putney Br)	3¼	5.2	✔	✔	

Northern bank (Kingston Bridge to Putney Bridge)

Place name	miles	km	Bank/ATM	Post office	TIC
Teddington Lock	2	3.2			
Twickenham	1½	2.4	✔		
Richmond Bridge	2	3.2			
Isleworth	1¼	2	✔		

Note: where there is no ATM shops/supermarkets may offer **cashback** as long as you spend some money

(cont'd on p34)

PLANNING YOUR WALK

TOWN FACILITIES

(cont'd from p31)

Eating place	Food	Campsite	Hostels	B&B-style	Place name
✔ = one	store	(✔)=no official	YHA	accommodation	(Places in
✔✔ = a few		campsite but a	hostel/	✔ = one	brackets are a
✔✔✔ = three +		tent can be	H=Ind	✔✔ = two	short walk off
(✔✔) = seasonal		pitched	Hostel	✔✔✔ = three+	the path)
✔					Mapledurham Lock
✔✔✔	✔	✔		✔✔✔	Caversham (Reading)
✔✔✔				✔✔✔	Sonning
✔	✔			✔	Lower Shiplake
✔✔✔	✔	✔		✔✔✔	Henley-on-Thames
✔				✔	Aston
✔✔✔	✔	✔		✔✔	Hurley
✔✔✔	✔			✔✔✔	Marlow
✔	✔				Bourne End
✔✔✔	✔	✔		✔	Cookham
✔✔✔	✔			✔✔	Maidenhead
✔✔✔	✔	✔			Dorney Reach/(Bray)
✔✔✔	✔			✔✔✔	Eton
✔✔✔	✔			✔✔✔	Windsor
✔✔	✔			✔	Datchet
✔					Old Windsor
✔✔					Runnymede
✔				✔	Bell Weir Lock
✔	✔			✔	Egham
✔✔				✔	Staines
✔	✔	✔			Laleham
✔✔	✔	✔		✔	Chertsey (Bridge)
✔✔					Shepperton Lock
✔				✔	Shepperton
✔✔✔	✔			✔	Walton-on-Thames
					Molesey Lock
✔✔✔	✔			✔	Hampton Crt/E Molesey
✔✔✔	✔			✔✔	Hampton Wick
✔✔✔	✔			✔✔✔	Kingston upon Thames
		Southern Bank (Kingston Bridge to Putney Bridge)			
✔✔✔	✔				Richmond
✔✔✔	✔				Mortlake
✔					Barnes
✔✔✔	✔		YHA (Earl's Ct)	✔✔	Putney (Putney Br)
		Northern Bank (Kingston Bridge to Putney Bridge)			
✔✔✔					Teddington Lock
✔✔✔	✔			✔	Twickenham
✔					Richmond Bridge
✔✔					Isleworth

(cont'd on p35)

PLANNING YOUR WALK

VILLAGE AND

(cont'd from p32)

Place name (Places in brackets are a short walk off the path)	Distance from previous place approx miles km		Bank/ ATM (cash machine)	Post office	Tourist Information Centre/Point (TIC/TIP)/Visitor Info Centre (VIC)
Northern bank (Kingston Bridge to Putney Bridge) *(cont'd from p32)*					
Brentford	2¼	3.6	✔		
Strand on the Green	1¼	2			
Hammersmith	3¼	5.2	✔		
Fulham (Putney Br)	2¾	4.4	✔		
Southern bank (Putney Bridge to Tower Bridge)					
Wandsworth	1½	2.4 (bridge)	✔		
Battersea	2½	4			
Lambeth	2	3.2			
Southwark	2	3.2			
Tower Bridge (Southern Bank)	1¼	2			
Northern bank (Putney Bridge to Tower Bridge)					
Chelsea (Battersea Bridge)	3½	5.6			
Pimlico	1¼	2	✔		
Westminster	2¼	3.6			
City of London	2	3.2			
Tower Bridge (Northern Bank)	1	1.6			
Northern bank (Tower Bridge to Greenwich)					
Wapping	1¼	2			
Limehouse	1¼	2	✔		
Canary Wharf	1	1.6			
Isle of Dogs	3¼	5.2 (includes to Greenwich Foot Tunnel)			
Southern bank (Tower Bridge to Greenwich)					
Bermondsey	1	1.6			
Rotherhithe	1	1.6			
Greenwich	3¾	6	✔		TIC
Southern bank (Greenwich to Thames Barrier)					
(Charlton) Thames Barrier	4.5	7.2			

TOWN FACILITIES

(cont'd from p33)

Eating place ✔ = one ✔✔ = a few ✔✔✔ = three + (✔✔) = seasonal	Food store	Campsite (✔)=no official campsite but a tent can be pitched	Hostels YHA hostel/ H=Ind Hostel	B&B-style accommodation ✔ = one ✔✔ = two ✔✔ = three+	Place name (Places in brackets are a short walk off the path)
Northern bank (Kingston Bridge to Putney Bridge *(cont'd)***)**					
✔✔✔	✔			✔✔	Brentford
✔✔					Strand-on-the-Green
✔✔✔	✔				Hammersmith
✔			YHA (Earl's Ct)	✔	Fulham (Putney Br)
Southern bank (Putney Bridge to Tower Bridge)					
✔✔	✔			✔	Wandsworth
✔✔	✔				Battersea
✔✔✔					Lambeth
✔✔✔				✔	Southwark
✔✔✔	✔				Tower Bridge (south)
Northern bank (Putney Bridge to Tower Bridge)					
✔✔	✔				Chelsea
✔	✔			✔	Pimlico
✔✔✔					Westminster
✔✔			YHA		City of London
✔✔				✔✔	Tower Bridge (north)
Northern bank (Tower Bridge to Greenwich)					
✔✔	✔				Wapping
✔✔	✔				Limehouse
✔✔					Canary Wharf
✔					Isle of Dogs
Southern bank (Tower Bridge to Greenwich)					
✔					Bermondsey
✔✔✔			YHA		Rotherhithe
✔✔✔	✔				Greenwich
Southern bank (Greenwich to Thames Barrier)					
✔✔					Thames Barrier (Charlton)

PLANNING YOUR WALK

NOTES: In the **London** area only services mentioned in the route guide because they are on or very near the path are summarised in this table; there are plenty of additional ATMs, post offices, food shops and supermarkets as well as places offering accommodation and meals.

CAMPING AND HOSTELS

Night	Relaxed — Place	Approx Distance miles	km	Medium — Place	Approx Distance miles	km	Fast — Place	Approx Distance miles	km
0	Kemble			Kemble			Kemble		
1	Cricklade§	12¼	19.7	Cricklade§	12¼	19.7	Castle Eaton	16½	26.6
2	Lechlade	11	17.7	Lechlade	11	17.7	Radcot	13½	21.7
3	Radcot	6¾	10.9	Rushey Lock	9½	15.3	Bablock Hythe	14	22.5
4	Shifford Lock	7	11.25	Northmoor Lock	9¼	14.9	Oxford**	12	19.3
5	Bablock Hythe	7	11.25	Oxford**	14	22.5	Clifton Hampden	13	20.1
6	Oxford**	12	19.3	Clifton Hampden	13	20.1	Streatley(YHA)	15¼	24.5
7	Abingdon (bus back to Oxford)	7¾	12.5	Wallingford§	8¼	13.3	Henley-on-T	20	32.2
8	Day's Lock (Dorchester)	8	12.9	Pangbourne§ (train to Streatley YHA)	11	17.7	Dorney Reach	17¼	27.75
9	Wallingford§	5½	8.9	Henley-on-T	16	25.75	Chertsey	17½	28.2
10	Streatley (YHA)	7	11.25	Hurley	6¼	10.1	Kingston§#	11¼	18.1
11	Reading§ (train to Streatley YHA)	11	17.7	Dorney Reach	11	17.7	Fulham§# (Putney§# 13½ 21.75)	16¼	26.2
12	Henley-on-T	9	14.5	Windsor§	5½	8.9	Tower Br N§• (Tower Br S§• 9¼ 14.9)	10	16.1
13	Hurley	6¼	10	Chertsey	12	19.3	Thames B N/S§° (Thames B S§° 10¼ 16.5)	11	17.7
14	Dorney Reach	11	17.7	Kingston§#	11¼	18.1			
15	Windsor§	5½	8.9	Fulham§# (Putney§# 13½ 21.75)	16¼	26.2			
16	Chertsey	12	19.3	Tower Br N§• (Tower Br S§• 9¼ 14.9)	10	16.1			
17	Kingston§#	11¼	18.1	Thames B N/S§° (Thames B S§°10¼ 16.5)	11	17.7			
18	Brentford§# (Richmond)§# 4¾ 7.6)	5½	8.9						
19	Fulham§# (Putney)§# 8¾ 14)	10¾	17.3						
20	Tower Br N§• (Tower Br S§• 9¼ 14.9)	10	16.1						
21	Thames B N/S§° (Thames B S§° 10¼ 16.5)	11	17.7						

Nearest hostel:
= YHA London Earl's Court
• = YHA London St Paul's
° = YHA London Thameside

Notes: * Once past Kingston the places and distances in brackets are those on the southern bank path; those not in brackets are for the northern bank.

** Distances to and from Oxford include/deduct the two miles from Osney Bridge to the turning for the campsite.

§ In places where there is neither a hostel nor a campsite the only accommodation option will be a B&B, guesthouse, pub or hotel.

Tower Br = Tower Bridge; **Thames B** = Thames Barrier; **N/S** = northern/southern bank

Thames B N/S = the route to the Thames Barrier starts on the northern bank but ends on the southern.

STAYING IN B&B-STYLE ACCOMMODATION

Night	Relaxed Place	Approx Distance miles	km	Medium Place	Approx Distance miles	km	Fast Place	Approx Distance miles	km
0	Kemble			Kemble			Kemble		
1	Ashton Keynes	7	11.25	Cricklade	12¼	19.7	Cricklade	12¼	19.7
2	Cricklade	5¼	8.5	Lechlade	11	17.7	Lechlade	11	17.7
3	Lechlade	11	17.7	Radcot	6¾	10.9	Newbridge	16¾	27
4	Radcot Bridge	6¾	10.9	Newbridge	10	16.1	Dorchester#	17¾	28.6
							(¼ mile off path)		
5	Newbridge	10	16.1	Oxford	14	22.5	Pangbourne	16½	26.5
6	Eynsham	7½	12	Abingdon	9¾	15.7	Henley	16	25.75
7	Oxford	6½	10.5	Wallingford	13½	21.7	Marlow	8½	13.7
8	Abingdon	9¾	15.7	Pangbourne	11	17.7	Windsor	14¼	23
9	Shillingford	10¼	16.5	Henley-on-T	16	25.75	Shepperton	14½	23.3
10	Goring/Streatley	10¼	16.5	Marlow	8½	13.7	Brentford	15	24.1
							(Richmond	14¼	23)
11	Caversham (Reading)	11	17.7	Windsor	14¼	23	Fulham	10¾	17.3
							(Putney	8¾	14.1)
12	Henley-on-T	9	14.5	Chertsey	12	19.3	Tower Br N	10	16.1
							(Tower Br S 9¼		14.9)
13	Marlow	8½	13.7	Kingston	11¼	18	Thames B N/S	11¼	18.1
							(Thames B S	10¼	16.5)
14	Maidenhead	7¾	12.5	Fulham	16¼	26.1			
				(Putney	13½	21.7)			
15	Windsor	6½	10.5	Tower Br N	10	16.1			
				(Tower Br S	9¼	14.9)			
16	Staines	8½	13.7	Thames B N/S	11¼	18.1			
				(Thames B S	10¼	16.5)			
17	Shepperton	6	9.7						
18	Kingston	9½	15.3						
19	Brentford	9	14.5	# Dorchester = Dorchester-on-Thames					
	(Richmond	4¾	7.6)						
20	Fulham	7¼	11.7						
	(Putney	8¾	14.1)						
21	Tower Br N	10	16.1						
	(Tower Br S	9¼	14.9)						
22	Thames B N/S	11¼	18.1						
	(Thames B S	10¼	16.5)						

Notes: * Once past Kingston the places and distances in brackets are those on the southern bank path; those not in brackets are for the northern bank.

Tower Br = Tower Bridge; **Thames B** = Thames Barrier; **N/S** = northern/southern bank

Thames B N/S = the route to the Thames Barrier starts on the northern bank but ends on the southern.

PLANNING YOUR WALK

SUGGESTED ITINERARIES

The itineraries on pp36-7 are based on different accommodation types (camping/hostel and B&B-style accommodation), each divided into three options depending on your walking speed. They are only suggestions so feel free to adapt them. Don't forget to **add on your travelling time** before and after the walk. If using public transport a **map and service details** are on pp55-60.

Once you have an idea of your approach, turn to Part 4 for detailed information on accommodation, places to eat and other services in each village and town on the route. Also in Part 4 you will find summaries of the route to accompany the detailed trail maps.

WHICH DIRECTION?

Whilst this book follows the Thames Path from west to east – ie downstream from source to sea – there is really no reason why you can't walk in the opposite direction. You would, of course, lose the dramatic effect of witnessing the river's growth and you'll also be walking against the flow of the river; it's often said, too, that by walking east you'll have the weather (the prevailing wind and the sun) on your back for most of the time. But many folk – those three men in that boat for example (see p49) – have tackled the river by leaving London and following the waters westward, in search of the source.

FESTIVALS AND EVENTS

Before leaving home it is wise to be aware of any cultural or sporting events which could turn your peaceful riparian stroll into something much more boisterous. You may wish to consider either avoiding or participating in the following events whilst planning your walk. Note that, as well as those mentioned, many other major sporting events – such as rugby matches at Twickenham – and cultural events occur in or near to places on the Thames Path and these may push up the price of accommodation and also mean it gets fully booked.

A useful website for information about festivals and major events in and around London is: 🖥 visitlondon.com/things-to-do (click on Events calendar).

For events along the tidal part of the river between Teddington and the Estuary see: 🖥 pla.co.uk/Events/Annual-Events-Calendar.

March/April
● **The Boat Race** (BNY Mellon/Cancer Research Boat Races; 🖥 theboatrace .org; see the box on p209) Probably better known as the Oxford and Cambridge Boat Race; this is held on a Saturday near Easter and the Women's Boat Race is now held on the same day. The races start in Putney and finish in Mortlake.

May
● **Lechlade Music Festival** (🖥 lechladefestival.co.uk) Three days of family-friendly music; held over the Bank Holiday weekend at the end of May.
● **Cookham Festival** (🖥 cookhamfestival.org.uk) Ten days of music, poetry, drama and art; held alternate years (odd years so the next is 2019) early in May.

● **RHS Chelsea Flower Show** (🖳 rhs.org.uk/shows-events/rhs-chelsea-flower-show) England's premier flower show, a 5-day event in mid to late May that has been held since 1913.

June/July

● **Cricklade Festival** (🖳 crickladefestival.com) Day-long street party in mid June.

● **GAP Festival** (🖳 goringandstreatleyfestival.org) Ten days of music, art, dance, theatre, comedy, poetry, workshops held in the villages of the Goring Gap (ie Goring and Streatley) in late June/early July on alternate years, the next being in 2018.

● **Henley Royal Regatta** (🖳 hrr.co.uk) Held early July; see the box on p160.

● **Henley Festival** (🖳 henley-festival.co.uk) Hosts some of the biggest names in music and comedy, many of them performing on their floating stage. Held over five days in early to mid July.

● **Marlow Town Regatta and Festival** (🖳 marlowtownregatta.org) Includes canoe and dragon boat races over a weekend in mid June.

● **Wimbledon Lawn Tennis Championships** (🖳 wimbledon.com) Not technically on the river though it may impact on your trip nevertheless, with astronomical price hikes for accommodation in and around Wimbledon. Held over two weeks starting late June and running until early July.

● **RHS Hampton Court Palace Flower Show** (🖳 rhs.org.uk/shows-events/rhs-hampton-court-palace-flower-show) Six days of floral displays and plants for all gardening fans, usually held in late June or early July.

● **Greenwich & Docklands International Festival** (🖳 festival.org) Free nine-day long festival of outdoor performing arts in late June/early July.

● **Swan Upping** (🖳 www.royalswan.co.uk) An annual event in the third week of July during which the unmarked mute swan (and cygnets) on the Thames are counted and also checked in terms of their health and to see if they have any injuries. These unmarked swans are owned by the Queen. The Royal Swan Uppers wear a scarlet uniform and travel in a rowing skiff between Sunbury and Abingdon.

August/September

● **Reading Festival** (🖳 readingfestival.com) Three days of music over the Bank Holiday weekend at the end of August.

● **BunkFest**, Wallingford (🖳 bunkfest.co.uk) Free family festival also held over three days over the August Bank Holiday weekend or early September.

● **Windsor Festival** (🖳 windsorfestival.com/autumn-festival) Fortnight-long music and arts festival.

● **Totally Thames Festival** (🖳 totallythames.org) Arts, cultural and river events along the 42-mile stretch of the Thames in London held throughout September.

You are also likely to come across numerous smaller events such as beer festivals, races, carnivals and fêtes occurring along the river.

PLANNING YOUR WALK

What to take

What – and how much – you should take are very personal choices. For those who are new to long-distance walking the suggestions below will help you reach a balance of comfort, safety and minimal weight.

KEEP YOUR LUGGAGE LIGHT

When packing your rucksack it cannot be emphasised enough that the less weight you are carrying the more you will enjoy your walk. If you pack a lot of unnecessary items you will probably find yourself gradually discarding them as you go. If you are in doubt about taking something, be ruthless and leave it at home.

Rucksack

If you are staying in B&Bs or hostels you will need a medium-sized pack of about 40-60 litres' capacity; just big enough to hold several changes of clothes, a waterproof jacket, a few toiletries, a water bottle/pouch and a packed lunch. Hostellers may require a few extras such as a towel, food for cooking and possibly a sleeping bag. Those camping are going to need a rucksack big enough to carry a tent, sleeping bag, towel, cooking equipment and food; a pack of about 70 litres should be ample in this case.

If you are walking with an organised tour (see pp25-8) you will be able to pack the bulk of your gear into a suitcase or holdall and carry just a daypack with you on the trail itself, containing a spare jumper, waterproof jacket, water bottle/pouch, this guidebook and lunch, though the fully equipped walker may also want to bring a camera, map, walking pole(s), binoculars and first-aid kit.

It's advisable to pack everything inside a large plastic bag for protection against the rain; there are few things worse than discovering at the end of the day that all your clothes and sleeping bag have got wet. Most outdoor shops stock large bags made from tough plastic or you can use bin bags instead.

FOOTWEAR

A comfortable, sturdy pair of leather or fabric **boots** are ideal for walking the Thames Path. If you don't already own a pair and the cost of purchasing them is prohibitive you could get by with a lightweight pair of trainers or trail shoes between late spring and early autumn. Certainly, if you're carrying a heavy rucksack, you would be wise to invest in boots although you do see people wearing trainers on the trail.

If you are walking in the winter you'll be much more comfortable if your boots are waterproof; wet feet equals cold feet and blisters are more of a concern too. These days most people opt for a synthetic waterproof lining (Gore-Tex or similar). Cover leather boots in a layer of wax to waterproof them and take the wax with you so you can redo them a couple of times during your walk.

Gaiters are not really necessary but if you have a pair you may find them useful when it's wet and muddy.

CLOTHING

Even if you are just on a day walk you should always have suitable clothing to keep you warm and dry, however nice the weather is when you set out. Most walkers pick their clothes according to the versatile layering system, which consists of an outer layer or 'shell' to protect you from the wind and rain, a mid-layer or two to keep you warm, and a base layer to 'wick' (ie to remove) sweat away from your skin.

The most important item is a **waterproof/windproof jacket**. Even in summer it can rain for a week and if the sun isn't out any breeze can make it feel distinctly chilly. The most comfortable jackets are those made from breathable fabrics that let moisture (ie your sweat) out but don't let moisture (ie rain) in.

A polyester **fleece** or **woollen jumper** makes a good middle layer as they remain warm even when wet. The advantage of fleece is that it is lightweight and dries relatively quickly. In winter you may want to carry an extra jumper to put on when you stop or you may find yourself getting cold very quickly.

In summer, cotton T-shirts are fine for a **base layer** but at other times of the year you will be more comfortable wearing a **thin thermal layer**. Those made from synthetic material such as polypropylene are now less popular because they retain smells and there are several new, technical and natural fabrics available. One of the best is merino wool which is lightweight, high-wicking, quick-drying and washable. Cotton absorbs sweat, trapping it next to the skin which will chill you rapidly when you stop exercising. Modern synthetic fabrics on the other hand, 'wick' sweat away from the body and dry rapidly.

Shorts are great to walk in during the summer, although you'll probably want to bring a pair of **long trousers** for cooler days. Also, some sections of the path can become overgrown with stinging nettles and you may appreciate having your legs covered. Don't wear jeans; if they get wet they become incredibly heavy and stick uncomfortably to your skin and they take forever to dry.

How much **underwear** you bring comes down to personal preference. Women may find a **sports bra** more comfortable because a backpack can cause bra straps to dig into your shoulders.

If you haven't got a pair of the modern hi-tech walking **socks** the old system of wearing a thin liner sock under a thicker wool sock is just as good. Bring a few pairs of each.

A **hat** is always a good idea: during the summer a sunhat helps to keep you cool and prevent sunburn, in the winter a woolly hat can help to keep you warm. In the cooler months I would also recommend a pair of **gloves**.

You will also need a **change of clothing** for the evening. If you're staying in B&Bs and eating out you may feel more comfortable with something smart. A spare pair of shoes such as lightweight sandals or trainers is also worth carrying,

PLANNING YOUR WALK

even if they do add a bit of weight. There's nothing worse than having to put wet, dirty (not to mention smelly) boots back on after you've showered and changed. If you're camping, early spring and late autumn nights can be decidedly chilly so pack something warm.

TOILETRIES

Take only the minimum. Essentials are **toothbrush**, **toothpaste**, **soap** (especially if camping), **shampoo**, any **medication** you may need and, for women, **tampons/sanitary towels**. **Loo paper** is generally provided in public toilets but bring a roll just in case and carry a small lightweight **trowel** for burying excrement if you get caught out far from a toilet (see p71 for the code of the outdoor loo). **Sunscreen** and something to put on cracked lips is also a good idea. Deodorants, hair brushes, razors and so forth are up to you. If you are hostelling, or camping you will also need a **towel**.

FIRST-AID KIT

Medical facilities in Britain are good so you need to take only a basic first-aid kit to deal with minor injuries. In a waterproof bag or container you should have: **scissors** for cutting tape and cutting away clothing; **aspirin** or **paracetamol** for treating mild to moderate pain; one or two **stretch bandages** for holding dressings or splints in place and for sprained ankles or sore knees; if you think your knees will give you trouble **elastic supports** are invaluable; a **triangular bandage** for broken/sprained arms; a small selection of **sterile dressings** for wounds and **porous adhesive tape** to hold them in place; **plasters/Band Aids** for minor cuts; a sturdier, preferably waterproof **adhesive tape** for blister prevention; **Compeed**, **Second Skin** or **Moleskin** for treating blisters; **safety pins**; **antiseptic cream** or **liquid**; **tweezers**; and possibly **Imodium** for acute diarrhoea – you never know when it might come in handy.

GENERAL ITEMS

Other **essential** items you should carry are: a **torch** (flashlight) in case you end up walking in the dark; a **compass**, assuming you can use one, to stop you getting lost; a **whistle** to attract attention if you do get lost, or find yourself in trouble (see p76); a **water bottle or pouch** (two litres is the best size); a **watch**; and a **plastic bag** for carrying any rubbish you accumulate. You should also carry some emergency **food** with you such as chocolate, dried fruit and biscuits.

   Walking poles are now widely used and can help in taking some of the weight off your feet. Using them requires some practice but once you get used to them they become a normal, indeed vital, part of your equipment.

   Useful items to carry are: a **pen-knife**; a **camera**; a **notebook** to record your impressions; **sunglasses** to protect your eyes on sunny days; **binoculars**; something to **read**; and a **vacuum flask** for hot drinks (worth the investment if you're on a budget as buying all those cups of tea or coffee can get expensive).

A **map-case** can be a useful extra for protecting your map and guidebook in the rain, which can very quickly reduce both to pulp.

CAMPING GEAR

Campers will need a decent lightweight **tent** able to withstand wind and rain; a **sleeping mat**; a two- or three-season **sleeping bag** (you can always wear clothes inside your sleeping bag if you are cold); a **camping stove** and **fuel**; **cooking equipment** (a pot with a pot-grabber and a frying pan that can double as a lid is enough for two people); a **bowl**, **mug**, **cutlery** (don't forget a can-opener), **pen-knife** and a **scrubber** for washing up.

MONEY

It is most convenient to carry your money as **cash**. A **debit card** with a PIN is the easiest way to withdraw money either from banks, post offices or cash machines; debit and credit cards can also be used to pay in larger shops, restaurants, most YHA hostels and hotels.

❏ **Digital mapping**
There are several software packages on the market today that provide Ordnance Survey maps for a PC or smartphone. The two best known are Memory Map and Anquet but more suppliers join the list every year. Maps are supplied not in traditional paper format but electronically, on DVD, USB media, or by direct download over the Internet. The maps are then loaded into an application, also available by download, from where you can view them, print them and create routes on them.

Digital maps are normally purchased for an area such as a National Park but the Thames Path is available as a distinct product from some vendors. When compared to the nine OS Explorer maps that are needed to cover the walk, these digital maps are very competitively priced. Once you own the electronic version of the map you can print any particular section of it – as many times as you like.

The real value of the digital maps, though, is the ability to draw a route directly onto the map from your computer or smartphone. The map, or the appropriate sections of it, can then be printed with the route marked on it, so you no longer need the full versions of the OS maps. Additionally, the route can be viewed directly on the smartphone or uploaded to a GPS device, providing you with the whole Thames Path in your hand at all times while walking. If your smartphone has a GPS chip, you will be able to see your position overlaid onto the digital map on your phone. Many websites now have free routes you can download for the more popular digital-mapping products.

Taking OS-quality maps with you has never been so easy. Most modern smartphones have a GPS receiver built in to them and almost every device with built-in GPS functionality now has some mapping software available for it. One of the most popular manufacturers of dedicated handheld GPS devices is Garmin, who have an extensive range of map-on-screen devices. Prices vary from around £100 to £600.

Smartphones and GPS devices should complement, not replace, the traditional method of navigation (a map and compass) as any electronic device can break or, if nothing else, run out of battery. Remember that the battery life of your phone will be significantly reduced, compared to normal usage, when you are using the built-in GPS and running the screen for long periods. **Stuart Greig**

Always keep your money and documents in a safe place and in a waterproof container. In particular, those camping or staying in hostels should take care not to leave them lying around; it's much safer to carry them on you.

MAPS

It would be perfectly possible to walk long stretches of the Thames Path unaided by map or compass: just keep the river alongside you and you can't go too far off track. The **hand-drawn maps in this book**, which cover the trail at a scale of 1:20,000, should provide sufficient aid in areas where navigation is slightly more problematic. Nevertheless, having other maps will paint a more complete picture of your surroundings and will allow you to plan much more effectively for any accommodation or other facilities that lie off the trail.

❏ FACTS AND FIGURES ABOUT THE THAMES

The etymology of 'The Thames'

'Thames' is one of the most ancient names recorded in England. It is thought to derive from the Celtic words Tam and Isa (or possibly esa); the two put together describing something which is 'smooth' or 'wide spreading' and consists of 'running water'. The Celts knew the river as Tamesa or Tamesis; later, Caesar and the Romans called it the Thamesis, while the Anglo-Saxons who followed them knew it as the Temes or Temese. Along the upper stretches of the river it is given two names, **Thames** and **Isis**, both of which would seem to derive from the ancient Celtic words. However, it has been speculated that originally there were actually two separate rivers, the Isis being the waters that flow between the source and Dorchester, while the Thames was the name of the river between the River Thame – a tributary of the Thames – and the sea. You'll notice that on Ordnance Survey maps the river in the upper reaches is often labelled as being both, describing it as 'River Thames or Isis'; meaning, I suppose, that even they aren't sure!

The Thames in numbers

The Thames, at 215 miles (346km) in length, is the longest river in England. (The title for being the longest river in the United Kingdom, by the way, goes to the Severn, which begins in Wales and is 220 miles/354km in length). To put these distances in a global context, the Amazon stretches for approximately 4345 miles (6992km) across three South American countries while the Mississippi is a relatively paltry 2340 miles (3766km) in length, though it traverses 10 of the states that make up the USA.

Between its source and the Nore, where the Thames meets the North Sea, the river falls 105m, its current moving at between 0.5 and 2.75 miles per hour (0.8-4.4kmph). The mean depth of the Thames is approximately 9 metres (30ft) and its mean width is 305m (1000ft), although this average is somewhat skewed by the fact that the river is 5½ miles wide at the Nore. At Lechlade, 191 miles away from the sea, the Thames becomes navigable, although it does not become tidal until the outskirts of London at Teddington Lock, the last (or first) of the 45 locks which exist along the non-tidal Thames. Along the length of the river there are over 200 bridges. Between Lechlade and Teddington the river holds some 4500 million gallons of water. Teddington is the river's largest lock, coping with approximately 1145 million gallons of water flowing through it each day. In spring as much as 5500 million gallons of water can be processed per day whilst in late summer the amount can be below 600 million gallons.

Ordnance Survey (OS; 🖥 www.ordnancesurvey.co.uk) produce their maps to two scales: the 1:25,000 Explorer series in orange and the 1:50,000 Landranger in pink (which is less useful for walking purposes).

Alongside the paper versions OS also produce an 'Active' edition of both which is 'weatherproof' (ie covered in a lightweight protective plastic coating). Those needed for the Thames Path are as follows: **Explorer**: 168 Stroud, Tetbury and Malmesbury; 169 Cirencester and Swindon; 170 Abingdon, Wantage and Vale of White Horse; 180 Oxford; 171 Chiltern Hills West; 172 Chiltern Hills East; 160 Windsor, Weybridge and Bracknell; 161 London South; 162 Greenwich and Gravesend (162 covers just the final stretch to the Thames Barrier so is not really necessary). If you don't feel such precise cartography is needed the **Landranger** may be sufficient: you will need 163 Cheltenham and

Finally, it is said that every drop of water which falls in the Cotswolds and joins the Thames will have been drunk by eight different people before it reaches the ocean – though quite how they know this is anyone's guess!

The geography and pre-history of the Thames
The Thames can broadly be divided into three sections: the Upper Thames, between the source and Goring Gap, a primarily rural landscape; the Middle Thames, between Goring and Teddington, where the river is lined with commuter and tourist towns; and the Lower Thames, where the river's tidal waters flow through London and beyond, cutting through the Kent and Essex marshes and out to sea.

The river runs through nine counties: Gloucestershire, Wiltshire, Oxfordshire, Berkshire, Buckinghamshire, Surrey, the Metropolitan county of Greater London (historically Middlesex), Essex and Kent. In fact, it often acts as the border between them, separating Wiltshire from Gloucestershire, for example, or Oxfordshire from Berkshire, Surrey from Middlesex and Essex from Kent. Indeed, virtually since Homo sapiens first came into contact with the Thames it has always acted as a border, a geographical feature acting as both a separator and protector of man. Yet the river's tale begins well before man's arrival.

The river was formed by the flow of the oceans of the Jurassic period, some 170 million years ago, though back then it followed a different route: the river's forerunner, the 'proto-Thames', actually flowed via the Vale of St Albans and into the North Sea at Harwich. During this period Britain was still connected to the Continent and the Thames was a tributary of a vast river which ran across Europe; a tropical river in which turtles paddled and crocodiles swam. But 250,000 years ago, during an extreme Ice Age, the river, finding its course blocked by glaciers, pushed southwards instead and burst through a weak point between the southern Downs and the Chilterns (a point that today is known as Goring Gap; see p142) flowing along the valleys, a course which it pretty much still follows to this day. As the temperatures rose, following the end of the last Ice Age approximately 12,000 years ago, the improved climate attracted hippos and elephants to the river. Mesolithic settlers, too, began to appear along the river's banks and ever since their arrival the Thames Valley has been permanently occupied. This is true despite the monumental events of c5500BC, when the rising waters submerged the land which joined the continent to Britain, the English Channel met the North Sea – and Britain became an island.

Cirencester; 164 Oxford; 175 Reading and Windsor; 176 West London; 177 East London. OS also offers **digital maps** (see box p46).

Harvey Maps (🖳 harveymaps.co.uk) produce a series of waterproof maps that cover all the designated National Trails to a scale of 1:40,000. Their paper Thames Path map is also available digitally from their website.

Rather than purchasing a number of maps the best option for walkers unconcerned by anything other than the path and its immediate environs is A-Z's **Thames Path Adventure Atlas** (🖳 az.co.uk) which is lightweight, cheap and includes the whole trail using Ordnance Survey's mapping on the same 1:25,000 scale as their Explorer series; it also includes an index.

RECOMMENDED READING

The river has been muse for many a writer and numerous books have been penned which take the Thames either as their central subject or use it as a backdrop to their tale. What follows is a selection of those most useful and well known.

❏ The cultural Thames

The Thames has been the muse of many an artist. The river has inspired painters and poets, sculptors... and punks. In their 1979 song *London Calling*, The Clash boasted of how they 'live by the river.' Before them, in 1967 The Kinks sang of the sunsets over London's *Waterloo Bridge* making them 'feel fine.'

Rock and Punk **music** are both a far cry from the concert performed on a barge afloat the Thames for King George I in 1717, a highlight of which was a performance of Handel's *Water Music*, or the songs compiled by Alfred Williams in his book *Folk Songs of the Upper Thames* in 1923.

Though these works may differ in genre, they all clearly share an affinity for the river. And it is not just composers that the river has inspired. The Thames attracts **sculptors** too. Indeed, one of the first pieces of art you'll see along the river is the statue of *Old Father Thames* at St John's Lock (see box p76). Meanwhile, situated at Rainham – and so unfortunately east beyond the Thames Path – is John Kaufman's eight-metre high steel statue, *The Diver*, completed in 2000. The only sculpture actually *in* the river, it is completely submerged by spring and neap tides. Apart from such extravagant pieces you'll pass numerous other smaller statues, metal-works and carvings.

Painters particularly associated with the river include the Italian, Canaletto (Giovanni Antonio Canal; *Westminster Bridge*, 1746; *Old Walton Bridge*, 1754); the American, James Abbott McNeill Whistler (*Nocturne: Blue and Silver – Chelsea*, 1871; *Nocturne: Blue and Gold – Old Battersea Bridge*, 1872); and the Frenchman, Claude Monet, who produced a series of paintings of the Houses of Parliament, with the river in the forefront, between 1901 and 1905.

The two painters most connected to the Thames, however, are Englishmen: Stanley Spencer, who dedicated much of his life to painting the river near Cookham (see box p174); and JMW Turner who is also particularly famous for his images featuring the Thames. Many of them, such as *Rain, Steam, and Speed* (1859-61; see p174) and *England: Richmond Hill, on the Prince Regent's Birthday* (1819), are well worth stopping off to view in London at Tate Britain (see p233) – where you'll also find several of Spencer's works.

Guidebooks

There have been innumerable guidebooks published about the River Thames. One of the oldest is *The Royal River: The Thames, from Source to Sea*, first published in 1885. Newer editions are available in libraries but unfortunately the book is quite large so it's not really practical to take with you. It includes some wonderful illustrations and is beautifully written.

Another 19th-century book which may be of interest is *Dickens' Dictionary of the Thames*, written by the great man himself and compiled by his son in 1887. Described as 'an unconventional handbook', Dickens' lovers should be warned that there are no orphans pleading for more, or convicts hiding in the marshes, in this tome.

Factual

For a magnificent introduction to the river try Peter Ackroyd's *Thames, Sacred River* (Vintage Books, 2008) and Andrew Sargent's *The Story of the Thames*

PLANNING YOUR WALK

As for **literature**, the river has inspired many more books than the two mentioned on p49 by Kenneth Grahame and Jerome K Jerome. It is aboard a boat ('a cruising yawl') anchored on the Thames that Joseph Conrad's Marlow narrates his tale of another river, the Congo, in *Heart of Darkness* (1899). The Thames also inspired Lewis Carroll's *Alice in Wonderland* (1865) and William Morris's *News from Nowhere* (1890; see box p100). The river also features as the backdrop to a Sherlock Holmes mystery in Arthur Conan Doyle's *The Sign of Four* (1890) and, more recently, as the setting for a story of intrigue in William Boyd's *Ordinary Thunderstorms* (2009).

Perhaps the author who was most bewitched by the Thames, however, was Charles Dickens; he based scenes from several of his novels on the river. His last complete novel, *Our Mutual Friend* (1864-65), begins, rather morbidly, with a dead man being pulled from the river near to London Bridge. It is along the Thames estuary that *Great Expectations* (1861) begins and amongst the slums along the southern bank of the river that his tale of an orphan, *Oliver Twist* (1838), ends. Indeed, Dickens even wrote a dictionary to the Thames (see above).

Then there's **poetry**. As well as featuring in William Blake's *London* (1794), in which the poet wanders the 'charter'd streets, near where the charter'd Thames does flow', the river has also appeared in the work of many of England's other great poets. From the idyllic, 'silver streaming' Thames of Edmund Spenser (*Prothalamion*; 1596) and the riparian scene which made William Wordsworth purr, 'Ne'er saw I, never felt, a calm so deep' (*On Westminster Bridge*; 1802); to the river which makes Matthew Arnold crave for the days when 'life ran gaily as the Thames; before this strange disease of modern life' (*The Scholar Gypsy*; 1853), it has generally been used to summon a pastoral sense of contentment.

Possibly the most famous line of poetry penned about the river, however, comes from an American quill (though the owner of the quill was by this stage a naturalised Englishman) and is more concerned with encroaching change. In TS Eliot's *The Waste Land* (1922) he begins a stanza by beseeching the river, 'Sweet Thames run softly, till I end my song.' Fearful of the consequences of industrialisation which he saw sweeping through the Western World, Eliot would hopefully be appeased by the efforts being made to conserve the river today.

❏ SOURCES OF FURTHER INFORMATION

Online Information

The most useful online resource for planning your journey is the official National Trail website (🖳 nationaltrail.co.uk/thames-path) which has a wealth of information and includes an interactive map, route descriptions, downloadable leaflets and information on geocaching.

The unofficial online guide, 🖳 thames-path.org.uk, may be of interest to those planning on walking the Thames Path from east to west as it includes route guides which follow the path starting from the Thames Barrier. It also includes the 10-mile extension route to Crayness.

Useful information on facilities, river conditions, lock closures and much more can be found at the Environment Agency's website, 🖳 gov.uk/government/organisations/environment-agency, while lots of general information about the river can be found at the website of the River Thames Society (🖳 riverthamessociety.org.uk).

Another website which may be of interest for day walks in the London area is 🖳 tfl.gov.uk/modes/walking/thames-path as that has maps for the routes mentioned and basic public transport information.

Though not specifically for walkers 🖳 visitthames.co.uk includes practical information as well as facts and figures about the Thames.

Tourist information

Many of the towns and villages along the Thames Path have places where you can get information: **Tourist information centres (TICs)** provide all manner of locally specific information for visitors and some offer an accommodation-booking service; most also have information about public transport services.

Visitor information centres (VICs) often have a range of information but staff may be volunteers and therefore may not be allowed to do accommodation booking. **Tourist information points (TIPs)** have leaflets but are not staffed. For details on where to find these consult the **Village and town facilities table**, while in Part 4 of this book you'll find their location and the relevant contact details.

London's official **tourist board**, Visit London (🖳 visitlondon.com), can provide assistance for all aspects of your time in the capital. Other websites worth looking at are 🖳 experienceoxfordshire.org and 🖳 visitsoutheastengland.com/places-to-visit/berkshire.

Organisations for walkers

● **The Long Distance Walkers' Association** (🖳 ldwa.org.uk) An association for people with the common interest of long-distance walking in rural, mountainous and moorland areas. Membership includes a journal, *Strider*, three times per year giving details of challenge events and local group walks as well as articles on the subject. Membership costs £13 per year.

● **Ramblers** (formerly Ramblers' Association; 🖳 ramblers.org.uk) Looks after the interests of walkers. They publish a large amount of useful information including their quarterly *Walk* magazine, access to the Ramblers Routes online library and a full directory of services for walkers. Individual/joint membership costs £35/46.50.

● **Backpackers' Club** (🖳 backpackersclub.co.uk) A club aimed at people who are involved or interested in lightweight camping through walking, cycling, skiing, canoeing, etc. They produce a quarterly magazine, provide members with a comprehensive advisory and information service on all aspects of backpacking, organise weekend trips and also publish a farm-pitch directory. Membership costs £15 per year.

(Amberley, 2013). Both explore all facets of their topic. Ackroyd is also the author of *London, The Biography* (Vintage, 2001). A rather less academic work, Christopher Winn's *I never knew that about the River Thames* (Ebury Press, 2010) makes for an entertaining read.

In *Mudlark River* (2015) Simon Wilcox recounts his walk along the Thames using a Victorian map. Mudlarks were what the Victorians called people who scavenged the banks of the river at low tide.

River Thames: From source to sea by Steve Wallis (2017) focuses on unusual and interesting features illustrated with colour photos.

There are numerous books specific to the Thames in London. A concise introduction is *London's Thames* by Gavin Weightman (John Murray, 2004). Concerned purely with traversing the river are *Cross River Traffic: A History of London's Bridges* (Roberts; Granta Books, 2005), *Crossing London's River* (Pudney; JM Dent & Sons, 1972) and *Crossing the River: The History of London's Thames River Bridges from Richmond to the Tower* (Cookson; Mainstream, 2006). This last one is especially good.

Also of interest may be *Front-Line Thames* by Michael Foley (The History Press, 2008), which takes the river's strategic significance as its central subject, or *Liquid History: The Thames through Time* (Croad; Batsford, 2003), a book of black and white photos of the river accompanied by some explanatory text.

With the Thames having played such an important role in the country's history, it's certainly worth brushing up on your wars, kings and beheadings. *A Short History of England* by Simon Jenkins (Profile Books, 2011) is as concise as the title suggests.

Biography and fiction

Undoubtedly the two books most associated with the River Thames are Kenneth Grahame's *The Wind in the Willows* (1908; see box p148), featuring Mr Toad of Toad Hall, Mole, Ratty and Badger, and Jerome K Jerome's *Three Men in a Boat*. Originally published in 1889, the latter tells the comedic tale of three men – J (the narrator) and his two friends Harris and George – as they journey upriver from Kingston accompanied by the dog Montmorency. Many of the pubs mentioned by Jerome still exist and it's a rare walker who manages the whole trail without hearing the book mentioned at least once per day!

More recent Thames-side biographies which are particularly readable are the light-hearted *Boogie Up the River* (Mark Wallington; Arrow Books, 1989) and Pauline Conolly's witty and informative *All Along the River: Tales from the Thames* (Hale Books, 2013).

In *From source to sea: Notes from a 215-mile walk along the River Thames* Tom Chesshyre (2017) covers the journey he undertook just after the Brexit vote in Britain. The book covers the history of the various places he passes but he also describes the people he met and strange experiences he had as he walked the length of the River Thames.

For more information on the River Thames's cultural significance see the box on pp46-7.

Flora and fauna field guides

For identifying obscure plants and peculiar-looking beasties as you walk, Collins and New Holland publish a pocket-sized range to Britain's natural riches. The Collins Gem series are tough little books; current titles include guides to *Trees*, *Birds*, *Mushrooms*, *Wild Flowers*, *Wild Animals*, *Insects* and *Butterflies*. There is also a handbook to the stars for those who are considering sleeping under them. In the Collins series, there's an adapted version of Richard Mabey's classic bestseller *Food for Free* – great for anyone intent on getting back to nature, saving the pennies, or just with an interest in what's available to eat without going into a shop.

New Holland's Concise range covers much the same topics as the Gem series; each one comes in a waterproof plastic jacket and includes useful quick reference foldout charts.

There are also several field guide **apps** for smartphones and tablets, including those that can aid in identifying birds by their song as well as by their appearance.

❏ Getting to Britain

● **By air** The best international gateway to Britain for the Thames Path is London with its five airports: **Heathrow** (the main airport), Gatwick, Stansted, Luton and **London City**. Both TfI Rail (🖥 tfl.gov.uk/modes/tfl-rail; daily 2/hr) and Heathrow Express (🖥 heathrowexpress.com; daily 4/hr) provide train services from Heathrow to London Paddington; also see box opposite. A train journey to Kemble from Heathrow Airport (via Paddington) takes approximately two hours.

London City Airport is particularly convenient for the end of the official path as it is a stop on the Docklands Light Railway (see box p23).

However, some airlines fly to **Bristol** (🖥 bristolairport.co.uk) and **Birmingham** (🖥 birminghamairport.co.uk) airports, although from the latter it may take up to three hours to get to Kemble by train. Both serve destinations all over the UK as well as Europe; Birmingham also receives flights from all over the world.

● **From Europe by train** Eurostar (🖥 eurostar.com) operates a high-speed passenger service via the Channel Tunnel between Paris, Brussels and Amsterdam (and additional places at certain times of the year) and London. The Eurostar terminal in London is at St Pancras International station with connections to the London Underground and all other main railway stations in London. Trains to many Thames Path destinations leave from both Paddington and Waterloo stations; see box pp52-3.

For more information about rail services from the Continent to Britain contact your national rail operator, or Railteam (🖥 railteam.eu).

● **From Europe by coach** Eurolines (🖥 eurolines.com) have a wide network of long-distance bus services connecting over 500 destinations in 25 European countries to London's Victoria Coach Station. Visit their website for details of services from your country.

● **From Europe by ferry (with or without a car)** There are numerous ferries plying routes between the major North Sea ports as well as across the Irish Sea and the English Channel. A useful website for information about the routes and the ferry operators is 🖥 directferries.co.uk.

● **From Europe by car** Eurotunnel (🖥 eurotunnel.com) operates 'le shuttle' train service for vehicles via the Channel Tunnel between Calais and Folkestone, taking one hour between the motorway in France and the motorway in Britain.

Getting to and from the Thames Path

Travelling to the start of the Thames Path by public transport makes sense. There's no need to worry about the safety of your temporarily abandoned vehicle while you walk along the trail, there are no logistical headaches about how to return to your car afterwards and it's one of the biggest steps you can take towards minimising your ecological footprint. Quite apart from that, you'll feel your holiday has begun the moment you step out of your front door rather than having to wait until you've slammed the car door behind you.

NATIONAL TRANSPORT

The best way of getting to Kemble, the nearest settlement to the source of the River Thames, is by rail. But other options are by coach/bus or by car.

By rail

Most of the major stops along the Thames Path, other than in London, lie on either the main or branch line services run by **Great Western Railway (GWR)**. Kemble is 80-100 minutes from London Paddington.

The trains which run through Charlton – the nearest stop to the Thames Barrier – are run by **Southeastern** and take less than half an hour to get to central London (terminating at Cannon St/London Bridge or Charing Cross stations).

Between Reading and London, and in London, you may find you need to use **South Western Railway** to reach some destinations.

Other operators providing train services to places on or near the path include: **Southern**, **Thameslink**, **London Overground/Tfl Rail**, **Docklands Light Railway** and **c2c** – and also the **CrossRail Elizabeth line** (see box below).

In the box on pp52-3 there is a list of the relevant destinations for these services along the Thames Path as well as contact details for the various rail operators. *(cont'd on p54)*

(right margin, vertical) PLANNING YOUR WALK

❏ **CrossRail Elizabeth Line**
When fully open this new line will provide services right across London. One part of the line will start from Reading and another from Heathrow Airport; they will join at Hayes & Harlington and then divide again at Whitechapel with a southern spur going to Abbey Wood and a northern one to Shenfield. Stations served will include **Reading**, Twyford, **Maidenhead**, **Taplow**, Slough, Ealing Broadway, London Paddington, London Liverpool Street, **Canary Wharf** and Woolwich.

The Liverpool Street to Shenfield and Heathrow to Paddington services are currently operated by Tfl Rail. The Elizabeth Line Paddington to Heathrow (replacing Tfl Rail's services), Paddington to Abbey Wood and Paddington to Shenfield services are scheduled to start in December 2018. The line from Reading is due to open in December 2019 and then services will be fully operational.

❏ TRAIN SERVICES

Great Western Railway (GWR; ☎ 0345-7000 125, 🖳 gwr.com)
● Paddington* to Didcot Parkway via Slough, **Maidenhead**, Twyford, Reading, **Tilehurst**, **Pangbourne**, **Goring & Streatley** & Cholsey, Mon-Sat 2/hr, Sun 1/hr
● **Reading** to Didcot Parkway via **Tilehurst**, **Pangbourne**, **Goring & Streatley** & Cholsey, Mon-Fri 1-3/hr, Sat 2/hr, Sun 1/hr
● **Reading**/Didcot Parkway to **Oxford**/Banbury, Mon-Sat 2/hr, Sun 1/hr (early morning and late afternoon services call at **Appleford, Culham** & **Radley** but otherwise during the day there are limited services to these stations.
● Paddington* to **Oxford** via **Reading**, Mon-Sat 2/hr, Sun 1/hr; plus Reading to **Oxford**, daily 2/hr (some services stop at Slough and/or Didcot Parkway)
● Slough to **Windsor** & Eton Central, daily 2-3/hr
● Paddington* to Cheltenham Spa via **Reading**, Didcot Parkway, Swindon, **Kemble**, Stroud & Gloucester, Mon-Fri 8/day, Sat & Sun 7/day for direct services to Kemble; additional services from Swindon Mon-Fri 10/day, Sat 8/day, Sun 5/day
● **Maidenhead** to **Marlow** via **Cookham** & **Bourne End**, daily 1-2/hr
● Twyford to **Henley-on-Thames** via Wargrave & **Shiplake**, daily 1-2/hr

South Western Railway (☎ 0345-6000 650, 🖳 southwesternrailway.com)
● Waterloo* to **Hampton Court** via **Vauxhall**, Clapham Junction, Earlsfield, Wimbledon, Raynes Park, New Malden, Surbiton & Thames Ditton, daily 2/hr
● **(Kingston Loop line)** Waterloo* circular route via **Vauxhall**, Clapham Junction, Earlsfield, Wimbledon, **Kingston**, **Hampton Wick**, **Teddington**, Strawberry Hill, **Twickenham**, St Margarets, **Richmond**, **Mortlake**, Barnes, **Putney**, **Wandsworth Town**, Clapham Junction, **Queenstown Road** & Vauxhall, daily 1-2/hr
● **Waterloo*** to Hounslow via **Vauxhall**, **Queenstown Road**, Clapham Junction, **Wandsworth Town**, **Putney**, Barnes, **Barnes Bridge**, **Chiswick**, **Kew Bridge**, Brentford, **Syon Lane** & Isleworth, daily 2/hr
● **(Hounslow Loop Line)** Waterloo* circular route via **Vauxhall**, Queenstown Road, Clapham Junction, **Wandsworth Town**, Putney, **Barnes**, **Barnes Bridge**, **Chiswick**, **Kew Bridge**, Brentford, **Syon Lane**, Isleworth, Hounslow, Whitton, **Twickenham**, St Margarets, North Sheen, **Mortlake**, Barnes, **Putney**, **Wandsworth Town**, Clapham Junction, Queenstown Road & **Vauxhall**, daily 2/hr
● **Waterloo*** to **Shepperton** via **Vauxhall**, Clapham Junction, Earlsfield, Wimbledon, Raynes Park, New Malden, Norbiton, **Kingston**, **Hampton Wick**, **Teddington**, Fulwell, **Hampton**, Kempton Park & Sunbury, Mon-Sat 2/hr, Sun 1/hr
● **Waterloo*** to **Twickenham** via **Vauxhall**, Clapham Junction, **Wandsworth Town**, **Putney**, Barnes & **Richmond**, Mon-Sat 4/hr, Sun 2/hr
● **Waterloo*** to **Twickenham** via Clapham Junction & **Richmond**, daily 2/hr
● **Waterloo*** to Reading via Clapham Junction, **Richmond**, **Twickenham**, Feltham, **Staines**, **Egham**, Virginia Water, Ascot, Bracknell & Wokingham, daily 2/hr
● **Waterloo*** to Virginia Water via Clapham Junction, **Richmond**, **Twickenham**, Feltham, **Staines** & **Egham**, daily 2/hr
● **Waterloo*** to Weybridge via **Vauxhall**, Clapham Junction, **Wandsworth Town**, **Putney**, Barnes, **Barnes Bridge**, **Chiswick**, **Kew Bridge**, Brentford, **Syon Lane**, Isleworth, Hounslow, **Staines**, **Egham**, Virginia Water & **Chertsey**, daily 1-2/hr
● **Waterloo*** to **Windsor & Eton Riverside** via **Vauxhall**, Clapham Junction, **Putney**, **Richmond**, **Twickenham**, **Staines** & **Datchet**, daily 2/hr
● **Waterloo*** to Woking via **Vauxhall**, Clapham Junction, Earlsfield, Wimbledon, Surbiton, Esher, Hersham, **Walton-on-Thames** & Weybridge, daily 2/hr

Southeastern (☎ 0345-322 7021, 🖥 southeasternrailway.co.uk)
● **Charing Cross*** to Dover Priory via **Waterloo East**, **London Bridge**,
Tonbridge, Ashford International & Folkestone (West & Central), daily 1/hr
● **Charing Cross*** to Canterbury West via **Waterloo East**, **London Bridge**,
& Ashford International, daily 1/hr (some services continue to Ramsgate)
● **Charing Cross*** to Gillingham via **Waterloo East**, **London Bridge**,
Dartford, Gravesend, Strood, Rochester & Chatham, daily 1/hr
● **Charing Cross*** to Sevenoaks via **Waterloo East** & **London Bridge**, Mon-Sat
1-2/hr (**Note**: the evening and Sunday (2/hr) services depart from Cannon St).
● **Charing Cross*** to Gillingham via **Waterloo East**, **London Bridge**, **Charlton**,
Woolwich Arsenal, Dartford, Gravesend, daily 1-2/hr
● **Cannon Street*** to Dartford via **London Bridge**, **Greenwich**, **Charlton**,
Woolwich Dockyard & Woolwich Arsenal, daily 2/hr

Southern (☎ 0345-127 2920, 🖥 southernrailway.com)
Note: at the time of writing new timetables/routes were being introduced for services
operated by the **Govia Thameslink** group (Southern, Thameslink and Great
Northern); see 🖥 railplan2020.com for details. Basic details are given below:
● Milton Keynes Central to East Croydon via Watford Junction, **Imperial Wharf** &
Clapham Junction
● Victoria* to **Crystal Palace** via **Battersea Park** & Clapham Junction
● Victoria* to West Croydon via **Battersea Park** & Clapham Junction
● **London Bridge** to Beckenham Junction via **South Bermondsey**
● **London Bridge** to East Croydon via **South Bermondsey** & Tulse Hill
● **London Bridge** to Epsom via Sutton
● St Pancras International to Sutton via Farringdon, City Thameslink & **Blackfriars**
● Bedford to Gatwick Airport via Luton, St Pancras International, **Blackfriars**,
London Bridge & East Croydon

Thameslink Railway (☎ 0345-026 4700, 🖥 thameslinkrailway.com)
● Luton to Rainham via Luton Airport Parkway, St Pancras International,
Blackfriars*, London Bridge, Greenwich, Charlton & Woolwich Arsenal, Mon-Fri
1/hr direct

c2c (☎ 0345-744 4422🖥 c2c-online.co.uk)
Fenchurch Street to Shoeburyness via **Limehouse**, daily 2-4/hr

London Overground (☎ 0343-222 1234, 🖥 tfl.gov.uk/modes/london-overground)
● Dalston Junction to Clapham Junction via **Wapping**, **Rotherhithe**, Canada Water
& Surrey Quays, daily 3/hr
● Clapham Junction to Stratford via **Imperial Wharf**, daily 4/hr
● **Richmond** to Stratford via **Kew Gardens** & Willesden Junction, daily 4/hr

Docklands Light Railway (DLR; ☎ 0343-222 1234, 🖥 tfl.gov.uk/modes/dlr)
● Stratford International to Woolwich Arsenal via London City Airport
● Bank to Lewisham via **Limehouse**, **Canary Wharf**, **Island Gardens**, **Cutty
Sark for Maritime Greenwich** & Greenwich
● Stratford to Woolwich Arsenal

NOTES Not all stops are listed and only the main services are included

* Paddington = London Paddington; Waterloo = London Waterloo; Victoria =
London Victoria, Charing Cross = London Charing Cross, Waterloo East = London
Waterloo East, Blackfriars = London Blackfriars

Fare and timetable information Fares and timetable information can be found on the websites listed in the box on pp52-3 and at **National Rail Enquiries** (☎ 0345-748 4950, 🖵 nationalrail.co.uk). A marvellous way to save some money is by booking your train travel online and (well) in advance either through the relevant operator or via 🖵 thetrainline.com; the latter may be a particularly good option if your journey involves using more than one operator.

Most rail companies as well as National Rail and trainline have **apps for smartphones** which are worth downloading in order to keep up to date with train times and fares as well as any changes which may have occurred.

By coach

Both Stroud and Cirencester are just a short train or bus journey from Kemble, near to the river's source, and both are connected to London via **National Express** coaches. National Express also has services from most major cities to Oxford, Reading-Calcot, Heathrow Airport and London Victoria. Local bus services (see pp58-9) operate from these to places on, or near, the path.

See the box below for a selection of the many coach services relevant to the Thames Path. For further details consult National Express's website.

Megabus (🖵 uk.megabus.com) also operates services to Oxford.

By car

With such extensive public transport networks available there's really no need to drive; the risks of leaving a car somewhere (and probably having to pay to do so) surely outweighing the minor additional inconvenience typically suffered by those travelling by public transport. If you do choose to, you may save money by seeking long-term parking in London via 🖵 justpark.com, from which you can organise to rent people's driveways and garages for significantly less than

---

❑ **Coach services**
Note not all stops are listed.

National Express (☎ 0871-781 8181, 🖵 nationalexpress.com)
NX200 Bristol to Gatwick via **Reading** & Heathrow, 3/day
NX401 London to Gloucester via Swindon, **Cricklade**, Chalford & Stroud, 1/day
JL737 Stansted Airport to **Oxford** via Luton Airport, 8/day
NX304 Birmingham to Weymouth via **Oxford** & Southampton, 1/day
NX539 Edinburgh to Bournemouth via Birmingham, **Oxford** & Southampton, 1/day
NX445 London to Hereford via Cirencester, Stroud & Gloucester, 1/day

Stagecoach Oxford Tube (☎ 01865-772250, 🖵 oxfordtube.com)
    London Victoria to **Oxford**, 1-5/hr, most frequently during the day

Oxford Bus Company (☎ 01865-785400, 🖵 oxfordbus.co.uk)
● **the Airline** (🖵 airline.oxfordbus.co.uk) Heathrow & Gatwick airports to **Oxford** 2/hr between about 8am and 8pm, less frequently outside these hours
● **X90** (🖵 x90.oxfordbus.co.uk) London to **Oxford** 1-3/hr during the day, less frequently at night and at weekends

Green Line Coaches (now operated by Reading Buses 🖵 reading-buses.co.uk)
702   London Victoria to Bracknell via Slough & **Windsor**, daily 1/hr

❏ **Boats along the Thames**

While they can't really be considered public transport, there are regular boats serving towns along the Thames that provide a leisurely and scenic way of travelling between places along the river as well as a fresh perspective on the river. The main company behind these 'cruises' is Salters Steamers (☎ 01865-243421, 🖥 salterssteamers.co.uk) which have been plying their trade on the river for over 150 years. Their routes cover Oxford to Windsor. The boats (Apr/May-Sep/Oct) travel once a day each way most days but they're not particularly cheap (Oxford to Abingdon is £13.40, for example).

Other services are provided by Turk's Launches (🖥 turks.co.uk; Apr-end Oct; Hampton Court to Kingston) and Thames River Boats (🖥 wpsa.co.uk; Apr-end Oct; Hampton Court to Westminster). See also River bus p60.

paying at a car park or meter. Near to the river's source you can leave your vehicle at Kemble railway station's car park (£3 per day, £2 on Sat & Sun; £15-17 for 7 days if booked online at 🖥 apcoaconnect.com); but you will – of course – have to go back to get it at the end of your trip. Kemble is located on the A429 between Cirencester and junction 17 of the M4 motorway. For accurate directions and timings from your location to Kemble – or anywhere else that you may wish to start your walk – 🖥 theaa.com/route-planner is a wonderful resource.

LOCAL TRANSPORT

Getting to and from most parts of the Thames Path is generally pretty simple thanks to a relatively comprehensive public transport network.

The **public transport maps** (pp56-7) give an overview of routes which are of particular use to walkers. The **bus services and operators table** on pp58-9 gives the approximate frequency of bus services, the relevant stops and contact details for the operators; see box pp52-3 for details of **rail services**.

If the enquiry lines for bus information prove unsatisfactory contact **traveline** (☎ 0871-200 2233, 🖥 traveline.info) which has public transport information for the whole of the UK. Tourist information centres provide timetables and all other relevant details around the areas which they serve. Smartphone users can also download two traveline **apps** (South West and South East England) which may prove useful; see also opposite for additional app details.

Apart from in London you will find **bus stops** either marked on the map, or their position described in the text. The nearest **railway stations** are also marked on the maps and relevant service details included in the text.

Transport in London

Between Hampton Court Bridge and Charlton (the nearest railway station to the Thames Barrier) you have London's **extensive transport system** at your disposal. The combination of National Rail, Tfl Rail/London Overground, Docklands Light Railway (DLR) and London Underground (the 'Tube') trains, Thames Clipper river bus services, the city's famous red double-decker as well as single-decker buses means every point along the river can be accessed with relative ease by using either one or a mixture of the above. (cont'd on p60)

PLANNING YOUR WALK

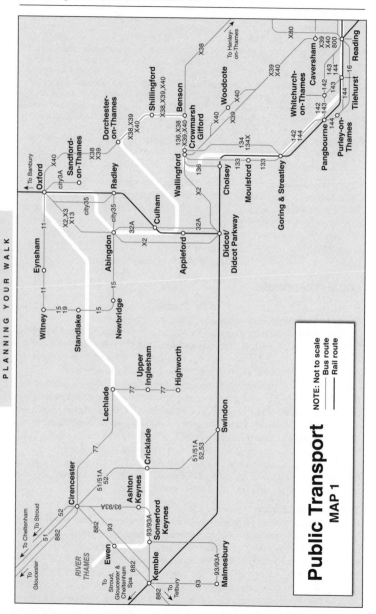

PLANNING YOUR WALK

Public Transport
MAP 1

NOTE: Not to scale
—— Bus route
—— Rail route

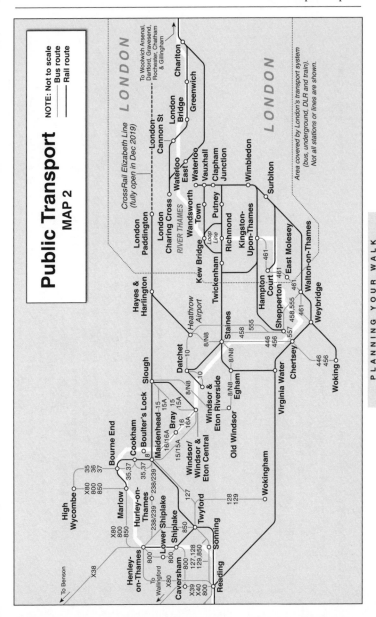

Public Transport
MAP 2

NOTE: Not to scale
— — — Bus route
———— Rail route

CrossRail Elizabeth Line
(fully open in Dec 2019)

LONDON

To Woolwich Arsenal,
Dartford, Gravesend,
Rochester, Chatham
& Gillingham

Charlton

Greenwich

London
Bridge

London–
Cannon St

Waterloo
East

Waterloo

Vauxhall

Clapham
Junction

Wimbledon

LONDON

Area covered by London's transport system
(bus, underground, DLR and train).
Not all stations or lines are shown.

London
Paddington

London
Charing Cross

RIVER THAMES

Wandsworth

Putney

Surbiton

Hayes &
Harlington

Kew Bridge

Richmond

Kingston-
Upon-Thames

Loop
Line

Twickenham

East Molesey

Walton-on-Thames

Hampton
Court

461

461

461

461

Heathrow
Airport

Staines

8/N8

555

461

Shepperton

458,555

Weybridge

Slough

Datchet

10

8/N8

446
456

Chertsey

557

446
456

Woking

Windsor &
Eton Riverside

8/N8

Egham

Virginia Water

8/N8

Old Windsor

Boulter's Lock

8

Maidenhead

15

15A

Bray

15

16/16A

16

16A

15/15A

Windsor/
Windsor &
Eton Central

Wokingham

Bourne End

High
Wycombe

35

36

37

X80
800
850

Marlow

35,37

Cookham

35,37

238/239

238/239

Hurley-on-
Thames

X80
800
850

127

850

Twyford

128
129

Lower Shiplake

800

Shiplake

850

Sonning

Henley-
on-Thames

To
Wallingford

800

X80
800

Caversham

X39
X40
800

127,128

129,850

Reading

To Benson

X38

PLANNING YOUR WALK

☐ BUS SERVICES & OPERATORS

Note: not all stops are listed

No	Operator	Route and frequency details
882	PC	Gloucester to Tetbury via Cirencester & **Kemble**, Mon-Sat 1-2/day plus 1/day from Cirencester stopping at **Ewen**; also plus 2/day to Kemble
93	CS	Malmesbury to Cirencester via **Kemble**. Mon-Sat 1/day
93/93A	CS	Malmesbury to Cirencester via **Ashton Keynes** (1/day) & **Somerford Keynes** (3/day). Mon-Sat 4/day
51	SC	Cheltenham to Swindon via Cirencester & **Cricklade**. Mon-Sat 1/hr, Sun 5/day
51A	SC	Stratton to Swindon via Cirencester & **Cricklade**. Mon-Sat 4/day
52	SC	Stroud to Swindon via Cirencester & **Cricklade**. Mon-Fri 4/day, Sat 3/day
53	SC	Swindon to **Cricklade**. Mon-Sat 7/day
77	SC	Cirencester to Highworth via **Lechlade** & **Upper Inglesham**, Mon-Fri 5/day, Sat 2/day plus 1/day to Lechlade
15	SC	Witney to Abingdon via **Standlake** & **Newbridge**. Mon-Sat 5/day
11	SC	Witney to **Oxford** via North Leigh & **Eynsham**, Mon-Fri 3/day plus 2/day from North Leigh
19	SC	Witney to Carterton via **Standlake** & Aston, Mon-Sat 8/day
city 3A	SC/OBC	Oxford to **Sandford-on-Thames**, Mon-Sat 2/hr (Stagecoach & Oxford Bus Company each provide an hourly service)
X3/X13	OBC	Oxford to **Abingdon**. Mon-Fri 6/hr
city 35	OBC	Oxford to **Abingdon** via Kennington & **Radley**, Mon-Sat 3/hr, Sun 1-2/hr
X2	TT	Oxford to **Wallingford** via Abingdon & Didcot Parkway, Mon-Sat 2/hr, Sun 1/hr
32A	TT	Abingdon to Wantage via **Culham**, Sutton Courtenay & Didcot Parkway, Mon-Sat 1/hr
X38	TT	(River Rapids) **Oxford** to **Henley-on-Thames** via Nuneham Courtenay, Berinsfield Layby (for **Dorchester-on-Thames**), **Shillingford**, **Benson**, **Crowmarsh** & **Wallingford**. Mon-Sat 1/hr
X39	TT	(River Rapids) **Oxford** to **Reading** via Nuneham Courtenay, Berinsfield Layby (for **Dorchester-on-Thames**), **Shillingford**, **Benson**, **Crowmarsh**, **Wallingford** & **Caversham**. Mon-Sat 1/hr
X40	TT	(River Rapids) **Oxford** to **Reading** via Nuneham Courtenay, Berinsfield Layby (for **Dorchester-on-Thames**), **Shillingford**, **Benson**, **Crowmarsh**, **Wallingford**, **Woodcote** & **Caversham**, daily 1/hr
133	TT	**Goring/Streatley** to **Wallingford** via Moulsford, Mon-Fri 1-3/day
136	TT	Benson to Cholsey via Crowmarsh **Gifford** & **Wallingford**, Mon-Fri 10/day, Sat 7/day
143	TT	Pangbourne to Reading via Kentwood Circle for **Tilehurst** station, Mon-Sat 4/day
134/134X	GF	**Goring**/Wallingford via Cleeve, South Stoke, North Stoke & **Crowmarsh Gifford**. Mon-Sat 9/day
142/144	GF	Goring to Reading via **Streatley**, **Pangbourne** & **Whitchurch-on-Thames**, Mon-Sat 3/day plus Mon-Fri 1/day

144	GF	Goring to Reading via **Streatley**, **Pangbourne**, **Purley-on-Thames** & **Tilehurst**, May-Oct Sun 4/day
16	RB	**Purley-on-Thames** to central Reading, Mon-Fri 4/hr, Sat & Sun 2/hr
800	ABB	Reading to High Wycombe via **Caversham**, **Shiplake**, **Lower Shiplake**, **Henley-on-Thames** & **Marlow**, daily 1-2/hr
850	ABB	Reading to High Wycombe via **Sonning**, Twyford, Wargrave, **Henley-on-Thames** & **Marlow**, Mon-Sat 1/hr
128/129	CB	Wokingham to Reading via Twyford & **Sonning**, Mon-Fri 10/day, Sat 5/day
127	CB	**Maidenhead** to Reading via Twyford & **Sonning**, Sat 5/day
X80 Regatta	Crl	High Wycombe to Reading via **Marlow**, **Henley-on-Thames** & **Lower Shiplake**, Mon-Sat 1/hr plus 1/hr to Marlow
238/239	CB	**Maidenhead** to **Hurley-on-Thames**, Mon-Fri 7/day (3/day continue to Henley). **Maidenhead** to **Henley** Sat 2/day
36	Crl	High Wycombe to **Bourne End**, Mon-Sat 2/hr (evening service operated by Arriva as No 35)
35/37	ABB	High Wycombe to **Maidenhead** via **Bourne End** & **Cookham**, Mon-Sat 1/hr (No 37), Sun 1/hr to **Bourne End** (No 35)
8	CB	**Maidenhead** to **Boulter's Lock**, Mon-Sat 11/day
10	CB	Dedworth to Heathrow Terminal 5 via **Windsor**, **Datchet** & **Wraysbury** (railway station), Mon-Sat 8/day but mostly morning and evening, plus Dedworth to Wraysbury 3/day and Windsor to Heathrow 2/day, Sun 8/day
15/15A	CB	**Maidenhead** circular route via Slough, **Eton**, **Eton Wick** & Dorney, Mon-Sat 2/day plus to Eton Wick 1/day
16/16A	CB	**Maidenhead** to Windsor via **Bray** & Dedworth, Mon-Sat approx 1/hr
8/N8	FBTTV	Slough to Heathrow Airport Terminal 5 via **Old Windsor**, **Egham** & **Staines**, daily 1-2/hr
458	CB	**Staines** to Kingston via **Laleham**, **Shepperton**, **Walton-on-Thames**, daily 1/hr plus Mon-Sat 1/hr to Walton-on-T
446	WB	Woking to **Staines** via **Chertsey**, daily 1/hr
456	FC	Woking to **Staines** via West Byfleet, **Addlestone** & **Chertsey**, Mon-Sat 1/hr
555	HB	Heathrow Airport to Whiteley Village via Ashford, Sunbury, **Shepperton**, **Walton-on-Thames** & Hersham, daily 1/hr
557	HB	**Addlestone** to Sunbury via **Chertsey**, **Shepperton** & Upper Halliford, Mon-Sat 1/hr
461	AS	**Addlestone** to Kingston via **Weybridge**, **Walton-on-Thames**, West Molesey, East Molesey & Hampton Court, daily 1-2/hr

Operator contact details: PC (Pulham's Coaches; ☎ 01451-820369, ▢ pulhamscoaches.com); **CS** (Coachstyle; ☎ 01249-782224, ▢ www.coachstyle.ltd.uk); **SC** (Stagecoach; ☎ 01865-785400, ▢ stagecoachbus.com); **OBC** (Oxford Bus Company; ☎ 01865-785400, ▢ city.oxfordbus.co.uk); **TT** (Thames Travel; ☎ 01865-785400, ▢ thames-travel.co.uk); **GF** (Going Forward Buses; ☎ 07484 605888, ▢ goingforwardbuses.com); **RB** (Reading Buses; ☎ 0118-9594000, ▢ reading-buses.co.uk); **ABB** (Arriva in Beds & Bucks; ☎ arrivabus.co.uk); **CB** (Courtney Buses; ☎ 0118-973 3486, ▢ courtneybuses.com); **Crl** (Carousel; ☎ 01494-450151, ▢ carouselbuses.co.uk); **FBTTV** (First Berkshire & The Thames Valley; ▢ firstgroup.com); **WB** (White Bus; ☎ 01344-882612, ▢ whitebus.co.uk); **FC** (Falcon Coaches; ☎ 01932-787752, ▢ fal concoachhire.com); **HB** (Hallmark Buses; ☎ 0845-519 9987, ▢ hallmarkbus.com); **AS** (Abellio Surrey; ▢ abellio.co.uk/surrey).

(*cont'd from p55*)   London is divided into **zones** and for the most part the **fare** you pay depends on the zone(s) you travel through. When it comes to paying for your journey, you can use an Oyster card, or a debit card as long as it is contactless. For the underground, or any train service, simply hold your card against the reader by the ticket gate and do the same as you exit the network, and you'll be charged the correct fare for your journey. If you forget to tap your card on the way out you'll be charged the maximum possible fare for your journey; the same applies if you inadvertently use a different card. For buses, you just need to tap your card against the reader on entering the bus.

There is a **daily cap** on most fares – at the time of writing this was £12.50 for travel in zones 1-6. However, any river bus journeys (see below) and 'flights' on the Emirates cable car (see p241) are not included in the daily cap.

For **information on all routes**, details of prices, timetables and up-to-date maps, contact **Transport for London** (🖥 tfl.gov.uk). A useful **app** for navigating the city's transport networks is #app# Citymapper.

Trains   The nearest and most useful railway (overground), underground (tube) and DLR stations are marked on the maps and mentioned in the text which accompanies them. See also box pp52-3 for rail and DLR routes.

Where a London Underground station is included the text also states which line it is on: for example **Charing Cross** (Northern/Bakerloo lines).

Buses   London buses do not take cash. If you intend to use them it is imperative you get an Oyster card (see box below) if you don't have a contactless debit card. **Hopper fares** enable you to hop on and off a bus (or tram) for free for up to an hour after paying for the first fare.

Since there are almost always bus stops outside or near both underground and railway stations, as well as at many places in between, bus stops are not marked on the maps for London. Nor are bus service details included in the text as there are so many options.

River bus   MBNA **Thames Clippers** (🖥 thamesclippers.com) operate various river bus routes between Putney and Woolwich (though no service covers the whole route) and they are a great way to see London from the river. Some services operate Monday to Friday only, or just in peak hours, but the main ones operate daily (approx 2/hr) from early morning till early evening. Oyster cards are valid and entitle you to a 10-20% discount. Piers to access the river bus are marked on the maps.

❏ **Oyster cards**
Oyster cards (🖥 tfl.gov.uk/oyster) are smart cards which provide discounted travel on most of London's travel network. You can get an Oyster card from numerous travel and information centres in London as well as from London Underground stations and newsagents. You will need to pay a £5 (refundable) deposit and put some credit on the card. You can then use it to swipe in and out of underground and DLR/railway stations and also on the buses and river buses. It can be topped up as and when required. For further details see the website.

Flora and fauna

The following is not in any way a comprehensive guide – if it were, you would not have room for anything else in your rucksack – but merely a brief rundown of the more commonly seen flora and fauna on the trail, together with some of the rarer and more spectacular species.

INSECTS

Of course, while you walk there is another world in existence all about you of which you'll largely be oblivious: that of the insect. Whizzing past your ears will be the **dragonfly** (*Anisoptera*) and the smaller **damselfly** (*Zygoptera*), the brilliant-green **banded demoiselle** (*Calopteryx splendens*) and the rare and relatively slow flying **club-tailed dragonfly** (*Gomphus vulgatissimus*).

Also airborne are the splendidly named **marmalade hoverfly** (*Episyrphus balteatus*), the amber-winged **brown hawker** (*Aeshna grandis*), **mayfly** (*Ephemeroptera*) and the ubiquitous **bees** and **wasps**. Meanwhile, on the ground you may come across one of the 70 species of **longhorn beetle** (*Cerambycidae*) native to Britain, the yellow and black **Cinnabar caterpillar** (*Tyria jacobaeae*) and **yellow meadow ants** (*Lasius flavus*).

The singing of grasshoppers and crickets is ubiquitous in summer; those you'll possibly see springing about in the grass include **meadow grasshoppers** (*Chorthippus parallelus*), **field grasshoppers** (*Chorthippus brunneus*) and **Roesel's bush-crickets** (*Metrioptera roeseli*).

BUTTERFLIES

One of the most pleasant sights whilst walking anywhere in the spring and summer is that of the butterfly which will suddenly appear, flitting about in the air, appearing to dance alongside you as you pace along the trail.

The meadows and waterside pathways of the Thames Path are rich in many species. You'll frequently see the **common** (*Polyommatus icarus*) and **adonis blue** (*Polyommatus bellargus*), the **large** and **small white** (*Pieris brassicae*/*Pieris rapae*), **small copper** (*Lycaena phlaeas*), **meadow brown** (*Maniola jurtina*) and, in early summer only, the **orange tip** (*Anthocharis cardamines*). All of these are relatively easy to distinguish thanks to their descriptive names.

Others commonly spotted but without such self-explanatory monikers include the striking lemon-yellow **brimstone** (*Gonepteryx rhamni*), the **gate-keeper** (*Pyronia tithonus*), which has orange wings rimmed with brown, the light-brown **small heath** (*Coenonympha pamphilus*) and the migrant **painted lady** (*Cynthia cardui*), the multicoloured wings of which will have carried it approximately 800 miles from North Africa; meaning, you'd imagine, that you're more likely to see it resting on a leaf, and probably asleep.

WILD FLOWERS AND SHRUBS

The river's waters are vital to the life of the local flora, of course, and many plants and wild flowers thrive along the banks and in the meadows which line the Thames.

By the river

Close to the water you're likely to come across an array of colours: **yellow iris** (*Iris pseudacorus*), the pink flowers of the **flowering rush** (*Butomus*), the lilac of the **water violet** (*Hottonia palustris*), an abundance of white-flowered **water crowfoot** (*Ranunculus aquatilis*) – and all watched over by **purple loosestrife** (*Lythrum salicaria*), which can grow up to 1.5m tall. You may also see **hemp-agrimony** (*Eupatorium cannabinum*), the reddish stem of which displays small dull pink flowers; whilst below them reside the dark green kidney-shaped leaves of **marsh-marigold** (*Caltha palustris*); the blue petals of **water forget-me-nots** (*Myosotis scorpioides*) and the floating oval leaves of **yellow water-lilies** (*Nymphaea lutea*), a good sign of nutrient-rich water. Finally, if walking between June and October, perhaps the most common plant you'll see are the pink flowers of the non-native **Himalayan balsam** (*Impatiens glandulifera*) dotted along the bank.

Meadows and woodland

Synonymous with spring and the start of the walking season are **bluebells** (*Hyacinthoides non-scripta*), the bluish-purple bell-shaped flowers of which carpet the woodland and hedgerows about the Thames. Appearing at a similar time of year are **cowslips** (*Primula veris*), **cuckooflower** (*Cardamine pratensis*), aka Lady's Smock, and **meadow buttercups** (*Ranunculus acris*); the latter can grow up to one metre in height.

By June the pinkish-lilac petals of the **common valerian** (*Valeriana officinalis*) should be on display in the meadows, as should the yellow-centred white-petalled **oxeye daisies** (*Leucanthemum vulgare*), the purple florets of the **common** (*Centaurea nigra*) and **greater knapweed** (*Centaurea scabiosa*), **bird's foot trefoil** (*Lotus corniculatus*), the tall and fragrant **meadowsweet** (*Filipendula ulmaria*), the golden-yellow **lady's bedstraw** (*Galium verum*), and the highly poisonous bright yellow flowers of the invasive **common ragwort** (*Senecio jacobaea*), which, sensibly avoided by grazing animals, thrives, particularly in pastures.

A relatively rare wild flower which is particularly exciting to see is the **purple snakeshead fritillary** (*Fritillaria meleagris*); this can be found carpeting North Meadow (Map 6), Iffley Meadow (Map 26) and Clifton Meadow (Map 32) in April. A plant you're unlikely to see any further north than the Thames is the **summer snowflake** (*Leucojum aestivum*), which can be spotted amongst the meadows and along the banks from April; complimenting the two you may also come across **yellow meadow vetchling** (*Lathyrus pratensis*), **red clover** (*Trifolium pratense*), **adder's tongue fern** (*Ophioglossum*), and a range of **orchids** such as the pink **southern marsh** (*Dactylorhiza praetermissa*) and **pyramidal orchids** (*Anacamptis pyramidalis*). Especially worth looking out for is the **bee orchid** (*Ophrys apifera*), the flowers of which are a mixture of pink, maroon, yellow and green; a distinctive colour scheme that is believed to attract a particular species of bee (*Andrena hattorfiana*) that pollinates the flowers.

TREES

The tree most associated with the river is the **willow** (*Salix*) and a number of varieties thrive along the banks of the Thames. The most easily identified is the **weeping willow** (*Salix x sepulcralis*), the leaves of which you'll often find yourself wandering beneath as they hang lazily over the river. Other varieties encountered include the **white willow** (*Salix alba*), which can be easily identified by its long and narrow leaves which taper to curled tips and are hairy underneath, and the **crack willow** (*Salix fragilis*), with its bright green leaves.

As well as **black poplar** (*Populus nigra*), **silver birch** (*Betula pendula*) and **ash** (*Fraxinus excelsior*) – the only native tree of the olive family – you may also come across **whitebeam** (*Sorbus aria*) and **elder** (*Sambucus nigra*) along the banks. **Hawthorns** (*Crategus monogyna*) are common as, especially along

---

❑ The capital's gentle giants – the London plane tree

It's a little-known fact that the London plane (*Platanus X Hispanica*) is the most common tree in the capital. Most easily distinguished by its olive, grey, cream and brown bark that forms a camouflage-like pattern on the tree, the plane is particularly common in London parks, and you'll walk through avenues of them in Wandsworth and Battersea parks (on the Thames's south side) as well as Bishop's Park in Fulham (on the north side).

Believed to be a hybrid between the American sycamore and the Oriental plane, the London plane is thought to have first appeared in the renowned nursery of John Tradescant the Younger, in Vauxhall, in the 17th century. But it really found popularity in the 18th and 19th centuries thanks to the unique property of its bark. London at the time was filled with soot and smog as the Industrial Revolution reached its peak, and many trees were unable to cope with the pollution. The plane tree, however, could shed large patches of its bark when it became too clogged with soot – thereby 'cleansing' itself of pollutants.

Those walking on the southern side of the Thames Path should look out for a plaque in the garden of Gaucho Restaurant on the way into Richmond (see map p208). Here, so the plaque boasts, is the tallest 'of its kind' in London – though experts say that there is one in Carshalton, a suburb of Sutton, that is taller.

the Chiltern stretch of the river, are **beech** (*Fagus sylvatica*). If walking in August you may see the tiny bright scarlet fruits of the **rowan** (*Sorbus aucuparia*) tree.

BIRDS

A common occurrence – especially while walking in the upper Thames – is the sudden scattering of waterfowl, shocked into action by your unexpected appearance as you make your way along the bank. Whilst birds are almost omnipresent on the river it's also worth keeping your eyes on the trees which line the shore as well as on the skies above as there are plenty to be spotted there too.

Waterfowl

Most of the waterfowl happily mingle and they are generally quite easy to identify. Needing no introduction, it's highly likely that the first bird you'll see gracefully gliding on the water is a **mute swan** (*Cygnus olor*, see Swan Upping on p39). To pass the time while walking we attempted to count how many we could spot and came up with the rough figure of 557, give or take a few. Be wary of getting too close, especially if they have cygnets in tow. If you do invade their territory you'll soon discover that they're not actually mute at all as they'll warn you off with a threatening hiss. Often to be seen socialising with the swans are **mallard** (*Anas platyrhynchos*) – say the word 'duck' and it's a mallard most people immediately envisage with their shimmering green heads – and **tufted duck** (*Aythya fuligula*). The commonest diving duck, the tuft on the back of their heads (which gives them their name), along with their grey black-tipped bill, makes them easily identifiable. Tufted ducks are especially prevalent in winter.

Never ones to shy away from any form of riverborne congregation are **Canada geese** (*Branta canadensis*). Introduced to the estates of wealthy landowners approximately 300 years ago, the population has exploded since and they're now the most common goose in southern Britain. Their large brown bodies, black necks and distinctive white 'chinstraps' make them easy to spot. You'll also see the **greylag goose** (*Anser anser*), sometimes mixed in with the flocks of Canada geese. The greylag is the ancestor of the domestic goose. A more recent migrant is the pinkish-brown **Egyptian goose** (*Alopochen aegyptica*).

Likely to be spotted about the river during the winter months are **black-headed gull** (*Larus ridibundus*) and **pochard** (*Aythya ferina*), while other birds which may make an appearance include the **wigeon** (*Anas penelope*) – brown with a white belly and small pale blue-grey bill – and the **long-tailed duck** (*Clangula hyemalis*). A small sea duck, it's unusual for them to make a foray inland but they are seen on the Thames. Another rare visitor – it is reckoned that fewer than 100 make the trip between November and March each year from Scandinavia and Siberia – is the **smew** (*Mergus albellus*). The male is distinguishable by its black 'bandit' mask whilst the females have red heads.

Waders observed along the river include the **snipe** (*Gallinago gallinago*), with its extremely long and straight bill, the larger **curlew** (*Numenius arquata*),

(cont'd after colour section)

Above, clockwise from top left: Pochard (©BT), mallard (©HS), Egyptian geese (©HS), Canada goose (©HS), greylag goose (©HS), mute swan (©HS), black-headed gull (©BT), curlew (©BT).

Above: The fields of many of the farms along the Thames come right down to the water. For the

nimals, the river is a useful source of drinking water and a place to cool off on a hot summer's day.

Peacock
Inachis io

Small Tortoiseshell
Aglais urticae

Common Blue
Polyommatus icarus

Large Garden/Cabbage White
Pieris brassicae

Small Heath
*Coenonympha
pamphilus*

Red
Admiral
Vanessa atalanta

Small Garden/Cabbage White
Pieris rapae

Painted Lady
Cynthia cadui

Small Copper
Lycaena phlaeas

Meadow
Brown
Maniola jurtina

Brimstone
*Gonepteryx
rhamni*

Himalayan Balsam
Impatiens glandulifera

Red Admiral butterfly (*Vanessa atalanta*) on
Hemp Agrimony (*Eupatorium cannabinum*)

Common Vetch
Vicia sativa

Herb-Robert
Geranium robertianum

Red Campion
Silene dioica

Lousewort
Pedicularis sylvatica

Meadow Cranesbill
Geranium pratense

Common Dog Violet
Viola riviniana

Common Knapweed
Centaurea nigra

Common Centaury
Centaurium erythraea

Old Man's Beard
Clematis vitalba

Common Ragwort
Senecio jacobaea

Yarrow
Achillea millefolium

Hogweed
Heracleum sphondylium

Gorse
Ulex europaeus

Meadow Buttercup
Ranunculis acris

Marsh Marigold (Kingcup)
Caltha palustris

Bird's-foot trefoil
Lotus corniculatus

St John's Wort
Hypericum perforatum

Tormentil
Potentilla erecta

Primrose
Primula vulgaris

Cowslip
Primula veris

Honeysuckle
Lonicera periclymemum

Harebell
Campanula rotundifolia

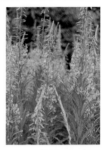

Foxglove
Digitalis purpurea

Rosebay Willowherb
Epilobium angustifolium

Rowan (tree)
Sorbus aucuparia

Dog Rose
Rosa canina

Forget-me-not
Myosotis arvensis

Scarlet Pimpernel
Anagallis arvensis

Self-heal
Prunella vulgaris

Germander Speedwell
Veronica chamaedrys

Ramsons (Wild Garlic)
Allium ursinum

Bluebell
Hyacinthoides non-scripta

Ox-eye Daisy
Leucanthemum vulgare

Above, clockwise from top left: Grey heron (©HS), red kite, chaffinch, reed bunting, coot, skylark, pied wagtail (all ©BT).

and the **lapwing** (*Vanellus vanellus*). Sightings of all of these are rather uncommon but one bird you'll definitely spot, thanks in part to its tendency to stand motionless and pose on riverbanks and mooring posts, watching for prey, is the **grey heron** (*Ardea cinerea*). Related to it, but much rarer, is the **bittern** (*Botaurus stellaris*); a type of heron, by 1997 they were nearly extinct but major conservation efforts since mean that there are currently over 100 males in existence in the south of England. On a still night the males' distinctive 'booming' mating call can be heard for up to five kilometres – meaning you're much more likely to hear it than see it.

Other birds you may see enjoying the river are: **moorhen** (*Gallinula chloropus*), comparable in size to a pigeon but black in colour and with a yellow-tipped red bill and long legs; similarly sized and shaped **coots** (*Fulica atra*), which are all black but for their white bill; the long thin neck and pinkish bills of the **great-crested grebe** (*Podiceps cristatus*); **cormorant** (*Phalacrocorax carbo*), which are dark-coloured with a hook-tipped bill; and, during summer, the **common tern** (*Sterna hirundo*).

In the woods and trees

A sure sign of spring and easily identifiable by its song is the **cuckoo** (*Cuculus canorus*), which will often give your journey along the river's upper reaches a musical accompaniment. Also resident on the Thames are: Britain's largest woodpecker, the **green woodpecker** (*Picus viridius*), which has a red head, black 'moustache' and a greenish-yellow lower back; and the commonest, the black, white and red **great spotted woodpecker** (*Dendrocopos major*). You may also see **swallows** (*Hirundo rustica*); their smaller relative, the **sand martin** (*Riparia riparia*), which is usually one of the earliest summer visitors to arrive; and Britain's most exotically coloured bird, the **kingfisher** (*Alcedonatthis*). They can be hard to spot (we saw six on our trek though those with more time and a keener eye will doubtless be able to spot many more), but with their iridescent blue colouring they're unmistakable once you do. Introduced from Asia and more commonly seen the closer you get to London are **ring-necked parakeets** (*Psittacula krameri*). Britain's only parrot is green, certainly offering competition to the kingfisher in the colour stakes. First recorded in the wild in 1969, you're most likely to see them perched in a tree top or hear their squawk (*kree, kree, kree, kree*); we saw our first one in Runnymede, but they're pretty ubiquitous east from there to Richmond and beyond. Indeed, they have become so common that one pub, The Anglers at Walton (see p194), now has one on its sign – a sure indication that they've become part of the landscape and fabric of this part of the country.

Common birds that are generally resident in Britain and which you should see on your walk include **blue tits** (*Cyanistes caeruleus*), the slightly larger but no less colourful **great tit** (*Parus major*) and the rarer – at least along the river – **long-tailed tit** (*Aegithalos caudatus*). Near to the water you may spot the sedentary **reed bunting** (*Emberiza schoeniclus*), clinging to a branch or singing from the top of a bush, or the **grey wagtail** (*Motacilla cinerea*), which breeds along tree-lined sections of the river and commonly nests close to

THE ENVIRONMENT AND NATURE

weirs. A relatively uncommon summer visitor to the meadows is the **yellow wagtail** (*Motacilla flava*), identifiable by its bright yellow underparts and brownish wings, whilst the black and white **pied wagtail** (*Motacilla alba*) also nests near water but is equally associated, especially in winter, with urban areas.

Other birds often spotted include Britain's smallest, the **goldcrest** (*Regulus regulus*), the **goldfinch** (*Carduelis carduelis*), the **bullfinch** (*Pyrrhula pyrrhula*), usually seen in woodland, as well as the sparrow-like **dunnock** (*Prunella modularis*), **skylark** (*Alauda arvenis*), **house sparrow** (*Passer domesticus*), and of course, the very common **robin** (*Erithacus rubecula*) and **blackbird** (*Turdus merula*).

Then there are the **warblers**. Sometimes spotted on their summer vacation are **blackcap** (*Sylvia atricapilla*), as well as the **garden** (*Sylvia borin*), **reed** (*Acrocephalus scirpaceus*) and **sedge warblers** (*Acrocephalus schoenobaenus*). You may also hear **chiffchaff** (*Phylloscopus collybita*), their olive-green feathers identifying them as they stand on branches and rather arrogantly sing their own names ... *chiff chaff chiff chaff chiff chaff* ... as if boasting of their successful immigration from the Mediterranean or West Africa.

Birds of prey

One bird which today you'll probably see hunting over the farmland, woodland and meadows which line the river – but which just 25 years ago you most definitely wouldn't – is the **red kite** (*Milvus milvus*). Persecuted almost to the point of extinction by the start of the 20th century, young birds from Europe were reintroduced to parts of England in 1989, since when numbers have been increasing exponentially. Similar in size to the **buzzard** (*Buteo buteo*), the kites are distinguishable by their 'scooped' tail and more graceful, 'shapely' silhouette than the rather clumsy, galumphing buzzard. They are also of a more russet/orange colour compared to the rather dull brown plumage of the buzzard – though it's doubtful you'll be able to distinguish this while they are in flight.

Smaller birds of prey you may spot standing on telephone wires or swooping down on their unexpecting prey include **kestrels** (*Falco tinnunculus*). There's also a chance, if wandering along in the evening, that you'll see – or, at least hear the distinctive 'snoring' or screeching calls of – a **barn owl** (*Tyto alba*).

MAMMALS

The character of Ratty in *The Wind in the Willows* (see box p148) is based on a **water vole** (*Arvicola terrestris*), and along with the other mammalian heroes and villains of Kenneth Grahame's tale, **badgers** (*Meles meles*), **moles** (*Talpa europaea*), **stoats** (*Mustela ermine*) and **weasels** (*Mustela nivalis*), all – with a little luck – can still be seen in the vicinity of the river.

The 'plop' of the water vole diving into the Thames nearly became a thing of the past as they suffered a devastating drop in population due to the arrival in the English countryside of the **American mink** (*Neovison vison*), which had successfully adapted to living in the wild after escaping from fur farms.

Unfortunately, the mink not only hunts water voles but is small enough to slip inside their burrows, thus being able to wipe out an entire river's population in a matter of months.

The consequences of the mink's arrival made the survival and protection of **otters** (*Lutra lutra*) along the Thames all the more important as they are believed to hunt mink. Shy and nocturnal; spotting an otter is unlikely but not impossible, thanks in large part to the huge conservation efforts to reintroduce them following a steep decline in their numbers during the middle of the 20th century. While still seldom spotted, their distinctive pad and toe prints are sometimes seen in the mud and their musk-scented droppings are occasionally seen left on prominent rocks to mark their territory. Indeed, so successful has the conservation effort been that some people, particularly the owners of the fishing lakes around Newbridge and Radcot, consider them a nuisance, as they deplete the stocks of carp in the lakes.

Usually measuring 60-90 centimetres in length, the otter would be the largest mammal living by the Thames if it weren't for the introduction in 2005 of six **Eurasian beaver** (*Castor fiber*) to the lake at Lower Mill Estate in Gloucestershire (see Map 3, p83). There are known to be at least 16 now gnawing away at the local trees.

Likely to be watching the beaver's gnawing with great trepidation from the branches above, a number of **bat** species frequent the habitat about the river, including the **soprano pipistrelle** (*Pipistrellus pygmaeus*), **natterer's bat** (*Myotis nattereri*), and **daubentons's bat** (*Myotis daubentonii*). The latter will fly along the surface of the river foraging for food before using their webbed feet to catch prey.

Back on all fours, common mammals that are more likely to be encountered include **foxes** (*Vulpes vulpes*), **hares** (*Lepus europaeus*), **hedgehog** (*Erinaceus europaeus*), **grey squirrel** (*Sciurus carolinensis*), **rabbits** (*Oryctolagus cuniculus*) and any number of species of **mice**, **voles** and **shrews**.

Aquatic mammals

The largest aquatic mammal to grace the Thames – at least, in recent times – was a female **bottle-nosed whale** (*Hyperoodon ampullatus*), which in January 2006 was seen swimming in the river as far upstream as Chelsea. Approximately five metres long and weighing in the region of seven tonnes, her appearance in the Thames was extremely unusual as such creatures typically stick to deeper sea waters. While crowds gathered to catch a glimpse of the surprise visitor the whale swam within yards of the bank, crashing into a boat and injuring itself. Throughout the following two days attempts were made to rescue the whale; alas they proved to be unsuccessful and she eventually died on a barge.

You're extremely unlikely to see whales from the banks of the London Thames, though there is a slim chance of catching a glimpse of a **harbour porpoise** (*Phocoena phocoena*), while also occasionally spotted are **grey seal** (*Halichoerus grypus*), **harbour seal** (*Phoca vitulina*) and **bottlenose dolphins** (*Tursiops truncatus*).

THE ENVIRONMENT AND NATURE

REPTILES AND AMPHIBIANS

The amphibians you're most likely to come across during the day are **frogs** (*Rana temporaria*), whilst at dusk **toads** (*Bufo bufo*) become more conspicuous.

The only poisonous snake in Britain is the **adder** (*Vipera berus*). They pose very little risk to walkers – indeed, you should consider yourself extremely fortunate to see one, providing you're a safe distance away, of course. They bite only when provoked, preferring to hide instead. The venom is designed to kill small mammals such as mice, voles and shrews, so deaths in humans are very rare but a bite can be extremely unpleasant and occasionally dangerous to children or the elderly. You are most likely to encounter them in spring when they come out of hibernation and during the summer when pregnant females warm themselves in the sun. They are easily identified by the striking zigzag pattern on their back. Should you encounter one, enjoy it but leave it be.

Locks are the perfect habitat for **grass snakes** (*Natrix natrix*) and you may see one swimming in the river. They're harmless but if you touch them it's likely to leave a nasty smell on your hand, the foul odour being their choice of defence rather than venom.

A treat for **gastropod** enthusiasts will be Kew Riverside Park Snail Reserve (Map 74, p210), home to the **two-lipped door snail** (*Balea biplicata*).

FISH

Unless you've a trained eye, it's unlikely you'll be able to identify many of the fish which exist in the Thames from the quick glimpse that you may catch of them as they swim by. Indeed, you're probably more likely to experience one on a plate than in the river. The following, however, are there beneath the surface and thrive in today's cleaner Thames (see box p70).

Smaller fish (usually 15-30cm) include **ruffe** (*Gymnocephalus cernua*), **gudgeon** (*Gobio gobio*), **dace** (*Leuciscus leuciscus*), **roach** (*Rutilus rutilus*), **grayling** (*Thymallus thymallus*), **rudd** (*Scardinius erythrophthalmus*), **perch** (*Perca fluviatilis*), **bullhead** (*Cottus gobio*), and the jawless **brook lamprey** (*Lampetra planeri*).

Common medium-sized fish (usually 30-60cm) include **chub** (*Squalius cephalus*), **bream** (*Abramis brama*), **tench** (*Tinca tinca*), **barbel** (*Barbus barbus*), **brown trout** (*Salmo trutta*) and **carp** (*Cyprinus carpio*).

Larger fish (usually 60cm or above) to frequent the river include **salmon** (*Salmo salar*), **pike** (*Esox lucius*) and **eel** (*Anguilla anguilla*), some of the latter growing up to two metres long. The crown, however, for the largest freshwater fish to frolic in the river's waters goes to the **Wels catfish** (*Silurus glanis*), which can be anything between one and five metres in length.

MINIMUM IMPACT & OUTDOOR SAFETY

3

ENVIRONMENTAL IMPACT

A walking holiday in itself is an environmentally friendly approach to tourism. The following are some ideas on how you can go a few steps further in helping to minimise your impact on the environment while walking the Thames Path.

Use public transport whenever possible

Public transport along the Thames Path is readily available (though it can be a little infrequent at times along the upper reaches). Public transport is always preferable to using private cars as it benefits everyone: visitors, locals and the environment.

Never leave litter

'Pack it in, pack it out'. Leaving litter is antisocial so carry a degradable plastic bag for all your rubbish, organic or otherwise (you could even pick up other people's too) and pop it in a bin in the next village. Or better still, reduce the amount of litter you take with you by getting rid of packaging in advance.

● **Is it OK if it's biodegradable?** Not really. Apple cores, banana skins, orange peel and the like are unsightly, encourage flies, ants and wasps and ruin a picnic spot for others; they can also take months to decompose. In high-use areas such as the Thames Path either bury them or take them away with you.

Buy local

Look and ask for local produce to buy and eat. Not only does this cut down on the amount of pollution and congestion that the transportation of food creates (so-called 'food miles'), it also ensures that you are supporting local farmers and producers.

Erosion

● **Stay on the main trail** The effect of your footsteps may seem minuscule but when they're multiplied by several thousand walkers each year they become rather more significant. Avoid taking shortcuts, widening the trail or taking more than one path, especially across meadows and ploughed fields.

● **Consider walking out of season** Maximum disturbance by walkers coincides with the time of year when nature wants to do most of its growth and repair. In high-use areas, like that along much of the Thames Path, the trail is often prevented from recovering.

Walking at less busy times eases this pressure while also generating year-round income for the local economy. Not only that but it may make the walk a more relaxing experience with fewer people on the path and less competition for accommodation.

Respect all flora and fauna

Care for all wildlife you come across along the path; it has as much right to be there as you. Tempting as it may be to pick wild flowers, leave them so the next people who pass can enjoy them too. Don't break branches off trees. If you come across wildlife keep your distance and don't watch for too long. Your presence can cause considerable stress, particularly if the adults are with young, or in winter when the weather is harsh and food is scarce. Young animals are rarely abandoned. If you come across young birds keep away so that their mother can return.

❏ The environment and conservation

Throughout much of its history the Thames and its tributaries acted as natural sewers for the industrial and domestic waste created by the settlements which had sprung up alongside it. For generations, the river's natural cycle had dispersed this waste, aerating the waters before flushing them out on the tides. By the 18th century the population bulge in the Thames Valley (and especially in London) had overwhelmed the river's innate ability to self-heal and pollution had become endemic. In the early 19th century a dramatic decline in the amount of fish in the river (always a good indicator of a river's condition) was followed by four significant cholera epidemics in London (1832, 1849, 1854, 1865). Despite evidence collated that linked the 1854 epidemic with the city's water, it would take the Great Stink of 1858 (during which the smell seeped in through the windows of the House of Commons) before Parliament finally acted and sewage systems were constructed to divert the city's waste away from the metropolis and further out towards the sea. Even with such efforts, however, by the 1950s there were still 28 sewage works emptying into the Thames and much industrial waste continued to leak into the river. Levels of oxygen in the water were at an all-time low; the lower Thames was dying.

The closure of London's docks (see box p236) along with increased investment and the application of higher water-quality standards have, since the 1960s, led to the natural life of the river going through something of a renaissance and today it is healthier than at any point in the past half-millennium. A good indicator of an unpolluted environment is the presence of otters (see p67), and their return to the river in around 2001 – along with the recent identification of over 125 species of fish – is testament to the ongoing conservation efforts of the organisations responsible for the enduring health of the River Thames.

Today, a variety of bodies watch over the river and its immediate environs. Legally responsible for taking care of the stretch between the source and Teddington is the **Environment Agency** (see box p48), whilst the Thames in London is the responsibility of the **Port of London Authority** (🖳 pla.co.uk). Other organisations heavily involved in the river's upkeep include the **National Trust** (🖳 nationaltrust.org.uk) and **Natural England** (🖳 gov.uk/government/organisations/natural-england). The latter is responsible for managing the **National Nature Reserves** (NNRs) – such as North Meadow (p82) and Chimney Meadows (see p98) – and the almost 150 **Sites of Special Scientific Interest** (SSSIs) that exist within three miles of the Thames.

The code of the outdoor loo

'Going' in the outdoors is a lost art worth reclaiming, for your sake and everyone else's. As more and more people discover the joys of the outdoors this is becoming an important issue. In some parts of the world where visitor pressure is higher than in Britain, walkers and climbers are required to pack out their excrement. This might one day be necessary here. Human faeces are not only offensive to our senses but, more importantly, can infect water sources.

● **Where to go** Wherever possible **use a toilet**. Public toilets are marked on the trail maps in this guide and you'll also find facilities in pubs, cafés, libraries and campsites along the path. Many pubs in London and other businesses have signed up to the 'Community Toilet Scheme' – this means they are happy for anyone to use their toilet facilities without making a purchase. There are also toilet (and water tap) facilities at some of the locks.

If you do have to go outdoors, avoid ruins which can otherwise be welcome shelter for other walkers, as well as sites of historic or archaeological interest, and choose a place that is at least **30 metres away from running water**. Use a stick or trowel to **dig a small hole** about 15cm (6") deep to bury your excrement. It decomposes quicker when in contact with the top layer of soil or leaf mould. Stirring loose soil into your deposit speeds up decomposition. Do not squash it under rocks as this slows down the composting process. If you have to use rocks to cover it make sure they are not in contact with your faeces.

● **Toilet paper and tampons** Toilet paper takes a long time to decompose whether buried or not. It is easily dug up by animals and may then blow into water sources or onto the path.

The best method for dealing with it is to **pack it out**. Put the used paper inside a paper bag which you then place inside a plastic bag. Then simply empty the contents of the paper bag at the next toilet you come across and throw the bag away. If this is too much bother, light your used toilet paper and watch it burn until the flames are out – you don't want to start a wild fire. Pack out **tampons** and **sanitary towels**; they take years to decompose and may also be dug up and scattered about by animals.

ACCESS

Britain is a crowded island with few places where you can wander as you please. Most of the land is a patchwork of fields and agricultural land and the terrain through which much of the Thames Path flows, at least outside London, is no different. However, there are countless public rights of way, in addition to the Thames Path, that criss-cross the land.

Right to roam

The Countryside & Rights of Way Act 2000 (CRoW), or 'Right to Roam' as dubbed by walkers, came into effect in 2005 after a long campaign to allow greater public access to areas of countryside in England and Wales deemed to be uncultivated open country; this essentially means moorland, heathland, downland and upland areas. Some land is covered by restrictions (ie high-impact

❏ THE COUNTRYSIDE CODE

The Countryside Code, originally described in the 1950s as the Country Code, was revised and relaunched in 2004, in part because of the changes brought about by the CRoW Act (see p71); it was updated again in 2012, 2014 and also 2016. The Code seems like common sense but sadly some people still appear to have no understanding of how to treat the countryside they walk in. An adapted version of the 2016 Code, launched under the logo 'Respect. Protect. Enjoy.', is given below:

Respect other people

● **Consider the local community and other people enjoying the outdoors** Be sensitive to the needs and wishes of those who live and work there. If, for example, farm animals are being moved or gathered keep out of the way and follow the farmer's directions. Being courteous and friendly to those you meet will ensure a healthy future for all based on partnership and co-operation.

● **Leave gates and property as you find them and follow paths unless wider access is available** A farmer normally closes gates to keep farm animals in, but may sometimes leave them open so the animals can reach food and water. Leave gates as you find them or follow instructions on signs. When in a group, make sure the last person knows how to leave the gate. Follow paths unless wider access is available, such as on open country or registered common land (known as 'open access land'). Leave machinery and farm animals alone – if you think an animal is in distress try to alert the farmer instead. Use gates, stiles or gaps in field boundaries if you can – climbing over walls, hedges and fences can damage them and increase the risk of farm animals escaping. If you have to climb over a gate because you can't open it always do so at the hinged end. Also be careful not to disturb ruins and historic sites.

Stick to the official path across arable/pasture land. Minimise erosion by not cutting corners or widening the path.

Protect the natural environment

● **Leave no trace of your visit and take your litter home** Take special care not to damage, destroy or remove features such as rocks, plants and trees. Take your litter with you (see p69); litter and leftover food doesn't just spoil the beauty of the countryside, it can be dangerous to wildlife and farm animals.

Fires can be as devastating to wildlife and habitats as they are to people and property – so be careful with naked flames and cigarettes at any time of the year.

● **Keep dogs under effective control** This means that you should keep your dog on a lead or keep it in sight at all times, be aware of what it's doing and be confident it will return to you promptly on command.

Across farmland dogs should always be kept on a short lead. During lambing time they should not be taken with you at all. Always clean up after your dog and get rid of the mess responsibly – 'bag it and bin it'. (See also p28 and pp244-5).

Enjoy the outdoors

● **Plan ahead and be prepared** You're responsible for your own safety: be prepared for natural hazards, changes in weather and other events. Wild animals, farm animals and horses can behave unpredictably if you get too close, especially if they're with their young – so give them plenty of space.

● **Follow advice and local signs** In some areas there may be temporary diversions in place. Take notice of these and other local trail advice. Walking on the Thames Path is pretty much hazard-free but you're responsible for your own safety so follow the simple guidelines outlined on pp74-6.

activities such as driving a vehicle, cycling and horse-riding are not permitted) and some land is excluded (such as gardens, parks and cultivated land). Full details are given on 🖳 jncc.defra.gov.uk/page-1378.

With more freedom in the countryside comes a need for more responsibility from the walker. Remember that wild open country is still the workplace of farmers and home to all sorts of wildlife. Have respect for both and avoid disturbing domestic and wild animals.

Outdoor health and safety

STAY HEALTHY

You will enjoy your walk more if you have a reasonable level of fitness. Carrying a pack for 5-7 hours a day is demanding and any preparation you have done beforehand will pay off.

Water

You need to drink lots of water while you're walking: 2-4 litres per day, depending on the weather. If you start to feel tired, lethargic or get a headache it may be that you are not drinking enough. Thirst is not a good indicator of when to drink; stop and have a drink every hour or two at the very least. A good indication of whether you are drinking enough is the colour of your urine – the lighter the better. If you are not needing to urinate much and/or your urine is dark yellow you need to increase your fluid intake.

Blisters

It's essential to try out new boots before embarking on your long trek. Make sure they're comfortable and once on the move try to avoid getting them wet on the inside and remove any small stones or twigs that get in the boot. Air and massage your feet at lunchtime, keep them clean, and change your socks regularly. As soon as you start to feel any hot spots developing, stop and apply a few strips of low-friction zinc oxide tape. Leave them on until the foot is pain free or the tape starts to come off. As you're walking continuously the chances are it won't get better – but it won't get worse so quickly either. If you know you have problems apply the tape pre-emptively. If you've left it too late and a blister has developed you should apply a plaster such as Compeed (or the slightly cheaper clone now made by Boots). Many walkers have Compeed to thank for enabling them to complete their walk. Popping a blister reduces the pressure but can lead to infection. If the skin is broken keep the area clean with antiseptic and cover with a non-adhesive dressing material held in place with tape.

Blister-avoiding strategies include rubbing the prone area with Vaseline or wearing a thin and a thick sock as well as adjusting the tension of your laces. All are ways of reducing rubbing and foot movement against the inside of the boot.

Hypothermia, hyperthermia and sunburn

Also known as **exposure**, **hypothermia** occurs when the body can't generate enough heat to maintain its normal temperature, usually as a result of being wet, cold, unprotected from the wind, tired and hungry. Hypothermia is easily avoided by wearing suitable clothing, carrying and consuming enough food and drink, being aware of the weather conditions and checking the morale of your companions. Early signs to watch for are feeling cold, tired and shivering involuntarily. If allowed to worsen, erratic behaviour, slurring of speech and poor co-ordination will become apparent and the victim can very soon progress into unconsciousness, followed by coma and death. Of course, on the Thames Path you're seldom far from civilisation and your first action should be to seek help or call the emergency services. But if for some reason this isn't possible, find some shelter as soon as possible and warm the victim up with a hot drink and some chocolate or other high-energy food. If possible give them another warm layer of clothing and allow them to rest until feeling better. Quickly get the victim out of wind and rain, improvising a shelter if necessary. Rapid restoration of bodily warmth is essential and best achieved by bare-skin contact: someone should get into the same sleeping bag as the patient, both having stripped to the bare essentials, placing any spare clothing under or over them to build up heat.

Not an ailment that you would normally associate with southern England, hyperthermia (heat exhaustion and heatstroke) is a serious problem nonetheless.

Symptoms of **heat exhaustion** include thirst, fatigue, giddiness, a rapid pulse, raised body temperature, low urine output and, if not treated, delirium and finally a coma. The best cure is to drink plenty of water. **Heatstroke** is another matter altogether and even more serious. A high body temperature and an absence of sweating are early indications, followed by symptoms similar to hypothermia (see above) such as a lack of co-ordination, convulsions and coma. Death will follow if treatment is not given instantly. Sponge the victim down, wrap them in wet towels, fan them – and get help immediately.

Sunburn can happen, even in England, and even on overcast days. The best ways to avoid it are either to stay wrapped up or smother yourself in sunscreen (with a minimum factor of 15), reapplying it regularly throughout the day. Don't forget your lips, nose, the back of your neck and even under your chin to protect you against rays reflected from the ground.

SAFETY

Sadly every year people are injured walking along the trail, though usually it's nothing more than a badly twisted ankle. Parts of the upper reaches of the River Thames are pretty remote, and it certainly pays to take precautions when walking. Abiding by the following rules should minimise the risk.

● Avoid walking on your own if possible.

● Make sure that somebody knows your plans for every day that you're on the trail. This could be a friend or relative whom you have promised to call every night, or your accommodation at the end of each day's walk. That way, if you fail to turn up or call that evening, they can raise the alarm.

● If the weather closes in suddenly and fog or mist descends while you're on the trail and you become uncertain of the correct trail, do not be tempted to continue. Just wait where you are and you'll find that mist often clears, at least for long enough to allow you to get your bearings. If you're still uncertain, and the weather does not look like improving, return the way you came to the nearest point of civilisation. If it is misty or foggy be careful you don't fall in the river.

● Fill up with water at every opportunity and carry some high-energy snacks.

● Always carry a torch, compass, map, whistle, mobile phone and wet-weather gear with you.

● Wear sturdy boots or shoes, not trainers.

● Be extra vigilant if walking with children.

Walking alone

If you are walking alone you must appreciate and be prepared for the increased risk. Take note of the safety guidelines below.

Swimming

The laws regarding swimming outdoors are a little ambiguous in England and Wales. Currently, as long as you are not trespassing, you are fine to swim in 'navigable' waters such as the **non-tidal Thames**. This does not mean that you should just dive in anywhere. It cannot be stressed highly enough that when choosing to have a dip you must do so with both the upmost respect for the river and highest regard for your own **personal safety**.

An informative online resource for potential Thames swimmers is 💻 oudoorswimmingsociety.com.

The dangers of swimming in the **tidal Thames** (downriver of Teddington Lock) are significant; as you walk you may notice memorials to people who have lost their lives swimming in the Thames. Any ramblers hoping to take a dip in the London Thames should note that it is illegal to swim in the Thames between Putney Bridge and the Thames Barrier without permission from the harbour master.

For information on swimming in the tidal Thames see 💻 pla.co.uk/Safety/Swimming-in-the-Tidal-Thames.

Top safety tips include

● Do not swim alone

● Wear a bright coloured hat (preferably red) so that boats and other swimmers can see you

● If possible, ask local advice first before plunging in

● Acclimatise to cold water gradually

● Have warm clothes available for when you get out

● Make sure you know your exit point

● Always step in; whether you can see the bottom or not, do not jump in.

Avoidance of hazards

With good planning and preparation most hazards can be avoided. This information is just as important for those out on a day walk as for those walking the

MINIMUM IMPACT & OUTDOOR SAFETY

entire Thames Path. Always make sure you have suitable **clothing** (see pp41-2) to keep you warm and dry, whatever the conditions when you set off, and a change of inner clothes too. Carrying plenty of food and water is vital too.

Dealing with an accident

● Use basic first aid to treat the injury to the best of your ability.

● Try to attract the attention of anybody else who may be in the area. The **international distress (emergency) signal** is six blasts on a whistle, or six flashes with a torch; both are best done when you think someone might see the light flashes or hear the whistle blasts.

● Work out exactly where you are. If possible leave someone with the casualty while others go to get help. If there are only two people, you have a dilemma. If you decide to get help leave all spare clothing and food with the casualty.

● In an emergency dial ☎ 999 (or the EU standard number ☎ 112). Make sure you know exactly where you are before you call and report the position of the casualty and their condition.

WEATHER FORECASTS

The weather along the Thames Path is as unpredictable as the rest of England and you'd be well advised to always prepare for the worst. Along the river's upper reaches, and especially during winter, **flooding** can be an issue. Before you set off for the day, look at the Government's flood information page 💻 flood-warning-information.service.gov.uk should you have concerns about the area in which you plan to go walking. Flooding along the tidal Thames in London is an issue and it would be worth consulting 💻 tidetimes.org.uk before you set out, although diversion signs will be in place anywhere where flooding occurs regularly.

Most hotels, some B&Bs and tourist information centres will have a summary of the **weather forecast** somewhere. Alternatively you can get a forecast either through 💻 bbc.co.uk/weather, or 💻 metoffice.gov.uk/public/weather.

Pay close attention to the weather forecast and alter your plans for the day accordingly. That said, even if the forecast is for a fine sunny day, this is the British Isles and you should always pack some wet weather gear.

❏ **Old Father Thames**
The statue of Old Father Thames, at St John's Lock (see p95) near Lechlade, is by the Italian sculptor Rafaelle Monti and one of several originally commissioned to adorn the fountains at the Crystal Palace in Sydenham in 1854. When fire destroyed the palace in 1936 the statue was rescued, eventually finding a new home at Thames Head, the river's source, in 1958. A victim of vandalism, it was  moved to St John's Lock in 1974; thus, whilst Old Father Thames guards the river, the statue itself can be kept under the watchful eye of the lock-keeper.

© Joel Newton

Using this guide

The following guide follows the Thames Path from west to east (ie downstream), beginning at the source of the river and concluding at the Thames Barrier. It is split into 15 stages; these do not have to be followed rigidly and with so much accommodation available en route you can pretty much divide your walk into as few or as many days as you want. See pp36-7 for some suggested itineraries.

To provide further help, practical information is provided on the trail maps, including walking times, places to stay and eat, public toilets as well as shops and supermarkets. Further service details are given in the text under the entry for each settlement.

For a condensed overview of this information see the **village and town facilities table** on pp30-5; for cumulative **distance charts** see pp250-3; and for **overview maps** and **map profiles** see the colour pages at the end of the book.

TRAIL MAPS   [for key maps see inside back cover]

Scale and walking times

The trail maps are drawn to a scale of 1:20,000 (1cm = 200m; $3^{1/8}$ inches = 1 mile). Walking times are given along the side of each map and the arrow shows the direction to which the time refers. Black triangles indicate the points between which the times have been taken.

The time bars are a tool and are not there to judge your walking ability. There are so many variables that affect walking speed, from the weather conditions to how many beers you drank the previous evening. After the first hour or two of walking you will be able to see how your speed relates to the timings on the maps.

Up or down?

Other than when on a track, bridleway, or road, the trail is shown as a dashed line. In Trailblazer guidebooks an arrow across the trail

---

❏ **Important note – walking times**
Unless otherwise specified, **all times in this book refer only to the time spent walking**. You will need to add 20-30% to allow for rests, time to stop and stare, photography, checking the map, drinking water etc. When planning the day's hike count on 5-7 hours' actual walking.

indicates the gradient; two arrows show that it's steep. However, as there is only one gradient of note on this entire trail, you won't see this symbol much. Note that the *arrow points uphill*, the opposite of what OS maps use on steep roads. Reversed arrow heads indicate a downward gradient.

Other features

Features are marked on the map when of possible interest or pertinent to navigation. In order to avoid cluttering the maps not all features have been marked each time they occur.

The numbered **GPS waypoints** refer to the list on pp246-8.

Accommodation

Apart from larger towns (and especially for the London area) where some selection of places has been necessary, almost every place to stay that is on, or very close to, the actual trail is marked on the map. Details of each place are given in the accompanying text.

The number of **rooms** of each type is stated, ie: **S** = Single, **T** = Twin room (with two single beds), **D** = Double room (with one bed), **Tr** = Triple room and **Qd** = Quad. Note that most of the triple/quad rooms have a double bed and one/two single beds (or bunk beds); thus for a group of three or four, two people would have to share the double bed, but it also means the room can be used as a double or twin. See also p20.

Rates quoted for B&B-style accommodation are **per person (pp) based on two people sharing a room** for a one-night stay; rates are usually discounted for longer stays. Where a **single room (sgl)** is available the rate for that is quoted if different from the rate per person. The rate for **single occupancy (sgl occ)** of a double/twin may be higher, and the per person rate for three/four sharing a triple/quad may be lower. Unless specified, rates are for bed and breakfast. At some places the only option is a **room rate**; this will be the same whether one or two people (or more if permissible) use the room. See p22 for more information on rates.

Unless otherwise stated you can assume that the accommodation described has **en suite facilities** in all its rooms. The text only mentions where places have **private**, or **shared, facilities** (in either case this may be a bathroom or shower room just outside the bedroom). In the text ✇ signifies that at least one **bath** is available – either in an en suite room or in a separate bathroom – for those who prefer a relaxed soak at the end of the day.

Also noted is whether the premises have **wi-fi** (WI-FI) and if **dogs** (🐾 – see also pp244-5) are welcome in at least one room (often places only have one room suitable for dogs), or at campsites, subject to prior arrangement. Some places make an additional charge while others may require a deposit which is refundable if the dog doesn't make a mess or cause damage.

If arranged in advance many B&B proprietors are happy to collect walkers from the nearest point on the trail and deliver them back again next morning; they may also be happy to transfer your **luggage** to your next accommodation place on the map. Some may make a charge for either or both of these services. Check the details at the time of booking.

The route guide

KEMBLE [Map 1, p80]

The source of the River Thames (see box below) – and thus the start of the Thames Path itself – is approximately 1¾ miles (2.8km; 35-45mins) from the village of Kemble; for directions between Kemble and the source see p81. We have also marked on the map the route from The Thames Head Inn (see Map 1).

The site of 7th-century Anglo-Saxon cemeteries and, before them, where the Romans buried their dead too, Kemble's name has evolved from *Kemele*, meaning boundary. The village sits at a junction of several historical transport routes including the Thames, the Roman Fosse Way (which links Exeter with Bath and Lincoln) and the Great Western Railway. A local politician, Robert Gordon, was so affronted by the arrival of the railway at Kemble that he insisted that the new line be hidden from view when it passed in front of his house. A tunnel was thus built over the track to conceal it from his view.

The main attraction in the village, the **church** on its southern edge, has a Norman door and tower dating from 1250.

On Windmill Rd, **Kemble Stores** (Mon-Fri 8am-1pm & 2-6pm, Sat 8am-1pm & 2.30-7pm, Sun 9am-noon) provides any basic necessities required; the **post office** (Mon, Tue, Thur & Fri 9am-1pm & 2-5.30pm, Wed & Sat 9am-1pm) is part of the shop and cash can be withdrawn depending on what debit card you have (see pp24-5).

For **B&B** in the village, *Willows* (☎ 01285-770667, 🖳 kmw.kemble@gmail .com; 1T en suite shower/1D private bathroom; 🍺; WI-FI) is tucked away down a quiet cul-de-sac at 2 Glebe Lane. The rate is £35-40pp (sgl occ from £60).

Between the village and the river source, there's no more appropriate place for Thames Path trekkers to stay and eat than *The Thames Head Inn* (☎ 01285-770259, 🖳 thamesheadinn.co.uk; 3D/1T; 🍺; WI-FI; 🐾; Tetbury Rd). **B&B** costs from £40pp (sgl occ from £50; room only rates also available). **Camping** (£20 per pitch) is an option and shower/toilet facilities are available. **Food** is available daily (Mon-Sat 11am-9.30pm, Sun from noon), Bob's bubble & squeak (£11.50) being

ROUTE GUIDE AND MAPS

❏ The source of the River Thames

Approximately one mile from Kemble the source of the river Thames is hidden deep in a Gloucestershire field known as **Trewsbury Mead**. Lying 105 metres (356ft) above sea level, the river's origin is marked by an **inscribed stone** next to an ancient ash tree. Thought to be two centuries old, the tree once had the initials 'TH' (Thames Head) carved in its bark; letters some beady-eyed folk still claim to be able to see. Despite photos from the 1960s showing young boys canoeing beneath the tree's boughs you will most likely see no water. Fear not though, deep in the earth below, the river's journey *is* beginning – as is yours, though at ground level.

There is some dispute over the source of the River Thames, an alternative origin being Seven Springs at the head of the River Churn. Joining the Thames at Cricklade (Map 7) this would make the Thames 12 miles longer and 91 metres further above sea level. Historically, however, the Churn has always borne its own name so it is considered to be merely a tributary rather than the river itself. The honour of being the official source of the Thames thus goes to Thames Head.

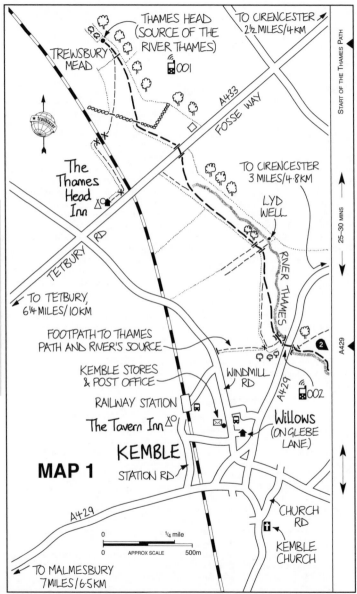

ROUTE GUIDE AND MAPS

TO CIRENCESTER
2½ MILES/4 KM

THAMES HEAD
(SOURCE OF THE
RIVER THAMES)

TREWSBURY
MEAD

001

trailblazer

The
Thames
Head
Inn

A433

FOSSE WAY

TO CIRENCESTER
3 MILES/4·8 KM

LYD
WELL

RIVER THAMES

START OF THE THAMES PATH

25–30 MINS

TETBURY RD

TO TETBURY,
6¼ MILES/10 KM

FOOTPATH TO THAMES
PATH AND RIVER'S SOURCE

KEMBLE STORES
& POST OFFICE

WINDMILL
RD

A429

RAILWAY STATION

The Tavern Inn

KEMBLE

STATION RD

002

Willows
(ON GLEBE
LANE)

MAP 1

A429

0   ¼ mile
0   APPROX SCALE   500m

CHURCH
RD

KEMBLE
CHURCH

TO MALMESBURY
7 MILES/6·5 KM

particularly popular and the homemade steak, kidney & ale pie (£13.95) is terrific.

The second option is *The Tavern Inn* (☎ 01285-770216, 🖥 arkells.com; WI-FI; 🐾), situated next to the railway station, a more informal affair. **Food** (Mon-Fri noon-2.30pm & 6-9pm, Sat noon-9pm, Sun noon-5pm) is available: at lunch you'll get a baguette for £6.95, whilst the most expensive meal in the evening is the 8oz rib-eye steak (£17.95). If arranged in advance **camping** may be available.

Kemble is a stop on GWR's (Paddington–Cheltenham Spa; see box pp52-3) **train** service and on **bus** service No 882 and also the 93 (see box pp58-9).

There are a couple of small **taxi firms** advertised on the door of The Tavern Inn, including Reliance Taxis (☎ 0778 779 0644, 🖥 reliancetaxiscirencester.co.uk).

THAMES HEAD TO CRICKLADE   [MAPS 1-7]

Your first day on the Thames Path is a tranquil **12¼-mile (19.7km, 4¼-5hrs)** stroll from Thames Head (see box p79), through meadows and farmland to the village of Cricklade.

From **Kemble** follow one of the footpaths shown on Map 1 to the actual path. You will have to do some walking just to get to the start of the trail, and if you're starting from the railway station at Kemble it's easiest to walk along the National Trail to the source, then turn around and walk back towards the village again! The official stage begins with scarcely any water to be seen (unless it's raining, of course), but it is not long before you pass **Lyd Well** – the spring from which, after rainfall, the nascent Thames often introduces itself (if it hasn't already done so); it seems strange to think that almost every footstep from now to the Thames Barrier is accompanied by the river as its crystal clear waters slowly deepen and spread.

Cotswold meadows lead you through the hamlet of **Ewen** (see p82; Map 2) and on to the Cotswold Water Park (Map 4), a huge expanse of man-made lakes rich in flora and fauna. As the trail cuts its way through the lakes you pass the outskirts of **Somerford Keynes** (see p82; Map 3) before arriving at **Ashton Keynes** (see p82; Map 4), both of which offer good options for lunch.

ROUTE GUIDE AND MAPS

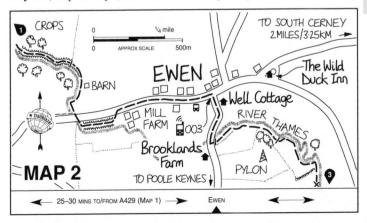

A final wander through the ancient and uncultivated **North Meadow NNR** (Map 6) – abundant in butterflies and wild flowers – brings you to **Cricklade** (see p86; Map 7).

EWEN [Map 2, p81]

Once the site of the first mill on the Thames – now called Mill Farm – Ewen provides an attractive alternative to a first night in Kemble. It is home to a great pub; although not technically on the trail, the 16th-century **Wild Duck Inn** (☎ 01285-770310, 🖥 the luckyonion.com; WI-FI; 🐾; food Mon-Fri noon-3pm & 6-9pm, Sat & Sun noon-4pm & 6-9pm is well worth finding an excuse to visit. Quality, of course, attracts custom and you'd be wise to book a table in advance, especially for weekends; although whatever time you pass by, a stop for a coffee or one of a fine selection of real ales or ciders – in either the shaded beer garden or quirky bar – is an opportunity worth taking. There's even an open fire in winter. The

new owners hope to provide accommodation, possibly from late 2018, so check this.

B&B can be found at **Well Cottage** (☎ 01285-770212, 🖥 wellcottagebandb.co.uk; 2D/1D or T; WI-FI; from £40pp, sgl occ £65), where, if requested in advance, they will try to cater for any special dietary requirements; and at the more rustic **Brooklands Farm** (☎ 01285-770487; 1S/1D; WI-FI; May-Sep; from £40pp). Both are on the road to Poole Keynes which the Thames Path follows out of the village.

The 882 **bus** service (Mon-Fri 1/day) stops in Ewen in the morning en route from Kemble and in the afternoon en route from Cirencester (see pp58-9).

SOMERFORD KEYNES [Map 3]

The site of a 'summer ford' (ie where the river was fordable during the summer months when it was at its lowest), 19th-century ramblers would at this point have been entering Wiltshire, though in 1897 the village opted to join neighbouring Gloucestershire instead. The village's 'surname' derives from Sir Ralph de Keynes, the local landowner in the time of King John (1199-1216). Near its northern end lies **All Saints Church** which has a number of interesting features including a Saxon doorway and a Viking carving.

Of more interest to thirsty ramblers may be **The Baker's Arms** (☎ 01285-861298, 🖥 thebakersarmssomerford.co.uk; **food** Mon-Sat noon-9pm, Sun noon-4pm,

also 6-8pm on bank hol weekends and in school holidays; 🐾). A 10-minute walk from the path, the 17th-century pub is a friendly place, lacking in wi-fi but with a good-sized beer garden which can get busy at weekends. The food can be described as superior pub fare though we suspect that most trekkers would prefer it if the food was less refined and more hearty. Still, it *is* undoubtedly tasty and the menu may include such mouth-watering prospects as slow-roasted rolled pork belly & mash (£14.50). Note that the kitchen generally closes for an hour in the afternoon (Mon-Sat).

The 93/93A **bus** (Malmesbury to Cirencester) service calls here (see pp58-9).

ASHTON KEYNES [Map 4, p84]

As you leave Gloucestershire for Wiltshire you arrive at the first village actually on the river: Ashton Keynes has over 20 bridges that cross the infant Thames as it flows through the village.

Those with time to loiter may be interested in visiting the remains of four 14th-century 'preaching crosses' scattered about

the village, though each one was damaged by Cromwell's Roundheads during the Civil War.

On High Rd both the **village shop** (Mon-Fri 7.45am-7pm, Sat 8.30am-7pm, Sun 9.30am-12.30pm) and **The White Hart Inn** (☎ 01285-861247, 🖥 thewhite hartashtonkeynes.com; **food** served Tue-Sat

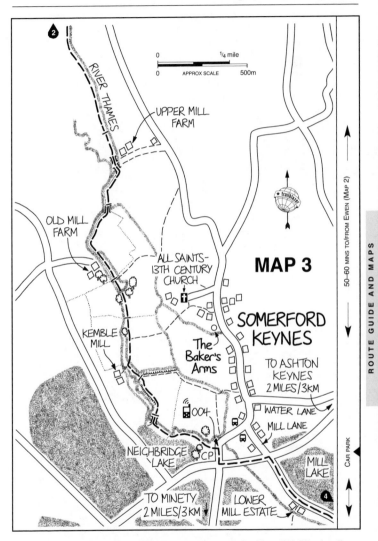

MAP 3

SOMERFORD KEYNES

RIVER THAMES

UPPER MILL FARM

OLD MILL FARM

ALL SAINTS-
13TH CENTURY
CHURCH

KEMBLE MILL

The Baker's Arms

004

NEIGHBRIDGE LAKE

CP

TO MINETY
2 MILES/3KM

LOWER MILL ESTATE

TO ASHTON KEYNES
2 MILES/3KM

WATER LANE

MILL LANE

MILL LAKE

CAR PARK

ROUTE GUIDE AND MAPS

50-60 MINS TO/FROM EWEN (MAP 2)

¼ mile
500m
APPROX SCALE

noon-2pm & 6-9pm, Sun noon-3pm; WI-FI; bar area) provide sustenance for walkers. At the pub, which has refreshingly cheerful décor for a local, the lunch menu includes soup with crusty bread (£4.95) and ham, eggs & chips (£10.95); the dinner menu consists largely of pub classics including fish & chips (£8.50 or £11.95). Note that on a Monday the bar is only open from 6pm and food is not served.

(cont'd on p86)

ROUTE GUIDE AND MAPS

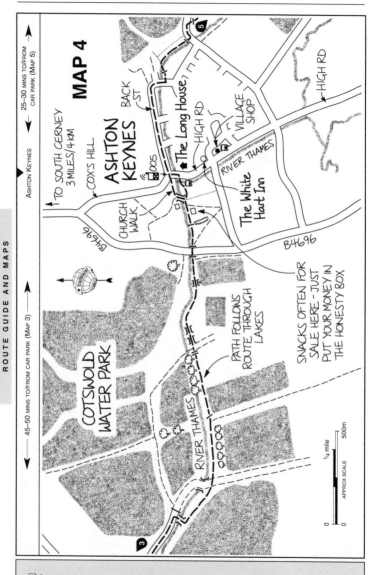

45-50 MINS TO/FROM CAR PARK (MAP 3)

ASHTON KEYNES

25-30 MINS TO/FROM CAR PARK (MAP 5)

MAP 4

TO SOUTH CERNEY 3 MILES/4 KM

COX'S HILL

ASHTON KEYNES

BACK ST

The Long House

HIGH RD

HIGH RD

VILLAGE SHOP

HIGH RD

RIVER THAMES

The White Hart Inn

CHURCH WALK

B4696

B4696

COTSWOLD WATER PARK

PATH FOLLOWS ROUTE THROUGH LAKES

RIVER THAMES

SNACKS OFTEN FOR SALE HERE - JUST PUT YOUR MONEY IN THE HONESTY BOX

¼ mile

500m

APPROX SCALE

0   0

❏ **Important note – walking times**
All times in this book refer only to the time spent walking. You will need to add 20-30% to allow for rests, photography, checking the map, drinking water etc.

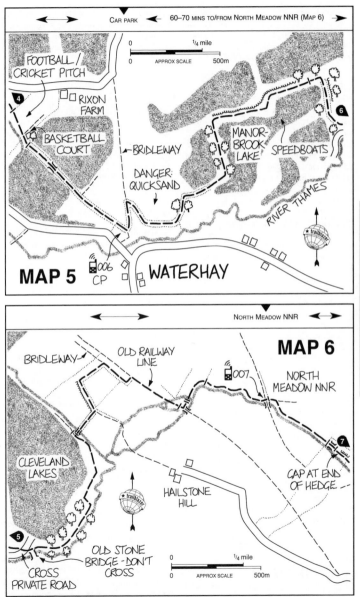

CAR PARK ← 60–70 MINS TO/FROM NORTH MEADOW NNR (MAP 6) →

0 ¼ mile

0 APPROX SCALE 500m

FOOTBALL / CRICKET PITCH

4

RIXON FARM

BASKETBALL COURT

←BRIDLEWAY

DANGER: QUICKSAND

MANOR-BROOK LAKE

SPEEDBOATS

6

RIVER THAMES

★ trailblazer

MAP 5

006 CP

WATERHAY

NORTH MEADOW NNR ←→

MAP 6

BRIDLEWAY

OLD RAILWAY LINE

007

NORTH MEADOW NNR

CLEVELAND LAKES

★ trailblazer

HAILSTONE HILL

7

GAP AT END OF HEDGE

5

CROSS PRIVATE ROAD

OLD STONE BRIDGE – DON'T CROSS

0 ¼ mile

0 APPROX SCALE 500m

ROUTE GUIDE AND MAPS

Ashton Keynes *(cont'd from p83):* **B&B** is available close to the path at friendly ***The Long House*** (☎ 01285-861317, 🖳 thelong house-ashton keynes.co.uk; 1S/2D/1T, shared bathroom; 🖤; WI-FI; 17 High Rd), a

Grade II-listed building built in the 17th century. The rate (from £30pp, sgl/sgl occ from £45) includes a continental breakfast.

The 93/93A **bus** service calls here (see pp58-9).

CRICKLADE

The first *town* on the Thames Path, and the only one in Wiltshire, Cricklade started out as a small Anglo-Saxon community back in the 9th century. Alfred the Great fortified the town against the Danes in AD890 and a century later it became the site of Cricklade Mint, which operated between AD979 and 1100 and produced coins bearing such well-known figures from England's past as King Cnut (AD995-1035).

The four corner pinnacles of Cricklade's almighty **St Sampson's Church** are the town's dominant feature. There has been a church on this site since the 9th century, though the current edifice, including the tower, is 16th century in origin.

In addition to its illustrious history, there are some legends about Cricklade that survive to this day. For one thing, there are suggestions that the town is located on the

site where St Augustine converted Wessex's Anglo-Saxons to Christianity in AD597; while some folk believe that the town's name originates from 'Greeklade' and espouse the theory that Cricklade is actually the site of England's first university, having been founded by the Mercians in AD650 – making it a mere 600 years older than any of Oxford's venerable colleges. Oddly, or possibly not, attempts to prove either claim has thus far proved inconclusive.

Services

The **tourist information point** (Mon-Fri 10am-12.45pm & 1.45-4pm) is in the town council building (☎ 01793-751394, 🖳 crick-ladetowncouncil.gov.uk) at 113 High St.

There is a Lloyds **bank** next door with an **ATM**. Another ATM can be found at the Tesco **supermarket** (Mon-Sat 6am-11pm, Sun 7am-10.30pm) which also hosts the local **post office** (Mon-Fri 9am-5.30pm, Sat 9am-12.30pm).

On the other side of High St you'll find **Cricklade Stores** (Mon-Sat 6am-8pm, Sun 6am-4pm) and a Boots the **chemist** (Mon-Fri 9am-6.30pm, Sat 9am-2pm).

The 51/51A & 53 **buses** (see pp58-9) call here as does National Express's 401 coach service (see box p54).

Where to stay

You have three accommodation options in Cricklade, all reasonably priced pubs within in easy walking distance of the trail. Indeed, the path goes past the front door of ***The Red Lion*** (☎ 01793-750776, 🖳 the redlioncricklade.co.uk; 5D; 🖤; WI-FI; 🐾; from £45pp, sgl occ from £85; 74 High St), which is brimming with character and also serves delicious food (see Where to eat).

Further along High St, ***The White Hart Hotel*** (☎ 01793-750206, 🖳 thewhite hartcricklade.co.uk; 1S/7D/4T/1Tr/1Qd; 🖤; WI-FI; 🐾) is another fine option which

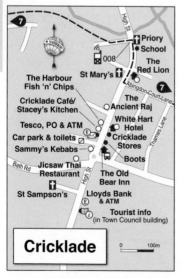

The Harbour Fish 'n' Chips

Cricklade Café/ Stacey's Kitchen

Tesco, PO & ATM

Car park & toilets

Sammy's Kebabs

Bath Rd — Jicsaw Thai Restaurant

St Sampson's

High St

St Mary's

Priory
School
The Red Lion

Abingdon Court Lane

The Ancient Raj

White Hart Hotel

Cricklade Stores

Boots

The Old Bear Inn

Lloyds Bank & ATM

Tourist info
(in Town Council building)

Thames Lane

Cricklade

0   100m

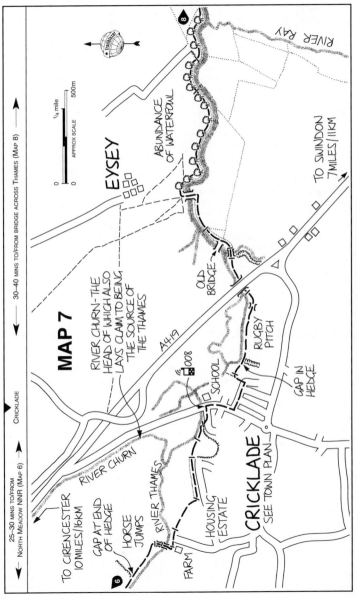

ROUTE GUIDE AND MAPS

← 25–30 MINS TO/FROM NORTH MEADOW NNR (MAP 6) ← CRICKLADE → 30–40 MINS TO/FROM BRIDGE ACROSS THAMES (MAP 8) →

MAP 7

APPROX SCALE
0 — ¼ mile
0 — 500m

EYSEY

TO CIRENCESTER 10MILES/16KM

RIVER CHURN—THE HEAD OF WHICH ALSO LAYS CLAIM TO BEING THE SOURCE OF THE THAMES

A419

008

SCHOOL

RUGBY PITCH

GAP IN HEDGE

OLD BRIDGE

ABUNDANCE OF WATERFOWL

RIVER RAY

TO SWINDON 7MILES/11KM

RIVER CHURN

GAP AT END OF HEDGE

HORSE JUMPS

RIVER THAMES

FARM

HOUSING ESTATE

CRICKLADE
SEE TOWN PLAN

also serves food (see Where to eat). The rate, including a continental breakfast, is around £37.50pp (sgl/sgl occ from £65); a cooked breakfast costs £6pp.

At 101 High St, *The Old Bear Inn* (☎ 01793-750005, 🖥 theoldbearinn.com; 3D/ 2T; WI-FI; 🐾) charges from £32.50pp (sgl occ from £50) for room only. Breakfast costs an additional £8.50pp but they are generally prepared to cook whatever is requested. The bar is open daily (Mon-Fri 5pm to late, Sat & Sun noon to late) but unlike the other two pubs in the town there is no other food served here.

Where to eat and drink

If you opt for a room-only rate at one of the pubs you have the perfect opportunity to visit *Cricklade Café/Stacey's Kitchen* (☎ 01793-750754; Mon-Sat 8am-2pm; 42 High St). It's an unpretentious place but the food is nonetheless pretty tasty, with a 6-item cooked breakfast for £4.95 (served all day).

For a **pub meal** both *The White Hart Hotel* (see Where to stay; food Mon-Sat noon-2.30pm & 6-9pm, Sun noon-3pm), with unusual items such as kangaroo fillet

steak and ostrich steak (both £17.95) on the menu, and *The Red Lion* (see Where to stay; food Mon-Sat noon-2.30pm, Sun to 3pm, daily 6.30-9pm) are decent options. The latter has a **micro brewery**, 🖥 hopket tlebrewery.co.uk) so not surprisingly serves real ales; it also has a big beer garden. It dishes up hearty food such as a cajun-spiced chicken burger (£13) and pan-fried sea bass (£18). This is a very popular place and one that isn't averse to putting on a bit of live music now and then.

Spicier morsels can be found at both *Jicsaw Thai* (☎ 01793-752838, 🖥 jicsaw thai.com; Tue-Sun & Bank Holiday Mon noon-2.30pm & 6-10.30pm; WI-FI; 32 High St), with a chicken Thai green curry costing £7.99; and *The Ancient Raj* (☎ 01793-750303; food Mon-Fri 5.30-11.30pm, Sat & Sun to midnight; 47 High St), with either sit-down or **takeaway** Indian meals.

Takeaway food is also available from *The Harbour* (Mon-Sat 11.30am-2pm & 4.30-10pm), which does decent fish 'n' chips, and the longstanding *Sammy's Kebabs* (☎ 01793-751177; daily noon-11.30pm).

CRICKLADE TO LECHLADE   [MAPS 7-12]

As with yesterday's stage, this **11-mile (17.7km, 3¾-4¾hrs)** section of the trail primarily consists of agrarian rambling through flora-rich meadows, although it does stray from the river for much of the day and there's some road walking too.

As the four 'spirelets' of St Sampson's Church bid you farewell, so the swans and meadows welcome you back and accompany you to the village of **Castle Eaton** (see p90; Map 9), from which a short jaunt along a country lane returns you to the banks of the Thames, with **St Mary's church**, **Kempsford**, visible on the opposite bank.

A further spell spent deep in the meadows of Wiltshire (the northern bank, incidentally, is in Gloucestershire) leads to a new section of trail that means Upper Inglesham and the busy A361 are avoided altogether; the only reason to go to Upper Inglesham now is to take **bus** No 77 (see pp58-9).

This new path opened after the time of research but is marked, roughly, on Maps 10-12. You'll need to follow the signs closely to keep to the trail through this short section but they are certain to see you safely to **Inglesham** (Map 12), where the 13th-century **Church of St John the Baptist** is well worth a visit.

Much to the chagrin of the waterfowl that live along here, the final, sublime stretch to **Lechlade** (see p90) has the first boats on the river since you started your walk.

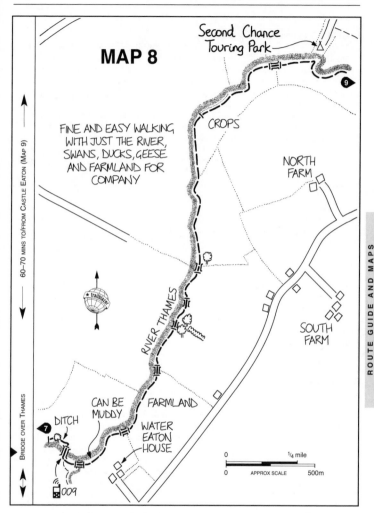

MAP 8

Second Chance
Touring Park

9

FINE AND EASY WALKING
WITH JUST THE RIVER,
SWANS, DUCKS, GEESE
AND FARMLAND FOR
COMPANY

CROPS

NORTH
FARM

SOUTH
FARM

60–70 MINS TO/FROM CASTLE EATON (MAP 9)

* trailblazer

RIVER THAMES

FARMLAND

CAN BE
MUDDY

DITCH

7

WATER
EATON
HOUSE

009

BRIDGE OVER THAMES

0   ¼ mile

0   APPROX SCALE   500m

On the opposite bank a **roundhouse** marks the Thames's **head of navigation** (the point at which the river becomes navigable for boats) as well as one end of the ill-fated **Thames-Severn Canal** (see box p90). The circular abode was the accommodation for the lock-keeper, who would have controlled the traffic between the two waterways.

❏ The Thames-Severn Canal

Opened in 1789, the Thames-Severn Canal was part of a system of waterways linking London with Bristol. Thirty miles long, the canal carved its way through the landscape from **Lechlade to Stroud**, from where it went on to connect with the River Severn. Passing just to the north of the Thames's source, the canal also travelled through Sapperton Tunnel which, at just over two miles in length, was, for a spell at least, the longest tunnel in Britain.

Beset by leaks due to the porous nature of the Cotswold limestone and struggling to compete with the nascent railway network the canal was last used commercially in 1911 and the last (non-commercial) boat made the journey between the two rivers in 1927. Many blame the lack of water at the Thames's source on the canal; the waterway's pumping station, so it is alleged, drew all the water away from the underground springs that had once risen in Trewsbury Mead (Map 1).

CASTLE EATON   [Map 9]

Shortly before you leave the village the 12th-century **Church of St Mary**, tucked away down a footpath, is worth a peek.

Far harder to miss is the first pub to line the Thames's banks: *The Red Lion* (☎ 01285-810280, 🖳 red-lion.co.uk), built around 1730, provides **B&B** (1D/1T share facilities, room sleeping up to six en suite; 🍺; WI-FI; 🐾 bar only; from £32.50pp, £45 sgl occ) and home-cooked **food** (Mon-Fri noon-2.30pm & 6-9pm, Sat noon-9pm & Sun to 7pm). If here on a Sunday it would

be a shame to miss out on one of their roast dinners (£9.25).

The first **campsite** along the Thames Path is on the opposite side of the river. *Second Chance Touring Park* (Map 8; ☎ 01285-810675, 🖳 secondchancetouring.co .uk; 🐾 on lead; Mar-end Nov) charges £6pp including use of shower facilities and is a half-mile stroll from the village. The site is adding lodges and chalets but these are for longer stays.

LECHLADE   [map p94]

So named because of its proximity to the River Leach, this market town used to be a bustling port due to its privileged location as the first place from which large commercial barges could head downstream carrying their wares to Oxford and London. One of the primary commodities traded was sage cheese, whilst the stone required to construct the dome of London's St Paul's Cathedral was also loaded here.

The town's two main features are **Halfpenny Bridge**, opened in 1792 to help deal with the influx of traders following the creation of the Thames-Severn Canal and taking its name from the toll taken from walkers who wished to cross; and **St Lawrence Church**, the view of which from the opposite bank is one photographers will not want to miss.

Services

All services can be found on High St. The **visitor information centre** is staffed by volunteers and is in the same building as the community-run library (☎ 01367-252631; Mon 10am-4pm, Tue-Thur & Sat 10am-1pm, Fri 1-5pm); information is also available on 🖳 lechladeonthames.co.uk.

The **post office** (Mon-Fri 7am-5.30pm, Sat 7am-3pm, Sun 7am-noon) is nearby and on the other side of the road are: **Lechlade Pharmacy** (Mon-Fri 9am-6pm, Sat 9am-5pm); a Barclays **bank** with **ATM**; and a Londis **shop** (daily 6.30am-10pm).

The 77 **bus** links Lechlade with Cirencester (see pp58-9).

(cont'd on p94)

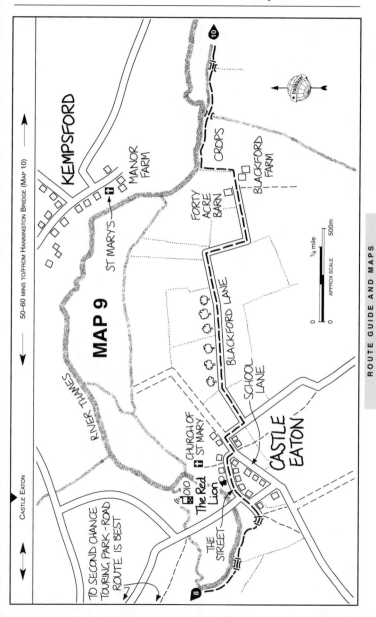

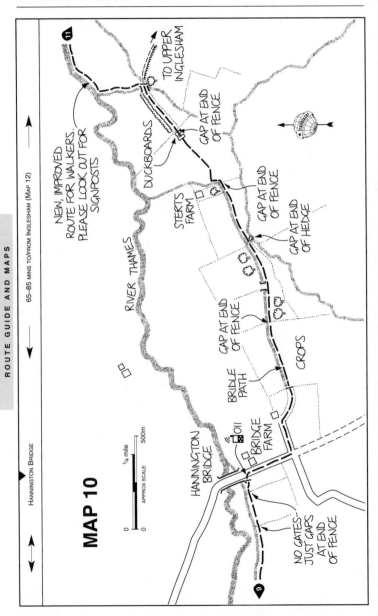

ROUTE GUIDE AND MAPS

HANNINGTON BRIDGE ◀ ▶ 65–85 MINS TO/FROM INGLESHAM (MAP 12) ◀ ▶

MAP 10

¼ mile
APPROX SCALE
0 — 500m

NEW, IMPROVED ROUTE FOR WALKERS. PLEASE LOOK OUT FOR SIGNPOSTS

TO UPPER INGLESHAM

DUCKBOARDS

GAP AT END OF FENCE

RIVER THAMES

STERTS FARM

GAP AT END OF FENCE

GAP AT END OF HEDGE

GAP AT END OF FENCE

CROPS

BRIDLE PATH

HANNINGTON BRIDGE

☎ 011

BRIDGE FARM

NO GATES– JUST GAPS AT END OF FENCE

11

9

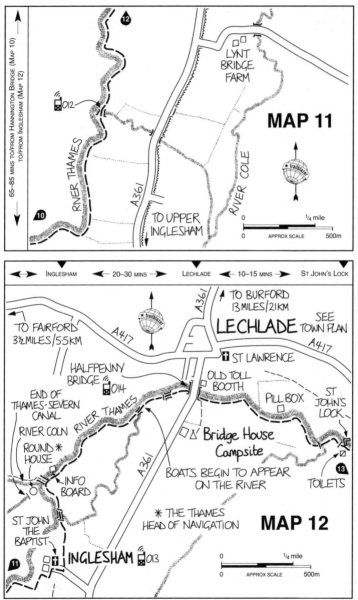

Where to stay

Campers need not cross the river. *Bridge House Campsite* (Map 12; ☎ 01367-252348, 🖳 bridgehousecampsite.co.uk; 🐾 on lead; Apr-end Oct but open in Mar if Easter is then; reception Sat-Thur 9am-7pm, Fri 9am-9pm) is a friendly, clean and efficiently run place. The cost is £9pp; payment must be in cash or by cheque with the relevant debit card number on. Note that there is a £20 key deposit for a fob which allows access to the showers; if you wish to leave very early in the morning you'll have to arrange repayment of the deposit (possibly by post) with the management. If requested in advance they may be willing to stay open later in the evening.

B&B is available at *Leventen House* (☎ 01367-252592, 🖳 emreay@hotmail .co.uk; 1Tr en suite, 1D with private bathroom; 🛁; WI-FI; 🐾; from £35pp, sgl occ £45-50; High St) and, a little further out of

town, at *Cambrai Lodge* (☎ 01367-253173, 🖳 cambrailodgelechlade.com; 2D/1D or T; 🛁; WI-FI; 🐾; £37.50-42.50pp, sgl occ £60-70; Oak St). At the latter, set well back from the road, there is a lovely garden and well-furnished rooms each with their own entrance. They will take on luggage for a fee of approximately £1 per road mile for the return journey.

A few **pubs** also offer **B&B**. Wonderfully situated right on the riverbank and next to the bridge is *The Riverside* (☎ 01367-252534, 🖳 riverside-lechlade.com; 1S private facilities, 1D/2Tr/1T/3Qd; 🛁; WI-FI; 🐾). Rates vary but expect to pay around £35-50pp (sgl/sgl occ from £40/60).

Another option is *The New Inn Hotel* (☎ 01367-252296, 🖳 newinnhotel.co.uk; 3S/27D or T; 🛁; WI-FI; 🐾) which enjoys both a frontage on High St and a huge beer garden which backs directly on to its own private section of the river. Rates for B&B here also depend on demand but £32.50-60pp (sgl £65-75, sgl occ from £75) is a guideline.

Away from the Thames on Burford St, *The Old Swan Inn* (☎ 01367-253571, 🖳 swaninnlechlade.co.uk; 3D/1T; 🛁; WI-FI; 🐾; £39-49pp, sgl occ £68-88) not only has four-poster beds but also real ales and some parts of the pub date from the 16th century. *The Crown Inn* (☎ 01367-252198, 🖳 crownlechlade.co.uk; 1D/2T; WI-FI; 🐾; from £27.50pp, sgl occ from £45; High St) is the only pub in Lechlade not to serve food, beer being their passion (bar daily noon-11pm); they have a microbrewery but it wasn't operating at the time of writing. There is live music most Saturdays.

Where to eat and drink

At *The Tea Chest* (☎ 01367-253015; Mon-Sat 9.30am-5pm, Sun 10am-4.30pm; 🐾; early Feb to late Dec) sandwiches, soups, salads and toasties are less than £5, the coffee is great and dogs are welcome; note, however, that the wi-fi here isn't reliable.

If you're prepared to walk a bit further into the centre of Lechlade the smart *Lynwood & Co Café* (☎ 01367 253707, 🖳 lynwoodandco.com (Mon-Sat 8am-4pm, Sun 8am-2pm; WI-FI; 🐾) does the best

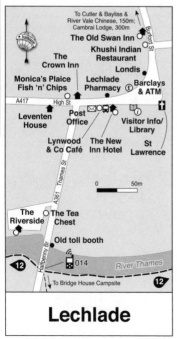

To Cutler & Bayliss &
River Vale Chinese, 150m;
Cambrai Lodge, 300m

The Old Swan Inn

Burford St

Khushi Indian
Restaurant

The
Crown Inn

Londis

Monica's Plaice
Fish 'n' Chips

Lechlade
Pharmacy

Barclays
& ATM

A417   High St

Leventen
House

Post
Office

Visitor Info/
Library

Lynwood
& Co Café

The New
Inn Hotel

St
Lawrence

Thames St

0   50m

The
Riverside

The Tea
Chest

Old toll booth

A361

Halfpenny Br

12   014   River Thames   12

To Bridge House Campsite

Lechlade

breakfasts of anyone in town including a fantastic plate of French toast, vanilla mascarpone & maple syrup (£5.95).

The menus at the town's pubs are, in all honesty, pretty unimaginative and seldom stray from the usual pub classics. *The New Inn Hotel* (see Where to stay) serves pub standards (daily noon-2.15pm & 6-9pm) including steak & ale pie for a tenner. Other pub options include *The Riverside* (see Where to stay; breakfast 8-11am, meals Mon-Sat summer noon-9pm, winter Mon-Sat noon-2pm & 6-9pm, Sun noon-8pm all year), which, given its location and name may be the most appropriate place to enjoy wholetail scampi & chips (£10); and the *The Old Swan Inn* (see Where to stay; food Mon-Sat noon-9pm, Sun noon-5pm), where you will find pub grub such as ham, egg & chips (£8.95). Remember that, no matter how good these pubs are, you may want to wait until St John's Lock and the

famous *Trout Inn* (see p98; Map 13). If you're planning on a picnic (not a bad idea given the paucity of eateries on the next leg) *Cutler & Bayliss* (☎ 01367-252451, 🖳 cutlerandbayliss.co.uk; Mon-Fri 8am-5pm, Sat to 4.30pm, Sun to noon; 4 Oak St) are a family-run butcher and greengrocer that will make fresh, high-quality sandwiches to order, the price depending on the ingredients you select.

Traditional Indian meals (£6.90-13.90) can be enjoyed at *Khushi* (☎ 01367-252956; Mon-Sat 5.30-11.30pm, Sun noon-5pm; Burford St) and Chinese meals at *River Vale* (☎ 01367-250033; Tue-Sun 5-11pm; 6 Oak St), with dishes costing from £3.70. Both offer a **takeaway** option.

Fish & chips for about a fiver can be purchased at *Monica's Plaice* (Mon & Tue 11.30am-10pm, Wed-Sat to 10.30pm, Sun noon-9.30pm; High St).

LECHLADE TO NEWBRIDGE   [MAPS 12-19]

Truly the lonely Thames, this **16¾-mile (26.7km, 5-6½hrs)** stage is the longest and most isolated along the whole path. Unlike yesterday's trek, today the path hugs the river close, holding on tight to every twist and time-consuming turn. Apart from the occasional riverside pub or lock, your only companionship on this stage is likely to be provided by the swans, with the call of the cuckoo a constant presence in the background.

The relative wildness of this stretch of the river also means **a paucity of services**. There *are* several pubs on the trail that serve food but unless you're willing to add some (otherwise unnecessary) mileage to your journey you should purchase any supplies in Lechlade – as the next shop is over thirty miles and two days away in Oxford!

From Lechlade the Thames becomes navigable and locks and weirs (see box pp96-7) become a frequent point of reference from now on. The first you encounter is **St John's Lock** (Map 12); be careful not to miss the **statue of Old Father Thames** (see box p76). As well as locks you'll also notice the ubiquity of another new feature on the river: **the pill box**. The result of a panic in 1940 over a presumed imminent invasion by the Germans, these small concrete buildings are just one way that the river – the 'artery of England' – has been defended and are a reminder of its strategic significance.

From St John's Lock you get the sense that the Thames seems to know that it is now navigable and begins to indulge in some rather intense meandering, passing **Buscot** (Map 13) on the opposite bank, its 13th-century **St Mary's Church** visible amongst the trees.   *(cont'd on p98)*

ROUTE GUIDE AND MAPS

Goring Lock

❏ LOCHS AND WEIRS

While small boats can journey downriver from Cricklade, the Thames becomes navigable for larger craft only from Lechlade. Between here and Teddington (from where the Thames becomes tidal), the Thames falls approximately 70 metres and there are 45 **locks** along the way, each with at least one accompanying **weir**.

Weirs are nothing more than a barrier placed across a waterway to alter the river's flow. They have existed on the Thames in one form or another for centuries, used by fishermen to persuade fish towards nets and by millers to power their mills.

By blocking the river, however, the millers and fishermen created problems for the boats that needed to travel round them. An early solution to this was the introduction of the **flash lock**, where several boards (or a gate) are placed in the weir which, when a boat approached, could be removed, thus allowing the vessel to be swept through on the resulting surge – or 'flash' – of water.

Unfortunately, this method only really worked for those travelling downstream; those travelling upriver, of course, would need to be winched or towed through the gap against the flow. Furthermore, flash locks were hazardous for everyone involved. So eventually, in the 17th century, these flash locks were replaced by **pound locks**, which is the type of lock you see to this day on the river. Pound locks operate by using two gates, one at either end of a 'pound' or chamber of water. The water level within the pound can thus be controlled by removing one of the gates (ie it can be raised by removing the gate upstream of the chamber, or lowered by removing the

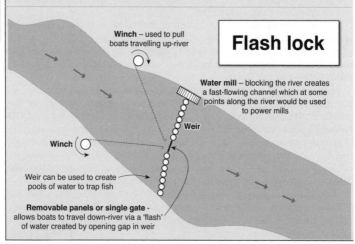

Winch – used to pull boats travelling up-river

Flash lock

Water mill – blocking the river creates a fast-flowing channel which at some points along the river would be used to power mills

Weir

Winch

Weir can be used to create pools of water to trap fish

Removable panels or single gate - allows boats to travel down-river via a 'flash' of water created by opening gap in weir 'downstream gate'). Once a boat has manoeuvred its way into the lock the two gates are then closed, thereby trapping the boat in the pound. The water in the pound is then raised or lowered, depending on which way the boat is travelling, using 'paddles' in the gates; so that the water level within the pound is equal to the water level above the lock (if the boat is travelling upstream) or below it (if travelling downstream). The first locks of this kind to be used on the Thames were constructed in 1633 and located at Iffley, Sandford and Abingdon, while the last, King's and Eynsham locks, were installed in 1928.

The pound lock is still the main design used on the river. All locks are run by the Environment Agency and many have tearooms and campsites nearby. For a list of the facilities available at each lock see 🖥 www.gov.uk/river-thames-bridges-locks-and-facilities-for-boaters#facilities-at-river-thames-locks.

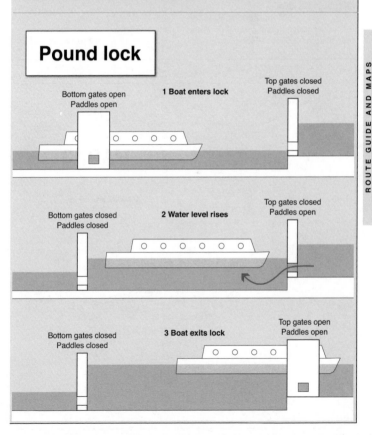

Pound lock

1 Boat enters lock

Bottom gates open
Paddles open

Top gates closed
Paddles closed

2 Water level rises

Bottom gates closed
Paddles closed

Top gates closed
Paddles open

3 Boat exits lock

Bottom gates closed
Paddles closed

Top gates open
Paddles open

(cont'd from p95) Buscot Village Shop and Tea Room (☎ 01367-250329; Tue-Sun and bank hol Mon 10am-5pm, winter Wed-Sun; 🐾; WI-FI) is on the opposite side of the river and serves teas. However, note that the village shop part is more for postcards and the like than groceries.

For a break along the way you have the option of a visit to **Kelmscott** (see p100; Map 14) and the estate of William Morris (see box p100). There are pubs worthy of a lunch stop by both **Radcot Bridge** (see p100; Map 15) and **Tadpole Bridge** (see p104; Map 17). Having visited the 1000-acre **Chimney Meadows National Nature Reserve** (Map 17), you then pass the hamlet of **Shifford** (see p104; Map 18) – the site at which the Anglo-Saxon King Alfred held the first recorded English Parliament in AD890 – before the river leads you to **Newbridge** (see p104; Map 19) and your first night in Oxfordshire.

ST JOHN'S LOCK
[Map 12, p93; Map 13]

Across the bridge from the trail, *The Trout Inn* (☎ 01367-252313, 🖳 thetroutinn.com;

food Mon-Sat noon-2pm, Sun to 2.30pm, daily 7-9.30pm; WI-FI; 🐾 bar only) has a history almost as long as the river. Once a

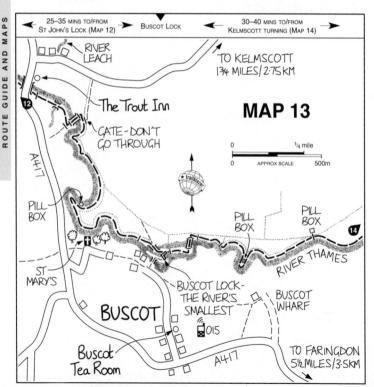

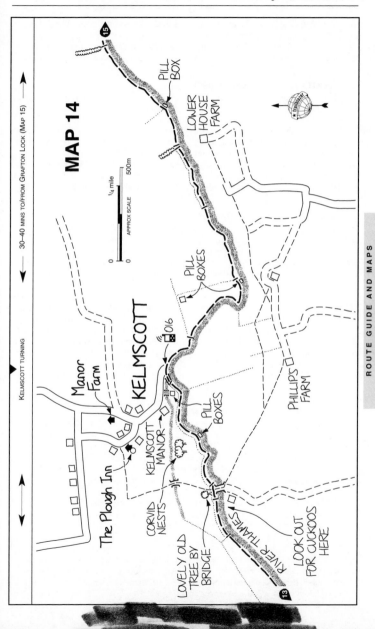

MAP 14

← 30-40 MINS TO/FROM GRAFTON LOCK (MAP 15) →

15

PILL BOX

LOWER HOUSE FARM

¼ mile
APPROX SCALE
500m
0

PILL BOXES

016

KELMSCOTT TURNING

Manor Farm

KELMSCOTT

The Plough Inn

Kelmscott Manor

CORVID NESTS

PILL BOXES

PHILLIPS FARM

LOVELY OLD TREE BY BRIDGE

RIVER THAMES

LOOK OUT FOR CUCKOOS HERE

13

ROUTE GUIDE AND MAPS

priory's almshouse, it was converted to an inn in 1472, gaining its current name in 1704. Today you'll find an extensive menu of snacks, pizzas and burgers as well as

dishes with locally sourced meat and a good selection of responsibly sourced fish, including local Bibury trout, grilled and served with potatoes & vegetables (£15).

KELMSCOTT   [Map 14, p99]

For those considering shortening this lengthy third stage a stop in Kelmscott is an option.

B&B (£55-70pp, sgl £90-110, sgl occ room rate) is available at *The Plough Inn* (☎ 01367-253543, ☐ theploughinnkelmscott.com; 1S/7D; ✔; WI-FI; 🐾 bar only). You'll also discover some splendid **food** here (Tue-Thur noon-2.30pm & 6-9.30pm,

Fri & Sat noon-3pm & 6-10pm, Sun noon-3.30pm); their menu is constantly changing but always imaginative (eg slow-cooked shoulder of lamb, crispy haggis, braised pearl barley & swede purée for £16).

Manor Farm (☎ 01367-252620, ☐ kelmscottbandb.co.uk; 2D/1Tr; ✔; WI-FI; from £40pp (sgl occ from £50) offers B&B in a 17th-century National Trust farmhouse.

RADCOT   [Map 15]

The **bridge** here lays reasonable claim to being the oldest over the Thames, with much of the stone that makes up its pointed Gothic arches dating from approximately 1200. Indeed, there is even evidence of there being a bridge here as far back as the 10th century, Radcot having been an important crossing point between the Saxon kingdoms of Mercia and Wessex.

Ye Olde Swan (☎ 01367-810220, ☐ yeoldeswan.co.uk; WI-FI) used to be called the Swan Hotel, the closure of their accommodation necessitating the name change. They still have **camping** (£8 per tent),

however, and while it used to be basic there are now showers and they also have 10 **glamping tipis** sleeping up to four (£90-120 inc breakfast & bedding). Breakfast is available (end Mar-end Oct 8.30-11.30am). **Food** (daily noon-9pm, winter Mon-Fri noon-2.30pm & 6-8.30pm) such as fish finger sandwiches (£5.95) or, in the evening, minted lamb burger (£11.50), is tasty, the portions generous and the large beer garden, which extends down to the river, is a lovely spot to wait the sometimes interminably long time for them.

(cont'd on p104)

❏ William Morris and Kelmscott Manor

Poet, novelist, translator, textile designer, social reformer and founder of the Victorian Arts and Crafts movement, William Morris (1834-1896) was a man of many talents. Though he owned several homes during his lifetime; he will forever be most associated with Kelmscott Manor, which was first built in 1570 as a farmhouse. Morris first laid eyes on the Manor in 1871; believing it to be the perfect retreat from his hectic life in London, he began renting it the same year, entertaining such guests as George Bernard Shaw and WB Yeats.

The manor would go on to become famous as the place where he would pen some of his finest work, including *News from Nowhere* (1890) and *The Well at the World's End* (1896). But the building itself also inspired him to found the Society for the Protection of Old Buildings – a forerunner to the National Trust – in 1877.

Now open to the public, Kelmscott Manor (☐ sal.org.uk/kelmscott-manor; Apr-Oct Wed & Sat 11am-5pm, last entry 4pm; £10, garden only £3.50) displays collections of furniture, furnishings and artwork owned by Morris as well as other former occupants. There is also a **tearoom** (Wed & Sat 10.30am-5pm) which serves lunches (noon-2.30pm) and supplies water for dogs.

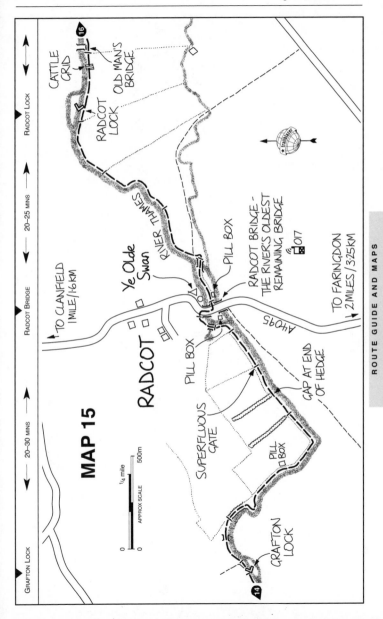

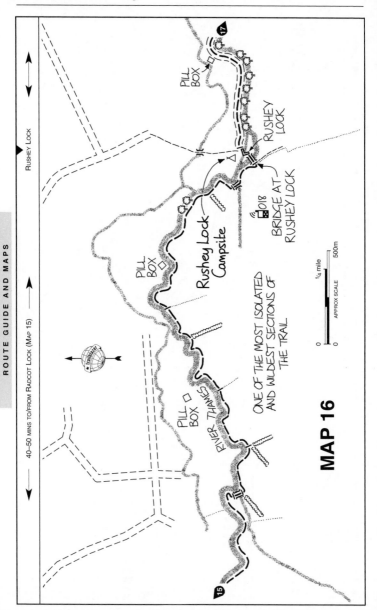

40–50 MINS TO/FROM RADCOT LOCK (Map 15)

RUSHEY LOCK

PILL BOX

17

PILL BOX

RUSHEY LOCK

BRIDGE AT RUSHEY LOCK

1018

Rushey Lock Campsite

PILL BOX

ONE OF THE MOST ISOLATED AND WILDEST SECTIONS OF THE TRAIL

PILL BOX

RIVER THAMES

0

0

¼ mile

APPROX SCALE

500m

MAP 16

15

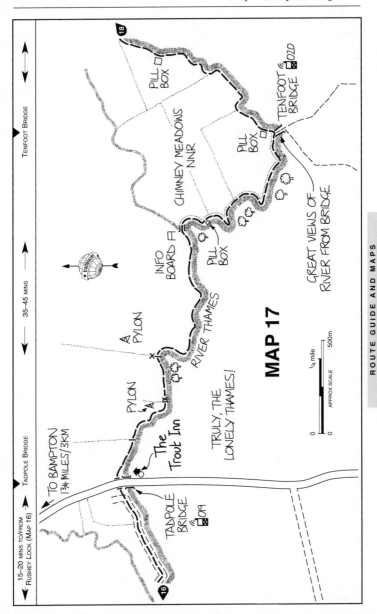

15–20 MINS TO/FROM RUSHEY LOCK (MAP 16)

TADPOLE BRIDGE

35–45 MINS

TENFOOT BRIDGE

TO BAMPTON
1¾ MILES/3KM

PYLON

PYLON

INFO BOARD

CHIMNEY MEADOWS NNR

PILL BOX

PILL BOX

PILL BOX

RIVER THAMES

The Trout Inn

TRULY THE LONELY THAMES!

TADPOLE BRIDGE 🏨 019

MAP 17

¼ mile

500m

0

0

APPROX SCALE

TENFOOT BRIDGE 🏨 020

GREAT VIEWS OF RIVER FROM BRIDGE

16

18

trailblazer

RUSHEY LOCK   [Map 16, p102]

Rushey Lock Campsite (☎ 01367-870218; 🐾 on lead; Apr-end Oct) is the first on the river that is run by the Environment Agency. There are 10 pitches and each costs £11; booking is recommended.

Water and a toilet are always available but access to the showers is limited to when

the lock-keeper is on duty (hours variable but generally 9am-5pm) as he's the man you need to pay (£3.50 per token). Note there is no road access to the site.

For food, the nearest pub, The Trout at Tadpole Bridge (see below), is one mile downstream.

TADPOLE BRIDGE   [Map 17, p103]

The setting of the award-winning *The Trout at Tadpole Bridge* (☎ 01367-870382, 🖳 trout-inn.co.uk; 2D/3D or T/1Tr; 🛏; WI-FI; 🐾) is pure Thames-side splendour, with a beer garden rolling down to a riverbank lined with barges. The cost of **B&B** (£49.50-85pp, sgl occ room rate) reflects both the standard of the location and the exquisite establishment itself. Note, too,

that there is a minimum two-night stay at weekends. Their **food** (daily noon-2.30pm & 6.30-8.30pm) is not for those keeping an eye on their bank balance. The menu changes regularly but if it is on the menu it's doubtful you'll rue the day you ate Dorset dressed crab (£19.95); always on the menu though are fish (usually haddock) & chips (£14.50).

SHIFFORD LOCK   [Map 18]

If you wish to stay at *Shifford Lock Campsite* (☎ 01367-870247; well-behaved 🐾; Good Friday to end Sep) you'll need to carry your food as there's no shop or pub within reasonable walking distance. The

five pitches available on the island cost £11 each (for up to two people and a tent), there are toilet and shower facilities. Booking is recommended.

NEWBRIDGE   [Map 19, p106]

This is the second oldest bridge over the Thames, its name deriving from the fact that it is 'new' compared to its venerable neighbour in Radcot – though even then it's only younger by 50 years. Originally built by monks to carry Cotswold wool across to customers in the south, the bridge now carries the A415 – a road on which you should be careful. There are a couple of places to rest and have a drink here.

The Maybush (☎ 01865-300101, 🖳 themaybush.com; food Mon-Sat noon-2.30pm & 6-9pm, Sun noon-5pm, Nov-Easter closed Mon; WI-FI; 🐾) is, in all honesty, not particularly cheap (burger of the day with chips £14.50, for example) but at least there's now some competition for The Rose Revived.

Crossing the bridge, the Path drops you at *The Rose Revived* (☎ 01865-300221, 🖳 oldenglishinns.co.uk; 5D/2D or T; WI-FI; 🐾

bar area only), the more established of the two with B&B varying in price but from around £50pp (sgl occ room rate). **Food** is served (daily 10am-10pm) though we don't think it's the best value on the trail – £5.49 for three calamari rings, for example.

They also, rather wonderfully, have a lovely **shepherd's hut** (1D; £32.50-50pp, sgl occ full rate; WI-FI; 🐾; Feb-Nov) by the river, called Swan's View, which you have to book through 🖳 airbnb.co.uk. There are separate toilet and shower facilities.

Rather than walk along the busy A415, **campers** would be well advised to take Stagecoach's No 15 **bus** service (see pp58-9) to get to **Standlake** (see p107), five minutes away. The No 15 also travels to Abingdon (see p126), which provides the closest accommodation should The Rose Revived be full.

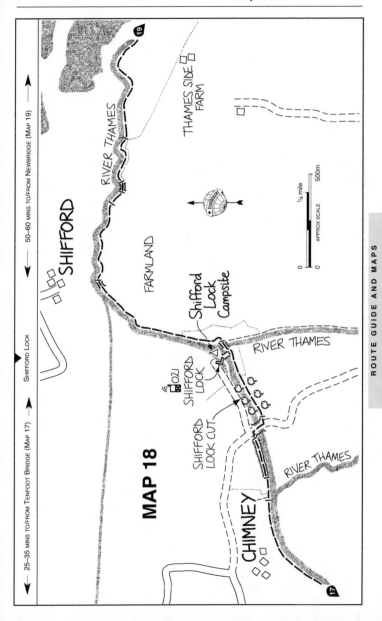

MAP 18

← 25–35 MINS TO/FROM TENFOOT BRIDGE (MAP 17) → SHIFFORD LOCK ← 50–60 MINS TO/FROM NEWBRIDGE (MAP 19) →

19

SHIFFORD

RIVER THAMES

THAMES SIDE FARM

FARMLAND

Shifford Lock Campsite

RIVER THAMES

SHIFFORD LOCK

SHIFFORD LOCK CUT

RIVER THAMES

CHIMNEY

17

¼ mile   500m
APPROX SCALE
0   0

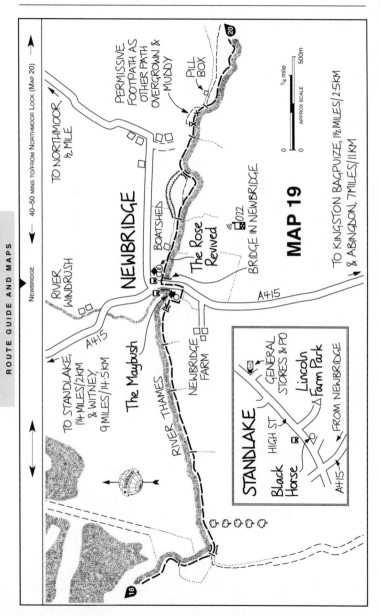

NEWBRIDGE

40–50 MINS TO/FROM NORTHMOOR LOCK (MAP 20)

TO NORTHMOOR, ½ MILE

PERMISSIVE FOOTPATH AS OTHER PATH OVERGROWN & MUDDY

PILL BOX

Boatshed

RIVER WINDRUSH

The Rose Revived

002

BRIDGE IN NEWBRIDGE

A415

A415

MAP 19

TO KINGSTON BAGPUIZE, 1½MILES/2·5KM & ABINGDON, 7MILES/11KM

¼ mile

500m

APPROX SCALE

The Maybush

RIVER THAMES

NEWBRIDGE FARM

TO STANDLAKE, 1¼MILES/2KM & WITNEY, 9 MILES/14·5KM

STANDLAKE

Black Horse

HIGH ST

GENERAL STORES & PO

Lincoln Farm Park

FROM NEWBRIDGE

A415

STANDLAKE [Map 19]

Lincoln Farm Park (☎ 01865-300239, ▣ lincolnfarmpark.co.uk; WI-FI; ☞; Feb-early Nov) is the best option in the area for **campers** but it is aimed at families so walkers should book in advance; there is a backpacker/cyclist rate of £10pp for anyone arriving without a vehicle. The facilities are tremendous, the staff friendly and informative; there's a shop too.

Stagecoach's No 15 **bus** service (see pp58-9) calls here; many trekkers will find this convenient especially as services operate in the late afternoon and also early in the morning (though Mon-Sat only). Their No 19 bus service also stops here.

A short walk from the site is the village

General Stores (Mon-Sat 8am-7pm, Sun 8am-5pm) which includes a **post office** (Mon-Fri 9am-5.30pm, Sat 9am-12.30pm).

Next to the campsite's entrance, *The Black Horse* (☎ 01865-300307, ▣ the blackhorsestandlake.com; WI-FI; ☞; **food** Tue 6.30-9.30pm, Wed-Sat noon-2.30pm & 6.30-9.30pm, Sun noon-4pm; 81 High St) is a typical country boozer, full of joviality and hearty food; their dish of lamb rump with mash & honey-roasted veg (£15) is certainly large enough to keep you warm as you doze off under canvas. Note that the pub is only open 5-10pm on Monday and Tuesday and closes during the afternoon (Wed to Fri).

NEWBRIDGE TO OXFORD [MAPS 19-25]

This **14-mile (22.5km, 4½-5½hrs)** hike is as wonderfully riparian as yesterday's stage, the path continuing to hug the riverbanks closely. The route scythes its way through meadows, passing **Northmoor Lock** (see p110; Map 20) before arriving at **Bablock Hythe** (see p110; Map 21).

From here, there is a brief diversion from the river before you return to pass **Pinkhill Lock** (see p110; Map 22) and arrive at **Swinford Toll Bridge**, one of just two such bridges remaining on the Thames (the other being at Whitchurch); don't let the toll put you off – walkers cross for free. Crossing the bridge (and a bit of a walk from the trail) will bring you – eventually – to the historic village of **Eynsham** (▣ eynsham-pc.gov.uk), once home to a great 11th-century abbey, which – like most of its age – was a victim of Henry VIII's dissolution. On the trail you will soon reach **Eynsham Lock** (see p110).

Continuing on, the river toys with the edge of **Wytham Woods** (Map 23), the last resting place for at least one victim in the *Inspector Morse* novels. The river and trail now wend their way via **King's Lock** – the northernmost point on

---

❏ **Godstow Abbey**
In between Godstow Bridge and Lock are the **remains of Godstow Abbey**. Established in 1133 and once a magnificent nunnery, the outer walls and ruins of the abbess's chapel are all that now remain. Young girls of the nobility were often sent here for 'finishing' and it is thought to be where Henry II met Rosamund Clifford. Famed for her beauty, 'Fair Rosamund' would go on to become the king's mistress and, according to rumour, bear him two children. Following her death in 1176 and burial here, the abbey grew in size due to the significant endowments lavished on it by the bereft king. In 1541 Henry VIII's dissolution saw most of the buildings destroyed. Those that remained found themselves involved in a political rather than a religious conflict a century later when the Royalists used them in the English Civil War to assist in their defence of Godstow Bridge.

❏ **Port Meadow**
Thought to have been grazed for over 4000 years and never touched by plough or pesticide, this 350-acre area of land was gifted to Oxford by Alfred the Great for the locals' help in resisting the Danes in the 10th century. The liberty to graze animals freely on the meadow was recorded in the *Domesday Book* in 1086 and has remained in place ever since. The cows quenching their thirst in the river obviously know their rights as they continue to stubbornly sup, unbothered by the endless stream of rowers who scull past on the water.

the Thames – and onwards past the turn-off to **Lower Wolvercote** (see p112; Map 24) and right by **Godstow Lock** and the remains of its nearby **Abbey** (see box p107). It's a lovely end to the day with the vast vista of **Port Meadow** (see box above) opening up on the opposite bank and Oxford's rowers accompanying you onwards. **Binsey** (see p112) offers the last chance for a pub-stop before you arrive in **Oxford** (see pp112-23; Map 25) which, if you plan for a rest day, is an absorbing place to take one. Where you plan to stay in Oxford will determine which route you should take to enter into the city (see box p115).

MAP 20

40–50 MINS TO/FROM NORTHMOOR LOCK (MAP 20)   NORTHMOOR LOCK

PYLON

023
NORTHMOOR LOCK

EATON ROAD

Northmoor Lock Paddocks Campsite

TO APPLETON & THE PLOUGH INN (FOOD), ½ MILE

MEADOWS

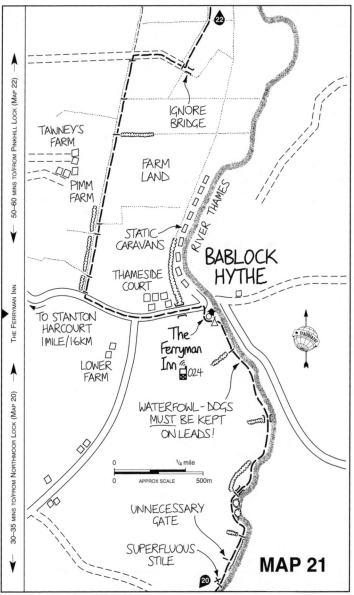

50–60 MINS TO/FROM PINKHILL LOCK (MAP 22)

The Ferryman Inn

30–35 MINS TO/FROM NORTHMOOR LOCK (MAP 20)

ROUTE GUIDE AND MAPS

★ trailblazer

22

IGNORE BRIDGE

TAWNEY'S FARM

PIMM FARM

FARM LAND

STATIC CARAVANS

RIVER THAMES

BABLOCK HYTHE

THAMESIDE COURT

TO STANTON HARCOURT 1 MILE/1·6KM

LOWER FARM

The Ferryman Inn 024

WATERFOWL – DOGS **MUST** BE KEPT ON LEADS!

0   ¼ mile
0   APPROX SCALE   500m

UNNECESSARY GATE

SUPERFLUOUS STILE

MAP 21

20

NORTHMOOR LOCK [Map 20, p108]

Northmoor Lock Paddocks (⌨ barefoot campsites.co.uk; ⚑ campers only; late May-Sep) is as splendidly isolated a **campsite** as you'll find along the River Thames. However, sadly, tent pitches are now only available 28 days a year and are only offered on specified weekends between May and August due to planning permission issues related to flooding. There is also a minimum 2-night booking policy, though single-night booking may be possible on restricted pitches for walkers/canoeists depending on campsite capacity. A pitch costs £12.50pp per night (£10pp for walkers/canoeists on a restricted pitch). You can also hire one of their two **wooden cabins** called '**log pods**' (£35 per night plus £12.50pp; no dogs). There is space in each to sleep up to four people but bedding is not provided so you need to have an air-bed or sleeping mat. People staying at the weekend (2-night bookings) have access to a fire pit for open fires; firewood must be bought on site. With cars being banned the atmosphere is one to be relished. Booking is essential; requests should be through the website but call ☎ 07961 514047 (May to Sep) for same-day availability and ☎ 07974-309958 for on-site emergencies.

For food, a civilised pub meal can be had approximately half-a-mile away in **Appleton** at *The Plough Inn* (☎ 01865-863535; WI-FI; ⚑; **food** Tue-Sat noon-2.30pm & 6.30-9pm, Sun noon-3pm; Eaton Rd), where you'll find real ales and home-cooked meals.

BABLOCK HYTHE [Map 21, p109]

Situated at what was once an important crossing point between Oxford and the West Country, Bablock Hythe is said to have played host to a ferry across the Thames for almost a thousand years, with the earliest record of one dating back to 1279. Before then, the Romans are known to have forded the river here too.

Despite such history the closest you'll get to a helping hand over the Thames these days is the name of the local pub. *The Ferryman Inn* (☎ 01865-880028, ⌨ ferrymaninn.co.uk; 2D/2T/2Tr; WI-FI; ⚑ in Fisherman's bar only) provides **B&B** and meals. For £42.50pp (sgl occ room rate) you get a room and a breakfast of toast and cereal; a full English is an extra £4.50pp.

Camping (£5 per tent; ⚑ on lead) for walkers is provided but it's basic with just a toilet and water supply. Dogs must be kept on a lead because of the local duck/goose population. The pub is closed on Tuesdays and in the afternoon in the winter months but otherwise is open for lunch and dinner (**food** Wed-Mon noon-2pm & 7-9pm). A free house, there are plenty of real ales to sip as you succumb to the smell of a steak & ale pie (£9.75) or choose one of their pub standards (£9.50 to £15.25 for the 8oz sirloin).

PINKHILL LOCK [Map 22]

Pinkhill Lock Campsite (☎ 01865-881452; ⚑ on a lead; Apr-Oct) is run by the Environment Agency. A pitch (tent and up to two people) costs from £11 (inc the cost of a shower); toilet facilities are available. Note that there is no vehicle access. The nearest pub is in Eynsham.

EYNSHAM LOCK [Map 22]

Another of the Environment Agency's sites, *Eynsham Lock Campsite* (☎ 01865-881324; open year-round unless the site is flooded; well-behaved ⚑) has 10 pitches (£7.50 irrespective of the number of people or tent size). There are toilets (code required) and a drinking water tap. The showers also operate on a token basis (£3.50) and open fires are allowed. Booking is recommended at weekends and in July & August.

Right by the path, *Swinford Manor Farm* (☎ 01865-881368, ⌨ swinfordmanor farmoxford.co.uk; 1S/1T/4D, private bathrooms; ☎; WI-FI) sits in a lovely spot and has equally lovely rooms, all with their own

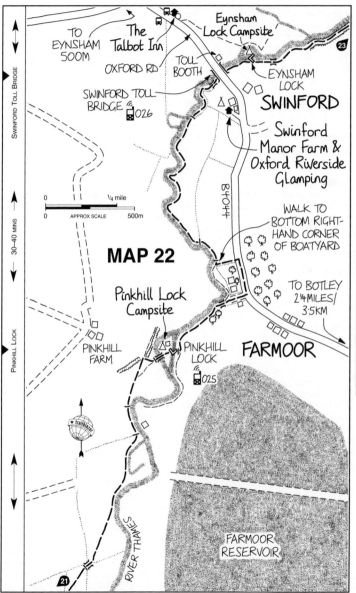

TO
EYNSHAM
500M

The
Talbot Inn

Eynsham
Lock Campsite

OXFORD RD

TOLL
BOOTH

SWINFORD TOLL
BRIDGE 📱026

Eynsham
Lock

SWINFORD

△

Swinford
Manor Farm &
Oxford Riverside
Glamping

B4044

WALK TO
BOTTOM RIGHT-
HAND CORNER
OF BOATYARD

0   ¼ mile

0   500m
APPROX SCALE

MAP 22

Pinkhill Lock
Campsite

TO BOTLEY
2¼ MILES/
3·5KM

PINKHILL
FARM

△   PINKHILL
        LOCK

📱025

FARMOOR

★ trailblazer

RIVER THAMES

FARMOOR
RESERVOIR

21

23

facilities and charges £50-60pp (sgl from £75, sgl occ room rate). On the same site is **Oxford Riverside Glamping** (🖥 swinford manorfarmoxford.co.uk/oxford-riverside-glamping; end Mar-early Oct); they have 10 fully fitted **bell tents** sleeping up to four people and complete with electric heater, though there's a 2-night minimum stay here (£170 for two people for the two nights plus £10pp).

Approximately 250 metres along Oxford Rd, between the lock and Eynsham, **The Talbot Inn** (☎ 01865-881348, 🖥 talbot

oxford.co.uk; 🛥; WI-FI; 🐾) provides **B&B** in either the original part of the pub (1D/1T share bathroom, 1T en suite; £33.75-47.50pp, sgl occ room rate) or in a new building called Wharf Side (2D/6D or T; around £50pp, sgl occ £100). There's also **food** (Mon-Fri noon-2.30pm & 6-9.30pm, Sat noon-9.30pm, Sun noon-9pm). The menu includes such saliva-inducing delights as Thai red curry chicken (£12.50).

The No 11 **bus** service (see pp58-9) stops by The Talbot and can be taken to get to Oxford.

KING'S LOCK   [Map 23]

If you wish to stay here (☎ 01865-553403; 🐾 on lead; Apr-Oct) you can put up a **tent** (a pitch costs £7.50) but the term 'basic' is taken to a new extreme: there's a water tap but no showers or toilets – and there's no

vehicle access either. Booking is recommended. The nearest pub on the Path is The Trout Inn (see below) approximately one mile further along the river.

LOWER WOLVERCOTE
[Map 24, p114]

As you cross **Godstow Bridge** you'll come to **The Trout Inn** (☎ 01865-510930, 🖥 the troutoxford.co.uk; **food** Mon-Fri noon-10pm, Sat noon-10.30pm, Sun 10am-9pm;

WI-FI; 🐾 bar only); it has a lovely terrace on which to relax and indulge in such exotic delights as caramelised fig & whipped goat's curd pizza (£10.95) for lunch or, for evening dining, spit-roast chicken (£12.95).

BINSEY   [Map 24, p114]

Following a signposted and magnificent willow-arched path, illuminated by fairy-lights, away from the river will bring you to **The Perch** (☎ 01865-728891, 🖥 the-perch .co.uk; **food** Sun-Thur noon-9pm, Fri & Sat to 10pm; 🐾), certainly one of the trail's quirkier places. Sitting beneath one of

their huge weeping willows on a sunny day, this is a lovely place to eat lunch; the menu is limited (with only four mains to choose from, for example) and the quality variable, though we loved their starter of crisp-fried pork belly (£4.95) and the location and ambience make it an essential stop.

OXFORD   [map p119]

Originally the site of a simple Saxon 'ford' used to guide 'ox' across the river, 'modern' Oxford's story begins early in the 8th century with the founding of a priory. In AD872, while journeying upstream, King Alfred rested at the priory and fell into discussions with the resident monks. The debate purportedly lasted a few days and Oxford gained a reputation as a place where people could learn. Over the coming

centuries a fortified settlement developed, a mint was built and the fledgling city would host councils between the Saxons and the Danes, with the latter also opting to raid it as and when they felt the need. Heavily fought over during the Norman Conquest, William ordered a castle to be built to control the town. Originally wooden but gradually modified in stone, the Norman fortification would be Matilda's base during the

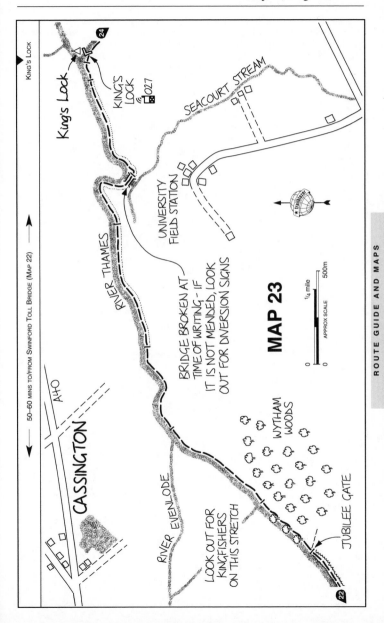

King's Lock

50-60 MINS TO/FROM SWINFORD TOLL BRIDGE (MAP 22)

King's Lock

24

KING'S LOCK

027

SEACOURT STREAM

RIVER THAMES

UNIVERSITY FIELD STATION

BRIDGE BROKEN AT TIME OF WRITING – IF IT IS NOT MENDED, LOOK OUT FOR DIVERSION SIGNS

MAP 23

APPROX SCALE

¼ mile

500m

0

0

Trailblazer

A40

CASSINGTON

RIVER EVENLODE

LOOK OUT FOR KINGFISHERS ON THIS STRETCH

WYTHAM WOODS

JUBILEE GATE

22

ROUTE GUIDE AND MAPS

Anarchy of 1141 (see p139) and also the primary fortification of the Royalists who would make Oxford their capital during the English Civil War.

The university's origins are as rooted in conflict as the city itself; specifically Henry II's troublesome relationship with his archbishop Thomas Becket. In 1167 Henry

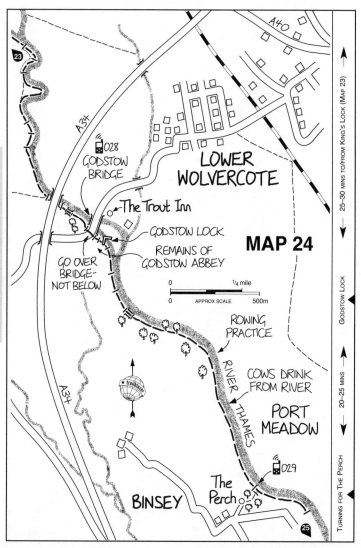

ROUTE GUIDE AND MAPS

028
GODSTOW
BRIDGE

LOWER
WOLVERCOTE

The Trout Inn

GODSTOW LOCK

MAP 24

REMAINS OF
GODSTOW ABBEY

GO OVER
BRIDGE-
NOT BELOW

0   ¼ mile

0   APPROX SCALE   500m

ROWING
PRACTICE

RIVER THAMES

COWS DRINK
FROM RIVER

PORT
MEADOW

trailblazer

029

The
Perch

BINSEY

25

25–30 MINS TO/FROM KING'S LOCK (MAP 23)

GODSTOW LOCK

20–25 MINS

TURNING FOR THE PERCH

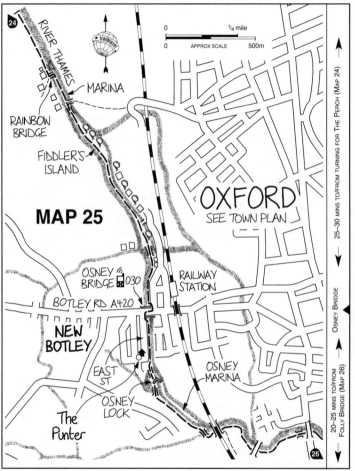

MAP 25

OXFORD
SEE TOWN PLAN

RIVER THAMES

MARINA

RAINBOW
BRIDGE

FIDDLER'S
ISLAND

OSNEY
BRIDGE 030

RAILWAY
STATION

BOTLEY RD A420

NEW
BOTLEY

EAST
ST

OSNEY
LOCK

OSNEY
MARINA

The
Punter

25–30 MINS TO/FROM TURNING FOR THE PERCH (MAP 24)

OSNEY BRIDGE

20–25 MINS TO/FROM FOLLY BRIDGE (MAP 26)

ROUTE GUIDE AND MAPS

❑ **Accessing Oxford**

Depending on where you are staying in Oxford there are different ways to reach your accommodation from the trail. Those staying near Osney Bridge and Oxford railway station, or in the city centre, should leave the path at Osney Bridge (Map 25), while those staying on Abingdon Rd should continue further along the river and Thames Path to Folly Bridge (Map 26). The bridge also provides a convenient access point for anyone staying in the city centre. **Campers** should continue two miles further along the Thames Path and follow the directions on Map 26.

ordered English students who were studying in France to come home: his motive? Becket was living in exile there and Henry was concerned that the students would side with the archbishop against him. Attracted by Oxford's reputation as a centre of learning, the scholars headed there and on arrival established halls of learning akin to the ones they had recently experienced in France. This led to the founding of Oxford's oldest college, **University College**, in 1249 – the first university in the English-speaking world. The **University Church of St Mary the Virgin** (see box below) became the university church as the scholars needed a central meeting place; the church was used for academic lectures as well as services.

Oxford today is a constant hive of activity and it's a great place to stroll amongst the throngs of students, locals and tourists who happily mingle beneath the 'dreaming spires'. An excellent way to see the sights is on a **walking tour**. Thoroughly recommended, the guides at Footprints Tours (☎ 020-7558 8706, 💻 footprints-tours.com) are knowledgeable, enthusiastic and great at adding the necessary sense of drama to the city's turbulent past. They operate a range of tours including a two-hour tour of the city (daily 11am, 12.30pm, 2pm & 3.30pm, also Sat at 10am &

3.30pm, and daily at 10am in Jul & Aug) which is free, though tips are appreciated. Guides can be found at 5 Broad St shortly before each tour begins.

If you'd rather see Oxford's attractions at your own pace you'll find most of them marked on the map on p119; the Tourist Information Centre also sells numerous pamphlets and further information can be found on their website (see Services).

The city's number one tourist attraction is **Ashmolean Museum of Art and Archaeology** (☎ 01865-278000, 💻 ashmolean.org; Tue-Sun & Bank Hol Mon 10am-5pm; free) on Beaumont St, established in 1683 and the oldest museum in England. Another history house is the **Museum of Oxford** (☎ 01865-252334, 💻 www.oxford.gov.uk/museumofoxford; Mon-Sat 10am-5pm, closed on Bank Hol Mons; free; St Aldates), whilst **Oxford Castle** (☎ 01865-260666, 💻 www.oxfordcastleunlocked.co.uk; daily 10am-5pm, guided tour only, every 20 mins, last tour 4.20pm; £11.50; New Rd) offers the best panorama of the city from its Saxon St George's Tower.

Services
In addition to providing information the **tourist information centre** (☎ 01865-686430, 💻 experienceoxfordshire.org; July & Aug Mon-Sat 9am-5.30pm, Sun 9.30am-

---

❏ **The Virgin Mary churches**
As you wander past the great churches and spires which watch over the river you may notice that many of them have more in common than just their fluvial location. For Cricklade, Castle Eaton, Buscot, Oxford, Wallingford, North Stoke, Streatley, Hurley, Henley-on-Thames, Putney and Lambeth all have a church dedicated to the Virgin Mary. Indeed, the list above is far from exhaustive, and there are more than 50 religious institutions devoted to St Mary along the banks of the Thames, an amount which equates to approximately one for every four-mile stretch of water! And of the few churches which no longer bear the name of Jesus's mother, several of them have been renamed and originally were St Mary's too – the Church of St Lawrence in Lechlade being one such example.

So why the fascination? Well, throughout history, water and rivers have long been associated with fertility. Indeed, women used to bathe in The Thames's waters believing that the river's power would increase their ability to produce offspring. Whether these riparian dips worked is unclear – but it did lead to numerous churches along the banks being dedicated to the most famous mother of them all – Mary, mother of the son of God.

4pm. Sep-June Mon-Sat 9.30am-5pm, Sun 10am-3.30pm; 15-16 Broad St) does accommodation booking and sells tickets for local events and attractions.

Also centrally located are branches of Sainsbury's **supermarket** (daily 7am-11pm or midnight depending on the store; St Aldates and Magdalen St) and Boots the **chemist** (Mon-Sat 8am-8pm, Sun 11am-5pm; Cornmarket St).

The **post office** (Mon-Sat 9am-5.30pm, Tue from 9.30am) is on St Aldates. Oxford has branches of all major High St banks and plentiful **ATMs**.

The closest **shop** to Osney Bridge is Westgate Stores (daily 8am-9.30pm; Botley Rd).

● **On Abingdon Rd (Map 26)** There are several **food stores** including a Tesco (daily 6am-11pm) with a free **ATM**.

For **camping supplies** visit Go Outdoors (🖳 gooutdoors.co.uk/oxford; 426 Abingdon Rd; Mon-Fri 9am-8pm, Sat 9am-6pm, Sun 10.30am-4.30pm).

Transport
Buses (see box pp58-9) connect the city with many of the towns and villages along the Thames Path. The services most likely to be of use are the: 11, X2, city 3A, X3/X13, city35, X38, X39 & X40; the latter run via stops along St Aldates and Abingdon Rd.

Oxford is easily accessed by **coach** (National Express, Oxford tube, Oxford Bus Company; see box p54) from airports in southern England as well as many other places in the UK. Most services operate to and from Gloucester Green Bus Station.

GWR **trains** (see box pp52-3) also operate regularly between Oxford and many other destinations along the Thames Path as well as to other areas of the UK.

Where to stay
There are loads of accommodation options in Oxford. In addition to the places listed below, in the summer months you can stay in some of the colleges (🖳 universityrooms .com/en/city/oxford/home).

Camping and hostels The city has three **hostels**. Next to the railway station is *YHA Oxford* (☎ 0345-371 9131 or ☎ 01865-727275, 🖳 yha.org.uk/hostel/oxford; 203 beds, 1-, 2-, 3-, 4- & 6-bed rooms, some en suite; WI-FI communal areas; 2a Botley Rd). Dorm beds cost from £18pp, private rooms from £28. The hostel is licensed and meals are available as are laundry and drying facilities; there is 24hr access.

The other two are a short stroll towards the centre of town: *Central Backpackers* (☎ 01865-242288, 🖳 centralbackpackers.co .uk; 4-, 6-, 8- & 12-bed mixed dorms, one 6-bed female only dorm; WI-FI; 13 Park End St). charges £19-28pp, with a 'light' breakfast available for £3. The rooms (mixed dorms and female only) at *Oxford Backpackers* (☎ 01865-721761, 🖳 hostels .co.uk; WI-FI; 9a Hythe Bridge St) have 4-18 beds; a bed costs £16-28.50pp and the rate includes a free continental breakfast. Lockers, Sky TV, kitchen and a pool table are available. Both hostels are clean and comfortable.

● **On Abingdon Rd (Map 26) Camping** is available at *Oxford Camping & Caravanning Club Site* (☎ 01865-244088, 🖳 campingandcaravanningclub.co.uk/ oxford; WI-FI; 🐕 on lead; 426 Abingdon Rd); the campsite is conveniently hidden behind a branch of Go Outdoors (see Services). It does lack charm but it's the only option in town; the official backpacker rate is £7.60-11.15pp but in the high summer season, a tent for two non-members cost

---

❏ **Where to stay: the details**
In the descriptions of accommodation in this book: unless otherwise stated the rooms described are en suite; ▼ means at least one room has a bath; Ⓛ means a packed lunch can be prepared if arranged in advance; 🐕 signifies that dogs are welcome in at least one room but also subject to prior arrangement, an additional charge may also be payable; WI-FI means wi-fi is available. See also p78.

£32. Booking is recommended in the peak season. Buses to central Oxford, Abingdon and Wallingford run from the stops outside the site.

B&Bs At *Becket House* (☎ 01865-724675, 🖳 becketguesthouse@yahoo.co.uk; 10D or T, mix en suite and shared facilities; WI-FI; 5 Becket St) a room costs from £37.50pp (sgl occ £60); breakfast is not served.

● **On Abingdon Rd (Map 26)** Most of Oxford's other B&Bs are on Abingdon Rd, amongst them *Newton House* (☎ 01865-240561, 🖳 newtonhouseoxford.co.uk; 8D/2T/2D or T/2Tr; WI-FI; £35-50pp, sgl occ from £80; Nos 82-84); *The Oxford Townhouse* (☎ 01865-511122, 🖳 theoxfordtownhouse.co.uk; 2S/2T/11D; WI-FI; £82.50-102.50pp, sgl/sgl occ from £135;

Nos 88-90) and the delectable *Lakeside Guesthouse* (☎ 01865-244725, 🖳 lakeside-guesthouse.com; 2D/2D or T/3Tr; most en suite but all with private facilities; WI-FI; f£50-67.50pp, sgl occ from £87; No 118).

Overlooking Folly Bridge is *The Head of the River* (☎ 01865-721600, 🖳 headoftheriveroxford.co.uk; 15D/2D or T/3Tr; ☛; WI-FI; 🐾; £60-125pp, sgl occ room rate). Owned by Fuller's Brewery and situated on the site at which – it is thought – the ancient ford that gave the town its name was located, this is urban Thames accommodation at its finest. Food is also available (see Where to eat).

Hotels Back down on Abingdon Rd, there's now a *Travelodge* (☎ 08715-591877, 🖳 travelodge.co.uk; 67D/14Tr; WI-FI) with room rates from £47 (see pp21-2).

ROUTE GUIDE AND MAPS

OXFORD – MAP KEY

Where to stay
2 River Hotel
5 Westgate Hotel
6 YHA Oxford
7 Becket House
9 Royal Oxford Hotel
10 Oxford Backpackers
12 Central Backpackers
19 Vanbrugh House Hotel
35 Bath Place Hotel

Where to eat & drink
1 The Punter
3 The One
8 The Jam Factory
11 Yellow Submarine
14 Café from Crisis
15 Kebab King
16 Jamie's Italian
17 George Street Social
18 Chutneys
20 The Three Goats Heads

Where to eat & drink (cont'd)
21 The Nosebag
25 The Eagle and Child
36 The Turf Tavern
48 The Bear

Services
4 Westgate Stores
22 ATM
23 Sainsbury's
26 Footprint Tours meeting place (5 Broad St)
27 Tourist Information
30 Blackwells Book Shop
45 Boots
46 Sainsbury's
49 Post Office

Other
13 Oxford Castle
24 Ashmolean
28 Balliol College
29 Trinity College
31 New Bodleian Library

Other (cont'd)
32 Museum of the History of Science
33 Sheldonian Theatre
34 Clarendon Building
37 Bridge of Sighs
38 Hertford College
39 Bodleian Library
40 Divinity School
41 Radcliffe Camera
42 All Souls College
43 University Church of St Mary the Virgin
44 Brasenose College
47 Museum of Oxford
50 Christ Church College & Cathedral
51 Corpus Christi
52 Merton College
53 University College
54 Magdalen College

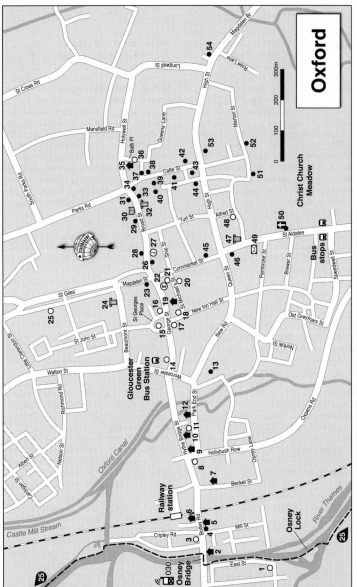

For those who want to stick near the river, accommodation is available at two hotels near Osney Bridge – neither will linger long in the memory but they won't break the bank either: *River Hotel* (☎ 01865-243475, 🖳 riverhotel.co.uk; 2S/8D/ 2T/5Tr all en suite, 1S/1D private bathroom; ☎; WI-FI; 17 Botley Rd) charges £56-62pp (sgl/sgl occ from £98) and there is a minimum two-night stay at weekends in the peak season; for a single-night stay it is best to call them in case they have availability. *Westgate Hotel* (☎ 01865-726721, 🖳 westgatehoteloxford.co.uk; 6S/5D/4T/ 3Tr/2Qd, mix en suite and shared facilities; ☎; WI-FI; 🐾; 1 Botley Rd) is on two sites, the main building has most of the en suite rooms (and baths) and there is a separate annex across the road where most rooms have shared facilities with showers. If you want a room with a bath it is best to call them as that can't be requested online, especially if booked through an agency. B&B costs £40-50pp (sgl/sgl occ from £70/85).

Hotels can also be found centrally. Between river and city is *Royal Oxford Hotel* (☎ 01865-248432, 🖳 royaloxfordho tel.co.uk; 1S/10T/13D/2Tr; ☎; WI-FI; Park End St), where the room only price varies depending on demand but is approximately £63.50pp (sgl from £127, sgl occ room rate; breakfast £13pp); while on St Michael's St (20-24) is the plush boutique *Vanbrugh House Hotel* (☎ 01865-244622, 🖳 van brughhousehotel.co.uk; 1S/3D or T/18D; ☎; WI-FI). Rates here are also very flexible; expect to pay at least £100pp (sgl from £180, sgl occ room rate). Both have restaurants.

Surreptitiously tucked away just off Holywell St is the well-established *Bath Place Hotel* (☎ 01865-791812, 🖳 bath place.co.uk; 15D/1Qd; ☎; WI-FI; 🐾; 4 & 5 Bath Place). Hiding practically next door to the famous Turf Tavern pub (see Pubs), this establishment is in a great central location from which to explore the city. The rate (£67.50-82.50pp, sgl occ from £105, but full room rate at weekends) includes a continental buffet; a cooked breakfast costs extra. Advance bookings for a single-night stay are not taken for Friday or Saturday

nights year-round but nearer the time may be considered.

Where to eat and drink
The city also has innumerable eateries of all type, amongst them...

Cafés and takeaways *Yellow Submarine* (☎ 01865-236119, 🖳 yellow submarine.org.uk; Mon-Thur 8am-4pm, Fri 8am-3pm; WI-FI; 🐾 if OK with manager; 12 Park End St) employs people with autism and learning difficulties. There's a limited breakfast but they prepare toasties (£2.90-4.10) at lunchtime as well as smashing coffees and cakes. *Café from Crisis* (☎ 01865-263972; Mon-Sat 8.30am-4pm; WI-FI; 40 George St) supports the homeless and provides decent breakfast options and has daily specials at lunch.

Takeaway is available centrally at *Kebab King* (🖳 kebabkingoxford.com; Mon-Sat 11am-4am, Sun 11am-3am) at 36 George St.

● **On Abingdon Rd (Map 26)** *Mediterranean Fish Bar* (☎ 01865-243822; Mon-Thur 11am-9.30pm, Fri & Sat to 10pm, Sun noon-9pm).

Pubs *'My happiest hours are spent with three or four old friends in old clothes, tramping together and putting up in small pubs.'* CS Lewis.

There are almost as many pubs as academics in Oxford; indeed, you could almost drown in the variation of ales, organic lagers and high-voltage ciders available. **They all also serve food** though in some cases almost as an afterthought – ale is definitely the priority at most of these establishments.

Ever-popular, *The Turf Tavern* (☎ 01865-243235, 🖳 greeneking-pubs.co.uk; WI-FI; 🐾; food daily 11am-9pm; Bath Place) has been a stalwart of Oxford's pub-scene for centuries and the section of old town wall which borders its back garden has witnessed many a peculiar event, from Bob Hawke (once prime minister of Australia) downing a yard of ale in eleven seconds to Bill Clinton 'not inhaling' something someone had lit. Other famous customers include Margaret Thatcher, Elizabeth Taylor and

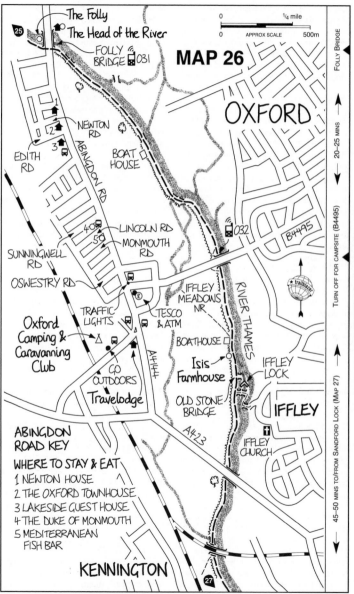

MAP 26

The Folly
The Head of the River
FOLLY BRIDGE 031

OXFORD

NEWTON RD
ABINGDON RD
BOAT HOUSE
EDITH RD

032

B4495

LINCOLN RD
MONMOUTH RD

SUNNINGWELL RD

OSWESTRY RD

IFFLEY MEADOWS NR

RIVER THAMES

TRAFFIC LIGHTS
TESCO & ATM

Oxford Camping & Caravanning Club

BOATHOUSE

Isis Farmhouse

IFFLEY LOCK

GO OUTDOORS
Travelodge

A4144

OLD STONE BRIDGE

IFFLEY

A423

IFFLEY CHURCH

ABINGDON ROAD KEY

WHERE TO STAY & EAT
1 NEWTON HOUSE
2 THE OXFORD TOWNHOUSE
3 LAKESIDE GUEST HOUSE
4 THE DUKE OF MONMOUTH
5 MEDITERRANEAN FISH BAR

KENNINGTON

27

0 ¼ mile
0 APPROX SCALE 500m

FOLLY BRIDGE
20–25 MINS
TURN OFF FOR CAMPSITE (B4495)
45–50 MINS TO/FROM SANDFORD LOCK (MAP 27)

ROUTE GUIDE AND MAPS

Oscar Wilde – the pub even claims to have a ghost, Rosie, who hangs around the glass wash area, apparently still awaiting her husband's return from the English Civil War. There's a decent menu with some interesting sharing platters including a Fish & Chip Board of two fish sliders, Whitby scampi, devilled whitebait, triple-cooked chips & tartare sauce (£11.95).

Despite The Turf Tavern's claims, it seems most likely that the title of oldest watering hole in Oxford goes to *The Bear* (☎ 01865-728164, 🖳 bearoxford.co.uk; food daily noon-4pm & 5-9pm; WI-FI; 🐾 outside; 6 Alfred St). A mainstay of the city's walking tours, beverages were first served here in 1242. The pub has an interesting interior, the walls being adorned with club and college ties donated by alumni from all over England. Now owned by Fuller's Brewery there is their normal range of ales on tap as well as a menu which always includes burgers and pub classics as well as a ciabatta (London porter hot smoked salmon ciabatta £7.90) at lunchtime.

A home from home for hobbit-lovers, *The Eagle and Child* (☎ 01865-302925, 🖳 nicholsonspubs.co.uk; WI-FI; food Mon-Sat noon-10pm, Sun noon-9pm; 49 St Giles) was once the favoured drinking venue of The Inklings, a group of writers, including JRR Tolkien and CS Lewis, who would regularly meet here. One wonders if either ever tried their mixed leaf, brown rice, quinoa & lemon salad (£7.95); probably not.

For cheap pub-grub and drinks, *The Three Goats Heads* (☎ 01865-721523; food Mon-Sat noon-2.45pm & 5-8.45pm, Sun noon-8.45pm; 🐾 on lead; 3 St Michael's St) serves Samuel Smith beer. There's no music or TV but the lack of such distractions keeps prices low – indeed, you'll get a plate of Cumberland sausage & mash for just £8.45.

Though not strictly a pub, *George Street Social* (🖳 georgestreetsocial.com; food daily 9am-10pm; WI-FI) is a lively place that's open all day to feed and water the masses. If you really feel like indulging they do a 'bottomless brunch' for £25, where you can choose any item off their brunch menu and twin it with as much

prosecco or bloody Mary as you can within a two-hour slot! Their mains are more reasonable, with linguine dishes from just £8.50 and burger with wedges for £9.75.

Right on the trail, *The Punter* (☎ 01865-248832, 🖳 thepunteroxford.co.uk; food Mon-Fri noon-3pm & 6-10pm, Sat noon-10pm, Sun noon-9pm; WI-FI; 🐾) is a smart little place with a menu that changes daily, though it's reasonable value and it's one of the few places we found on the trail that serves mussels & fries (£11), though it isn't on the menu all year.

● **On Abingdon Rd (Map 26)** Libations by the Thames can be sunk at *The Head of the River* (see Where to stay; WI-FI; 🐾; food summer Mon-Fri 7am-10pm, Sat 8am-10pm, Sun 8am-9pm, winter 8/9am-9pm). There's plenty of outdoor seating peering out over the water and a decent menu (main courses £12-26) but it can get very busy especially in the summer months so it is worth booking then.

Campers and those residing on Abingdon Rd in particular may be interested in *The Duke of Monmouth* (☎ 01865-240294, 🖳 greeneking-pubs.co.uk; food daily noon-9pm; WI-FI; 🐾 bar area; No 260), another Greene King pub. The prices are particularly generous including sandwiches from £3.29 (Mon-Sat to 5pm) and 8oz rump steak with chips for £9.99.

Restaurants Nearest to Osney Bridge is jack-of-all-trades *The One* (☎ 01865-240018, 🖳 theoneoxford.co.uk; food daily noon-11pm; WI-FI; 2 Botley Rd), where you'll find not just Chinese, Thai and Western food but also tapas and takeaway.

Followers of cheeky chappy TV chef Jamie Oliver are in luck as there's a branch of *Jamie's Italian* (☎ 01865-838383, 🖳 jamieoliver.com/italian; Mon-Sat noon-11pm, Sun noon-10pm; WI-FI; 24-26 George St) in the city. Dishes such as Jamie's Italian burger (£14.55) are available; they also have a pizzeria (pizzas from £11.95).

The Jam Factory (☎ 01865-244613, 🖳 thejamfactoryoxford.com; food: breakfast daily 8-11.30am, lunch Mon-Sat noon-3pm, dinner 5-10pm, Sun noon-9pm) is a characterful place on Hollybush Row, a restaurant, bar and gallery all rolled into one. Food-wise, they do a wide range of burgers £11.50-15 and a lovely baked whole rainbow trout (£16.50).

Based at 6-8 St Michael's St, *Nosebag Restaurant* (☎ 01865-721033, 🖳 nosebagoxford.co.uk; Mon-Thur 9.30am-10pm, Fri & Sat 9.30am-10.30pm, Sun 9.30am-9pm) is a well-regarded independent place that's been serving up great home-cooked food for almost fifty years. Though they do cater for carnivores they are best-known for their vegetarian food; for lunch consider their lentil & sweet pepper lasagne (£9.20), while at dinner we recommend you get yourself on the outside of a paella with summer vine vegetables & toasted almonds (£11.50).

At the end of the street, for Indian lovers, *Chutneys* (☎ 01865-724241, 🖳 chutneysoxford.co.uk; daily noon-2.30pm, Sun-Thur 5.30-11pm, Fri & Sat to 11.30pm; 36 St Michael's St) is a must. Tandoori dishes (£9.70-13.95) and all the normal suspects are available at the city's oldest-surviving Indian restaurant.

● **On Abingdon Rd (Map 26)** On an island in the river is *The Folly* (☎ 01865-986131, 🖳 no1-folly-bridge.co.uk; food mid Mar to end Oct daily 10am-9pm, rest of year Mon-Fri 5-9pm, Sat & Sun 11am-9pm. The restaurant offers riverside dining on an outdoor floating pontoon. The menu changes regularly but may include seared fillet of red mullet (£18.95) and pan-seared bream (£18.95).

OXFORD TO ABINGDON [MAPS 25-29]

This **9¾-mile (15.5km, 3¼-3¾hrs)** stretch retains the sense of isolation from the previous stages, the bustle of Oxford notwithstanding; although the size and style of the houses that occasionally spring up on the opposite bank suggest that the solitude one finds downstream of Oxford is in a decidedly more affluent setting than that you've already encountered upstream.

Having left the spires and students behind, this is a straightforward and relatively short stroll along the riverbank. Passing **Iffley Meadows Nature Reserve** (Map 26) – host to thousands of snake's-head fritillaries in spring – you arrive at **Iffley Lock** (see below), the first 'pound' lock built on the Thames (see box pp96-7). **Sandford Lock** (Map 27) follows with its accompanying, infamous river, known as 'the Lasher' (see box p126). You'll find decent opportunities for food at both locks.

Having passed the turning to **Radley** (see p126; Map 28), you come across 18th-century **Nuneham House** (see box p126), staring down at you from the eastern bank. Then, shortly before you arrive at **Abingdon Lock**, on the opposite bank is one end of **Swift Ditch** (or Short Cut), also labelled as **Back Water** on OS maps. It is thought that this may be the river's original course, with the current route having been dug by the monks of Abingdon in the 10th century in order to divert the river past the abbey's doors. Today the lock boasts a small weekends-only café, *The Whippet Kitchen* (from 10am). Following the lock, an amiable amble sees you arrive in **Abingdon** (see p126).

IFFLEY LOCK [Map 26, p121]

Shortly before the lock, *Isis Farmhouse* (☎ 01865-243854, 🖳 theisisfarmhouse.co.uk; **food** Mon & Thur noon-9pm, Fri-Sun 10am-9pm, closed Tue & Wed all year; 🐕) is set in a magnificent location and has live music virtually every evening it is open and also jazz on Sunday afternoons (5-8pm). Note there is no vehicle access to the pub.

ROUTE GUIDE AND MAPS

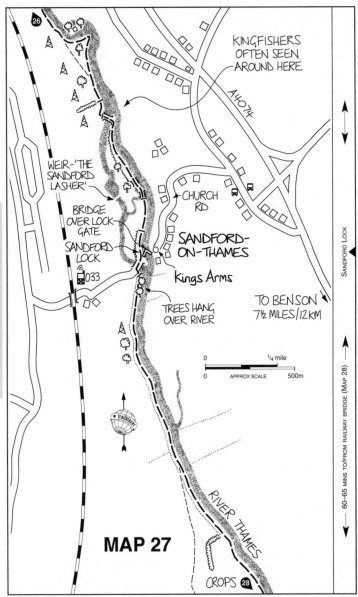

KINGFISHERS
OFTEN SEEN
AROUND HERE

A4074

WEIR-'THE
SANDFORD
LASHER'

BRIDGE
OVER LOCK-
GATE

SANDFORD
LOCK

📞033

CHURCH
RD

SANDFORD-
ON-THAMES

Kings Arms

TREES HANG
OVER RIVER

TO BENSON
7½ MILES/12KM

0   ¼ mile

0   500m
APPROX SCALE

★ trailblazer

MAP 27

RIVER THAMES

CROPS 28

26

ROUTE GUIDE AND MAPS

Sandford Lock

60-65 MINS TO/FROM RAILWAY BRIDGE (MAP 28)

SANDFORD-ON-THAMES [Map 27]

Kings Arms (☎ 01865-777095, 🖥 chefand brewer.com; WI-FI; 🐕 bar area) serves **meals** such as Caesar salad (£8.99) and slow-cooked pork belly (£13.29) all day (daily noon-9pm) and you can eat out in the garden that looks over lock and river.

The city 3A **bus** service (see pp58-9) stops here.

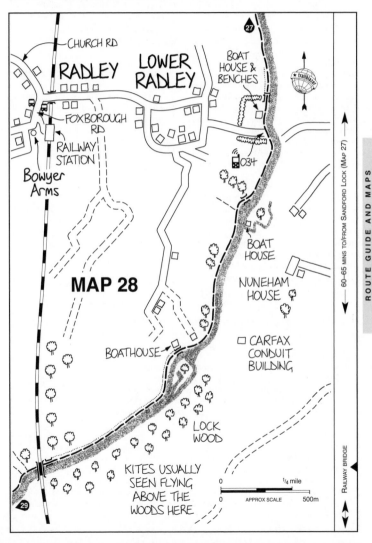

CHURCH RD

RADLEY

LOWER RADLEY

BOAT HOUSE & BENCHES

★ trailblazer

FOXBOROUGH RD

RAILWAY STATION

Bowyer Arms

☎ 034

MAP 28

BOAT HOUSE

NUNEHAM HOUSE

BOATHOUSE

CARFAX CONDUIT BUILDING

LOCK WOOD

KITES USUALLY SEEN FLYING ABOVE THE WOODS HERE

0   ¼ mile
0   500m
APPROX SCALE

← 60–65 MINS TO/FROM SANDFORD LOCK (MAP 27) →

ROUTE GUIDE AND MAPS

RAILWAY BRIDGE

❑ **The Sandford Lasher**
Just before Sandford Lock you pass an infamous weir known as 'the Lasher.' Described by Jerome K Jerome in *Three Men in a Boat* as 'a very good place to drown yourself', the weir's dramatic title has been gained due to the number of unfortunate souls who have lost their lives to this particular section of the river's fast and deadly undercurrents. Rather ironically, one of the Lasher's victims was the adopted son of JM Barrie and the inspiration for Peter Pan – not, alas, a boy who would live forever.

RADLEY [Map 28, p125]

Just shy of a mile away from the path, there is no need to divert to Radley unless you are utterly desperate for a railway station or pub; and even the latter, *Bowyer Arms* (☎ 01235-523452, 🖥 greeneking-pubs.co.uk; **food** daily noon-9pm; WI-FI; 🐾 on lead; Foxborough Rd) offers no real reason *not* to persist along the trek to Abingdon. If food is deemed essential the menu offers plenty of steaks, burgers, and scampi & chips (£8.69).

GWR **trains** (see box pp52-3) run between Radley, Oxford and a number of destinations along the Thames Path; the city 35 **bus service** calls at the railway station en route between Oxford and Abingdon (see box pp58-9).

ABINGDON [map p129]

With excavations uncovering evidence of Iron Age, Roman and Saxon communities, Abingdon (its official name is Abingdon-on-Thames) can lay reasonable claim to being the oldest continuously inhabited settlement in England. Wonderfully, this market town is as pretty as it is historic.

The town originally grew prosperous in the 7th century thanks to its abbey and continued to thrive even after Henry VIII's dissolution of the monasteries in 1538. In 1556 it was named the county town of Berkshire, though reorganisation of local government led to the town becoming part

❑ **Nuneham House and Carfax Conduit Building** [Map 28, p125]
This Grade II-listed Palladian Villa (ie a building inspired by the work of the 16th-century Italian architect Andrea Palladio) was built in 1756 by the 1st Earl Harcourt. Considering the view from his house to be spoilt by the nearby village of Nuneham Courtenay, he had the village demolished and commissioned the famed landscape architect Capability Brown to design some new and lavish gardens. During the Second World War the house and grounds were requisitioned by the Ministry of Defence and until the mid 1950s it was known as RAF Nuneham Park. On its return to the Harcourts they sold it to Oxford University who now lease it to Brahma Kumaris World Spiritual University.

Incidentally, as you continue east along the trail you may just be able to see, poking above the trees on the opposite bank, a sandstone Gothic construction. This is **Carfax Conduit Building**, that used to sit in the centre of Oxford. The conduit used to bring clean water from the nearby hills to the centre of Oxford. Unfortunately, by 1787 it had become too much of an obstacle for the ever-increasing traffic of the city and the decision was taken to demolish it and replace it with a smaller cistern. It was at this point that Earl Harcourt stepped in and brought the building to Nuneham, where it stands today.

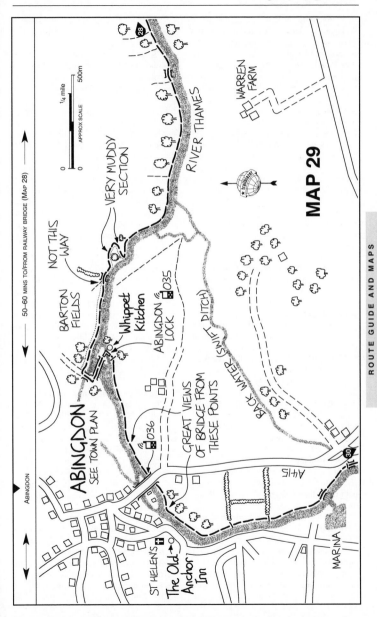

of Oxfordshire in 1974. The grandeur of Abingdon's sights means that they tend to introduce themselves. In the centre of the town is **St Nicolas Church**, parts of which date back to the 11th century; the archway next door was once the Abbey Gateway though now it leads to **Abbey Gardens**.

Dominating one side of Market Place is **County Hall**, in which you'll find the town's **museum** (☎ 01235-523703, 💻 abingdon.gov.uk/partners/abingdon-county -hall-museum; Tue-Sun & Bank Hol Mons 10am-4pm; free). A climb up on to the hall's roof (£2; closed if the weather is bad) presents magnificent views out over the town and back down towards the river.

You'll not be able to miss the tower and spire of the 10th-century **St Helen's Church**, which together with the town's **bridge** offer great photo opportunities.

Services

The **visitor information centre** (☎ 01235-522711, 💻 abingdon.gov.uk/discover-abing don; Mon-Sat 9.30am-3pm) is in Guildhall.

On West St Helen St there is a Co-op **supermarket** (daily 7am-10pm) which includes a **post office** (daily 7am-10pm), while on Bury St is a Boots the **chemist** (Mon-Sat 9am-5.30pm, Sun 10am-4pm).

Market Place has a branch of NatWest **bank** with **ATMs** outside.

Numerous **bus** services run between here (city 35/X2/X3/X13) and Oxford, while the X2 also runs to Wallingford; the 15 and 32A also call here; see box pp58-9 for details. Relevant bus stops are situated on Bridge St and High St.

Where to stay

Abingdon is not overrun with **B&B**-style accommodation but the two nearest to the path more than make up for this: both are on East St Helen St.

At No 22 is *Susie Howard Bed and Breakfast* (☎ 01235-550979, 💻 abingdon bedandbreakfast.com; 1D en suite, 2S/1D share bathroom; ☞; WI-FI), a colourful house with beamed ceilings. The owner has been in the business for 32 years. Room-only rates are £32.50-40pp (sgl/sgl occ £45-65) but on weekdays you have the

option of a breakfast for £10pp. There is also a kitchen for guests who wish to prepare their own food.

A little further along the road, *St Ethelwold's House* (☎ 01235-555486, 💻 ethelwoldhouse.com; 3S/3D/room sleeping up to six; shared bathroom; ☞; WI-FI; No 30) is a unique establishment here. The building is made up of a mixture of medieval and Georgian architecture and the gardens run down to the Thames. 'A place to find stillness in the world' according to the brochure and there are several 'quiet rooms' throughout the building, and meditation sessions are held regularly. Prices vary but the majority of guests pay from £35pp (sgl £27-40, sgl occ from £50); a continental breakfast is £7pp but this must be requested in advance. A couple of the rooms have some kitchen facilities so guests can prepare their own meals.

There are other accommodation options near to the river with the first a particularly quirky one. Hidden away from the town and set in its own magnificent grounds is the rather secretive *Coseners's House* (☎ 01235-523198, 💻 thecoseners house.co.uk; 20S/30D or T, most en suite some share shower facilities; ☞; WI-FI; 15-16 Abbey Close). B&B costs from £47.50pp (sgl from £75, sgl occ room rate) and evening meals are available (see Where to eat).

Hotel-wise *The Crown & Thistle* (☎ 01235-522556, 💻 crownandthistleleabing don.co.uk; 2D or T/14D/2Tr; ☞; WI-FI; 🐾; 18 Bridge St) offers the most expensive accommodation in town. It has some stunning rooms with the price for B&B reflecting the standard of the accommodation. The rate varies according to demand but is in the range of £64.50-72pp (sgl occ negotiable but full room rate in peak season).

Where to eat and drink

Centrally located and locally owned **cafés** include *Throwing Buns* (☎ 01235-533656, 💻 throwingbuns.com; daily 8am-5.30pm; 8 Market Place) and *Java & Co* (☎ 01235-526957, 💻 javaandco.co.uk; Sun-Thur 8am-5.30pm, Fri & Sat to 6pm; WI-FI; 🐾; 18/19 Market Place). At both you'll find friendly service and sandwiches and other typical café fare costing around £5.

Nearby, spacious *R&R* (☎ 01235-528472; WI-FI; daily 8am-5.30pm) offers paninis (£4.95-5.50), jacket potatoes (from £5.25), cakes and snacks. Next door, cheap baguettes (around £3) can be found at – where else? – *La Baguette* (☎ 01235-537070; Mon-Sat 9.30am-4pm).

The nearest **pub** to the path is actually on the island in the middle of The Thames. A winner of CAMRA awards, *The Nag's Head* (☎ 01235-524516; 🖥 thenagshead onthethames.co.uk; food Mon-Thur noon-3pm & 6-9pm, Fri & Sat noon-3.30pm & 6-9.30pm, Sun noon-3.30pm & 6-8pm; WI-FI; 🐾) stocks a wide range of local real ales and has a large outside riverside dining area. In the summer months (though this depends on the weather) you can sit by the water's edge and ponder the outdoor menu which includes pizza (from £12.95) and grill dishes using locally sourced produce; these are cooked in a pizza oven (Sat-Thur noon-3pm & 6-8.30pm, Fri noon-9pm).

At 10 East St Helen St, in what was once a 16th-century coaching inn, *Kings Head and Bell* (☎ 01235-525362, 🖥 kings headandbell-abingdon.com; food Mon-Fri noon-3pm & 5-9pm, Sat & Sun noon-9pm; WI-FI; 🐾) serves up old favourites such as bangers & mash (£10.95) with more unusual dishes on the specials board.

Down by the river and recently refurbished, *The Old Anchor Inn* (☎ 01235-412669, 🖥 oldanchorinn.co.uk; food Mon-Sat noon-3pm & 6-9pm, Sun noon-4pm; WI-FI; 🐾; 1 St Helen's Wharf) is beautifully set

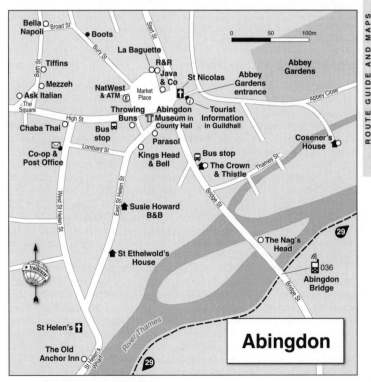

Abingdon

ROUTE GUIDE AND MAPS

in the shadow of the church. The pub is worth a visit for its location and the food, mainly pub classics such as gammon, egg & chips (£11.50), is good too. Note that food may not be served on a Monday in the winter. Another restaurant worth considering for its locality is *Cosener's House* (see Where to stay) where dinner is served 7-9pm.

The menu at *The Crown & Thistle* (see Where to stay; food Mon-Thur 7am-10pm, Fri to 10.30pm, Sat 8am-10.30pm, Sun 8am-9pm) has everything from eggs Benedict for breakfast (£8) to super-food salads for the health conscious (£10), pizzas, burgers and a delicious slow-cooked belly of pork (£15) during the day.

Gargantuan servings of Chinese food can be found at *Parasol* (☎ 01235-520700; Mon-Sat noon-2pm & 5.30-11.30pm, Sun noon-9pm; 5 Market Place) where they have an eat-as-much-as-you-can deal (Sun-Thur £17.50 plus service) as well as set menus (£9-12.50pp) and **takeaway**.

Across on Bath St is an Indian, *Tiffins* (☎ 01235-537786, 🖳 tiffins-tandoori.busi ness.site; daily noon-2.30pm & 6-11.30pm) with vegetarian mains for £6. A couple of doors away there's a Lebanese, *Mezzeh House* (☎ 01235-533551, 🖳 mezze-house .co.uk; Mon-Sat noon-3pm & 5-11pm, Sun 6-11pm) with tapas-style Middle Eastern dishes for £4.50-6, as well as mains for £10-15.

Round the corner on High St, *Chaba Thai* (☎ 01235-525540, 🖳 chabathai.co .uk; daily 6-11pm) open in the evenings only, with a chicken green curry (£7.95). Finally, there are a couple of Italian eateries, including *Bella Napoli* (☎ 01235-537676, 🖳 bellanapoliabingdon.co.uk; Tue 6-10pm, Wed-Sat noon-10pm, Sun to 9pm; 29a Broad St) and a branch of the national chain *Ask* (☎ 01235-529699, 🖳 askitalian .co.uk; Sun-Thur 11am-10pm, Fri & Sat to 11pm) on The Square.

ABINGDON TO WALLINGFORD   [MAPS 29-35]

This quite lengthy **13½-mile (22km, 4½-5½hrs)** stage is blessed. Not only does the trail start and end in two of the most picturesque of Thames-side towns but it also passes through a number of smaller settlements of interest. Furthermore, there's some wonderful scenery as you amble on through meadows between locks and hamlets, past ancient churches and villages, the path keeping to the water's edge for most of the stage.

Having utilised **Culham Cut** (Map 30) – dug in 1809 to bypass a section of the river that was notoriously awkward to navigate – you cross the road leading to **Culham**; the only services there now are bus (32A; see box p58-9) and train (see box pp52-3). Go under the railway line to reach **Clifton Cut** (Map 31) which in turn delivers you to the hamlet of **Clifton Hampden** (see p133; Map 32), ideally situated for lunch. As you approach you are treated to one of the finest vistas along the length of the river, with the hamlet's tiny 12th-century church nestled behind its red-brick bridge.

At **Day's Lock** (see p134; Map 33) – home to the annual World Pooh Stick's Championship – you cross the river and have the option of exploring the ancient settlement of **Dorchester-on-Thames** (see p134). Dorchester lies across the river from **Sinodun Hills**, more commonly known as **Wittenham Clumps** (see box p134), the second of two major landmarks – after the remaining towers of **Didcot Power Station** (Map 30) – that dominate the views to the south of the trail today. As you leave the clumps behind you cross the confluence of the rivers Thames and Thame (see box pp44-5). The only brief diversion from the river is on the approach to **Shillingford** (see p136; Map 34).

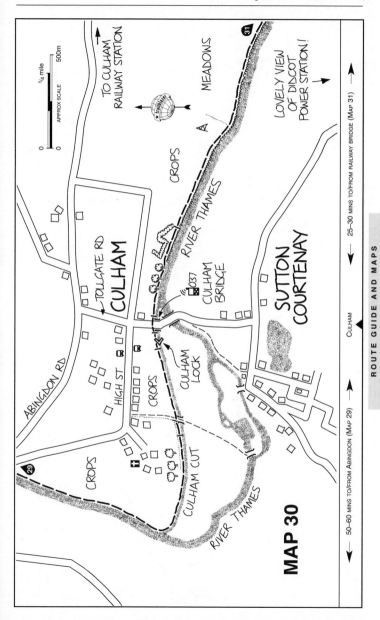

MAP 30

50-60 MINS TO/FROM ABINGDON (MAP 29)

CULHAM

25-30 MINS TO/FROM RAILWAY BRIDGE (MAP 31)

ROUTE GUIDE AND MAPS

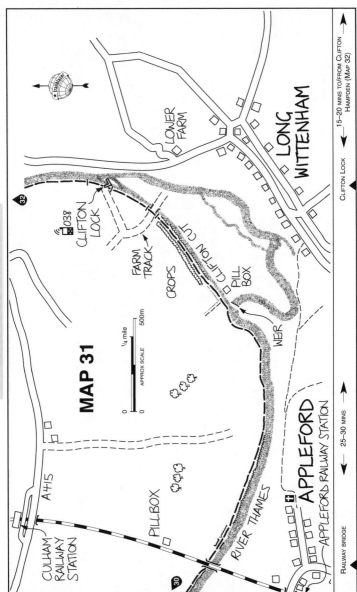

MAP 31

APPROX SCALE

¼ mile

0   500m

LONG WITTENHAM

LOWER FARM

☐ 038

CLIFTON LOCK

FARM TRACK

CROPS

CLIFTON CUT

PILL BOX

WEIR

CULHAM RAILWAY STATION

A415

PILLBOX

PILLBOX

RIVER THAMES

APPLEFORD

APPLEFORD RAILWAY STATION

◀ CLIFTON LOCK   15–20 MINS TO/FROM CLIFTON HAMPDEN (MAP 32) ▶

◀ 25–30 MINS ▶

RAILWAY BRIDGE

Benson (see p137; Map 35) is both the last settlement and final lock you pass by – and, on this occasion, cross – before the day's concluding stretch, flanked by river and peaceful meadow. The ground here has not always known such serenity, however, for until 1652 this was **the site of Wallingford Castle** (see box p139), one of the largest and most formidable fortifications in pre-Civil War England. At Wallingford Bridge you can decide to turn left for **Crowmarsh Gifford** (see p137) – really a viable option for campers only – or continue for **Wallingford** town (see p139).

CLIFTON HAMPDEN   [Map 32]

At this point the river passes over sandstone, the 'clif' in the village's name being made up of such. The village's 'surname' derives from John Hampden, cousin of Oliver Cromwell and one-time owner of the local manor.

In amongst the thatched cottages on the western bank you'll find **Stores** (Mon-Fri 6.30am-6pm, Sat 7am-1pm, Sun 8am-noon) with a **post office** (Mon-Fri 9am-5.30pm, Sat 9am-12.30pm).

Pristinely located by river and pub, **campers** can pitch up at *Bridge House Caravan & Campsite* (☎ 01865-407725; 🐾 on lead and under close control; Mar-end Oct); they charge from £12/15 for a tent and one/two people; the site has toilet & shower facilities, the latter with a coin meter. Booking is recommended for the peak season.

On the A415, *The Plough* (☎ 01865-409976, 🖥 ploughbnb.com; 6D; ●; WI-FI) offers **B&B** (£39.50-49.50pp, sgl occ £70-82) including a cooked breakfast.

On the opposite side of the river, *The Barley Mow* (☎ 01865-407847, 🖥 chefandbrewer.com; **food** daily noon-9pm; WI-FI; 🐾 bar area) has the usual Chef & Brewer menu, so if you visited the King's Arms at Sandford-on-Thames you'll know what to expect. This place can get busy in the evenings so you may have to wait for the usual pub fare, which is of variable quality and value; expect to pay £11.69 for fish & chips. Our only real gripe about this place is the piped music, which pervades every corner of the pub, inside and out – and which we find totally unnecessary.

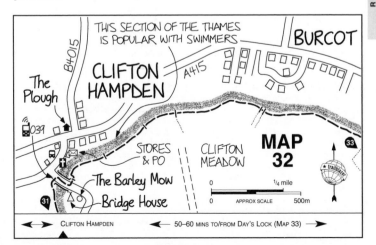

ROUTE GUIDE AND MAPS

THIS SECTION OF THE THAMES IS POPULAR WITH SWIMMERS

BURCOT

B4015

CLIFTON HAMPDEN

A415

The Plough

039

STORES & PO

CLIFTON MEADOW

MAP 32

33

The Barley Mow

Bridge House

31

0   ¼ mile

0   500m
APPROX SCALE

trailblazer

CLIFTON HAMPDEN   ◄— 50–60 MINS TO/FROM DAY'S LOCK (MAP 33) —►

ROUTE GUIDE AND MAPS

DAY'S LOCK [Map 33]

Campers (well-behaved 🐾) staying on the island here must arrive during the lock-keeper's working hours (☎ 01865-407768; from Good Friday/Mar by 3.30pm, Apr by 4.30pm, May by 5pm, June & Sep by 6pm, July-Aug by 6.30pm) in order to collect a key for the site, for which there is a deposit

(£10). A pitch (one tent and up to two people) costs £11 including use of the showers. Booking is recommended as the maximum number of people (including children) allowed to stay on the site each night is only 10. The nearest shop and pub are in Dorchester-on-Thames.

DORCHESTER-ON-THAMES
[Map 33]

Entering sleepy Dorchester-on-Thames, you'll find it hard to imagine that it was once a great city, home to a Roman garrison and entertained by an amphitheatre. The pretty village was – preceding Winchester – the primary city of Wessex and it was on the banks of the River Thame here that Bishop Birinius, sent by Pope Honorius I to convert the Saxons, baptised King Cynegils of Wessex (AD611-643). Converting Cynegils in the presence of the already Christian King Oswald of Northumbria united the two kingdoms against the pagan Mercians and established England as a Christian nation. A more recent claim to fame for the village occurred in 2017, when the local cricket side managed the unlikely feat of scoring 41 runs off the final over to win a game against a nearby village, an achievement that's particularly noteworthy when one considers that the maximum number of runs that one can normally score off an over is 36!

If, on entering the village, you get the feeling that you've visited Dorchester

before, that's probably not evidence that you are the reincarnation of King Cynegils of Wessex, but is instead more likely an indication that you've been watching *Midsomer Murders* recently; many of the TV drama's episodes were filmed in and around the village.

Dorchester Abbey (🖥 dorchester-abbey.org.uk; summer daily 8am-6pm, winter 8am to dusk) was founded in 1140 and was spared the worst of Henry VIII's wrath during the dissolution of the monasteries. Just outside the abbey there is a **museum** (early Apr-end Sep daily 2-5pm; free) housed in the medieval Abbey Guest House; this isn't a guest house at all but it describes itself as a 'place of hospitality' and does have a **tearoom** (Apr-Sep Wed 3-5pm, Thur, Sat, Sun & Bank Holiday Mon 2.30-5pm).

For services, on the High St there's a Co-op **supermarket** (Mon-Sat 7am-9pm, Sun 8am-9pm) that can provide **cashback**.

The No X38/X39/X40 **bus** services (see box pp58-9) stop at Berinsfield Layby but some school and other limited services call in the village.

❏ Wittenham Clumps [Map 33]

These twin chalk hills are part of Little Wittenham Nature Reserve, the 'clumps' being the small huddles of beech trees which cap them. Wittenham Clumps is the most common moniker used to refer to the Sinodun Hills; others being the Berkshire Bubs (the redrawing of the county boundaries in 1974 making this name somewhat redundant as they are now in Oxfordshire) and Mother Dunch's Buttocks, so named after the unpopular local Lady Dunch who was Oliver Cromwell's aunt. The name 'Sinodun' possibly derives from the Celtic *Seno-Dunum* meaning 'old fort' and indeed on top of one of the twin clumps, Castle Hill, there was an Iron Age hill fort, built in approximately 500BC.

Archaeological digs have also unearthed Bronze Age and Roman settlements so it would seem that the hills' strategic vantage point over the surrounding lands has long been exploited. Today the clumps are one of the most visited sites in Oxfordshire.

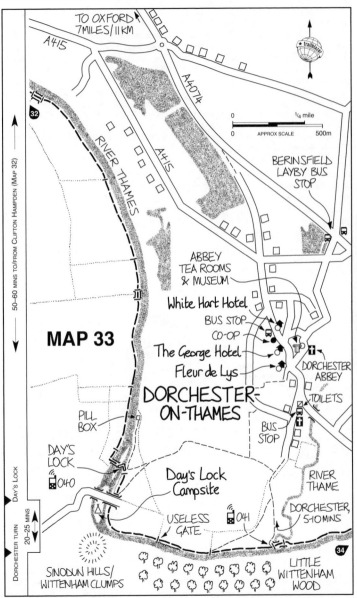

TO OXFORD
7 MILES/11 KM

A415

A4074

A415

RIVER THAMES

trailblaze

32

50-60 MINS TO/FROM CLIFTON HAMPDEN (MAP 32)

0   ¼ mile
0   APPROX SCALE   500m

BERINSFIELD
LAYBY BUS
STOP

ABBEY
TEA ROOMS
& MUSEUM

White Hart Hotel

BUS STOP

CO-OP

The George Hotel

Fleur de Lys

MAP 33

DORCHESTER-
ON-THAMES

DORCHESTER
ABBEY

TOILETS

PILL
BOX

BUS
STOP

DAY'S
LOCK
040

Day's Lock
Campsite

RIVER
THAME

041

DORCHESTER,
5-10 MINS

USELESS
GATE

34

DAY'S LOCK

DORCHESTER TURN   20-25 MINS

SINODUN HILLS/
WITTENHAM CLUMPS

LITTLE
WITTENHAM
WOOD

ROUTE GUIDE AND MAPS

The place closest to the Thames offering both accommodation and food is *Fleur de Lys* (☎ 01865-340502, 🖳 fleurdelys-dorchester.co.uk; 4D; 🍺 bar area; WI-FI; food Tue-Sat noon-2.15pm & 6-9pm, Sun noon-3pm); B&B costs £35-37.50pp (sgl occ from £60). The menu changes regularly but in the evening a two/three-course meal costs £20.50/23.50.

Slightly deeper into the village, on either side of High St are *The George Hotel* (☎ 01865-340404, 🖳 historicinnz.co.uk; 3S/16D/5T; 🍺; WI-FI; 🐕 in garden only; £42.50-60pp, sgl £70-100, sgl occ room

rate), a traditional 15th-century coaching inn which serves up some delicious dishes (**food** Mon-Sat noon-2.30pm & 6-9pm, Sun noon-9pm) including a fabulous belly pork with creamy mash (£14.95); and *White Hart Hotel* (☎ 01865-340074, 🖳 white-hart-hotel-dorchester.co.uk; 2S/6D or T/20D; 🍺; WI-FI; 🐕; from £52.50pp, sgl/sgl occ from £95). The menu (food Mon-Sat noon-2.30pm & 6.30-9.30pm, Sun noon-8pm) here is varied but in the evening may include breast of duck with fondant potato (£17).

SHILLINGFORD   [Map 34]

Between path and river, and not to be confused with its namesake in Clifton Hampden, *Bridge House* (☎ 01865-858540, 🖳 bridge-house.org.uk) is for those who

prefer a simple farm-style **campsite** (WI-FI; 🐕; Easter-end Sep) to those facility-filled family-friendly places that (over)charge those who simply want somewhere to set

← 35-40 MINS TO/FROM DORCHESTER TURN (MAP 33) →   SHILLINGFORD BRIDGE ←→

up their tent for the night. A field, a compost toilet, a simple shower, and a small room where you can make a cup of tea and charge your phone. Perfect. Rates are £10 for a one-/two-man tent, £15 for larger tents (Aug & bank hol weekends you have to pay for two nights even if you stay only one). They also have a fully equipped **bell tent** (£45 per night, two-night minimum stay; sleeps up to three) with a real double bed and a kitchenette. **B&B** (1D/1Tr; ✆; WI-FI; 🐾 but not in the room) is available in the farmhouse; the rate (from £27.50pp, sgl occ from £40) includes a simple self-service breakfast but if requested in advance they will provide a cooked breakfast for £5 (also an evening meal for £15).

The first place you reach in the village is **The Kingfisher Inn** (☎ 01865-858595,

🖳 kingfisher-inn.co.uk; 5D/1T; ✆; WI-FI; from £46.25pp, sgl occ from £69.50; 27 Henley Rd); it offers **B&B** but is more a guesthouse than a pub; evening meals for residents are available if requested in advance.

Fortunately, across the water, **Shillingford Bridge Hotel** (☎ 01865-858567, 🖳 shillingfordbridgehotel.co.uk; 9S/29D/12T; ✆; WI-FI; 🐾) *does* provide victuals for non-residents (daily noon-9pm) and the **food** is reasonably priced too, with mains from £9, rising to £17 for the 6oz sirloin or 8oz rump steak. Some rooms have four-poster beds and some are suites; the tariff (from £39.50pp, sgl/sgl occ from £79/ £94) includes breakfast.

Bus services X38, X39 and X40 stop here (see box pp58-9).

BENSON [Map 35, p138]

The site of a Saxon battle between the kingdoms of Wessex and Mercia, somnolent Benson offers little such excitement today.

Run by **Benson Waterfront** (🖳 benson waterfront.co.uk) are the riverside **Waterfront Café** (☎ 01491-833732, 🖳 water frontcafe.co.uk; daily 8am-6pm, Apr-Sep Tue-Sun to 10pm; WI-FI; 🐾 in conservatory only) – where a varied menu contains such

café stalwarts as baguettes (£6.50-7.25) and gourmet burgers (£8.95-10.50) – and a **campsite** (☎ 01491-838304; WI-FI; 🐾; Mar-Jan) with eight pitches (£25 per pitch; a discount may be available for walkers with a one-man tent); booking is advisable.

Bus services X38, X39 and X40 stop here as does the 136 (see pp58-9).

CROWMARSH GIFFORD [Map 35, p138]

The nearest **shop** for campers is Crowmarsh Stores (Mon-Sat 6.30am-7.30pm, Sat 7am-7.30pm, Sun 8am-2pm).

Bus services X38, X39, X40 & 136 stop here (see pp58-9) as do the No 134/ 134X.

Campers have two choices: by the river is **Riverside Park Campsite** (Apr/May-end Sep call ☎ 01491-835223, rest of year ☎ 01865-341035, 🖳 better.org .uk/leisure-centre/south-oxfordshire/river side-park-and-pool; Apr/May-end Sep) which, run by South Oxfordshire District

Council, is rather over-priced for what you get (pitch £15.50).

However, you'll find a better deal slightly further away from the water at **Bridge Villa** (☎ 01491-836860, 🖳 bridge villa.co.uk; WI-FI; 🐾; Feb to end Dec), a camping & caravan park charging £10-12/15-22 for a tent and a walker/two walkers. The facilities are very good and include a little shop. Also available on the site is one en suite twin **room** (year-round; from £25pp, sgl occ from £45; WI-FI) with tea- and coffee-making facilities – though breakfast is not included in the price.

❏ **Important note – walking times**
All times in this book refer only to the time spent walking. You will need to add 20-30% to allow for rests, photography, checking the map, drinking water etc.

ROUTE GUIDE AND MAPS

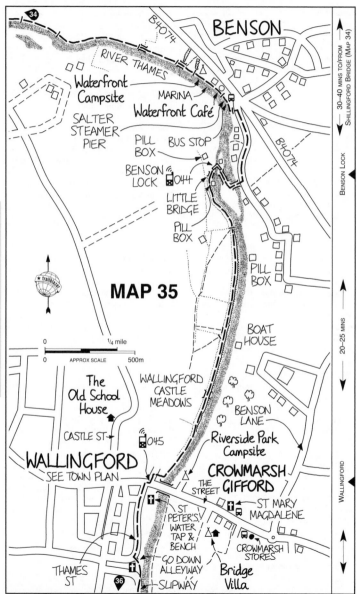

30–40 MINS TO/FROM SHILLINGFORD BRIDGE (MAP 34)

BENSON

B4074

RIVER THAMES

Waterfront
Campsite

MARINA

Waterfront Café

SALTER
STEAMER
PIER

PILL
BOX

BUS STOP

BENSON
LOCK ▯044

LITTLE
BRIDGE

PILL
BOX

PILL
BOX

B4074

BENSON LOCK

MAP 35

0   ¼ mile
0   500m
APPROX SCALE

BOAT
HOUSE

The
Old School
House

CASTLE ST

WALLINGFORD
CASTLE
MEADOWS

▯045

BENSON
LANE

Riverside Park
Campsite

20–25 MINS

WALLINGFORD

SEE TOWN PLAN

CROWMARSH
GIFFORD

THE
STREET

ST MARY
MAGDALENE

ST
PETER'S

WATER
TAP &
BENCH

CROWMARSH
STORES

WALLINGFORD

THAMES
ST

GO DOWN
ALLEYWAY

SLIPWAY

Bridge
Villa

36

ROUTE GUIDE AND MAPS

WALLINGFORD [map p140]

Steeped in history, Wallingford is the finest-surviving example of a Saxon *burh* (a fortified town) in England. Having previously been the site of a Roman settlement, the town's 9th-century importance is reflected by the defences whose construction was ordered by King Alfred to resist the Danes. Once as large as the Wessex capital of Winchester, by the time the Normans invaded in 1066 Wallingford was Berkshire's primary town (although, as with Abingdon, the town is now in Oxfordshire).

Deemed a safer place to cross the Thames than London Bridge, William the Conqueror led his freshly victorious army over the river here and in 1067 the Normans began the construction of **Wallingford Castle** (see box below). More recently, Wallingford has been perhaps better known for its association with Agatha Christie, who lived with her husband just outside the town at Winterbrook House for over forty years until her death in 1976; a blue plaque sits on the wall of her unremarkable home, which is now a private house, though **Wallingford Museum** (☎ 01491-651127, 🖳 www.wallingfordmuseum.org.uk; Mar-end Nov Tue-Fri & Bank Hols 2-5pm, Sat 10.30am-5pm, Jun-Aug

also Sun 2-5pm; £5; 52 High St) tells the town's tale and has an exhibition on Mrs Christie's associations with the town.

Services

Wallingford Town Tourist Information (☎ 01491-826972, 🖳 wallingford.co.uk; Mar-Nov Mon-Fri 10am-1pm & 1.30-4pm, Sat 10am-2pm, Dec-Feb Mon-Sat 10am-2pm) is in the town hall on Market Place. There's also a **post office** (Mon-Fri 9am-5.30pm, Sat 9am-12.30pm), Lloyds **Pharmacy** (Mon-Fri 9am-6pm, Sat 9am-5.30pm), a Boots the Chemist (Mon-Fri 8.30am-6pm, Sat to 5.30pm, Sun 10am-4pm), **ATMs** and a branch of Nat West as well as most other **banks**. On High St there is a Waitrose **store** (Mon-Fri 8am-9pm, Sat 8am-8pm, Sun 10am-4pm).

Wallingford is well connected by **bus**: the X2, X38, X39, X40, 133, 134/134X & 136 call in at various destinations along the Thames Path (see pp58-9). Buses run from Market Place.

Where to stay

A short walk from the town centre at 23 Castle St (Map 35) is a decent option for **B&B**, namely *The Old School House*

❑ **Site of the former Wallingford Castle** **[Map 35]**

The castle here was one of three built by the Normans to control the Thames Valley, the others being at Windsor and Oxford. The first castle was built between 1067 and 1071 and was made of wood. As the castle was passed down the Norman lineage it was gradually rebuilt with stone and would develop into one of the great royal castles of the 12th and 13th centuries. During The Anarchy (1135-1154), a civil war fought between Stephen (the nephew of Henry I) and Matilda (Henry I's daughter), who both laid claim to the English throne, the castle was one of Matilda's strongholds and one which would never be taken.

The lengthy war would end with Henry II – Matilda's son – on the throne and the castle converted into a luxurious royal residence. The castle went into decline after Henry VIII's reign but would be refortified in 1643 during the English Civil War (1642-1651) when it became a Royalist stronghold and part of a defensive ring surrounding the escaping king's Oxfordshire base.

Repeated Parliamentarian attacks and a 16-week siege failed to penetrate the castle's defences and it became the last Royalist stronghold to surrender, finally doing so only by royal command. So fierce and impenetrable had the defence of the castle been that Cromwell, never wishing to have to lay siege to such a formidable fortress again, ordered it destroyed in 1652.

(Map 35; ☎ 01491-839571, 🖥 bbwalling ford.co.uk; 1D en suite/1D private bathroom; ✎; WI-FI; £49-60pp, sgl occ room rate). Note that advance bookings between May and September must be for two nights but it's always worth enquiring to see if they are willing to provide a last-minute booking for a single night. In addition to the two advertised rooms they also offer a third double to family and friends of residents, and they charge £180 for all four people.

If you want to stay more centrally, a **pub** may be your best bet and *The Coach Makers Arms* (☎ 01491-838229, 🖥 www .coachmakersarmswallingford.co.uk; 1D/ 1D or T/1Tr; ✎; WI-FI; 🐾; £40-50pp, sgl occ £75-90; 37 St Mary's St) has rooms. Situated on the edge of the town centre, it

provides a reasonably peaceful night's sleep though note that breakfast is no longer served here.

Right on the path, *The Town Arms* (☎ 01491-599105, 🖥 thetownarms.com; 5D/ 1Tr; ✎; 🐾 not moulting and small (!); High St) is one of the friendlier places in town with rooms from £40pp (sgl occ £80); in peak season they may offer breakfast (additional charge).

While just up the road is *The George Hotel* (☎ 01491-836665, 🖥 peelhotels.co .uk; 9S/25D/4T; ✎; WI-FI; High St), though it's not cheap: they charge £65-75pp (sgl/sgl occ from £110) for room only. Breakfast costs £10pp if requested at the time of booking and £12.95 if you just turn up.

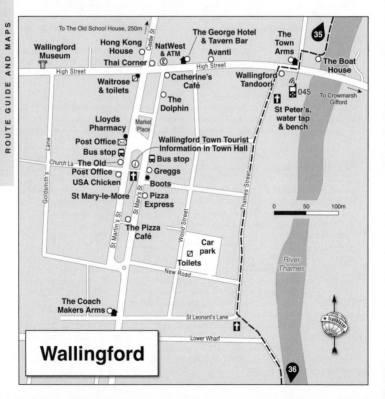

Where to eat and drink

If you can put up with the sometimes desultory service, food at *The Dolphin* (☎ 01491-837377, 🖳 thedollyinwally.co.uk; food Mon 8am-2pm, Tue-Sat 8am-8.30pm, Sun 9am-2pm; WI-FI; 🐾 bar area) is amongst the best value in the town, with a great Full English breakfast (£6). Their closest rival in this regard is their near-neighbour *Catherine's Café* (☎ 01491-838122; Mon-Sat 9am-5pm, Sun 10am-4pm; WI-FI; 28 High St), with their Full English just 5p cheaper. Their breakfast menu is in fact much more varied and includes bacon baps (£4) and beans on toast (£3.50) and has a welcoming upstairs area, complete with sofas to sink into and walls adorned in Hollywood memorabilia. On a hot day it's well worth considering the fruity coronation chicken salad (£6.25).

Pub food and real ales from the West Berkshire and White Horse breweries can be found at CAMRA award-winning *The Town Arms* (see Where to stay; food Tue-Sun noon-8pm; 102 High St). Before that, the first place you come to on entering Wallingford is *The Boat House* (☎ 01491-834100, 🖳 boathouse-pub.co.uk; WI-FI; 🐾; food daily 11am-9pm), right on the riverbank and with a sunny outdoor area. It's not the most characterful of places – and we could have done without the music piped throughout the place and with faster service – though the food is cheap enough for such an idyllic and convenient location, with sandwiches and wraps from £4.99, burgers from £9.99.

Away from the water at the *Tavern Bar* (see **The George Hotel**, Where to stay; food daily noon-1.45pm & 6-8.45pm), mains cost from £12.25 and there is sport on the telly. Food is also served in the **bistro** (daily 6-8.30pm).

Pub food is also on offer at *The Coach Makers Arms* (see Where to stay; WI-FI; 🐾

in bar; food Tue-Sun noon-3pm, Tue-Sat 6-8.30pm); their steak & Brakspear ale pie with chips or mash (£11.95) is bound to fill you up.

More good-value Eastern fare is available at *Thai Corner* (☎ 01491-825050; Mon-Sat 5.30-11pm; High St), offering two courses for £9.95 if you eat before 7pm; and, nearer to the river, *Wallingford Tandoori* (☎ 01491-836249, 🖳 wallingfordtandoori.com; Mon-Sat 5.30-11.30pm, Sun noon-11pm; 4 High St), with dishes costing less than £10.

The favoured Italian of local folk is *Avanti* (☎ 01491-835500, 🖳 avantiitalian.com; food Wed-Sat noon-2pm & Mon-Sat 6-10pm; WI-FI; 85 High St), where, unsurprisingly, there's plenty of pizzas (£7.60-11.50) and pasta dishes (£6.95-12.95). Flashier – but still serving good grub – *The Old Post Office* (☎ 01491-836068, 🖳 opo wallingford.co.uk; food Mon-Sat 8am-10pm, Sun 9am-9pm; WI-FI; 🐾 in bar area; St Martin's St) serves food all day. The outside tables are the perfect spot to watch the world of Wallingford go by whilst enjoying a pizza (from £8). There's also a branch of the national chain *Pizza Express* (☎ 01491-833431, 🖳 www.pizzaexpress.com; Mon-Fri 11.30am-11pm, Sat 11am-11pm, Sun 11.30am-10.30pm) at 12 St Mary St.

For **takeaway** try *The Pizza Café* (Mon-Thur 10am-2.30pm, daily 5.30-10.30pm, Fri & Sat to 11pm; 2 The Arcade), or the kebabs and burgers at *USA Chicken* (Tue-Thur & Sun 3-11pm, Fri & Sat to 11.30pm; St Martin's St); a branch of *Greggs* (Mon-Sat 7.30am-5.30pm, Sun 10am-4pm; Market Pl), the bakery; and a couple of Chinese takeaways including *Hong Kong House* (☎ 01491-835453, 🖳 hongkonghouse.org.uk; Sun-Thur 5-11.30pm, Fri & Sat noon-1.30pm & 5-11.45pm).

❏ Where to stay: the details

Unless specified, B&B-style accommodation is en suite; 🛏 means at least one room has a bath; 🐾 signifies that dogs are welcome in at least one room but always by prior arrangement; WI-FI means wi-fi is available. See also p78.

ROUTE GUIDE AND MAPS

WALLINGFORD TO PANGBOURNE [MAPS 35-40]

The centrepiece of this **11-mile (17.7km, 3¾-4¾hrs)** stage is **Goring Gap**. It was here, during an Ice Age a quarter of a million years ago, that the ancient course of the river (see box p45), finding its route blocked by glaciers, instead penetrated its way through the chalk at a weak spot between the Chiltern Hills and the Berkshire Downs, so forcing the river through the valley – the 'Gap' – and thereby permanently changing the river's course to that which it roughly follows today. The riverscapes surrounding the Gap are some of the finest along the whole length of the river.

This is also a day on which something most unfamiliar occurs: a **hill**.

Before you reach the Gap, the route keeps to the Thames as far as **Moulsford** (see below; Map 37), passing beneath two magnificent **double-arched railway viaducts** built by Isambard Kingdom Brunel in 1839. Though the path diverts from the river briefly, the water lures you back to the doorstep of one of the path's most famous pubs before a simple riverside stroll leads you to the twin towns of **Streatley** and **Goring** (see below; Map 38), the path first arriving in Streatley before crossing the river to Goring on the opposite bank. Having spent half a million years eroding its way through the chalk the Thames continues victoriously onwards. You, however, divert away from its banks for a while though the path is still rewarding as it flirts with the Chilterns, passing through some of the only woodland on the whole trail before heading up that solitary hill.

The final stretch is an unremarkable road walk, eventually guiding you back down to the river at **Whitchurch-on-Thames** (Map 40) and across it out of Oxfordshire and into Berkshire at **Pangbourne** (see p147) where tales of a rat, toad, badger and mole await (see box p148).

MOULSFORD [Map 37, p144]

At the end of Ferry Lane, *The Beetle & Wedge* (☎ 01491-651381, 🖥 beetle-andwedge.co.uk) deals in both **B&B** (1D/2D or T; ☛; WI-FI; £45-50pp, sgl occ from £75) and **food** (Apr-Dec daily noon-2pm & 7-9.45pm, Jan-Mar Tue-Sun only).

Between Monday and Thursday there's a set menu at lunch and dinner (2/3 courses £17.50/20).

The 133 (Goring–Wallingford) **bus** service calls here; see box pp58-9 for details.

GORING & STREATLEY [Map 38, p145]

Both the ancient Ridgeway and Icknield Way – Britain's oldest road – pass through the Goring Gap, the 'street' in Streatley referring to either of these paths, although there is some ambiguity over exactly which one. Such ancient features suggest the area was of considerable importance to early Britons and the twin villages are certainly worth a stop. Dropping off the bridge in Goring, you'll pass an alleyway filled with

flowers, plaques, balloons and cards – tributes to late pop singer George Michael, to whose former house the alley leads.

Services

In Goring, as well as a **shop**, McColls (Mon-Sat 6am-10pm, Sun 7am-10pm), which includes a **post office**, there is also a branch of Tesco Express (supermarket) by the station. Lloyds **pharmacy** (Mon-Fri 9am-6pm, Sat 9am-5pm) and an **ATM** are on the High St. *(cont'd on p146)*

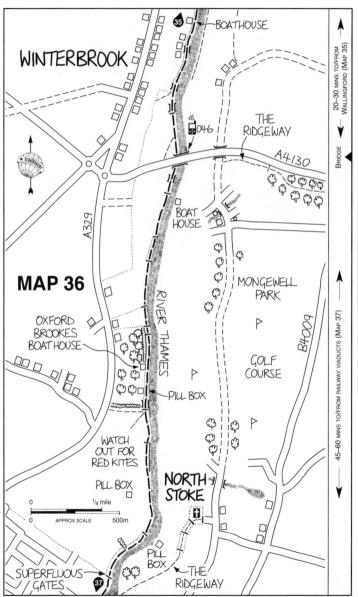

BOATHOUSE

35

WINTERBROOK

046

THE RIDGEWAY

A4130

20–30 MINS TO/FROM Wallingford (MAP 35)

BRIDGE

BOAT HOUSE

A329

MAP 36

MONGEWELL PARK

RIVER THAMES

OXFORD BROOKES BOATHOUSE

GOLF COURSE

B4009

45–60 MINS TO/FROM RAILWAY VIADUCTS (MAP 37)

PILL BOX

WATCH OUT FOR RED KITES

PILL BOX

NORTH STOKE

0 ¼ mile
0 500m
APPROX SCALE

SUPERFLUOUS GATES

PILL BOX

THE RIDGEWAY

37

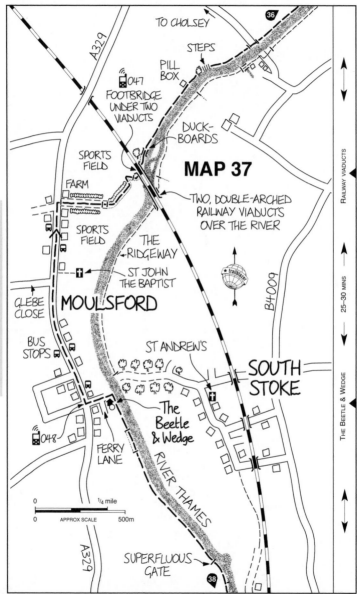

MAP 37

TO CHOLSEY

36

STEPS

A329

047
FOOTBRIDGE
UNDER TWO
VIADUCTS

PILL
BOX

DUCK-
BOARDS

SPORTS
FIELD

FARM

TWO, DOUBLE-ARCHED
RAILWAY VIADUCTS
OVER THE RIVER

SPORTS
FIELD

THE
RIDGEWAY

★ trailblazer

B4009

ST JOHN
THE BAPTIST

GLEBE
CLOSE

MOULSFORD

BUS
STOPS

ST ANDREW'S

SOUTH
STOKE

048

The
Beetle
& Wedge

FERRY
LANE

RIVER THAMES

0   ¼ mile
0   APPROX SCALE   500m

A329

SUPERFLUOUS
GATE

38

ROUTE GUIDE AND MAPS

RAILWAY VIADUCTS   25-30 MINS   THE BEETLE & WEDGE

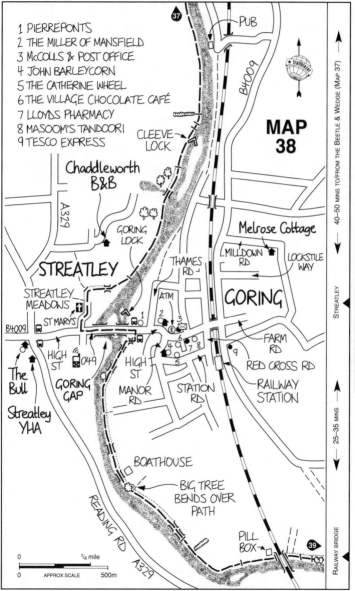

1 PIERREPONTS
2 THE MILLER OF MANSFIELD
3 McCOLLS & POST OFFICE
4 JOHN BARLEYCORN
5 THE CATHERINE WHEEL
6 THE VILLAGE CHOCOLATE CAFÉ
7 LLOYDS PHARMACY
8 MASOOM'S TANDOORI
9 TESCO EXPRESS

MAP 38

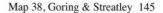

Chaddleworth B&B

CLEEVE LOCK

PUB

B4009

GORING LOCK

STREATLEY

A329

Melrose Cottage

MILL DOWN RD

LOCKSTILE WAY

THAMES RD

GORING

STREATLEY MEADOWS

ST MARYS

ATM

B4009

HIGH ST

GORING GAP

The Bull

Streatley YHA

HIGH ST

MANOR RD

STATION RD

FARM RD

RED CROSS RD

RAILWAY STATION

BOATHOUSE

BIG TREE BENDS OVER PATH

READING RD A329

PILL BOX

0   ¼ mile
0   APPROX SCALE   500m

40–50 MINS TO/FROM THE BEETLE & WEDGE (MAP 37)

STREATLEY

25–35 MINS

RAILWAY BRIDGE

ROUTE GUIDE AND MAPS

(cont'd from p142) GWR **trains** (see box pp52-3) run regularly from Goring to Pangbourne and Reading as well as other Thames Path destinations. **Bus** services (133, 134/134X, 142 & 144) also connect the twin villages with these towns (see box pp58-9) as well as Wallingford.

Where to stay and eat

Goring If an extra 15- to 20-minute walk doesn't put you off and you'd rather not stay above a pub, *Melrose Cottage* (☎ 01491-873040, 🖳 howarthr523@gmail .com; 1S/2T shared bathroom; 🛏; WI-FI; 36 Milldown Rd) is your only option; **B&B** is very reasonably priced (£32.50pp, sgl/sgl occ from £40) and all the rooms have a fridge and a microwave.

As for the pubs, *The Miller of Mansfield* (☎ 01491-872829, 🖳 millerof mansfield.com; 13D; 🛏; WI-FI; 🐾) has some glorious rooms although the price (£49.50-100pp, sgl occ rates on request) may put some off. The **food** (Mon-Sat noon-2pm & 6-9pm, Sun noon-2pm & 5-7pm) is as magnificent as the rooms but you're unlikely to get a main course in the evening for much less than £15 (eg saddle of wild rabbit £23.50).

Cheaper, *John Barleycorn* (☎ 01491-872509, 🖳 thejohnbarleycornpub.com; 3D; 🛏; WI-FI; 🐾 bar only) charges from £45pp (sgl occ from £75) for **B&B** and their menu (**food** Mon-Sat noon-2pm & 6.30-9pm, Sun noon-2pm) is also reasonable, the beer-battered haddock & chips costing £11.

Other food options include the unpretentious *The Village Chocolate Café* (☎ 01491-874264, 🖳 chocolatecafegoring.co .uk; Mon-Fri 8am-5pm, Sat 9am-5pm, Sun 10am-5pm; WI-FI; 🐾) – note that the sign still says The Village Café, its previous incarnation. They sell a decent range of sandwiches, baguettes and breakfasts, their wonderful breakfast baguette (sausage, egg & bacon) costing £6. Other than their hot chocolate (from £2.30), made using Belgian chocolate, the menu is light on

chocolate. Nearer to the bridge *Pierreponts Café* (☎ 01491-874464, 🖳 pierrepontsgor ing.co.uk; Tue-Sat 8am-5pm, also most Fri 6-9.30pm; dog hooks outside; WI-FI) cooks up full-English breakfasts (£8.75; 8-11.30am) and their popular spinach pancakes (£8.75) at lunchtime (11.30am-3pm).

The Catherine Wheel (☎ 01491-872379, 🖳 tcwgoring.co.uk; food Mon-Sat noon-3pm & 6-9pm, Sun noon-4pm; WI-FI; 🐾) serves pub classics such as ham, egg & chips (£12.50) as well as a menu that changes monthly; while *Masoom's Tandoori* (☎ 01491-875078, 🖳 masooms .co.uk; Sat-Thur noon-2pm, daily 5.30-11pm) is an Indian restaurant and **takeaway**.

Streatley *Streatley YHA* (☎ 0345-371 9044, or ☎ 01491-872278, 🖳 yha.org.uk/ hostel/streatley-thames; 1 x 2-, 4 x 4-, 2 x 5- & 3 x 6-bed rooms; WI-FI communal area; Ⓛ; Mar-Oct & midweek Nov-Feb) is on Reading Rd. There is a self-catering kitchen but meals are available and the hostel is licensed; facilities include a drying room. Note that the hostel may be booked for exclusive hire so individual bookings are only accepted three months in advance. Dorm beds cost from £13pp and private/ family rooms from £29/25.

The Bull at Streatley (☎ 01491-872392, 🖳 bullinnpub.co.uk; 4D/2T; 🛏; WI-FI; 🐾; £35-40pp, sgl occ full room rate) is also on Reading Rd but nearer to the crossroads. It provides **B&B** and also serves **food** (Mon-Sat noon-9pm, Sun noon-8pm). The menu has offers most nights of the week; Wednesday is their curry night (£7.45 inc a drink).

Chaddleworth B&B (☎ 07711 420586, 🖳 chaddleworthbedandbreakfast .com; 1D or T en suite, 1D or T private bathroom; 🛏; WI-FI; £45-55pp, sgl occ rates on request) is a few minutes from the path. Subject to prior arrangement they are happy to provide luggage transfer and a pick up/drop off service.

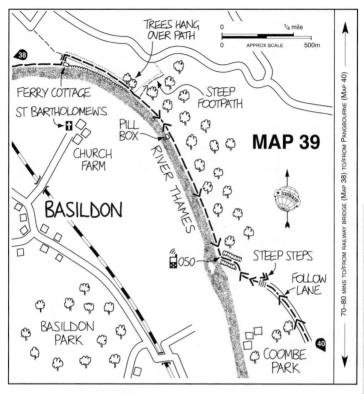

TREES HANG OVER PATH

0   ¼ mile
0   APPROX SCALE   500m

38

FERRY COTTAGE

ST BARTHOLOMEW'S

STEEP FOOTPATH

PILL BOX

MAP 39

CHURCH FARM

RIVER THAMES

BASILDON

trailblazer

050

STEEP STEPS

FOLLOW LANE

BASILDON PARK

40

COOMBE PARK

70–80 MINS TO/FROM RAILWAY BRIDGE (MAP 38) TO/FROM PANGBOURNE (MAP 40)

ROUTE GUIDE AND MAPS

WHITCHURCH-ON-THAMES
[Map 40, p149]

Whitchurch is possibly best known for its **toll bridge**; drivers still have to pay but it is free for walkers.

There are two **pubs** here serving food: *The Greyhound* (☎ 0118-343 3016, 💻 greyhoundwhitchurchonthames.co.uk; WI-FI; 🐾 on lead; food Mon-Sat noon-3pm & 5-9pm, Sun noon-4pm) serves standard pub food; *The Ferryboat* (☎ 0118-984 2161, 💻 theferryboatwhitchurch.com; WI-FI; 🐾 on lead and in bar area only; food Tue-Sat noon-2.15pm & 6-9pm, Sun noon-3pm) has a similar menu but a bit more extensive and expensive. Note that it is closed all day on Monday.

Whitchurch is also a stop on the 142 **bus** service (see box pp58-9).

PANGBOURNE
[map p150]

So-named due to the village's location on the River Pang, Kenneth Grahame, author of *The Wind in the Willows*, lived here following the death of his son (see the box on p148). A cultural hotspot, Jimmy Page – guitarist in Led Zeppelin – also resided in the village; indeed, it is said that in 1968, during a visit from Robert Plant – the powerhouse rockers' vocalist – it was actually here that the band formed.

Services
There is a Co-op **store** (daily 7am-10pm), **post office** (Mon-Sat 8.30am-5.30pm, Lloyds **pharmacy** (Mon-Fri 8.30am-6.30pm, Sat 9am-5.30pm) and **ATM**.

Pangbourne is a stop on some of GWR's **train** services (see box pp52-3). The 142, 143 &144 **bus** services (see box pp58-9) also call here.

Where to stay and eat
On the corner of Whitchurch Rd, and recently refurbished, is *The George Hotel* (☎ 0118-984 2237, 🖳 georgehotelpang bourne.com; 3S/12D/4T/3Tr; ☛; WI-FI; room rates from £38.25pp, sgl/slg occ from £60). Breakfast costs an extra £8pp if booked in advance (£10 on the day); **food**

(Mon-Sat noon-3pm & 6-9pm, Sun noon-6pm; 🐾 in bar only) is available in both the bar and the restaurant.

Those booking at least 30 days in advance can expect to pay £37.50-62.50pp (sgl/sgl occ £69-125) for B&B in a classic room at *The Elephant* (☎ 0118-984 2244, 🖳 elephanthotel.co.uk; 2S/18D/2D or T; ☛; WI-FI; 🐾; Church Rd). **Fine dining** (restaurant daily 6-9pm) is available; a pan-seared venison steak with sweet potato & beetroot gratin is £18.95. They also serve food in the bar (daily noon-2.30pm & 5-9pm).

The best location for **pub food** is next to the river at *The Swan* (☎ 0118-984 4494, 🖳 theswan-pangbourne.co.uk; WI-FI; 🐾 in bar area; Shooters Hill). Famous as the

---

❏ Kenneth Grahame & *The Wind in the Willows*
Born in Edinburgh in 1859, Kenneth Grahame spent most of his formative years living with his grandmother in the Thames-side village of Cookham – his mother having died of scarlet fever when he was very young, and his father being an alcoholic. During this early period of his life he would get to learn about the river, go boating and explore the countryside of the upper reaches of the Thames. His family could not afford for him to go to university so instead he moved to London where he worked at the Bank of England. Progressing through the ranks swiftly, it was during this period that he would begin to write. His early essays and short stories were much acclaimed – though they would all be overshadowed by what was to come.

Grahame married Elspeth Thomson in 1899 and their only son – Alastair – was born the following year. Unfortunately, Alastair was a sickly child, blind in one eye and of poor health, so his father created bedtime stories to help his disabled son to sleep. These anthropomorphic stories recounting the riverside adventures of Mole, Ratty, Badger and the troublesome Mr Toad were undoubtedly influenced to a large degree by Grahame's early childhood at Cookham. Eventually the tales were collected together and published in 1908 under the title *The Wind in the Willows*.

The book would, of course, go on to become one of the best loved in the English language. One particular fan who was instrumental in its mass publication was Theodore Roosevelt, then President of the United States, who on visiting Oxford in 1910 was so taken with the tales that he requested an audience with the author.

Tragedy struck the Grahames in 1920 when Alastair Grahame committed suicide. His devastated parents fled abroad, though they eventually returned to England – and the banks of the river – a few years later in 1924, moving into **Church Cottage** in Pangbourne, where Kenneth Grahame lived until his death in 1932.

It wasn't just the stories that were influenced by the scenery surrounding Pangbourne and Cookham; the book's illustrations, too, especially those completed by EH Shepard for the 1931 edition, were inspired by the area. Indeed, both Hardwick Estate and Mapledurham House (Maps 40 & 41), across the water from the path en route to Henley, lay claim to being the inspiration for Shepard's Toad Hall.

Look out for the plaque (see Map 67) quoting the most famous line from the book.

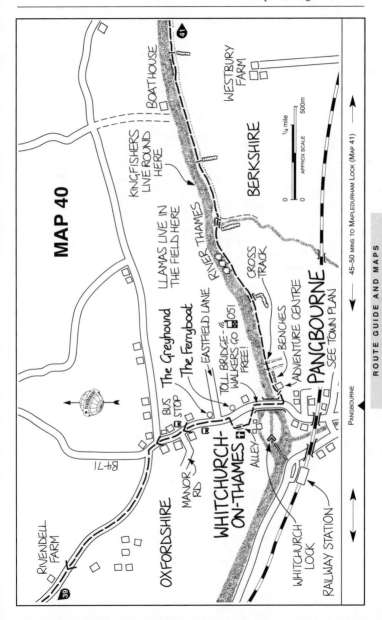

MAP 40

RIVENDELL FARM

39

OXFORDSHIRE

B4471

MANOR RD

WHITCHURCH-ON-THAMES

ALLEY

WHITCHURCH LOCK

RAILWAY STATION

BUS STOP

The Greyhound

The Ferryboat

EASTFIELD LANE

TOLL BRIDGE - WALKERS GO FREE!

051

LLAMAS LIVE IN THE FIELD HERE

KINGFISHERS LIVE ROUND HERE

RIVER THAMES

CROSS TRACK

BENCHES

ADVENTURE CENTRE

PANGBOURNE
SEE TOWN PLAN

BERKSHIRE

BOATHOUSE

41

WESTBURY FARM

¼ mile

APPROX SCALE   500m

0   0

← PANGBOURNE

45–50 MINS TO MAPLEDURHAM LOCK (MAP 41) →

★ trailblazer

ROUTE GUIDE AND MAPS

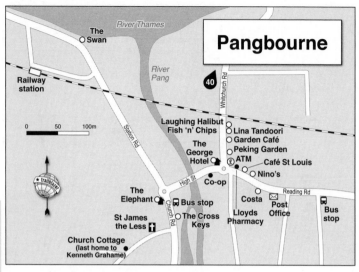

location where Jerome K Jerome's three men finally ditched their comedic boat, the setting is grand and the food (Mon-Sat 10am-9pm, Sun to 8pm) great too. The menu changes regularly but features both classic and contemporary dishes.

Equally imaginative meals such as chargrilled Cajun tuna steak (£12.95) are on the menu at *The Cross Keys* (☎ 0118-984 3268; food daily noon-2.30pm & 6-9pm). Their menu includes slow cooked belly pork (£15) and fish & chips (£12).

For pasta (£8.90-13.90) or pizza (from £8.50) look no further than *Nino's* (☎ 0118-984 1333, ⌨ ninos-trattoria.co.uk; Tue-Sat noon-2pm, Mon-Sat 6-10pm; 11 Reading Rd); while an all-you-can-eat Chinese buffet (£15.50pp, minimum 2 people; Sun & Mon noon-3pm & 6-10pm) is available at *Peking Garden* (☎ 0118-984 2669; Tue-Sat noon-2pm & 6-10pm, Sun & Mon noon-3pm & 6-10pm; 2-6 Whitchurch Rd). Nearby, at No 16, *Lina Tandoori* (☎ 0118-984 5577; daily noon-2.30pm & 5-11pm) is a standard Indian restaurant with lamb or chicken masala £7.45.

For more traditional British fare, *Laughing Halibut* (☎ 0118-984 1614; Mon-Sat 11.30am-2pm & 4.30-10pm, Sun & Bank Hols 4.30-10pm; 18 Whitchurch Rd) has **takeaway** fish & chips for around £6.

Alternatively, there are the cafés: *Café St Louis* (☎ 0118-984 2246, ⌨ cafe-st-louis.com; Mon-Fri 8am-5pm, Sat & Sun 9am-5pm; WI-FI; ☙) on Reading Rd. A good spot for lunch, they do a nice line in sandwiches and baguettes (£6.80-7.30) including a steak one with fries (£9.55).

For early risers, across the road there's a branch of the national chain *Costa* (Mon-Sat 6.30am-6.30pm, Sun 8am-6.30pm); while back on Whitchurch Rd is *Garden Café* (☎ 0118-984 1114; WI-FI; ☙; Mon-Sat 8am-4pm), which does a good line in food and hot and cold drinks including, when we were there, iced teas and frappés (both £2.65).

PANGBOURNE TO HENLEY-ON-THAMES [MAPS 40-48]

This **16-mile (25.7km, 5-6hrs)** section of the path boasts some impressive locks which bookend a long and surprisingly peaceful jaunt – surprising as for much of it you'll be accompanied by the Great Western Railway and will skirt around the outer reaches of **Reading** (see box p156), though the trail is usually separated from its companions by the obligatory meadow. Throughout the day red kites compete with the aeroplanes for dominance of the skies, the latter inflicted on the area by Heathrow – a timely reminder that the nation's capital gets ever closer.

As you follow the river out of Pangbourne the opposite bank is dominated by the Chilterns, as well as **Hardwick Estate** and **Mapledurham House** (Map 41), both of which claim to have been the inspiration for EH Shepard's illustrations for Kenneth Grahame's Toad Hall (see box p148).

The *café* at **Mapledurham Lock** (see below) offers refreshment before a suburban walk through **Purley-on-Thames** guides you back to the water's edge shortly before **Tilehurst** railway station (Map 42), where a sign welcomes you to Reading. Tilehurst is a stop on some of GWR's **train** services (see box pp52-3). The 143 & 144 **bus** services stop in Tilehurst; the 144 also calls in at Purley-on-Thames (see pp58-9). There are food and accommodation options near **Caversham Bridge** (see below; Map 43).

During the day's latter stages you switch counties again (from Berkshire to Oxfordshire) via the bridge at **Sonning** (see p157; Map 45).

A brief dalliance with the village of **Lower Shiplake** (see p159; Map 46) then follows, after which you reach **Marsh Lock** (Map 47). A final stretch along a path draped in willows to **Henley-on-Thames** (see p160; Map 48) ensues, a suitably pleasant reward for what has been a long day.

MAPLEDURHAM LOCK
[Map 41, p152]

Dog-friendly *Mapledurham Lock Café* (Apr-Oct daily 9.30am-5.30pm, open to 7pm in Aug, Oct-Apr weekends only; 🐾) happily provides hungry walkers with Full English breakfasts (£5) as well as sandwiches and cakes; only cash is accepted as payment.

CAVERSHAM (READING)
[map p154]

There is a BP petrol station with a **shop** (24hrs) and **ATM** on Richfield Ave. Further along the path is a branch of Tesco (Map 43; Mon-Sat 24hrs, Sun 10am-4pm). The only option for **campers** is *Wokingham Waterside Centre* (Map 43; ☎ 0118-926 8280, 🖥 wokinghamwatersidecentre.com/

❏ **Fish ladders**
Weirs are as much a hindrance to fish as they are to boats as they prevent the former from swimming upriver in their search for new waters in which to feed and breed. Since the 1980s fish ladders have been added to weirs in order to allow the fish such passage. Using metal plates to slow the water down at the edge of the weir allows fish the chance to bypass the weirs and continue their journey upstream.

camping; 🐾); the centre has two small fields where tents can be pitched (£10pp). A fob (available from reception) provides access to showers and toilets. There is also a kitchen with microwave ovens and a kettle. Booking is recommended as they can get full with groups.

For **accommodation** with a roof, by the bridge and looking over the river is

Crowne Plaza Reading (☎ 0118-925 9900, 🖳 cp-reading.co.uk; 122D or T; 🛒; WI-FI); expect to pay from £60pp for a room (sgl occ full room rate) but rates with breakfast, or dinner and breakfast, are also available.

Cheaper accommodation can be found at the *Premier Inn* (see p21; Reading (Caversham Bridge; ☎ 0871-527 8922, 🖳 premierinn.com; 60D/15D or T; WI-FI) with

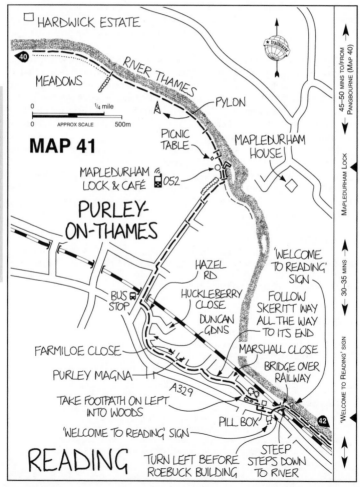

HARDWICK ESTATE

RIVER THAMES

MEADOWS

PYLON

PICNIC TABLE

MAPLEDURHAM HOUSE

MAP 41

0   ¼ mile
0   APPROX SCALE   500m

MAPLEDURHAM LOCK & CAFÉ   052

PURLEY-ON-THAMES

HAZEL RD

'WELCOME TO READING' SIGN

BUS STOP

HUCKLEBERRY CLOSE

DUNCAN GDNS

FOLLOW SKERITT WAY ALL THE WAY TO ITS END

FARMILOE CLOSE

MARSHALL CLOSE

PURLEY MAGNA

A329

BRIDGE OVER RAILWAY

TAKE FOOTPATH ON LEFT INTO WOODS

PILL BOX

'WELCOME TO READING' SIGN

READING   TURN LEFT BEFORE ROEBUCK BUILDING

STEEP STEPS DOWN TO RIVER

45-50 MINS TO/FROM PANGBOURNE (MAP 40)

MAPLEDURHAM LOCK

30-35 MINS

'WELCOME TO READING' SIGN

ROUTE GUIDE AND MAPS

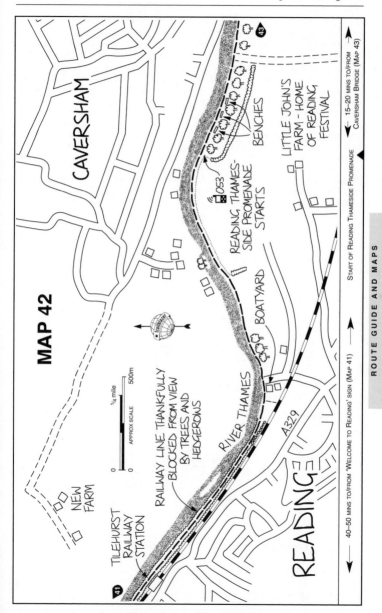

MAP 42

CAVERSHAM

NEW FARM

TILEHURST RAILWAY STATION

RAILWAY LINE THANKFULLY BLOCKED FROM VIEW BY TREES AND HEDGEROWS

¼ mile

0   500m

APPROX SCALE

RIVER THAMES

A329

READING

BOATYARD

Reading Thames-side Promenade starts

053

BENCHES

LITTLE JOHN'S FARM – HOME OF READING FESTIVAL

43

41

← 40–50 MINS TO/FROM 'WELCOME TO READING' SIGN (MAP 41) →

START OF READING THAMESIDE PROMENADE

← 15–20 MINS TO/FROM CAVERSHAM BRIDGE (MAP 43) →

Saver rates (see p21) from £37.50 for a room. Weekdays are more expensive but on average expect to pay £70-144 if you don't book in advance.

Caversham Rd is lined with places to stay, amongst them those run by Central Reading Hotels (☎ 0118-958 9900, ☐ centralreadinghotels.com). There are 30 rooms (8D/10T/7Tr/5Qd; WI-FI) in three buildings: *Caversham Bridge Lodge*, *Bridge Lodge* and *Caversham House Lodge*. Caversham House Lodge, at Nos 164-166, operates as the trio's reception. A room costs £25-30pp (sgl occ room rate) but **breakfast** isn't included; it is, however, available (£6.25 for a 'fry-up') at *Richfields Deli & Grill* (☎ 0118-939 1144, ☐ richfieldsdeli.com; Mon-Sat 7am-5.30pm, Sun 8am-3.30pm; WI-FI; No 211).

On the corner of Caversham Rd and Richfield Ave, *The Gorge Café* (☎ 0118-950 3446; Mon-Sat 6.45am-2.45pm, Sun from 7.45am), also provides breakfasts from £4.10.

Pub meals are on the menu at *The Moderation* (☎ 0118-375 0767, ☐ themodreading.com; food Mon-Fri noon-3pm & 6-9.30pm, Sat & Sun noon-4pm & 6-9pm; 213 Caversham Rd), where sausage & mash costs £9.50; and also at *Toby Carvery Caversham Bridge* (☎ 0118-950 5044, ☐ tobycarvery.co.uk; food daily 8am-9pm; WI-FI), which, like all branches of Toby Carvery, is cheap, with roast pork, stuffing & apple sauce costing just £6.99.

River Spice (☎ 0118-950 3355, ☐ riverspicereading.com; Mon-Sat noon-2.30pm & 6-11pm, Sun noon-11.30pm) is the local Indian restaurant. Located right next to the river there are seafood specialities such as tandoori monkfish masala (£13.95).

Takeaway can be found on Caversham Rd at *Mr Cod* (☎ 0118-957 4731; daily 10.30am-12.30am; No 155) and *Marmaris Kebabs* (☎ 0118-959 0363; Sun-Thur noon-1am, Fri & Sat noon-4am; No 169). From both you'll be able to eat for less than a tenner.

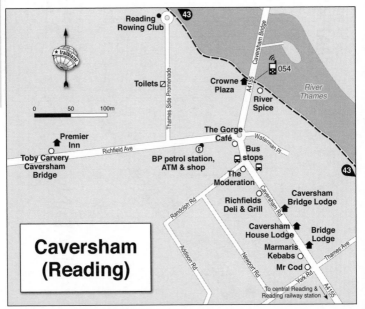

Caversham (Reading)

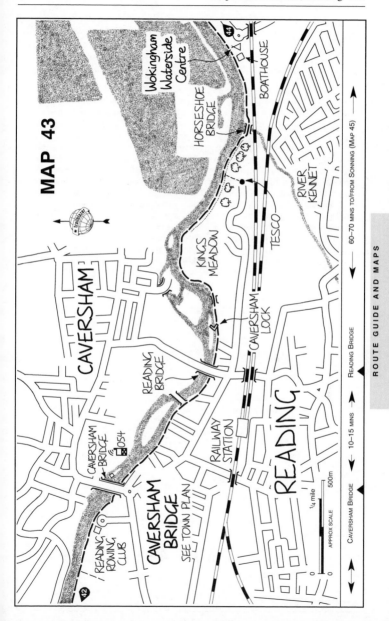

Caversham Rd is linked to central Reading by the X39/X40 **bus** service. Services from central Reading include the 16, 127, 128, 129, 143, 144, 800, 850 & X80. See box pp58-9 for details. Reading is also well connected by **train** (GWR; see box pp52-3) and it is a stop on the NX200 **coach** service (see box p54).

❏ **Reading – past and present**
Though Reading is widely believed to have been settled since Roman times, the first irrefutable evidence of Reading's existence dates 'only' to the 8th century when it was known as *Readingum*, a name which originated from Reada, a Saxon leader whose tribe had settled here. In AD870 King Alfred fought the Danes at Reading in a great battle which was recorded in the *Anglo-Saxon Chronicle*, the first written record of the town.

The Victorian era – and the arrival of the Great Western Railway – saw the town prosper due to the manufacturing of what famously became known as the **Three Bs**: **beer**, at Simond's Brewery; **bulbs**, at Suttons Seeds; and **biscuits**, at Huntley & Palmers, who once ran the world's largest biscuit factory. Today, however, the town is perhaps most famous/notorious as the place where in 1895 **Oscar Wilde** was incarcerated for 'committing acts of gross indecency with other male persons', his time immortalised in his poem *The Ballad of Reading Gaol*.

Oddly, for a town of such significance, Reading has no tourist information. Central Reading is a fair hike away from the river and walkers will likely be more than happy with the amenities near **Caversham Bridge** (Map 43). A night here is an option but you'd be better to follow **Jerome K Jerome**'s advice that 'one does not linger in the neighbourhood of Reading' and continue along the river to Henley or Sonning.

ROUTE GUIDE AND MAPS

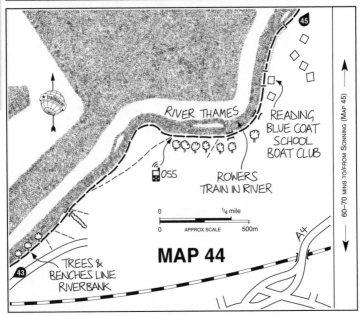

RIVER THAMES

READING BLUE COAT SCHOOL BOAT CLUB

☎ 055

ROWERS TRAIN IN RIVER

0   ¼ mile
0   APPROX SCALE   500m

MAP 44

TREES & BENCHES LINE RIVERBANK

60–70 MINS TO/FROM SONNING (MAP 45)

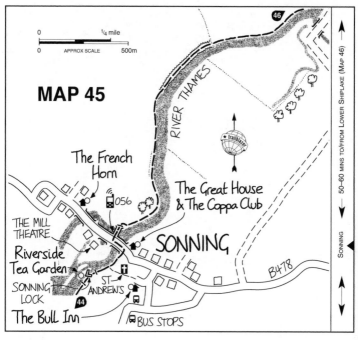

MAP 45

The French Horn

THE MILL THEATRE

Riverside Tea Garden

SONNING LOCK

The Bull Inn

RIVER THAMES

The Great House & The Coppa Club

SONNING

ST ANDREW'S

BUS STOPS

SONNING [Map 45]

One of the Thames's most eye-catching villages, there is evidence of there being a bridge here back in the Saxon era, though the current stone one was erected only in 1775. There is also evidence of a settlement here as far back as the Palaeolithic and Mesolithic eras: our predecessors must have seen the site as Jerome K Jerome described it as 'the most fairy-like little nook on the river'.

Sonning is a stop on the 127, 128, 129 & 850 **bus** services (see box pp58-9).

Three establishments provide **B&B** and **food**. Tucked away along a footpath shortly before you get to the bridge is *The Bull Inn* (☎ 0118-969 3901, 🖳 bullinnson ning.co.uk; 7D or T; WI-FI; 🐾 in bar only; High St). It's a very well-kept and popular place partly because of its mention in Jerome's *Three Men in a Boat*. B&B costs from £42.50pp, (sgl occ full room rate).

The menu (food Mon-Sat noon-9.30pm, Sun noon-8.30pm) may include pan-fried corn-fed chicken with sautéed potatoes, peas and bacon (£15.50). At the time of writing this was closed for refurbishment but it should be open again by the time you are passing.

The Great House (☎ 0118-969 2277, 🖳 greathouseatsonning.co.uk; 36D/7T; 🛏; WI-FI; 🐾) is yet another fine establishment near to the water's edge. B&B costs from £40pp (sgl occ room rate); the food in their restaurant/bar called *The Coppa Club* (☎ 0118-921 9890; Mon-Fri 6.30am-10pm, Sat 7.30am-10pm, Sun 7.30am-9.30pm) is surprisingly reasonable with flash steak & fries for £11.45.

Across the road bridge is *The French Horn* (☎ 0118-969 2204, 🖳 thefrench horn.co.uk; 18D/3D or T; 🛏; WI-FI; 🐾; £85-112.50pp, sgl occ £135-180). The

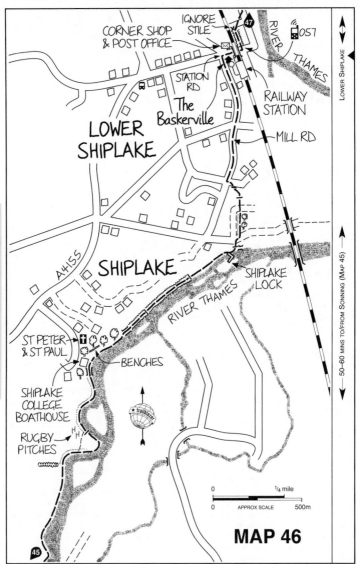

CORNER SHOP & POST OFFICE

IGNORE STILE

47

RIVER

057

THAMES

STATION RD

The Baskerville

RAILWAY STATION

MILL RD

LOWER SHIPLAKE

A4155

SHIPLAKE

SHIPLAKE LOCK

RIVER THAMES

ST PETER & ST PAUL

BENCHES

SHIPLAKE COLLEGE BOATHOUSE

RUGBY PITCHES

★ trailblazer

0   ¼ mile

0   APPROX SCALE   500m

MAP 46

45

LOWER SHIPLAKE

50-60 MINS TO/FROM SONNING (MAP 45)

rooms and meals (Mon-Sat noon-1.45pm & 7-9.30pm, Sun to 9pm) are simply staggering but the prices reflect this. At dinner half a spit-roasted Aylesbury duck costs £27.50. By **Sonning Lock** a most enjoyable place to stop for a 'cuppa', amongst other delights, is *Riverside Tea Garden* (☎ 0118-969 7178; 🐾 on lead; Apr-Sep/Oct daily 11am-5pm). They sell home-made sandwiches (£4.20) and cakes amongst other things.

LOWER SHIPLAKE [Map 46]

Shiplake itself is hidden from the trail by trees; its main claim to fame is that the author Eric Blair, aka George Orwell, grew up here. Another literary behemoth, Alfred Tennyson, got married in the church (**St Peter & St Paul**), paying the vicar for his services with a poem rather than a fee. You're unlikely to get away with that in the **corner shop** (Mon-Fri 7.30am-5.30pm, Sat 8am-12.30pm, Sun 8am-noon) or **post office** (Mon-Fri 9am-5.30pm, Sat 9am-12.30pm) which share a building on Station Rd, Lower Shiplake.

The Baskerville (☎ 0118-940 3332, 🖳 thebaskerville.com; 2D/1T/1Tr; WI-FI; 🐾; No 7). B&B is around £55pp (sgl occ from £100) and the **food** in their award-winning restaurant (Mon-Sat noon-2.30pm & 6-9pm, Sun noon-3pm), such as grilled swordfish (£18.50) is reasonably priced given its high quality.

Shiplake **railway station** is a stop on GWR's services (see box pp52-30) from Twyford to Henley; the 800 & X80 **bus** services (see pp58-9) call here, and at Shiplake, en route between Reading and High Wycombe.

MARSH LOCK

48

📶 058
START OF
LONG BRIDGE

★ trailblazer

JUNCTION
WITH
CHILTERN
WAY

MAP 47

0 .... ¼ mile
0 .... APPROX SCALE 500m

RIVER THAMES

PRIVATE GARDEN WITH ITS OWN MINI-RAILWAY AND EVEN ITS OWN STATION

46

MARSH LOCK

25-30 MINS TO/FROM LOWER SHIPLAKE (MAP 46)

ROUTE GUIDE AND MAPS

HENLEY-ON-THAMES   [map p163]

Host to the world-famous Henley Royal Regatta (see box below), the path's most stylish Thames-side town is not cheap; its sheer beauty, however, goes some way to mollifying your purse.

A market town since 1269, the town's most photogenic feature is its bridge, built in 1786. While perusing its arches note the sculpted faces of Old Father Thames peering downstream and of Isis staring back towards the source (see box p76).

As you approach Henley there is a **River and Rowing Museum** (Map 48; ☎ 01491-415600, ⬚ rrm.co.uk; daily 10am-5pm; £12.50) on your left.

Fans of The Beatles probably know that George Harrison lived at Friar Park, to the west of town; Dusty Springfield has a gravestone marker in St Mary's churchyard.

Services

Henley **Visitor Information Centre** (☎ 01491-578034, ⬚ visit-henley.com; Mon-Sat 9am-4pm) is in the town hall.

On Bell St there is a **chemist**, Boots (Mon-Sat 8.30am-6pm, Sun 10.30am-4.30pm), and for provisions Sainsbury's (daily 7am-11pm); a larger **supermarket**, Waitrose (Mon-Fri 8am-9pm, Sat 8am-8pm, Sun 10am-4pm) is located just off the same street.

The **post office** (Mon-Fri 8.30am-5.30pm, Sat 9am-12.30pm) is on Reading Rd. Henley has branches of most High St banks and **ATMs** can be found on Hart St.

Henley railway station (see Map 48) is at the end of the branch line from Twyford; **train** services are operated by GWR (see box pp52-3). **Bus** services X38, 238/239, 800, 850 & X80 call here; see pp58-9.

Where to stay

Campers have a short amble out of town to reach *Swiss Farm Touring & Camping* (Map 48; ☎ 01491-573419, ⬚ swissfarmcamping.co.uk; WI-FI; 🐕 except during August; Mar-end Nov). Solo campers should ask for the walker's rate (£15pp) but the tent pitch (£18-27.50) is better value for two sharing a tent. Note that for the Henley Regatta period they only accept bookings of at least two nights and it would be essential to book very early. It's a large family site where the staff are friendly and the facilities good, including a **shop** (daily 9am-5pm) and **café**.

❏ Henley Royal Regatta

Attracting rowers from all over the globe, The Royal Regatta at Henley is held annually over the first weekend in July and lays fair claim to being the world's most famous festival of rowing and boat races. Established in 1839, the event predates any form of national or international rowing organisation so abides by its own rules and regulations.

Attempts to make the course as fair as possible have led to the route changing over time and the advantages once offered – by, for example, bends in the river, riverside features which offered shelter from the wind and areas which had a stronger current – have all been eradicated. Since 1924, however, the course has remained fairly constant, the rowers setting off from **Temple Island** (see Map 49) before crossing the finishing line just short of **Henley Bridge** (Map 48), a distance of one mile and 550 yards – the longest naturally straight stretch of river in Britain. The patronage of Prince Albert enhanced its prestige and it became a royal regatta in 1851; since that time it has been one of the most popular occasions of the English social season. Beginning as a one-day event in 1839, the regatta has grown in length as well as popularity down the years and since 1986 has been spread over five days. The regatta's most prestigious event is the Grand Challenge Cup, raced by Men's Eights, which – the war years aside – has taken place every year since 1839 and been won by crews from all over the world.

For further information on the regatta visit ⬚ hrr.co.uk.

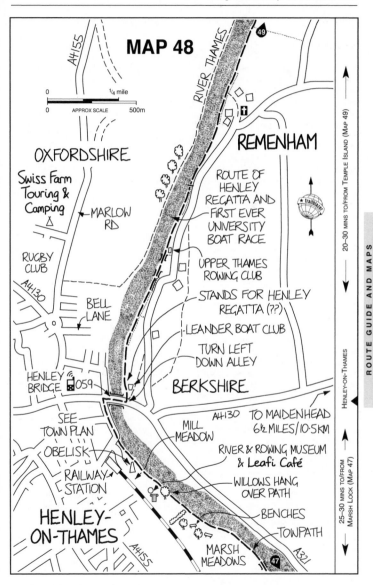

MAP 48

OXFORDSHIRE

Swiss Farm
Touring &
Camping

RUGBY
CLUB

A4130

MARLOW
RD

BELL
LANE

HENLEY
BRIDGE

SEE
TOWN
PLAN

OBELISK

RAILWAY
STATION

HENLEY-
ON-THAMES

A4155

A4155

RIVER THAMES

REMENHAM

ROUTE OF
HENLEY
REGATTA AND
FIRST EVER
UNIVERSITY
BOAT RACE

UPPER THAMES
ROWING CLUB

STANDS FOR HENLEY
REGATTA (??)

LEANDER BOAT CLUB

TURN LEFT
DOWN ALLEY

BERKSHIRE

A4130   TO MAIDENHEAD
6½ MILES/10·5KM

MILL
MEADOW

RIVER & ROWING MUSEUM
& Leafi Café

WILLOWS HANG
OVER PATH

BENCHES

TOWPATH

MARSH
MEADOWS

A321

49

47

059

0   ¼ mile
0   500m
APPROX SCALE

20–30 MINS TO/FROM TEMPLE ISLAND (MAP 49)

HENLEY-ON-THAMES

25–30 MINS TO/FROM
MARSH LOCK (MAP 47)

ROUTE GUIDE AND MAPS

There are two high standard **B&Bs**: *Denmark House* (☎ 01491-572028, ⌨ denmark-house.net; 2T/1D; ☞; WI-FI; £37.50-47.50pp, sgl occ £55-60; 2 Northfield End, Bell Lane) and *The Walled Garden* (☎ 01491-573142, ⌨ walled gard@aol.com; 1D/1T shared bathroom; ☞; WI-FI; £37.50pp, sgl occ from £70). The latter's two rooms are in an annexe set in the owner's half-acre garden. Walkers with dogs may be welcome but you need to phone and enquire.

Accommodation in **pubs** can be found centrally. *The Catherine Wheel* (☎ 01491-848484, ⌨ jdwetherspoon.com; 4S/16D/6T/4Tr; ☞; WI-FI; 7-15 Hart St) has plenty of rooms but some of them can be quite noisy, especially on Friday and Saturday nights when there is music until 2am in the Wetherspoon's-owned bar below them. Rates (£19.50-40pp, sgl from £60, sgl occ room rate) don't include breakfast but this is available (£3-6) from the restaurant downstairs, as is food throughout the day (see Where to eat). For a more peaceful forty winks, *The Row Barge* (☎ 01491-572649, ⌨ brakspear.co.uk/pub-finder/row-barge; 3D/1T; ☞; WI-FI; £45-50pp, sgl occ full room rate) is a better bet and food is also available (see Where to eat).

For **hotels**, *Red Lion* (☎ 01491-572161, ⌨ redlionhenley.co.uk; 26D/10T; ☞; WI-FI; 🐾) stands next to the bridge overlooking the Thames. The dog-friendly rooms are in a separate building. For up-to-date prices check the website, though a double room in summer will typically set you back in the region of £45pp (sgl occ room rate) with breakfast included.

Centrally, *The Loch Fyne Henley* (☎ 01491-845789, ⌨ oldenglishinns.co.uk; 7D; ☞; WI-FI; 20 Market Place) is a cheap-

er option, especially if landing in Henley on a Sunday night when they sometimes provide rooms for as little as £35pp including breakfast (normally £52.50-75pp, sgl occ room rate). The restaurant below has some mouth-watering food (see Where to eat).

Where to eat and drink

Henley has numerous eateries. For **breakfast** look no further than *Café Buendia* (☎ 01491-573706; WI-FI; Mon-Thur 8am-9pm, Fri & Sat 8am-10pm, Sun 9am-9pm; 8 Bell St). Primarily a pizza and pasta restaurant, it also cooks up a splendid full-English breakfast (from £5.50). If you can't be bothered to walk that far, *The Chocolate Café* (☎ 01491-411412, ⌨ thechocolate cafe.info; WI-FI; Mon-Thur 8am-5.30pm, Fri-Sun 8am-6pm) is right on the path and the riverfront. It's actually the sister of the café in Goring and it's a popular place with all-day breakfasts for a tenner and a great array of sandwiches (£5.95-7.50), cakes and hot drinks. They also offer takeaway.

In the same building as the rowing museum (see p160) is *Leafi* (Map 48; ☎ 01491-415602, ⌨ rrm.co.uk/visit/cafe; WI-FI; 🐾 outside; daily 10am-4.30pm); they serve sandwiches from £7.50, cakes from £2.50 as well as main courses.

Ten of Henley's **pubs** are owned by Brakspear Brewery (⌨ brakspear.co.uk). Best located for a pint after a hard day's walk is *The Angel on the Bridge* (☎ 01491-410678, ⌨ theangelhenley.com; WI-FI; 🐾; food Mon-Sat 11.30am-10pm, Sun to 7pm), which is ... by the bridge. Mains are good value, starting at a £10.50 for a vegetarian penne and rising to £13.50 for a whole rack of barbecue ribs with fries & salad.

For an evening meal, the town's locals rave about a trio of the Brakspear pubs. Pre-eminent amongst them, *The Bull on Bell St* (☎ 01491-576554, ⌨ bullonbell.co.uk; food Mon-Fri noon-10pm, Sat 10am-10pm, Sun 10am-9pm; WI-FI; 🐾 bar only; Nos 57-59), which is more restaurant than pub; mains cost from £11 and the lunch menu may include such dishes as seared fillet of sea bream (£16.95).

The other two are: *The Three Tuns* (☎ 01491-410138, ⌨ threetunshenley.co.uk;

> ❑ **Accommmodation alert**
> Note that during certain times of year – and especially during Henley Royal Regatta (late June to early July) – accommodation prices in the town rise to astronomical levels and it is essential to book months in advance.

food Tue-Thur noon-2.45pm & 6-9.30pm, Fri & Sat noon-2.45pm & 6-9.45pm, Sun noon-3.45pm; 5 Market Place), where pie mash & gravy costs £12.95 and a very good Sunday lunch is £12.95-13.95. (Note that the whole pub is closed on Mondays except sometimes bank holiday Mon); and *The Row Barge* (see Where to stay; 🐾 in bar on lead; food Wed-Sat noon-2pm & 7-9pm, Sun noon-3pm, in the summer they may also serve food Tue 7-9pm), which has a beer garden to relax in as you feast on their homemade pie of the day & veg (£11.50).

Also owned by Brakspear, *The Station House* (☎ 01491-578332, 🖳 stationhouse henley.co.uk; WI-FI; 🐾 in bar; 38 Market Place) is, as we go to press, on the market but still open and currently serves bar food only during the day.

Fish is the speciality at *The Loch Fyne Henley* (see Where to stay; food Mon-Thur 7.30am-10pm, Fri to 10.30pm, Sat 8am-10.30pm, Sun 8am-10pm). Despite the fresh and varied seafood and shellfish on offer the most popular dish remains their generously portioned fish & chips (£14.95).

Cheapest for standard pub food is *The Catherine Wheel* (see Where to stay; food daily 7am-10pm), although, being Henley, the food prices are slightly inflated above those of your average Wetherspoon's.

At 38 Hart St, *CAU* (☎ 01491-576729, 🖳 caurestaurants.com; Mon-Sat 9am-11pm, Sun to 10.30pm; WI-FI) is an Argentinian steak restaurant – and if you're going to eat steak, Argentinian steak is the best there is. Located just a few strides from the path, the price of the steak depends on

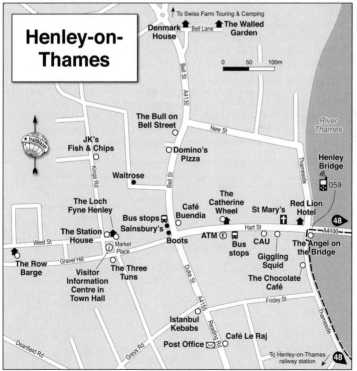

Henley-on-Thames

To Swiss Farm Touring & Camping

Denmark House — Bell Lane — The Walled Garden

0   50   100m

The Bull on Bell Street

New St

JK's Fish & Chips

Domino's Pizza

Waitrose

River Thames

Henley Bridge

059

The Loch Fyne Henley

Café Buendia

The Catherine Wheel

St Mary's

Red Lion Hotel

Bus stops

Sainsbury's

The Station House

Boots

ATM £

Bus stops

Hart St

CAU

48

A4130

West St

Market Place

The Angel on the Bridge

The Row Barge

Gravel Hill

Visitor Information Centre in Town Hall

The Three Tuns

Giggling Squid

The Chocolate Café

Friday St

Deanfield Rd

Istanbul Kebabs

Post Office

Café Le Raj

Greys Rd

Reading Rd

Thameside

To Henley-on-Thames railway station

48

the cut and the weight, with a sirloin starting at £15.50 for 220g, rising to £22.95 for 320g. While those who want to pig out can opt for the £89.95 CAU feasting plate, consisting of a 400g cut each of three different types of steak.

Nearby, heat seekers should consider *Giggling Squid* (☎ 01491-411044, 🖳 gigglingsquid.com; Mon-Thur noon-10pm, Fri & Sat to 10.30pm, Sun to 9.30pm; 40 Hart St), for chicken & cashew nut stir-fry (£7.95 at lunch) and other spicy Thai dishes; or *Café Le Raj* (☎ 01491-573337, 🖳

cafeleraj.co.uk; food daily noon-2.30pm & 6-11.30pm; 17 Reading Rd) which provides some of the best-value meals in Henley, with a chicken vindaloo £6.75.

Takeaway is also available at *Domino's Pizza* (☎ 01491-577666, 🖳 dominos.co.uk; daily 10am-11pm; 55 Bell St), *Istanbul Kebabs* (Mon-Thur 11am-1am, Fri 11am-3.30am, Sat noon-3.30am, Sun 1pm-1am; Greys Rd) and *JK's Fish and Chips* (Mon-Fri 11am-2pm & 5-10pm, Sat, Sun & Bank Hols 4-10pm; 54 Kings Rd).

HENLEY-ON-THAMES TO MARLOW [MAPS 48-52]

This short **8½-mile (13.5km, 3-3¾hrs)** stage begins by following the same stretch of river used by the races during the Henley Regatta (see box on p160) – albeit in reverse – to **Temple Island** (Map 49). From here the river sweeps swiftly round to **Hambleden Lock**, the starting point for the first-ever University Boat Race (see box p209).

Leaving the Thames at **Aston** (see p166; Map 50) the trail cuts its way past the 18th-century **Culham Court** and through a **deer park** before reuniting itself with the river. At **Hurley Lock** (Map 51) a footpath can be taken to **Hurley** village (see p166).

After you've crossed the river to Buckinghamshire – your third county of the day – **Temple Lock** is the last lock encountered before you follow the towpath to **Marlow** (see p168; Map 52), those pesky planes from Heathrow getting ever larger and noisier in the skies above. As you wander along be sure not to miss the view of **Bisham Church** on the opposite bank.

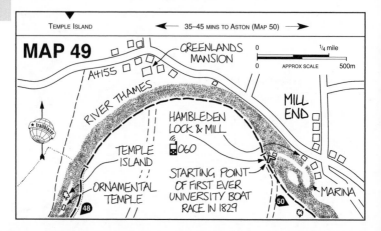

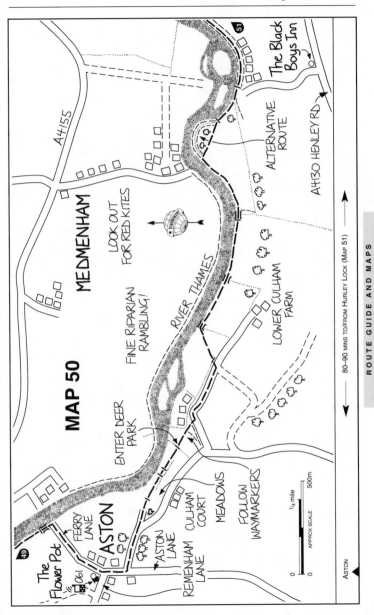

ASTON [Map 50, p165]

The Flower Pot (☎ 01491-574721, 🖳 brak spear.co.uk; 2D en suite/1T private bathroom; 🐾; WI-FI; 🐕 bar only) charges £40-60pp (sgl occ from £60) for **B&B**. The menu (**food** served Mon-Fri noon-2.30pm & 6-9pm, Sat noon-9pm, Sun noon-2.30pm) includes staples such as chicken curry with rice & naan (£10.50) as well as a long list of specials (venison steak with chips £17.50). Some may object to the hunting and fishing theme or to the caged parrot that sits in the corner; but for us, it was one of the most characterful pubs on the entire walk and we loved it.

HURLEY LOCK/HURLEY [Map 51]

There are two options for **campers** here. On the island here is *Hurley Lock Campsite* (☎ 01628-824334; pitch £11 for up to two people; 🐕 if on a lead and any messes cleaned up; Apr-end Sep). As with other sites operated by the Environment Agency it is gated so you'll need to arrive within the lock-keeper's hours (generally 9am-5pm) to get the key. There are shower and toilet facilities; booking is recommended especially for a weekend. Refreshments are available at a **tea shop** (Apr-end Sep Tue-Sun & Bank Hol Mon 11am-5pm), though the food is limited to cakes and biscuits (£6 for a cream tea for two).

You can also camp at the gargantuan *Hurley Riverside Park* (☎ 01628-824493, 🖳 hurleyriversidepark.co.uk; pitch £13-28 for up to two people; WI-FI; 🐕; Mar-Oct), the main entrance to which is on High St. There is a keycoded back entrance gate on to the Thames Path for campers who have already checked in (last check in is 8pm).

Hidden from the river, Hurley's **St Mary's Church** is built on the foundations of its Saxon predecessor which was founded by St Birinus – the first bishop of Dorchester – in AD635. Beneath the Norman nave rest the remains of Edward the Confessor's sister.

Opposite the church is the **Village Shop** (☎ 01628-824271; daily summer 8am-5pm, winter 8am-1.30pm) with limited **post office** (Tue 10am-12.30pm & Thur 9.30am-noon only) services.

The closest *indoor* accommodation to the path is at *Crazy Fox* (☎ 01628-825086, 🖳 crazyfoxhurley.com; 4D; 🐾; WI-FI; High St), a 'boutique' bed and breakfast with luxury king-size rooms; rates depend on demand but are around £67.50-92.50pp, with no discount for single occupancy.

As historic a pub as you'll come across on your Thames journey, *The Olde Bell* (☎ 01628-825881, 🖳 theoldebell.co.uk; WI-FI; 🐕 bar only) has both fine **rooms** (48D; 🐾), a bar with bar **food** (daily noon-9pm) and a restaurant (daily noon-3pm & 6-9pm). As you munch on grilled rainbow trout with Jersey royal potatoes (£16), it's worth contemplating that these same rooms have hosted Benedictine monks (there was a Benedictine abbey nearby and the pub was used as a guesthouse for its visitors), plotters against kings and even Winston Churchill and Dwight D Eisenhower as they planned the liberation of Europe. Check the website for rates as they offer a variety of deals; in general expect to pay anywhere from £32.50pp to over £100pp with no discount for single occupancy.

Rebellion Beer (see box p23) is almost always available at *The Rising Sun* (☎ 01628-825733, 🖳 risingsunhurley.co.uk; food Mon-Sat noon-3pm & 6-9pm, Sun noon-3pm; 🐕) and other ales are available at certain times of the year. The menu includes home-cooked meals such as ham or sausage and eggs with chips (£8.95), as well as baguettes and jacket potatoes (all £7.95).

Black Boys Inn (☎ 01628-316913, 🖳 blackboysinn.co.uk; WI-FI; 🐕) serves breakfast (daily 7.30-10.30am) and main meals (Mon-Sat noon-2.30pm & 6-9.30pm, Sun to 4pm) may be the most convenient pub for campers staying at Riverside Park.

The 238/239 **bus** calls here on week days; see box pp58-9.

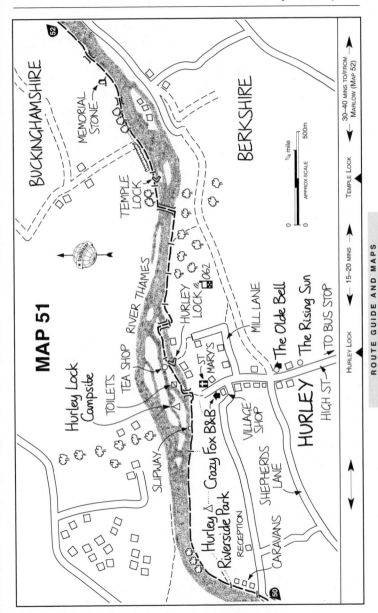

MAP 51

BUCKINGHAMSHIRE

BERKSHIRE

MEMORIAL STONE

TEMPLE LOCK

RIVER THAMES

Hurley Lock Campsite

TOILETS

TEA SHOP

HURLEY LOCK

1062

ST MARY'S

SLIPWAY

Hurley Crazy Fox B&B

Riverside Park

RECEPTION

CARAVANS

VILLAGE SHOP

SHEPHERDS LANE

HURLEY

HIGH ST

MILL LANE

The Olde Bell

The Rising Sun

TO BUS STOP

¼ mile

APPROX SCALE

0   500m

← HURLEY LOCK — 15-20 MINS → ← TEMPLE LOCK → 30-40 MINS TO/FROM MARLOW (MAP 52) →

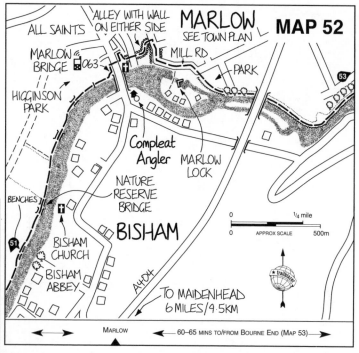

MARLOW

60–65 MINS TO/FROM BOURNE END (MAP 53)

MARLOW

Rich in literary association, this laidback market town is where Thomas Love Peacock's *Nightmare Abbey* and Mary Shelley's *Frankenstein* were both composed; the latter's husband, the poet Percy Bysshe Shelley, also penned *The Revolt of Islam* whilst floating on the river nearby and post-WW1 the town was the home of TS Eliot (see box p47). It may be time to start scribbling in your diary – there must be something in the air.

The town's significant features are its **19th-century bridge** and **All Saints Church**, the two combining to form yet another splendid riparian scene.

Services

Marlow Information Centre is in the library (Tue 10am-6pm, Wed & Fri to 5pm, Thur & Sat to 4pm) on Institute Rd; also on the same road is the **post office** (Mon-Fri 9am-5.30pm, Sat 9am-12.30pm).

On the High St are both **Marlow Pharmacy** (Mon-Fri 8.30am-5.30pm, Sat 9am-5pm, Sun 11am-4pm) and a Sainsbury's **supermarket** (daily 7am-11pm), near to which you'll find an **ATM**. There is also a branch of the **trekking outfitters** Mountain Warehouse (☎ 01628-487823; Mon-Fri 9am-5.30pm, Sat to 6pm, Sun 10.30am-4.30pm) at 36-38 High St.

Marlow is at the end of the branch **railway** line from Maidenhead; services are operated by GWR (see box pp52-3). **Bus** services X80/800/850 (see box pp58-9) also call in town.

Where to stay

Nearest to the river is a *Premier Inn* (☎ 01628-814310, 🖳 premierinn.com; 1S/16D;

•; WI-FI; The Causeway). For the best rates (as little as £35 per room but £80-90 is more likely) booking in advance and online is advised; see also p21.

B&B is on offer at *12 Lodge Close* (☎ 01628-473863, 🖳 bedbreakfast-marlow.co .uk; 1D/1T shared bathroom; •; WI-FI; from £35pp, sgl occ from £50) but cash payment is required.

Three **pubs** also offer accommodation. Close to the railway station is *The Prince of Wales* (☎ 01628-482970, 🖳 www.the-prince-of-wales.co.uk; 1S/1D/4T; WI-FI; £42.50-45pp, sgl/sgl occ from £75; 1 Mill Rd) where the breakfast is continental and is left in your room. *The Chequers* (☎ 01628-482053, 🖳 thechequersmarlow.co .uk; 7D/2D or T; •; WI-FI), in the heart of the action at 53 High St, has nine spanking new rooms; B&B costs from £50pp (sgl occ room rate).

A short walk from town, at 126 West St, is the plush *Hand & Flowers* (☎ 01628-482277, 🖳 thehandandflowers.co.uk; 8D; •; WI-FI; 🐾). The accommodation includes four double cottage suites and four more rooms in The Apple House, a five-minute walk away. B&B costs £97.50-137.50pp,

sgl occ full room rate: not cheap, but the rooms do belong to a Michelin award-winning pub (see Where to eat). However, you will need to book a long way in advance – see the website for details.

Across the river there are some magnificent **hotel** rooms at *The Compleat Angler* (☎ 01628-484444, 🖳 macdonald hotels.co.uk; 52D/12D or T; •; WI-FI; 🐾), part of the Macdonald chain, but they also are not cheap: you can expect to pay £140-255pp (sgl occ full room tariff) depending on demand and the season.

Where to eat and drink

Marlow has many options so finding somewhere to eat or drink won't be a problem.

On High St, two decent spots for **breakfast** are *Fego Caffé* (☎ 01628-475873, 🖳 fegocaffe.co.uk; Mon-Sat 8.30am-5pm, Sun 9am-4.30pm, bank holidays 10am-4pm; WI-FI) where you'll get a Full English breakfast for £9.95 (they also do gourmet sandwiches, £6.95-8.50) and *Café Copia* (🖳 cafecopia.co.uk; Mon-Sat 7.30am-5pm, Sun 9am-5pm; WI-FI; 🐾) which has bacon or sausage sandwiches (£4.45) on the menu.

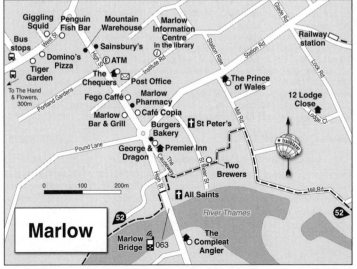

Also on High St you'll find a top-notch spot for a brew and a pastry at *Burgers Bakery* (☎ 01628-483389, 🖥 burgersarti sanbakery.com; Mon-Fri 8am-5pm, Sat 8.30am-5pm; WI-FI; note Burgers is pronounced 'Burjers'. Afternoon tea costs £12.50pp and hungry canines are allowed but at the outside tables only.

For those staying at the Premier Inn, the accompanying *George & Dragon* (☎ 01628-814312, 🖥 whitbreadinns.co.uk; WI-FI; food daily 6.30/7am-10pm), The Causeway) is ideal for those who want to set off on a full stomach; an all-you-can-eat breakfast (Mon-Fri 6.30-10.30am, Sat & Sun 7-11am) is available for £8.99.

Decent **pub meals** can be found at *The Chequers* (see Where to stay; food Mon-Thur 8-10am & noon-9.30pm, Fri 8-10am & noon-10pm, Sat 8-11am & noon-10pm, Sun 8-11am & noon-8.30pm; 🐾 in main bar only; 53 High St), a Brakspear pub where the menu focuses on steaks but also includes duck leg (£17) and standards such as fish & chips. Right on the trail, *Two Brewers* (☎ 01628-484140, 🖥 twobrewers marlow.co .uk; WI-FI; 🐾; food Mon-Thur noon-3pm & 6.30-9pm, Fri & Sat noon-9pm, Sun noon-6pm) is the oldest pub in Marlow. It is a smart and friendly place with a standard pub menu including peri peri chicken (£9.25), as well as a good selection of burgers (£9.25-10.50).

Fish and meat dishes such as steak & lobster for two (£28.75pp) can be reeled in at *Marlow Bar and Grill* (☎ 01628-488544, 🖥 individualrestaurants.com/bar-and-grill/marlow; food Mon-Sat noon-11pm, Sun noon-10.30pm; WI-FI; 92-94 High St). For solo trekkers, cheaper meals

such as slow-cooked free-range pulled pork (£13) also appear on the menu.

The **restaurant** receiving the highest accolades in Marlow is *The Hand & Flowers* (see Where to stay; food Mon-Sat noon-2.45pm & 6.30-9.45pm, Sun noon-3.15pm; WI-FI). An establishment run by stellar chef Tom Kerridge and awarded two stars in the Michelin Guide. The menu changes regularly and is not cheap, with a roasted scallop with preserved fennel, pollen & sauce bouillabaisse au beurre for £19.50, yet one suspects that if you plan to treat yourself just once during your time by the river this may well be the place to do it. Booking is essential though (see the website).

For more exotic fare, jungle curry (£8.95) and other **Thai** dishes can be found at *The Prince of Wales* (see Where to stay; food daily noon-2.30pm & 6-10pm; WI-FI; 🐾 bar area) and also at the town's branch of *Giggling Squid* (☎ 01628-483047, 🖥 gig glingsquid.com/branches/marlow; Mon-Thur noon-10pm, Fri & Sat to 10.30pm, Sun to 9.30pm; 24 West St), where a chicken & cashew nut stir-fry will set you back £7.50.

A highly recommended **Indian** restaurant is *Tiger Garden* (☎ 01628-482211, 🖥 tigergarden.co.uk; daily noon-2.30pm & 6-11pm; WI-FI; 41 West St). The food, whether eaten in the restaurant or taken away, will not disappoint.

Other **takeaway** options include *Domino's Pizza* (☎ 01628-477711, 🖥 dom inos.co.uk; daily 10am-11pm) and *Penguin Fish Bar* (Mon-Thur & Sat 11am-10.30pm, Fri 11am-11pm, Sun noon-9.30pm). Both are on West St and charge typical takeaway prices.

MARLOW TO WINDSOR [MAPS 52-59]

This varied **14¼-mile (22.7km, 5-6hrs)** stage passes through a number of towns, each separated from the other by the serenity of some fine riverside tramping. With the magnificent and imposing view of Windsor Castle (see box p182) dominating the final leg, this is one stage where you would be justified in setting off early.

The section begins with a quiet riparian stroll as far as **Bourne End** (see p172; Map 53) where you cross to the southern side to enter **Cock Marsh**, owned by the National Trust and a Site of Special Scientific Interest.

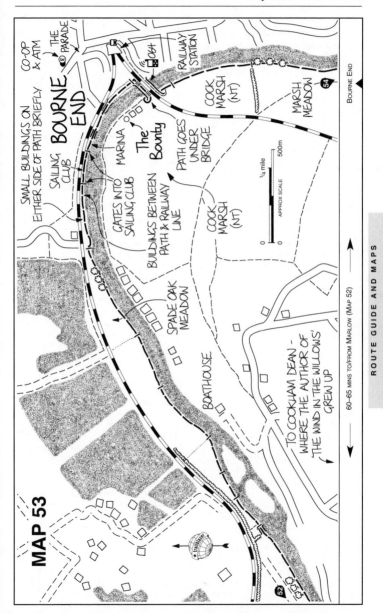

MAP 53

CO-OP & ATM

THE PARADE

BOURNE END

SMALL BUILDINGS ON EITHER SIDE OF PATH BRIEFLY

SAILING CLUB

MARINA

RAILWAY STATION

The Bounty

GATES INTO SAILING CLUB

BUILDINGS BETWEEN PATH & RAILWAY LINE

COCK MARSH (NT)

PATH GOES UNDER BRIDGE

COCK MARSH (NT)

MARSH MEADOW

BOURNE END

¼ mile

500m

0

0

APPROX SCALE

SPADE OAK MEADOW

BOATHOUSE

TO COOKHAM DEAN – WHERE THE AUTHOR OF 'THE WIND IN THE WILLOWS' GREW UP

60–65 MINS TO/FROM MARLOW (MAP 52)

After a short but worthwhile diversion from the river to collude with the village of **Cookham** (see below), an all-too-brief spell of woodland walking leads you to a hike through **Maidenhead** (see below; Map 55), a highlight of which is **Boulter's Lock** (the No 8 **bus** service, see box pp58-9, calls here).

Having crossed the river and left Maidenhead in its wake the path gradually regains a sense of isolation, passing, on the opposite bank, **Bray** (see p177; Map 56) – home to Heston Blumenthal's *Fat Duck* – the tranquillity of this stretch spoilt somewhat by the thunderous M4. With the sound of the motorway still resonant in your ears, **Dorney Lake** (Map 57), home to Eton College's rowers, appear on your left and having navigated its length you arrive at the intriguing **Church of St Mary Magdalene** in Boveney (Map 58).

Finally, as **Windsor** (see pp181-4) looms into view you have only the town of **Eton** (see pp180-1; Map 59) – a worthwhile stop in its own right – to wander through before you arrive at Windsor Bridge... and at a castle fit for a queen.

BOURNE END [Map 53, p171]

Author Enid Blyton once lived in this large commuter village. That aside, and the fact that food is available by the river, unless you require a Co-op **store** (daily 7am-10pm) or an **ATM** there's really nothing at Bourne End to encourage you to leave the trail.

Bourne End is a stop on the branch **railway** line between Marlow and Maidenhead; services are operated by GWR (see box pp52-3). The 35, 36 & 37 **bus** services (see box p58-9) call here.

Having crossed the railway line, by turning right off the Thames Path you arrive

at *The Bounty* (☎ 01628-520056, 🖳 the bountypub.com; WI-FI; 🐕; **food** Apr-Sep daily noon-8pm, Oct-Mar weekends only noon-5pm). One of the river's most colourful pubs, this popular free house welcomes walkers and all other folk who choose to follow the river. There's a vast range of burgers (£6.95-8.95) and their Rebellion (see box p23) selection of ales is especially popular. Dogs are welcomed as if long-lost friends and they provide dog snacks (£2 for a bowl of sausage chunks). The toilets are also free for walkers.

COOKHAM [Map 54]

Famous as the home of the artist Stanley Spencer (see box p174), Cookham has a long history. Bronze Age burial mounds exist nearby and abundant Roman and Saxon skeletons have been found, with the riverbed hiding relics from every period. Author of *The Wind in the Willows*, Kenneth Grahame (see box p148) grew up in nearby Cookham Dean.

The rate at *Cookham Lock Campsite* (☎ 01628-520752; £11 for up to two walkers; Apr-Sep) includes a shower and there are toilet facilities and a water tap. Booking is essential and campers must arrive by 5pm as the weir gate is locked then; a key (deposit £10) enables campers to go into the village in the evening.

One of the country's newer pub and restaurant chains has set up in one of the country's oldest coaching inns. *Bel and The*

Dragon (☎ 01628-521263, 🖳 belandthedra gon-cookham.co.uk; 10D; 🐕; WI-FI) is in a 600-year-old hostelry just a few steps from the path. Offering both **accommodation** (from £60pp; sgl occ room rate) and **food** (Mon-Sat noon-3pm & 6-10pm, Sun noon-9pm; 🐕 bar area), the hostelry's menu changes according to the season but you may find partridge (£16) or suckling pig (£19) being cooked on their rotisserie.

There are several other options for food. As you enter town, on your left along Sutton Rd you'll spot *The Ferry* (☎ 01628-525123, 🖳 theferry.co.uk; WI-FI; in parts of the bar and restaurant; food Sun-Thur noon-9pm, Fri & Sat to 10pm). The lunch menu includes spit-roast chicken (£12.95) as well as salads (£9.95-12.95) and there's a patio on which you can enjoy your meal as you gaze over the river.

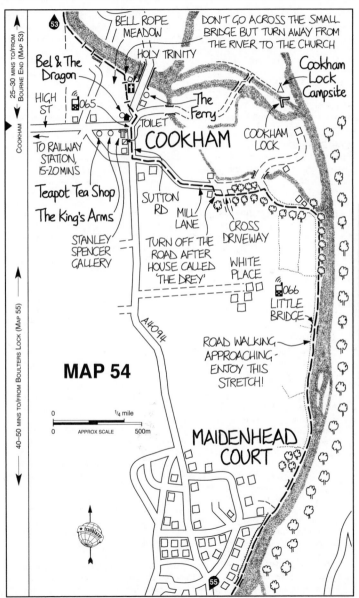

MAP 54

Back on the High St, the friendly and bright – if rather expensive – *Teapot Tea Shop* (☎ 01628-529514, 🖥 teapot-tea shop.co.uk; WI-FI; 🐾; daily 10am-5pm) sells baked potatoes with salad (£7.50), baguettes (£6.95) and slices of home-made cake, while for **pub food** look no further than *The King's Arms* (☎ 01628-530667, 🖥 thekingsarmscookham.co.uk; food Mon-Sat noon-10pm, Sun to 9.30pm; WI-FI; 🐾

bar area only) where there are real ales to help wash down home-made cod fishfinger sandwiches (from £7.95), or king prawn, crab & chorizo linguine (£13.25).

Cookham is on the Marlow to Maidenhead branch line; for details of GWR's **train services** see box pp52-3. The railway station is a 15- to 20-minute walk from the path. Cookham is also a stop on Nos 35 & 37 **bus** services (see box pp58-9).

MAIDENHEAD [Map 55]

Of note along the stretch of river which bypasses Maidenhead is the railway bridge you pass beneath. Designed by Isambard Kingdom Brunel in 1838, it features in JMW Turner's famous Thames-side painting *Rain, Steam and Speed* (see box p46).

Along the path there are several amenities for walkers, including a **Co-op** (daily 6am-11pm) and **ATM**; both are on Ray Mead Rd near the bridge.

On the same road is *Jenner's Café* (☎ 01628-621721, 🖥 jennerscafe.com; Apr-Aug daily 8am-5pm, Sep-Mar Mon-Fri to 3pm, Sat & Sun to 4pm) which sells cakes

and ice-cream as well as lunches such as gammon, egg & chips (£6.30).

On the island at **Boulter's Lock** is *Boulters* (☎ 01628-621291, 🖥 www.boul tersrestaurant.co.uk; food Mon-Sat 10am-9.30pm, Sun to 2.45pm; WI-FI); a brasserie and a bar. On the bar menu expect to see beer-battered haddock & chips (£14.30) and chicken Caesar salad (from £13.30).

Accommodation is available at two large old hotels, both with restaurants. Our favourite is the 19th-century *Thames Hotel* (☎ 01628-628721, 🖥 thameshotel.co.uk; 6S/15D/5T/3D or T/2Qd; ☎; WI-FI), with a

❏ Stanley Spencer

The Thames has been a constant source of inspiration for artists (see box p46) and none more so than Stanley Spencer (1891-1959). Born in and spending much of his life in Cookham, the village would appear frequently in his paintings. His style was very distinctive, with Biblical scenes superimposed on to the village and its inhabitants. Indeed, such was his affection for the village that his contemporaries at the Slade School of Art in London – amongst them the famous war artist Paul Nash – nicknamed him 'Cookham'. Having seen action in WWI, in 1918 he was invalided from the army and returned to his parents' house in the village to continue to work on his art. Leaving in April 1920 he briefly moved to Bourne End before leading a somewhat nomadic existence, painting wherever he went.

In 1923, whilst residing in Hampstead, he began work on one of his most celebrated paintings, *The Resurrection, Cookham*. Set in the grounds of Cookham's Holy Trinity Church, it depicts his family and friends emerging from the graves, all watched over by God, Christ and the saints. Having exhibited the picture in 1927, Spencer sold the painting, its purchaser eventually donating it to Tate Britain (see p233) where it resides to this day. Spencer returned to Cookham in 1932 and the village would form the backdrop to numerous of his other works including *View from Cookham Bridge* (1936) and *Christ Preaching at Cookham Regatta* (1952-59). Sadly, this last he would not live to complete.

A wealth of information on the artist can be found in Cookham at **Stanley Spencer Gallery** (☎ 01628-471885, 🖥 stanleyspencer.org.uk; Apr-Oct daily 10.30am-5.30pm, Nov-Mar Thur-Sun 11am-4.30pm, £6; High St).

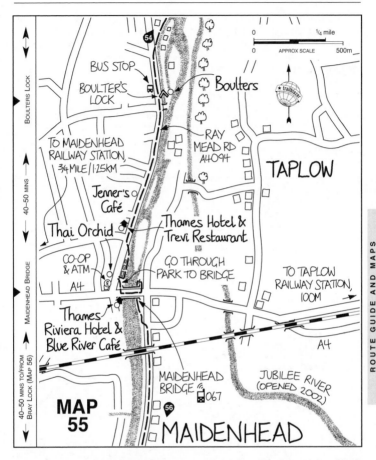

super-fast wi-fi connection and comfortable rooms that cost around £45pp (sgl from £75) but the rate varies depending on demand. **Trevi Restaurant** (Mon-Thur noon-2.30pm & 6.30-9.45pm, Fri & Sat to 10.15pm, Sun noon-3pm & 6-9.45pm), on the ground floor, serves good Italian food including *pollo alla Romana* (chicken topped with parma ham & sage; £15.95); English food is available in the bar.

Right by the bridge, **Thames Riviera Hotel** (☎ 01628-674057, 🖳 thamesriviera.com; 7S/37D/3T/5Qd; ☛; WI-FI). With

rates changing daily their website will tell you the precise cost and also any special deals; but as a barometer expect to pay £25-80pp for room only (sgl from £49, sgl occ room rate); if not included in your rate breakfast costs around a tenner. Food (Mon-Fri 7am-9pm, Sat 8am-9pm, Sun 8am-8.45pm) is available all day from their bar or in their **Blue River Café**.

In between the two hotels is **Thai Orchid** (☎ 01628-777555; Sun & Tue-Fri noon-2pm & 5.30-10pm, Sat 5.30-10.30pm) with mains around £10-14.

Maidenhead is a stop on GWR's **railway** services between London Paddington and Didcot Parkway; the branch line to Marlow starts here (see box pp52-3). **Bus services** 8, 15/15A, 16/16A, 35/37, 127, 238 & 239 also call here; see box pp58-9.

DORNEY REACH [Map 56]

For **campers**, near to the river and the M4 is *Amerden Caravan Park* (☎ 01628-627461, 🖥 amerdencaravanpark.com; WI-FI at reception; 🐾 on lead; £14/18 for a tent and one/two walkers; Apr-Sep). However, Amerden is expecting to close at the end of August (2018) for a year due to the M4 construction work and it is possible they

will also lose some of their land. If you do camp here note that there is no shop so you'll need either to carry any supplies required or head to Bray (crossing over the river on the footpath on the M4) for a meal; see opposite. Alternatively the caravan park has phone numbers for Indian, Chinese and pizza places that will deliver to the park.

ROUTE GUIDE AND MAPS

BRAY LOCK

45-55 MINS TO/FROM BOVENEY CHURCH (MAP 58)

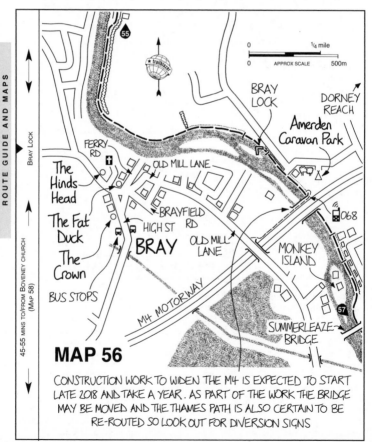

MAP 56

CONSTRUCTION WORK TO WIDEN THE M4 IS EXPECTED TO START LATE 2018 AND TAKE A YEAR. AS PART OF THE WORK THE BRIDGE MAY BE MOVED AND THE THAMES PATH IS ALSO CERTAIN TO BE RE-ROUTED SO LOOK OUT FOR DIVERSION SIGNS

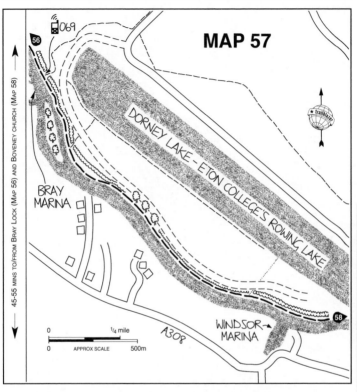

Culinary diversion to Bray – for a Heston Blumenthal restaurant

Chef Heston Blumenthal owns three of **Bray**'s restaurants, the most famous of which is *The Fat Duck* (🖳 thefatduck.co.uk). Not a place you just stroll into in muddy boots; if you plan to visit you'll need to book months in advance.

Of the other two, a meal at *The Hinds Head* (☎ 01628-626151, 🖳 hinds headbray.com; food Mon-Sat noon-2pm & 6-9pm, Sun noon-3.30pm) also requires some planning as booking is almost essential, although it's not quite as famous as The Fat Duck.

The best opportunity for walkers to enjoy a taste of Blumenthal's gastronomy is at *The Crown* (☎ 01628-621936, 🖳 thecrownatbray.co.uk; food Mon-Thur noon-2.15pm & 6-9.15pm, Fri noon-2.15pm & 6-9.45pm, Sat noon-2.45pm & 6-9.45pm, Sun noon-4.45pm & 7-9pm; WI-FI; 🐾 if booked in advance). Though still very busy (booking remains advisable especially at the weekend), The Crown is the most pub-like of the three and also has the cheapest of the menus, with Heston's special twists added to classics such as hamburgers (£17.50) and fish & chips (£17.95).

The No 16/16A **bus** services (see pp58-9) call in Bray. *(cont'd on p180)*

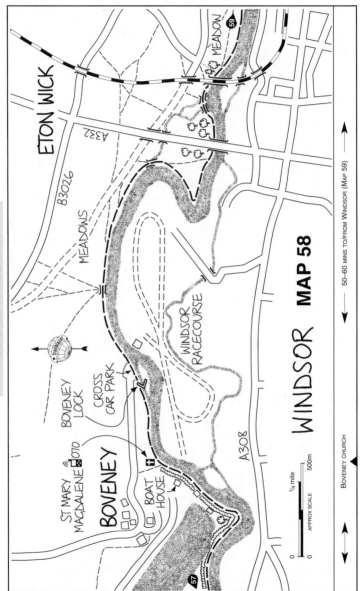

ETON WICK

MEADOW

59

A332

B3026

MEADONS

MEADONS

WINDSOR **MAP 58**

50–60 MINS TO/FROM WINDSOR (MAP 59)

WINDSOR RACECOURSE

A308

BOVENEY LOCK

CROSS CAR PARK

ST MARY MAGDALENE

BOVENEY

BOAT HOUSE

¼ mile

500m

APPROX SCALE

0

0

BOVENEY CHURCH

57

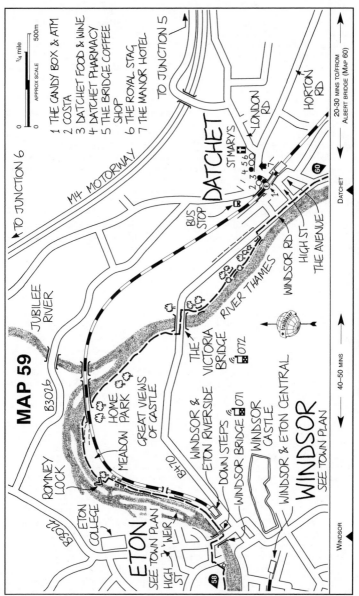

MAP 59

TO JUNCTION 6

M4 MOTORWAY

JUBILEE RIVER

B3026

1 THE CANDY BOX & ATM
2 COSTA
3 DATCHET FOOD & WINE
4 DATCHET PHARMACY
5 THE BRIDGE COFFEE SHOP
6 THE ROYAL STAG
7 THE MANOR HOTEL

APPROX SCALE
0 — ¼ mile
0 — 500m

TO JUNCTION 5

DATCHET

ST MARY'S

1 2 3 4 5 6 7

LONDON RD

HORTON RD

BUS STOP

RIVER THAMES

WINDSOR RD

HIGH ST

THE AVENUE

20-30 MINS TO/FROM ALBERT BRIDGE (MAP 60)

DATCHET

THE VICTORIA BRIDGE

O72

40-50 MINS

ROMNEY LOCK

ETON COLLEGE

HIGH ST

B3022

ETON WEIR

HOME PARK

GREAT VIEWS OF CASTLE

MEADOW PARK

B3010

WINDSOR & ETON RIVERSIDE

DOWN STEPS

WINDSOR BRIDGE O71

WINDSOR CASTLE

WINDSOR & ETON CENTRAL

WINDSOR

SEE TOWN PLAN

ETON

SEE TOWN PLAN

58

60

WINDSOR

ROUTE GUIDE AND MAPS

ETON

Synonymous with its college (see box below), Eton offers a good alternative stop if you don't wish to dally in Windsor. Far less hectic and with great views of Windsor Castle from the bridge which spans the river between the two, the town, despite being the smaller twin, still has everything a walker needs.

On High St is a **shop**: Eton Premier Stores (Mon-Sat 5.30am-8pm, Sun 7am-7pm). **Bus** services (15/15S) connect Eton with Slough and Maidenhead (see pp58-9); see Windsor (p182) for rail services.

Relatively reasonably priced **accommodation** can be found on High St. *The Crown and Cushion* (☎ 01753-861531, 🖳 thecrownandcushioneton.co.uk; No 84) offers **B&B** (8D; WI-FI; £35-47.50pp, sgl occ full room rate) and also dishes up pub classics (**food** Mon-Sat noon-9pm, Sun noon-6pm) and has a large range of burgers on the menu including 'The Hot One', topped with Swiss cheese, jalapeno & chilli sauce (£10.95).

More expensive, *The George Inn* (☎ 01753-861797, 🖳 georgeinn-eton.co.uk; 2S/3D/1T/2Tr; WI-FI; 🐾 bar area only; No 77) provides breakfast in with the price of your 'boutique' room (from £60pp, sgl from £90, sgl occ room rate). **Food** (May-Oct Mon-Fri 7-10am & noon-9.30pm, Sat 8-10am & noon-9.30pm, Sun 8-10am & noon-7pm, rest of year the kitchen closed Mon-Fri 3-6pm) is served all day in the summer months; the evening menu including pan-fried seabass fillet with baby potatoes (£15.50) and sausages & mash (£13.95).

Rates at *The Christopher Hotel* (☎ 01753-852359, 🖳 thechristopher.co.uk; 9S/8T/16D/1Tr; ☛; WI-FI; 🐾 in Courtyard rooms and bar; No 110) change throughout the year but in summer you can expect to pay about £80pp (sgl around £126, sgl occ room rate). Breakfast is not included but can be purchased from the restaurant (small continental £8.25, buffet £13.25, full English £17.50) where **meals** (daily noon-9.30pm), such as chicken/vegetarian curry (£14.95/12.95), are dished up throughout the rest of the day.

High St has a number of cafés, including a branch of *Costa* (🖳 costa.co.uk; Mon-Sat 6.30am-7pm, Sun 8am-6.30pm; WI-FI) and, a little further from the water, *Zero 3* (☎ 01753-864725; Apr-Nov Mon-Fri 8am-4pm, Sat 9am-4pm, Sun 10am-4pm, winter to 3pm; WI-FI; 🐾). You'll find full English breakfasts (£7.50) here and water is provided for dogs though you'll have to eat with your four-legged buddy at one of the tables outside.

As you enter Eton, the first **pub** you arrive at is *The Watermans Arms* (☎ 01753-861001, 🖳 watermans-eton.com; food Mon-Fri noon-3pm & 6-9pm, Sat noon-9pm, Sun noon-4pm; WI-FI; 🐾; Brocas St). Brimming with character, this place has up to eight locally brewed real ales to accompany your ploughman's lunch or portion of liver & bacon (both £10.95).

❏ Eton College

Eton College (Map 59) was founded by Henry VI in 1440, originally as a charity to educate underprivileged boys, many of whom then went on to King's College, Cambridge, which he founded the following year. Eton College remains an all-boys school to this day. It was originally one of nine independent English 'public' boarding schools, five of which still follow in the all-male boarding school tradition (others include Harrow and Winchester College). Eton – as it is commonly known – has educated much of the British aristocracy down the years as well as 19 prime ministers, amongst them Robert Walpole, William Pitt the Elder, Harold Macmillan and David Cameron. Other famous alumni, both real and imagined, include Boris Johnson (the former Mayor of London), Justin Welby (the Archbishop of Canterbury), authors George Orwell and Aldous Huxley, PG Wodehouse's Bertie Wooster, Ian Fleming's James Bond and even Tarzan; one imagines he did well at PE.

Next to the bridge and with great views of both river and castle is *Côte Brasserie* (☎ 01753-868344, 🖥 cote.co.uk; Mon-Fri 8am-11pm, Sat 9am-11pm, Sun 9am-10.30pm; WI-FI). On the menu are spinach & mushroom crêpes (£10.95) and

roast duck breast (£14.95). *Golden Curry* (☎ 01753-863961; Mon-Sat noon-3pm & 6pm-midnight, Sun noon-midnight; WI-FI; 46 High St) is Eton's Indian restaurant. Mains start at £8.95 and are available for **takeaway**.

WINDSOR

Windsor is dominated by its castle, which over the years has had many inhabitants but can now also be visited by ordinary mortals: **Windsor Castle** (see box p182; 🖥 royalcollection.org.uk/visit/windsorcastle; daily Mar-Oct 9.30am-5.15pm, Nov-Feb 9.45am-4.15pm) covers an area of approximately 13

acres and over 500 people live and work within its walls. The current Queen's favoured weekend escape, it is used as a venue for state visits and banquets. Many of the castle's apartments, collections and galleries can be visited (£21.20 inc audio tour, £11.70 when the state apartments are

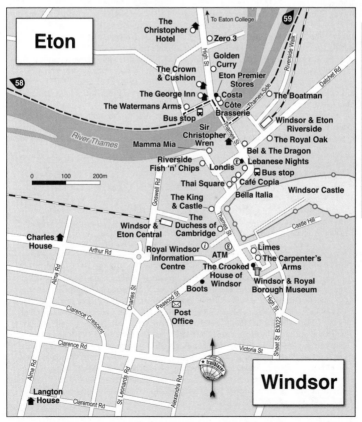

ROUTE GUIDE AND MAPS

closed), items from the Royal Collection are often exhibited and you may also be able to see the Changing of the Guard (usually Mon, Wed, Fri & Sat at 11am). The modern town which has grown below the castle is a vibrant and hectic place. Expect the soundtrack to your day to be that of clicking cameras and foreign voices, their owners gawping in awe at one of England's most impressive buildings.

Windsor and Royal Borough Museum (☎ 01628-685686; Tue-Sat 10am-4pm, Sun & Bank Hols noon-4pm; £2; High St) tells the local area's tale.

Services
Royal Windsor Information Centre (☎ 01753-743900, 🖥 windsor.gov.uk; daily 10am-4pm but sometimes open earlier and/or later) is in The Old Booking Hall, Windsor Royal Shopping, on Thames St.

On Peascod St there is a **post office** (Mon-Fri 9am-5.30pm, Sat 9am-4pm) and a Boots **pharmacy** (Mon-Sat 8am-7pm, Sun 11am-5pm), while closer to the river on Thames St is a Londis **supermarket** (Mon-Fri 6am-midnight, Sat 7am-midnight, Sun 7am-11pm) with **ATM**. There

are also ATMs along High St and scattered about the town.

Transport
Windsor is well-linked to the outside world as well as other Thames Path destinations by its **two railway stations** – GWR trains run from **Windsor and Eton Central** to London Paddington, while South Western Railway serves **Windsor and Eton Riverside** from London Waterloo (see box pp52-3) – as well as by **bus** (10 & 16/16A; see pp58-9). Green Line Coaches 702 service (see box p54) also calls here.

Where to stay
A couple of **B&Bs** exist within walking distance of the river. Recommended locally is *Langton House* (☎ 01753-858299, 🖥 langtonhouse.co.uk; 2D/1D or T/1Tr/1Qd, one en suite, rest with private facilities; WI-FI; 46 Alma Rd), where the rate (£37.50-52.50pp, sgl/sgl occ from £65/79) includes a continental breakfast; a full English is an additional £6.50.

Also worth considering is *Charles House* (☎ 01753-831433, 🖥 accommodationinwindsor.co.uk; 2D/2D or T; ☛; WI-FI;

❏ Windsor Castle
An official residence of Elizabeth II, Her Majesty the Queen, Windsor Castle is the oldest and largest occupied castle in Europe. Similar to the castles that the Normans built upstream at Wallingford and Oxford in order to control the river's populace in its upper reaches, the castle at Windsor was built between 1070 and 1086 both to protect the Thames valley and also to guard the western approaches to London.

As with other Norman fortifications, Windsor was originally designed as a motte-and-bailey castle and built with timber, the defences gradually being replaced with stone. Since the time of William the Conqueror's son, Henry I (1100-1135), Windsor Castle has been used by 39 English and British monarchs, many of whom have added extra buildings and rooms to it, each one contributing to its size and grandeur. During the English Civil War (1642-1651) it was controlled by the Parliamentarians who imprisoned Charles I within its walls and during the following Restoration (1660-1688) much of it was rebuilt by Charles II. Huge expense was lavished on the castle by George III (1760-1820) and George IV (1820-30) and much of the current design – including the magnificent State Apartments, which are one of the sections of the castle which can be visited – dates back to this time. Queen Victoria (1837-1901) used the castle to host bountiful royal events and the Second World War saw it used as a refuge for the royal family, protecting them from the might of the German war machine just as it had protected King John eight centuries earlier during the First Barons' War (1215-1217).

£40-57.50pp, sgl occ £70-105; 89 Arthur Rd). Breakfast is not provided but if requested in advance a 'quick' breakfast (£3 for cereal and juice) will be left in the fridge which is a feature of each of the rooms.

A **hotel** with some spectacular rooms overlooking the river is the *Sir Christopher Wren* (☎ 01753-442400, 🖳 sirchristopher wren.co.uk; 7S/102D/24D or T; 🛏; WI-FI; Thames St). B&B normally costs from £67.50pp (sgl/sgl occ from about £100) although these prices can fluctuate dramatically depending on the time of year.

Where to eat and drink
Windsor's streets are lined with cafés, pubs and restaurants: indeed, it is said that there are 140 places in which you can eat here.

If you have the energy to climb towards the castle, we think *Café Copia* (☎ 01753-424290, 🖳 cafecopia.co.uk; WI-FI; 🐾; Mon-Sat 8am-5pm, Sun 10am-5pm; 23 Thames St) is a good bet; it is dog-friendly and with comfortable chairs in which to enjoy a coffee and one of their tasty savoury wraps (from £5.95).

Further up the hill, *Limes* (☎ 07563-927024, 🖳 limesbakery.com; Mon-Fri 10am-3pm, Sat to 4pm, Sun 10.30am-4pm; 2 Market St) describes itself as a 'dine-in bakery' and the selection of cakes is unsurprisingly large, including a homemade scone with a filling of your choice and a hot drink for £5.95. But they also do lunches including Spanish omelette and homemade quiche of the day (both £7.25).

Amongst the **pubs** serving **food** are *The Carpenter's Arms* (☎ 01753-863739, 🖳 nicholsonspubs.co.uk; WI-FI; 🐾 bar area; food daily noon-10pm; Market St) with hearty dishes such as Gloucester Old Spot sausages & mash (£9.75) and grilled lamb chops (£14.25); and *The Royal Oak* (☎ 01753-865179, 🖳 royaloakwindsor .com; WI-FI; 🐾 in bar only; food Mon-Fri noon-3pm & 5-10pm, Sat noon-10pm, Sun to 9pm; Datchet Rd). The main menu, available in both the bar and the restaurant, includes pie of the day (£12-14). There's also another link in the *Bel and the Dragon* (☎ 01753-866056, 🖳 belandthedragon-windsor.co.uk; food Mon-Sat noon-5pm &

6-10pm, Sun noon-9pm) chain, conveniently situated on the corner of Thames St and Datchet Rd. In addition to their usual bar menu they also serve afternoon tea (from £26 for two people, up to £46 with champagne too) but this must be reserved in advance.

On the climb up to the castle via Thames St, one of the finest establishments in which to enjoy a meal is *The Duchess of Cambridge* (☎ 01753-864405, 🖳 the duchessofcambridgepub.co.uk; food Mon-Fri 11am-10pm, Sat 10am-10pm, Sun to 9pm; WI-FI; Nos 3-4). They offer tapas-style sharing bundles (£5.95 per dish, or £19.50 for four) including duck croquettes, and rolled vine leaves, as well as burgers, steaks and a decent vegetarian selection.

Amongst the cheapest pubs to eat in is Windsor's Wetherspoon's: *The King and Castle* (☎ 01753-625120, 🖳 jdwetherspoon .com; food daily 8am-11pm; WI-FI; 15-16 Thames St).

As the path follows the river out of Windsor you'll come across *The Boatman* (☎ 01753-620010, 🖳 boatmanwindsor.com; WI-FI; 🐾 on lead, bar only; food daily noon-9pm, winter Sun to 6pm) which opened in April 2015 and was previously called The Riverhouse. Serving what they describe as a Classic British menu, expect dishes such as fillet of salmon, creamy spinach & new potato cake (£15.95), and lamb shoulder, mash & green beans (£17.95).

Bella Italia (☎ 01753-852288, 🖳 bella italia.co.uk; Mon-Thur 11.30am-10pm, Fri 11.30am-11pm, Sat 9am-11pm, Sun 9am-9.30pm; WI-FI; No 30), at Royal Windsor Station, and *Thai Square* (☎ 01753-868900, 🖳 thaisq.com/restaurants; Mon-Fri noon-2.30pm & 6-10.30pm, Sat noon-10.30pm, Sun noon-10pm; WI-FI; No 29) represent their countries with pasta dishes (£8.29-13.29) and tasty Thai meals (eg chicken green curry £8.75) respectively.

For something completely different, *Lebanese Nights* (☎ 01753-832333, 🖳 leb anesenights.co.uk; Mon-Thur 5.30-10pm, Fri noon-3pm & 5.30-10pm, Sat & Sun noon-10pm; 41 Thames St) offers some delicious Middle Eastern fare, including *lahem meshwi* (char-grilled lamb cubes with shallots, tomatoes, peppers & flat bread; £12.95); note they have belly dancing most nights, and on Friday & Saturday there is a £15 minimum spend. They also offer a **takeaway**. Fish & chips can be sourced from either *Riverside Fish 'n' Chips* (daily 10am-6/7pm), or nearby *Mamma Mia* (☎ 01753-620166, 💻 mam mamiacafe.weebly.com; daily 8.30am-9.30pm).

WINDSOR TO CHERTSEY BRIDGE [MAPS 59-64]

This **12-mile (19.5km, 4-5¼hrs)** stage begins with a riverside stroll through **Home Park** (Map 59), the tranquillity of which feels a far cry from the tourist-packed streets of Windsor. En route there are some majestic views of Windsor Castle over your shoulder.

Having switched banks to skirt the village of **Datchet** (see below) the path crosses to the southern bank again, toying with the outskirts of **Old Windsor** (see p186; Map 60) before entering Surrey to arrive at **Runnymede** (see pp186-7; Map 61), the site of the signing of the Magna Carta in 1215 (see box p186).

Another, more modern reminder of humanity's progress soon appears as you pass below the roaring **M25 motorway** (Map 62). People have climbed up the bank, over the fence and onto the pavement of the M25 (there is one) for a better view (and photo opportunity) over **Bell Weir Lock**. Of course, I can't condone such actions but the possibility is there if you want...

The trail continues to hug the Thames, crossing the water again between **Egham** (see p187) and **Staines** (see p190) – this section actually offering some surprisingly attractive ambling – to arrive at **Penton Hook Lock** (Map 63). The adjacent **Penton Hook Island** was created by the construction of the lock in 1815 and is home to heron and water vole amongst other wildlife.

Having passed **Laleham** (see p190) and beneath the M3 motorway you arrive at **Chertsey Bridge** (see p190; Map 64). Chertsey is on the opposite bank; there are some services by the bridge but the main part of town is a 15- to 20-minute walk along the road.

DATCHET [Map 59, p179]

The Candy Box General Stores (Mon-Fri 5.50am-9pm, Sat & Sun 7am-9pm; High St) sells basic goods and has an **ATM** (£1.75).

Just up the street on the corner is a second and larger general store, **Datchet Food & Wine** (Mon-Sat 8am-10pm, Sun 9am-10pm) which when we visited was on the cusp of opening its own takeaway pizza service (£6.49-15.99 depending on size and number of toppings). On Horton Rd is Datchet **Pharmacy** (Mon-Fri 9am-6pm, Sat 9am-1pm).

Bus No 10 (see box pp58-9) runs between Datchet, Windsor and Heathrow Airport. Datchet is also a stop on South Western Railway's **train** services to Windsor & Eton Riverside (see pp52-3).

Hotel accommodation can be found at *The Manor* (☎ 01753-543442, 💻 themanor windsor.com; 2S/10T/43D; ➹; WI-FI; £50-120pp, sgl from £90, sgl occ room rate). Rates exclude breakfast (£9.95pp).

Centrally, caffeine fixes can be had at *Bridge Coffee Shop* (Mon-Fri 9am-5pm, Sat 9.30am-3pm; WI-FI), a very inexpensive place (a hot chocolate is only £1, for example, and sandwiches are only £2) with friendly staff. There's also a branch of *Costa* (Mon-Fri 6.30am-6.30pm, Sat to 4.30pm, Sun 8am-6.30pm); whilst for something more substantial *The Royal Stag* (☎ 01753-584231; food Mon-Sat noon-9.45pm, Sun to 7.45pm; WI-FI; 🐾) has plenty of dishes fit for walkers including burgers (from £9.95) and spicy Ligurian fish stew (£14.50).

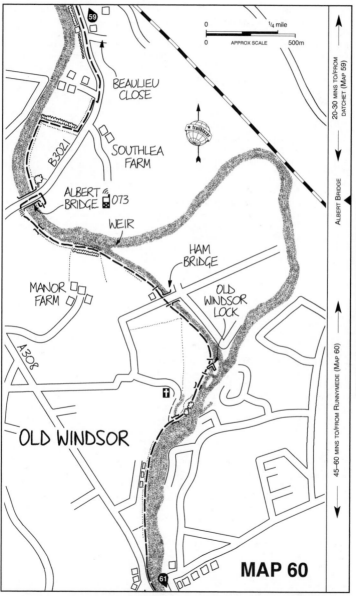

BEAULIEU
CLOSE

B3021

SOUTHLEA
FARM

ALBERT
BRIDGE 073

WEIR

HAM
BRIDGE

OLD
WINDSOR
LOCK

MANOR
FARM

A308

OLD WINDSOR

MAP 60

0 ¼ mile

0 500m

APPROX SCALE

★ trailblazer

20-30 MINS TO/FROM DATCHET (MAP 59)

◀ ALBERT BRIDGE

ROUTE GUIDE AND MAPS

45-60 MINS TO/FROM RUNNYMEDE (MAP 60)

59

61

OLD WINDSOR
[Map 60, p185; Map 61]

There is evidence that Windsor was inhabited long before the first wood was cut for the Conqueror's timber castle (see box p182). Recorded in the *Anglo-Saxon Chronicle*, the original Windsor was home to a Saxon palace owned by Edward the Confessor.

RUNNYMEDE [Map 61]

The **site of the signing of Magna Carta**, there is the opportunity here to divert from the path and view the John F Kennedy and Magna Carta monuments (see box below).

The Bells of Ouzeley (☎ 01753-861526, 🖳 harvester.co.uk/thebellsofouzeleyoldwindsor; **food** daily 9am-10pm; WI-FI) offers a huge range of food and several special deals including an earlybird special (Mon-Fri 11.30am-5pm) where all mains are £6.99.

Bus route No 8 (FBBTV; see pp58-9) stops outside the pub.

A good old-fashioned brew can be had at *National Trust Magna Carta Tearoom* (Apr-Oct daily 10am-5pm, limited hours in winter; WI-FI). There are plenty of picnic

---

❏ Runnymede and the Magna Carta

King Richard I (aka Richard the Lionheart; 1189-99) spent most of his reign abroad, crusading in Palestine and fighting in France. Following his death from a crossbow wound in 1199 the rule of England fell on the shoulders of his younger brother, King John (1199-1216). He would not be a popular monarch. In the early 13th century the country was run according to feudal law with the king relying on his barons for both money – which they gathered through taxation – and men to fight in his foreign wars. Tradition dictated that before new taxes were imposed on the populace they first had to have the consent of the barons. This relationship worked as long as the king's foreign escapades were successful. John, however, would not be a successful military campaigner and he began to lose his grip on the lands he owned in northern France.

Eager to win back these French territories, in 1214 John returned from France to oversee the imposition of even higher taxes on his subjects to fund his fighting. But on this occasion he did so without consulting his barons. As a result they rebelled and quickly captured London from the hapless monarch, though they failed to win a decisive victory against their king. A stalemate ensued until by the spring of 1215 the two sides were ready to discuss terms. They would meet at Runnymede in June and the terms to which both parties agreed would become known as the **Magna Carta**.

Latin for 'Great Charter', the document consisted of a number of guarantees given to the barons by the king. It was primarily concerned with the English legal system and amongst its clauses was one that gave everyone, irrespective of wealth, access to the courts of law. Future adaptations would state that no one could be imprisoned without first having the proper rule of law applied in deciding their guilt. Today the charter is seen as one of the foundations of civil liberty – indeed, a first step towards democracy itself – and it has influenced the constitutions of many nations.

In the meadows of **Runnymede** (☎ 01784-432891, 🖳 nationaltrust.org.uk/runnymede) today there are some monuments which are worth a detour from the path (Map 61). The **Magna Carta Monument** was erected by the American Bar Association in 1957 and is surrounded with informative boards for those who wish to know more. Commemorating a more willing supporter of civil liberty than King John, The **John F Kennedy Memorial**, along with the acre of land which surrounds it, was gifted to the people of the USA by Queen Elizabeth II in 1965. A series of 12 intricately worked bronze chairs by the artist Hew Locke, called *The Jurors*, was unveiled for the 800th anniversary of the signing of the Magna Carta in 2015.

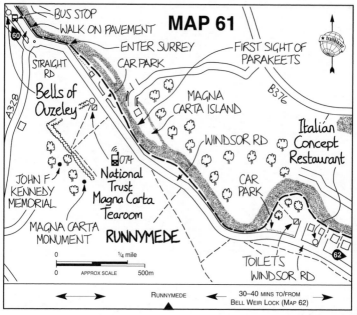

benches from which to gaze over the historic meadows and enjoy a hot drink or a cream tea; it's just a shame it's set by such a busy road. A more extensive menu is available at *Italian Concept Restaurant* (☎ 01784-432244, 🖳 italianconceptrestaurant .com; Tue-Thur 11.30am-2.45pm & 5.30-10pm, Sat 11.30am-10pm, Sun to 9pm; WI-FI; Windsor Rd) with pasta dishes and risottos (£8.95-12.95).

BELL WEIR LOCK [Map 62, p188]
Splendidly located overlooking the lock is *The Runnymede-on-Thames* (☎ 01784-220960, 🖳 runnymedehotel.com; 11S/131D/36D or T; ☞; WI-FI; 🐾 bedroom only), though the tariff (from £90pp, sgl/sgl occ from £145) is probably high enough to give the average Thames walker an aneurysm. The hotel has two **restaurants** for which booking is generally essential but you could always drop in and enquire about the possibility of afternoon tea (3-5pm; £25pp), though if you want to sit in the conservatory booking is recommended.

EGHAM [Map 62, p188]
On Egham's riverbank is *The Swan Hotel* (☎ 01784-452494, 🖳 swanstaines.co.uk; 14D/1Qd; ☞; WI-FI; 🐾; The Hythe). As well as accommodation (B&B around £63-70pp, sgl occ room rate), there is a somewhat eclectic menu (**food** Mon-Thur noon-3pm & 5-9.30pm, Fri & Sat noon-9.30pm, Sun to 8.30pm); it changes regularly but always includes standard items such as spiced green lentil curry (£12), burger (from £13) and fish & chips (£13). Close by is a **supermarket**, a large branch of Sainsbury's (Mon-Fri 7am-10pm, Sat to 9pm, Sun 10am-4pm).

Buses (FBTT 8/N8; see box pp58-9) operate to Windsor, Heathrow Airport and Staines. Egham is also a stop on several of South Western Railway's **train** services (see box pp52-3). *(cont'd on p190)*

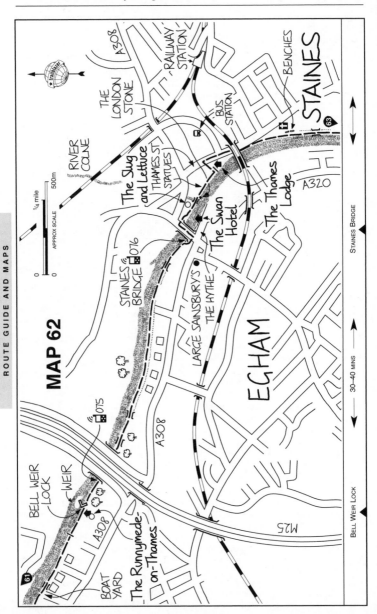

ROUTE GUIDE AND MAPS

MAP 62

APPROX SCALE

0 — 500m

0 — ¼ mile

A308

RAILWAY STATION

THE LONDON STONE

RIVER COLNE

The Slug and Lettuce

THAMES ST STATUES

BUS STATION

BENCHES

STAINES

A320

The Thames Lodge

The Swan Hotel

STAINES BRIDGE ⌂076

LARGE SAINSBURY'S

THE HYTHE

EGHAM

⌂075

A308

BELL WEIR LOCK

WEIR

The Runnymede-on-Thames

BOAT YARD

A308

61

63

STAINES BRIDGE

30-40 MINS

BELL WEIR LOCK

M25

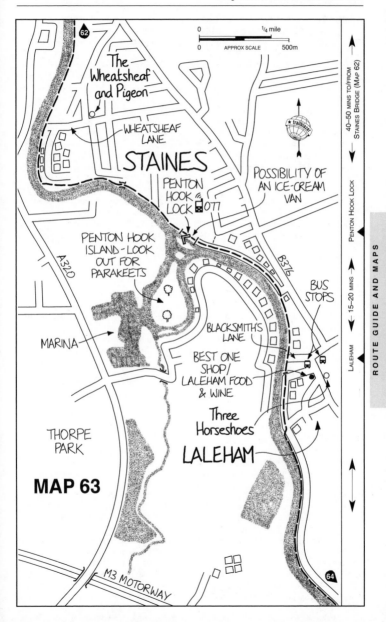

MAP 63

STAINES
[Map 62, p188; Map 63, p189]

The site of a Roman, Saxon and Norman bridge, Staines's current crossing was opened in 1832. The Roman town Ad Pontes ('By the Bridges') which once lay here is predated by evidence of a Neolithic settlement nearby. The London Stone (Map 62; see box p193) is also here. Officially the town's name is Staines-upon-Thames but it is generally referred to as Staines.

Staines is well connected by **train** (South Western Railway; see box pp52-3) to London and numerous other destinations along the Thames Path and also by **bus** (8/N8, 446 & 458); see box pp58-9.

Should you be tempted by a night by the river try *The Thames Lodge* (also known as *Mercure London Staines Hotel*; ☎ 01784-334800, 🖵 mercure.com; 78D/10D or T; 🍷; WI-FI; 🐾; Thames St). Rates vary but for a single night in summer on a room-only basis you should expect to pay from £45pp (sgl occ room rate); allow £15.50pp for breakfast.

Shortly after crossing to the Staines riverbank you pass a branch of *The Slug and Lettuce* (☎ 01784-456914, 🖵 slugand lettuce.co.uk; food daily 10am-10pm; WI-FI; 🐾 terrace area only) chain.

If you'd prefer a **pub** dealing in real ale and home-made food fear not: a short diversion from the path is *The Wheatsheaf and Pigeon* (Map 63; ☎ 01784-452922, 🖵 wheatsheafandpigeon.co.uk; food Tue-Fri noon-2.30pm & 6-9pm, Sat noon-9pm, Sun noon-4pm; WI-FI; 🐾). A bustling place with a great variety of house and guest ales and meals such as slow-roasted ribs (£9 for half a rack, £13 for a full rack), this is the type of place of which real-ale-powered ramblers dream.

LALEHAM   [Map 63, p189; Map 64]

On Shepperton Rd there is both a **shop**, Laleham Food & Wine (Mon-Sat 6am-6.30pm, Sun 9am-2pm) and a pub; *Three Horseshoes* (Map 63; ☎ 01784-455014, 🖵 threehorseshoeslaleham.co.uk; food Sun-Thur noon-9.30pm, Fri & Sat to 10pm; WI-FI; 🐾 bar area). The lunch menu includes a steak sandwich (£8.50) and Welsh rarebit (£8.95). **Bus** service No 458 (see box pp58-9) stops nearby.

Laleham Camping Club (Map 64; ☎ 01932-564149, 🖵 lalehamcampingclub.co.uk; from £10pp; WI-FI intermittent; 🐾 on lead and not unattended; Apr-early Oct; Thames Side) may seem tempting to some but it's a large family-orientated site and you're likely to find peace and relaxation far easier to come by if you continue to the site at Chertsey (see below).

CHERTSEY

Etymologically the 'island of Cerotus', Chertsey was originally a small parcel of land surrounded by marsh, the Thames and its tributary streams. Who Cerotus was remains a mystery; what *is* known, however, is that despite being pillaged twice by the Vikings – and rebuilt by Saxon King Edgar in AD964 – the Benedictine Abbey of St Peter, founded here in AD666, was once the wealthiest religious house in Surrey. The abbey's monks established the town here – one of England's oldest – in the 12th century. Keeping the story alive is **Chertsey Museum** (☎ 01932-565764, 🖵 www.chertseymuseum.org; Tue-Fri 12.30-4.30pm, Sat 11am-4pm; 33 Windsor St; free), about a 20-minute walk from the river.

Chertsey's **railway** station is a stop on South Western Railway's services (see box pp52-3) to London Waterloo; **bus** Nos 446, 456 & 457 (see box pp58-90) also call here.

Staying near to the river, however, you will find a BP petrol station on Bridge Rd which has a Spar **shop** (24hrs). *Chertsey Camping & Caravanning Club* (☎ 01932-562405, 🖵 campingandcaravanningclub.co.uk/Chertsey; WI-FI; 🐾) is perfectly located

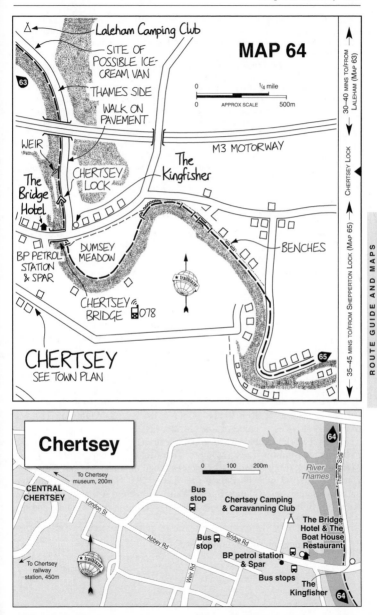

MAP 64

Laleham Camping Club

SITE OF POSSIBLE ICE-CREAM VAN

THAMES SIDE

WALK ON PAVEMENT

63

0   ¼ mile
0   APPROX SCALE   500m

30–40 MINS TO/FROM LALEHAM (MAP 63)

CHERTSEY LOCK

WEIR

M3 MOTORWAY

The Kingfisher

CHERTSEY LOCK

The Bridge Hotel

DUMSEY MEADOW

BENCHES

BP PETROL STATION & SPAR

CHERTSEY BRIDGE 078

65

35–45 MINS TO/FROM SHEPPERTON LOCK (MAP 65)

CHERTSEY
SEE TOWN PLAN

ROUTE GUIDE AND MAPS

Chertsey

To Chertsey museum, 200m

CENTRAL CHERTSEY

London St

Abbey Rd

To Chertsey railway station, 450m

Weir Rd

0   100   200m

Bus stop

Bus stop

Bridge Rd

Chertsey Camping & Caravanning Club

BP petrol station & Spar

Bus stops

River Thames

Thames Side

64

The Bridge Hotel & The Boat House Restaurant

The Kingfisher

64

a short way from the bridge. The rate for a non-member walker is £9·25pp. At weekends (Apr-Nov Fri & Sat evenings) there is often a **takeaway van** on site selling fish & chips and burgers; also breakfasts in peak season (July & Aug Sat & Sun mornings).

The most convenient **B&B** for trail walkers is *The Bridge Hotel* (☎ 01932-565644, 🖳 bridgehotelchertsey.com; 44D or T; ☞; WI-FI). The price (£20.50-56.50pp, sgl occ full room rate) can vary drastically depending on the season so booking online in advance is advised. Breakfast costs £7.50pp for residents if booked at the time of booking, £9 if booked at check in and £9.95 on the day. The hotel's restaurant,

The Boat House (Mon-Fri 7-10am & noon-9.15pm, Sat 8-10am & noon-9.30pm, Sun 8-10am & noon-9pm), overlooks the Thames; the food is classic British fare with braised beef cheek & creamy mash priced at £15.

Pub food by the bridge is available from *The Kingfisher* (Map 64; ☎ 01932-579811, 🖳 thekingfisherchertsey.co.uk; food Mon-Sat noon-9.45pm, Sun noon-8.45pm; WI-FI; 🐾 in bar area). There's a reasonable outside dining area from which you can consider both the river and the menu, which may include such delights as king prawn, crab & chorizo linguine (£13.50).

CHERTSEY BRIDGE TO KINGSTON UPON THAMES [MAPS 64-69]

This, your final stage before you arrive in London, includes the Thames Path's solitary **ferry** crossing (see box below). For any arch-landlubbers who would prefer to boycott the boat there is the option of sticking to dry land and following an **alternative route**. Utilising the ferry will lead to your day being **11¼ miles (18.2km, 3¾-4¾hrs)**, while undertaking the whole section on foot makes for a slightly longer **12-mile (19.5km, 4-5hrs)** hike.

The day begins by passing through **Dumsey Meadow** (Map 64), an SSSI (see box p70), before arriving at **Shepperton Lock** (see p194; Map 65) and the point at which you need to make a choice: foot or ferry? While the pedestrian option includes a visit to **Shepperton** (see p194), the route is convoluted and at times hard to follow; if you choose this option keep your eyes peeled for National Trail acorns and follow Map 65 carefully. For this reason you would be well-advised to take the ferry (see box below) if possible. Opting for this then involves a simple walk along the opposite riverbank before both routes eventually meet at **Walton Bridge**. Once at the bridge, **Walton-on-Thames** (see p194) provides amenities a short stroll away.

From the bridge the path embarks on a straightforward journey along the riverbank via **Sunbury Lock** (Map 66), **East Molesey** (see p194; Map 67) and **Molesey Lock** (Map 68) to the London Borough of Richmond and **Hampton Court** (see p194) with its **Palace** (see box p198). The path here skirts the palace's grounds and follows **Barge Walk**, an historic towpath, to arrive at **Kingston Bridge** (Map 69) – some 150 miles from the river's source and the

---

❏ **The Shepperton to Weybridge Ferry**
When requested (by ringing the bell), the ferry (£2.50/4 single/return; 🐾; Apr-Sep weekdays 8am-6pm, Sat 9am-6pm, Sun 10am-6pm; Oct-Mar weekdays 8.30am-5.30pm, Sat 9am-5pm, Sun 10am-5pm) runs every 15 minutes and takes less than five minutes to cross the river. For further information call ☎ 01932-221094.

gateway to **London** (see box below). However, if, after so long spent on the riverbank, the chaos of England's primary metropolis is too much to face, consider spending the night on the western bank in laidback **Hampton Wick** (see p200), or in **Kingston** itself (see p201).

❏ So where does London begin?

As you leave Staines on the Thames Path you come across several statues and monuments. One, however, though plain in design, causes many a walker to pause and examine it in greater detail. This is the **London Stone** (see Map 62), a pillar that once marked the limits of jurisdiction of the City of London. It could thus be interpreted as a border post between London and the rest of the country. The site of the stone was chosen because it was here, a couple of times a day, that the high tide could be perceived. Beyond this, therefore, the City had no rights over the land or the parishes that lay beyond. (The pillar is in fact a mere copy, the original having been moved to Spelthorne Museum in Staines in 2004.) But it did leave us to wonder where the actual border of the capital lies today?

As it transpired, there is no easy answer to this, though there are several candidates. **Teddington**, widely regarded as the home of the last lock on the Thames (we're ignoring Richmond here for the moment, whose lock is only usable at low tide) and from where, today, the Thames becomes tidal, is an obvious choice; there's a **monument** (see Map 71) just past the lock on the southern side of the Thames that marks the point where the Port of London Authority takes over from the Thames Conservancy (a body which is now part of the Environment Agency).

Another possibility is **Kingston-upon-Thames**, which describes itself as 'the Gateway to London' and which many walkers believe has a more metropolitan 'feel' than its upriver rivals. But there are those who consider everything that lies within the M25 as being part of London, and thus would argue that a Thames Path walker will enter the city just after Runnymede, on Map 62, where the motorway crosses the trail. And then, of course, a little further on there's **Staines**, which is the location of the London Stone and which enjoys many of the benefits of London living. These 'benefits' include being part of the London Transport network – further evidence, in some people's eyes, that Staines is part of the capital – with the No 290 bus running between it and Twickenham. But others will argue that you aren't actually in London unless you're can catch the Underground network into the centre – which means that **Richmond** would be the first place that Thames Path trekkers enter the city, it being the first place on the trail with a tube station.

As you can see from the above, the actual boundary of London depends on which definition of 'London' you use. If you're looking at the **Greater London** area, the administrative area that's organised into 33 government districts (32 boroughs and the City of London*) and covers an area of 1572 sq km (607 sq miles) and has a population of 8,174,000 according to the 2011-12 census, Thames Path walkers actually reach the border at West Molesey (see Map 67). Molesey is actually outside the boundary, though across the river the district of Hampton is *within* Greater London. However, those walking the Thames Path won't actually cross the border into Greater London until they cross the bridge before Hampton Court (see Map 68). If you're looking at the **Greater London Built-up Area**, however (which in 2011 had a population of 9,787,426), the boundaries are a little less clear. In this definition, however, Staines does form part of the metropolis, as do both Shepperton and Walton-on-Thames.

*The City of London, also known as the 'Square Mile', is the part of London which was originally within the city walls; it incorporates the central business district. See also p201.

SHEPPERTON LOCK [Map 65]

Just before the lock is *The Thames Court* (☎ 01932-221957, 🖳 vintageinn.co.uk; **food** served Mon-Sat noon-10pm, Sun noon-9.30pm; WI-FI; 🐾 bar only). The lunch menu includes a large smoked haddock kedgeree fishcake with broccoli, roasted vine tomatoes & a basil dressing (£10.95) as well as sandwiches and burgers (£5.95-12.75).

Actually at the lock is *Riverside Refreshments* (daily noon-5pm) where a mug of tea is £1.60.

SHEPPERTON [Map 65]

The final resting place of poet Thomas Love Peacock and also long the home of writer JG Ballard (1930-2009), this small village has a few fine establishments in which to eat and sleep; amongst them is *The Anchor Hotel* (☎ 01932-242748, 🖳 anchorhotel.co.uk; 1S/9D/2T; ☞; WI-FI in public area; 🐾 bar only; Church Sq) where **B&B** costs £25-35.50pp (sgl/sgl occ from £50). On the menu (**food** Mon-Sat noon-2pm & 6-9pm, Sun noon-4pm) are salmon fishcakes & fries (£11.50) and pork chop with apple fritter (£11.90).

Shepperton is a stop on the Nos 458, 555 & 557 **bus** services (see box pp58-9); it is also connected by **train** to London Waterloo (South Western Railway; see box pp52-3).

WALTON-ON-THAMES
[Map 65; Map 66, p196]

Take a five-minute walk away from the river along New Zealand Avenue and you'll find a **shopping plaza** with a Sainsbury's **supermarket** (Mon-Sat 7am-10pm, Sun 11am-5pm), a free **ATM** and branches of *Costa* (Mon-Sat 7am-7.30pm, Sun 8am-6.30pm) and *Starbuck's*. There are numerous other chain cafés and food outlets; however, if you want to stick by the river *Café Gino* (daily 8am-7.30pm; cash only), just before the bridge, is perfectly acceptable and has full English breakfasts for £6.50 as well as a clear view to the river.

For **accommodation**, shortly before Sunbury Lock, **B&B** (and food) can be found at *The Weir Hotel* (Map 66; ☎ 01932-784530, 🖳 weirhotel.co.uk; 4D/2T; ☞; WI-FI; 🐾 restaurant only; £47.50-70pp, sgl occ room rate). **Food** (Mon-Sat 11.30am-9.30pm, Sun 12.30-7.30pm) is available all day.

Keep to the river rather than heading along New Zealand Avenue and you'll soon arrive at **Walton Wharf** and two pubs: *The Anglers* (☎ 01932-223996, 🖳 classicinns .co.uk; WI-FI; 🐾; food daily 10am-10pm) has an imaginative menu which may include pear and pecorino pasta (£13.29); they also do sandwiches (from £8.49 for prawn focaccia) and also afternoon teas; whilst *The Swan* (☎ 01932-225964, 🖳 swanwalton.com; food Mon-Thur noon-9.30pm, Fri & Sat to 10pm, Sun to 8pm; WI-FI; 🐾 in bar) also has a plethora of dishes and even its own burger shack (May-Sep); try the soft-shell crab burger with Devon crab mayo & fries (£18) but beer-battered cod & chips (£14.50) is also available.

Bus services 458 & 461 (see pp58-9) call here as do **trains** on the London Waterloo to Woking line (South Western Railway; see box pp52-3).

EAST MOLESEY/HAMPTON COURT
[Map 67, p197; Map 68, p198]

Amongst the **cafés** here are *Thyme by the River Café* (Map 67; ☎ 020-8941 1777, 🖳 thymebytheriver.com; daily 8.30am-5.30pm; WI-FI; 🐾), which moved into Molesey Boat Club in March 2018; it produces some wonderful coffees and a mean Welsh rarebit (£6.95). A bit further along is *The Molesey Lock Café* (Map 68; ☎ 07836-296189, 🖳 molesey-lock-cafe.busi ness.site; Apr-mid Oct Tue-Sun 9am-5pm; WI-FI; 🐾), where baguettes (from £4) are also reasonably priced. Near the bridge are *Mada Deli* (Mon-Tue 7am-6pm, Wed-Sun

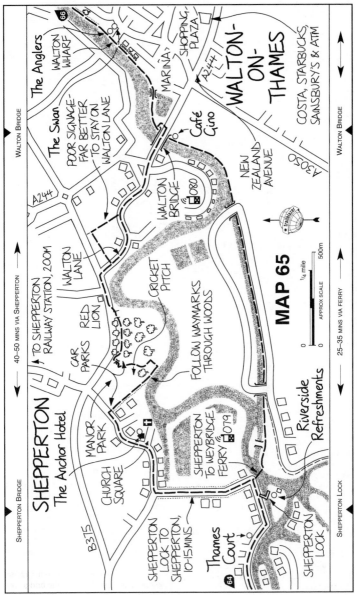

SHEPPERTON BRIDGE

SHEPPERTON
The Anchor Hotel

B315

Church Square

Manor Park

Shepperton Lock to Shepperton, 10–15 mins

Thames Court

64

Shepperton to Weybridge Ferry 079

Car Parks

Red Lion

TO SHEPPERTON RAILWAY STATION, 200M

Walton Lane

Cricket Pitch

Follow Waymarks Through Woods

Riverside Refreshments

40–50 MINS VIA SHEPPERTON

The Swan

The Anglers

Walton Wharf

Walton Bridge

POOR SIGNAGE– FAR BETTER TO STAY ON WALTON LANE

A244

Walton Bridge 080

MARINA

SHOPPING PLAZA

66

Café Cino

New Zealand Avenue

WALTON-ON-THAMES

A244

A3050

Costa, Starbucks, Sainsbury's & ATM

WALTON BRIDGE

MAP 65

0   ¼ mile
0   APPROX SCALE   500m

25–35 MINS VIA FERRY

SHEPPERTON LOCK

Shepperton Lock

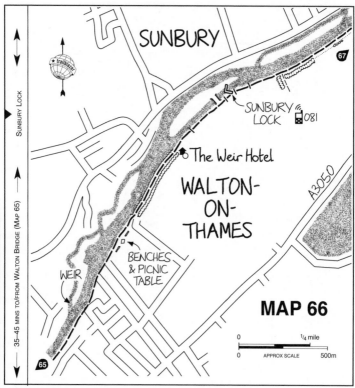

SUNBURY

SUNBURY LOCK 081

The Weir Hotel

WALTON-ON-THAMES

BENCHES & PICNIC TABLE

WEIR

MAP 66

0   1/4 mile

0   APPROX SCALE   500m

SUNBURY LOCK

35–45 MINS TO/FROM WALTON BRIDGE (MAP 65)

65

---

to 10.30pm; WI-FI; 🐾), where there is a fine mixture of gourmet open sandwiches (£7.80) such as spicy sausage with goat's cheese & roasted peppers; and *Henry's Kitchen* (☎ 020-8783 1020, 🖳 henrykitchen .co.uk; Mon-Tue 8am-6pm, Wed to 8.30pm, Thur-Sat 8am-10pm, Sun 8am-8pm; WI-FI), at which you'll find more substantial meals such as beef & guinness pie (£14.95).

Real ale and classic **pub food** such as gammon steak (£9.29) is to be found hidden a little further along Bridge Rd at *The Albion* (☎ 020-8783 9342, 🖳 emberinns.co .uk; food daily noon-9.45pm; WI-FI; 🐾).

Hampton Court Superstore (daily 8am-10pm) is a **convenience store** with an **ATM** £1.95).

Both Hampton (Map 67) and Hampton Court (Map 68) **railway stations** are stops on South Western Railway's services to London Waterloo but they are on different lines (see box pp52-3). The 411 & 461 **bus** services (see box pp58-9) stop at either end of Hampton Court Bridge.

In the summer months **Hampton Ferry** (🖳 hamptonferryboathouse.co.uk/ Ferry; Apr to end Oct Mon-Fri 7.45am-6pm, Sat & Sun 11am-6pm; £2/3 single/ return, 🐾 free) provides a convenient link from Hampton to Hurst Park (Map 67), though services are dependent on the weather and river conditions. This has operated since the 16th century and is the oldest ferry service on the Thames.

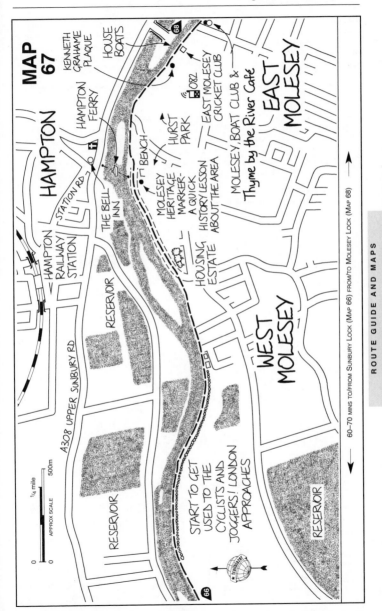

MAP 67

HAMPTON

KENNETH GRAHAME PLAQUE

HOUSE BOATS

HAMPTON FERRY

HAMPTON RAILWAY STATION

STATION RD.

A308 UPPER SUNBURY RD.

THE BELL INN

RESERVOIR

RESERVOIR

RESERVOIR

HOUSING ESTATE

WEST MOLESEY

BENCH

MOLESEY HERITAGE MARKER - A QUICK HISTORY LESSON ABOUT THE AREA

HURST PARK

EAST MOLESEY CRICKET CLUB

MOLESEY BOAT CLUB & Thyme by the River Café

EAST MOLESEY

START TO GET USED TO THE JOGGERS! LONDON APPROACHES

CYCLISTS AND

¼ mile
APPROX SCALE
0   500m

60–70 MINS TO/FROM SUNBURY LOCK (MAP 66) FROM/TO MOLESEY LOCK (MAP 68)

Hampton Court side Crossing the bridge you enter the London Borough of Richmond-upon-Thames (see box p193) and Hampton Court Palace (see box below). Opposite the palace gates is *Mitre*

Hotel (☎ 020-8979 9988, 🖳 mitrehampton court.com; 35D or T/1Qd; most en suite, rest private bathroom; ●; WI-FI; 🐾). The building was originally commissioned by Charles II in the 17th century to house the

---

❏ Hampton Court Palace

King Henry VIII's chief advisor Cardinal Wolsey began construction of the lavish palace here in 1514 and both the buildings and grounds are steeped in royal history.

Entry to the palace (☎ 020-3166 6000, 🖳 hrp.org.uk/HamptonCourtPalace; Mar-Oct daily 10am-6pm, Nov-Mar to 4.30pm), maze and gardens costs £22.70 (maze only £4.20, £7 with the magic garden in the summer months). The rates quoted above are what you would pay at the gate; if booked online in advance the cost is £19.20.

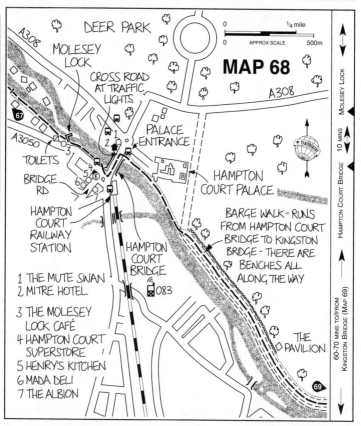

ROUTE GUIDE AND MAPS

DEER PARK

A308

MOLESEY LOCK

CROSS ROAD AT TRAFFIC LIGHTS

MAP 68

A308

67

A3050

TOILETS

PALACE ENTRANCE

BRIDGE RD

HAMPTON COURT RAILWAY STATION

HAMPTON COURT BRIDGE

HAMPTON COURT PALACE

★ trailblaze

BARGE WALK - RUNS FROM HAMPTON COURT BRIDGE TO KINGSTON BRIDGE - THERE ARE BENCHES ALL ALONG THE WAY

083

1 THE MUTE SWAN
2 MITRE HOTEL
3 THE MOLESEY LOCK CAFÉ
4 HAMPTON COURT SUPERSTORE
5 HENRY'S KITCHEN
6 MADA DELI
7 THE ALBION

THE PAVILION

69

0 ¼ mile
0 500m APPROX SCALE

MOLESEY LOCK

10 MINS

HAMPTON COURT BRIDGE

60-70 MINS TO/FROM KINGSTON BRIDGE (MAP 69)

guests who couldn't be accommodated at the palace. **B&B** rates vary depending on availability but as a guide expect to pay a minimum of £50pp (sgl occ full room rate) for B&B. Next door is *The Mute Swan* (☎ 020-8941 5959, 🖥 brunningandprice.co.uk; food

Mon-Sat noon-10pm, Sun to 9.30pm; WI-FI; 🐾). A classy joint, the sandwich menu (daily to 5pm; £6.95-9.95) may include a roast pepper, cream cheese & basil toasted bagel as well as a slow-roasted duck & plum sauce wrap.

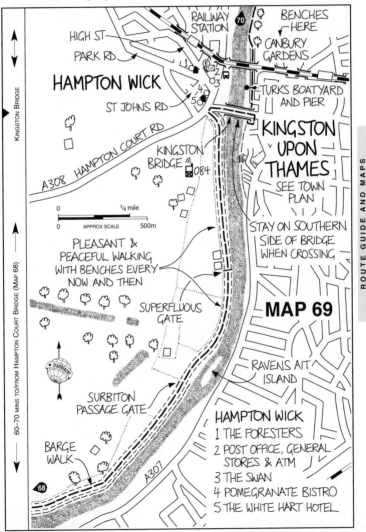

ROUTE GUIDE AND MAPS

HAMPTON WICK [Map 69, p199]

The site of a Roman ford, the first wooden bridge to cross the Thames here dates from 1219, though this is not the structure you see today, of course.

Once just a village, although now incorporated within the London Borough of Richmond-upon-Thames, Hampton Wick today remains a leafy and peaceful alternative to Kingston with a number of decent accommodation and dining options.

At 56-58 High St there is a **post office** and **general store** (both Mon-Sat 7am-7pm, Sun 8am-2pm) with **ATM**.

South Western Railway **trains** connect Hampton Wick to London Waterloo (see box pp52-3) and other places on the Thames Path.

Accommodation and excellent **food** are available at *The Foresters* (☎ 020-8943 5379, 🖳 the-foresters.com; 1S/2D/1T; WI-FI; 🐕 bar area only; 45 High St). The rates (£50-60pp, sgl occ room rate) are for room only; they do not provide breakfast but guests have a 10% discount in the restaurant. There are some splendid meals (food Tue-Sat noon-3pm & 6-10pm, Sun noon-5.30pm), such as lamb chops with rosemary-roasted sauté potatoes, buttered kale & jus (£17); see the hungry stampede through the door.

At 1 High St, *The White Hart Hotel* (☎ 020-8977 1786, 🖳 whitehart hoteluk.co.uk; 22D/10D or T/5Tr; 🐕; WI-FI; 🐕), a standard double costs from £42pp

---

❏ A brief history of London

The city of London owes its very existence to the Thames. When Julius Caesar and the **Romans** first arrived on the banks of what he referred to as Tamesis in 55BC (see box p44), they were not planning on settling in what was then the wild and sparsely populated Thames valley; his marching legions were merely searching for a place to ford the river. The location of this first Roman crossing point is open to much debate with Westminster and Brentford being two suggested sites. A century later, during the Roman Conquest of AD43, they again crossed the Thames, their traversal of the river a necessity in order to connect the Kent coast where they had landed with their garrison in Colchester. This time, however, it can be safely assumed, given the pattern of the surrounding Roman roads, that Westminster was where they crossed.

Having built a wooden bridge across the river in AD47 they then needed to establish defences to protect it, so a military encampment was placed on the northern bank to protect the crossing. With no defensive wall, this first encampment was vulnerable to attack and in AD61, the Iceni tribe of East Anglia – a force numbering around 100,000 and led by the inspirational Boudicea – destroyed the Roman settlement.

The Romans eventually regained control, of course, and rebuilt the town, adding stone defences in approximately AD100 to protect the encampment (on three sides) with the river demarcating its southern boundary. Incidentally, the area enclosed by the Romans' defensive wall measured approximately one 'square mile' – from which the city's financial district gets its nickname.

By the early 3rd century **Londinium**, as the Romans knew it, was a provincial capital and a lively port which traded with the rest of the Roman Empire. But in AD410 the Romans, with their empire in decline, left Britain and the city was abandoned. What they left behind, however, would not crumble so quickly.

The **Anglo-Saxons** from northern Europe and Scandinavia who followed in the Romans' wake initially chose not to repopulate the old Roman towns, opting instead to establish their own. **Lundenwic** – Anglo-Saxon London – was initially located approximately a mile up the river from the abandoned Roman walls (*wic* signifies a

(sgl occ rates on request) room only – but can easily climb to £100pp or more should you ramble into town during Wimbledon fortnight or one of the many other major events in the area (see pp38-9). Breakfast (Mon-Fri 7-9.30am, Sat & Sun 8-10am) costs £11.95 (£11 if booked in advance) for the full English. The place is also renowned for its **food** (daily noon-10pm); the dinner menu changes regularly but may include grilled lamb leg steak & sautéed potatoes (£21.95).

There are several **cafés** on High St, including *Pomegranate Bistro* (☎ 020-7998 8808, 🖳 pomegranatebistro.co.uk; Mon-Sat 8am-6pm, Tue-Sun 8am-10pm; WI-FI; 🐾 outside) where the menu offers an array of meals including the 'breakfast bomb' (two eggs, two rashers of bacon, two sausages, chips, tomatoes, beans & black pudding) for £7.95, to lunches (create-your-own panini for £4.95) and through to dinner (grilled salmon £10.20).

Classic **Thai food** (mains £10-15) is on offer at *The Swan* (☎ 020-8977 2644, 🖳 swanhamptonwick.co.uk; food daily noon-3pm & 5-10pm; WI-FI; 🐾; 22 High St).

KINGSTON UPON THAMES
[map p203]

With a name derived from either 'king's town' or 'king's stone' this place is undoubtedly of great historical significance. In AD838 Alfred the Great's grandfather, King Egbert, held a Great Council here and it remains the site of the first of England's

riverside trading point). The Venerable Bede (AD673-735), author of *The Ecclesiastical History of the English People*, described it as a 'bustling trading town'; but due to its location on the river, the settlement was always vulnerable to attack and the Vikings continually harassed the town.

Finally, having survived for 300 years, Lundenwic was abandoned by the Anglo-Saxon King Alfred (AD849-899) in AD886 and the settlement was moved back within the old Roman walls. From this point the city's development became one of almost continual growth until, by the early 11th century, it was by far the largest settlement in England. The Anglo-Saxons' seat of power had moved now from Winchester to London, though the Vikings, as was their wont, would continue to invade, pillage and burn down the town, on one occasion even pulling down one of the wooden Anglo-Saxon bridges (see pp228-9).

The **Viking Age** (AD793-1066) was, symbolically, at least, ended by King Harold (1022-66), whose men defeated the invading Norwegians in Yorkshire at the Battle of Stamford Bridge in 1066. But as the king's exhausted army celebrated a momentous victory, another threat was landing on England's southern shores...

Following the Battle of Hastings in 1066, the victorious Normans were refused entry to London via the city's bridge and instead had to cross upriver at Wallingford. The city, though, could not resist them for long and London inevitably fell, William the Conqueror being crowned King of England at Westminster Abbey. The arrival of the Normans would see stone used significantly for the first time since the departure of the Romans and they soon started work on the Tower of London and Old London Bridge (see pp228-9). Primarily a defensive line across the Thames rather than a crossing point, Old London Bridge prevented larger craft from continuing upriver, meaning that they had to moor – and so trade – east of the bridge. The expanse of water immediately east of London Bridge would become known as the Pool of London and develop into the greatest seaport in the world (see box p229 & p236).

Today, many of London's main historical sites are located on the river and can quite easily be incorporated into your walk along the Thames Path.

ROUTE GUIDE AND MAPS

thrones, the **king's stone**, on which at least seven of the Anglo-Saxon kings of Wessex were crowned. The actual king's stone can be seen outside the **Guildhall**.

Kingston lay on the border between the ancient kingdoms of Mercia and Wessex and following Athelstan's coronation here in AD925, and subsequent victory over the Northumbrians 12 years later, it was from this seat of power that he united and controlled the Kingdom of England – the first Saxon monarch to do so. Next to the 12th-century **All Saints Church**, the outline of the Church of St Mary – where the coronations occurred – is marked by a plaque.

Kingston Museum (🖳 kingston.gov .uk/museum; Tue, Fri & Sat 10am-5pm, Thur 10am-7pm; free; Wheatfield Way) hosts both permanent and guest exhibitions concerned with the history of the local area.

Services
Kingston has branches of most high street **banks** and **ATM**s can be found in Market Place. The **post office** is part of ARIS Convenience Store (Mon-Sat 7am-11pm, Sun 9am-10.30pm; 24-28 Eden St). The nearest **supermarket** to the bridge is Waitrose (Mon-Wed 8.30am-7pm, Thur 8.30am-9pm, Fri 8.30am-8pm, Sat 8am-7pm, Sun 11am-5pm), in the basement of the John Lewis store on Wood St, while more centrally there is an Aldi (Mon-Sat 8am-10pm, Sun 10am-4pm) just off Wheatfield Way. A **pharmacy**, Superdrug (Mon-Sat 8.30am-8pm, Thur to 9pm, Sun 11am-5pm), is on Clarence St.

The town is well connected by **bus** (services include the 411, 458 & 461; see box pp58-9) and **train** (South Western Railway; see box pp52-3) to places on the Thames Path and also the rest of London.

Where to stay
There are two branches of *Travelodge* (🖳 travelodge.co.uk) within easy walking distance of the river: London Kingston upon Thames Hotel (☎ 0871-984 6241; 27D/45D or T; 🛏; WI-FI; 🐾) at 21/23 Old London Rd; and Kingston upon Thames Central Hotel (☎ 0871-984 6428; 82D/5T/15Tr; 🛏; WI-FI; 🐾), on Wheatfield Way. Saver

rooms at both start at £35 (see p21) and booking early and online is the best way of securing a good deal.

Next door to the latter is a *Premier Inn* (☎ 0871-527 9586, 🖳 premierinn.com; 160D; 🛏; WI-FI) with Saver rates (see p21) starting from £49, but expect to pay more especially in the main season.

B&B is available at *Hermes Hotel* (☎ 020-8546 5322, 🖳 hermes-hotel.co.uk; 6S share facilities, 3D; 🛏; WI-FI; 🐾; 1 Portsmouth Rd) where the rate (£29.50-40.50pp, sgl/sgl occ from £49) depends on whether the room is en suite and/or has a river view.

If you prefer a hostel the closest is *YHA London Earl's Court* (see p220); it is less than an hour from the path by train to Wimbledon (South Western Railway; see box pp52-3) and then the District Line to West Brompton or Earl's Court; it is an easy walk from either station.

Where to eat and drink
Walkers will certainly not struggle to find food here. **Pubs** and **restaurants** line the riverbank to the south of the bridge, there are numerous **cafés** on Castle St and a selection of **food stalls** (Kingston Market) can often be found in Market Sq.

Ideally situated for **breakfast** for those staying in either of the Travelodges is *Lana's Coffee House* (Tue-Fri & Sun 8.30am-4pm, Sat & Mon to 5pm; 32 Wheatfield Way); you can get a breakfast bap (egg with sausage or bacon) for £3.50.

If you'd rather dine close to the bridge *Bill's* (☎ 020-8549 1410, 🖳 bills-website.co.uk; Mon-Sat 8am-11pm, Sun 9am-10.30pm; WI-FI; 🐾 outside; 2 Riverside Walk) is perfectly located. There's a varied breakfast menu including home-made blueberry & buttermilk pancakes (£6.95 for three). Options for the rest of the day include Bill's BBQ-style ribs (£15.50) and Thai green chicken curry (£13.50). Dogs are welcome to admire the river from the outside seating area.

There are also a few **pubs** near Kingston Bridge, amongst them is *The Bishop* (☎ 020-8546 4965, 🖳 thebishop kingston.co.uk; food Mon-Fri 11am-10pm,

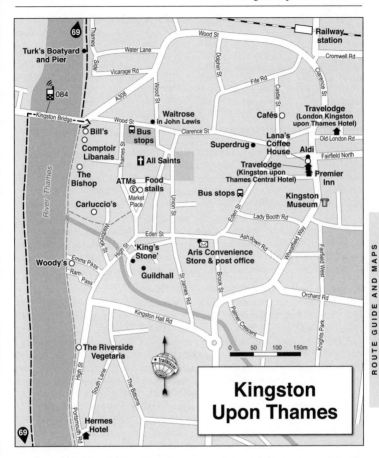

Kingston Upon Thames

Sat 10am-10pm, Sun 10am-8.30pm; WI-FI; 🐾). The menu changes regularly but usually includes a meat (£14) and fish board (£14.50), the latter including mackerel paté, scampi & cod goujons.

Also on the riverbank is *Woody's* (☎ 020-8541 4984, 🖳 woodyspubco.com; food Mon-Fri noon-10pm, Sat 10am-10pm, Sun 10am-9pm; WI-FI; 🐾) where there is a fairly standard pub menu including succulent lamb balls in a spicy tomato sauce with homemade tzatziki, Greek-style pita & mixed salad (£14).

A short way along the river (Map 70) is *The Boaters Inn* (☎ 020-8541 4672, 🖳 boaterskingston.com; food Mon-Thur noon-9pm, Fri & Sat to 10pm, Sun to 8pm; WI-FI; 🐾 on lead). Set in the perfect location for considering which side of the river to follow on the next stage, the menu varies but may offer other difficult choices such as that between the Valencian fish stew (consisting of salmon, cod, clams & a wedge of sourdough bread; £18) and pan-fried sea bream (£17). Hungry herbivores may be ecstatic to find *The Riverside Vegetaria* (☎

020-8546 7992, 🖳 riversidevegetaria.co
.uk; Mon-Sat noon-11pm, Sun to 10pm; 🐾
on terrace only; 64 High St). The award-
winning vegetarian restaurant has outdoor
tables by the river and generously priced
meals including a Caribbean casserole
(£9.95). Also near the river, *Carluccio's* (☎
020-8549 5898, 🖳 www.carluccios.com;
Mon-Sat 9am-11pm, Sun 9am-10.30pm;

WI-FI) specialises in authentic Italian meals
with most main dishes costing between
£9.50 and £15.95.
　　Lebanese cuisine is available right by
the bridge at *Comptoir Libanais* (☎ 020-
7657 1966, 🖳 comptoirlibanais.com; daily
10am-11pm; WI-FI); as well as breakfast
and lunches there's a fine variety of tagines
including a lamb kofta one (£10.95).

KINGSTON UPON THAMES TO PUTNEY BRIDGE　　　[MAPS 69-77]

Following an uncomplicated two-mile stretch to **Teddington Lock** (Map 70) –
from where the Thames becomes tidal – this stage leaves you with a decision to
make: whether to follow the southern bank (**13½ miles/21.7km** from Kingston,
4½-5¼hrs), or to cross to the northern bank (**16¼ miles/26km** from Kingston,
5¾-7hrs), to Putney Bridge. My advice, simply put, is this: take the southern
route (see below). The route along the northern bank (see pp215-20) is significantly longer and also involves a considerable amount of road walking, while
the southern bank of the Thames is also – for much of the way at least – more
'rural' (a relative term once you get this far along the path) and thus feels more
in tune with the river and path that you have already completed.

Kingston to Putney Bridge: southern bank

Having decided not to switch banks at Teddington, you follow the shores of
Ham Lands Nature Reserve (Map 71). As you cross **Petersham Meadows**
(Map 72), the gigantic **Star and Garter Home** (🖳 starandgarter.org) peers
down at you from the top of Richmond Hill. Taking the time to climb
Richmond's famous hill is a great opportunity to see one of the finest views of
the river – and the only one to be protected by an Act of Parliament! The view
has also been painted by JMW Turner and Joshua Reynolds and even inspired
the naming of Richmond, Virginia in the US, after the city founder thought the
curve in the river there resembled the meander of the Thames as seen from the
hill. From the attractive town of **Richmond** (see pp208-9) you pass round **Old
Deer Park** (Map 73), where there are no deer, hence the 'old'. After you've
appreciated the fine vista of **Syon House** (see box p217) on the opposing bank,
you'll follow the perimeter of **Kew's Royal Botanical Gardens** (Map 74; see
box p217) and arrive at **Kew Bridge** (Map 74). Kew has a couple of pubs serving food and drink, but otherwise few useful services by the river for walkers.
　　From this point the river embarks on one of its great sweeping snake-
shaped manoeuvres past **Mortlake** (see p209) and **Barnes** (see p214) to

---

❏ **WARNING**
Certain sections along this stage may flood at high tide and since the tide can rise as
fast as an inch a minute it is well worth checking 🖳 tidetimes.org.uk before setting off.
In some places alternative routes are signed away from the river, but sometimes the
flooding is unexpected – so you will need to find another way out or retrace your steps.

Hammersmith Bridge (Map 76). The walking is pleasant and feels undisturbed by the spread of modernity to your right. The boathouses of numerous rowing clubs welcome you to **Putney** (see p214; Map 77), with this stage ending at its famous bridge. *(cont'd on p208)*

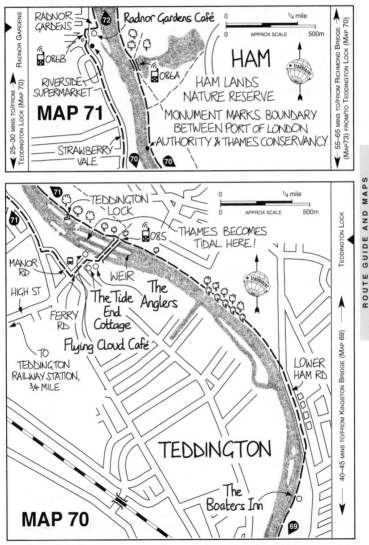

MAP 71

RADNOR GARDENS

Radnor Gardens Café

72

086B

RIVERSIDE SUPERMARKET

25–30 MINS TO/FROM TEDDINGTON LOCK (MAP 70)

RADNOR GARDENS

STRAWBERRY VALE

70 70

086A

HAM

HAM LANDS NATURE RESERVE

MONUMENT MARKS BOUNDARY BETWEEN PORT OF LONDON AUTHORITY & THAMES CONSERVANCY

0   ¼ mile
0   APPROX SCALE   500m

trailblazer

55–65 MINS TO/FROM RICHMOND BRIDGE (MAP73) FROM/TO TEDDINGTON LOCK (MAP 70)

MAP 70

71 71

TEDDINGTON LOCK

085

THAMES BECOMES TIDAL HERE!

MANOR RD

HIGH ST

FERRY RD

WEIR

The Tide End Cottage

The Anglers

Flying Cloud Café

TO TEDDINGTON RAILWAY STATION, ¾ MILE

LOWER HAM RD

TEDDINGTON

The Boaters Inn

69

0   ¼ mile
0   APPROX SCALE   500m

trailblazer

TEDDINGTON LOCK

40–45 MINS TO/FROM KINGSTON BRIDGE (MAP 69)

ROUTE GUIDE AND MAPS

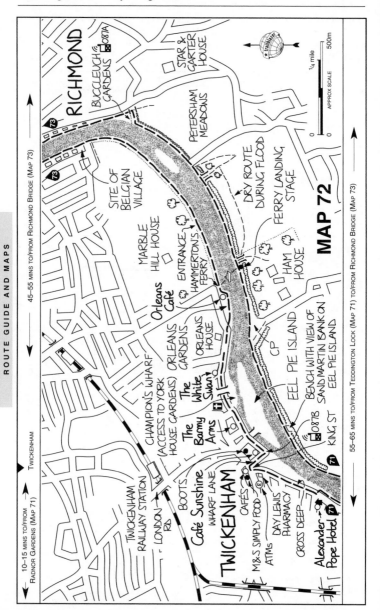

10-15 MINS TO/FROM
RADNOR GARDENS (MAP 71)

TWICKENHAM

45-55 MINS TO/FROM RICHMOND BRIDGE (MAP 73)

55-65 MINS TO/FROM TEDDINGTON LOCK (MAP 71) TO/FROM RICHMOND BRIDGE (MAP 73)

RICHMOND

BUCCLEUCH GARDENS

087A

STAR & GARTER HOUSE

PETERSHAM MEADOWS

SITE OF BELGIAN VILLAGE

DRY ROUTE DURING FLOOD

FERRY LANDING STAGE

MAP 72

MARBLE HILL HOUSE

ENTRANCE

HAMMERTON'S FERRY

HAM HOUSE

Orleans Café

ORLEANS GARDENS

ORLEANS HOUSE

CP

EEL PIE ISLAND

BENCH WITH VIEW OF SAND MARTIN BANK ON EEL PIE ISLAND

CHAMPION'S WHARF
(ACCESS TO YORK HOUSE GARDENS)

The White Swan

The Barmy Arms

087B

KING ST

71

TWICKENHAM RAILWAY STATION

LONDON RD

BOOTS

Café Sunshine

WHARF LANE

TWICKENHAM

CAFÉS

M&S SIMPLY FOOD

ATMS

DAY LEWIS PHARMACY

CROSS DEEP

Alexander Pope Hotel 71

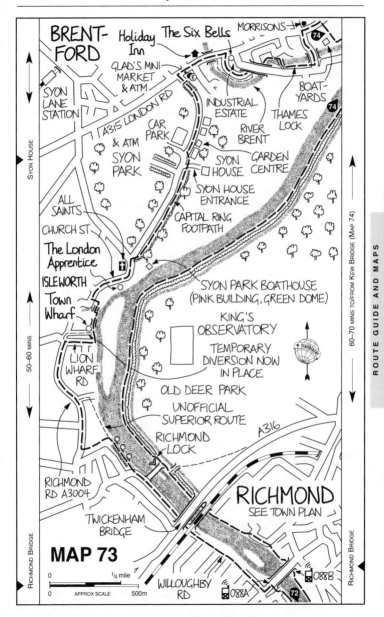

BRENT-FORD

Holiday Inn

The Six Bells

MORRISONS

GLAD'S MINI MARKET & ATM

SYON LANE STATION

A315 LONDON RD

INDUSTRIAL ESTATE

BOAT-YARDS

CAR PARK & ATM

RIVER BRENT

THAMES LOCK

SYON PARK

SYON HOUSE

GARDEN CENTRE

SYON HOUSE ENTRANCE

ALL SAINTS

CAPITAL RING FOOTPATH

CHURCH ST

The London Apprentice

ISLEWORTH

Town Wharf

SYON PARK BOATHOUSE
(PINK BUILDING, GREEN DOME)

KING'S OBSERVATORY

TEMPORARY DIVERSION NOW IN PLACE

LION WHARF RD

OLD DEER PARK

UNOFFICIAL SUPERIOR ROUTE

A316

RICHMOND LOCK

RICHMOND RD A3004

RICHMOND
SEE TOWN PLAN

TWICKENHAM BRIDGE

MAP 73

0   ¼ mile

0   APPROX SCALE   500m

WILLOUGHBY RD

088A

088B

72

74

trailblazer

SYON HOUSE

50-60 MINS

RICHMOND BRIDGE

RICHMOND BRIDGE

60-70 MINS TO/FROM KEW BRIDGE (MAP 74)

ROUTE GUIDE AND MAPS

RICHMOND

Recorded in the *Domesday Book* as part of an area called Sheen, the town gained its modern name from Henry VII's Richmond Palace, built in 1501. The palace was one of Elizabeth I's favourite residences and she died there in 1603. Following the execution, in 1649, of Charles I – who fled to Richmond to escape the plague – the palace fell into decay and little remains of it now.

Richmond Bridge is London's oldest, having been built between 1774 and 1777. The town is now synonymous with its **hill**, from where there are some great views over the river.

The **Museum of Richmond** (☎ 020-8332 1141, 🖳 museumofrichmond.com; Tue-Sat 11am-5pm, Sat to 4pm in winter; free; Whittaker Ave) is in the town hall and well worth a visit. As you walk into

Richmond look out for the **plaque** about the London Plane tree here, in the grounds of Gaucho Restaurant; see also box p63.

Services

For those not wishing to stray far from the bridge the nearest **shop** is Best-one (24hrs) on Hill Rise. Other services: Tesco **supermarket** (Mon-Sat 6am-midnight, Sun 11am-5pm), a Boots **pharmacy** (Mon-Fri 8am-7pm, Sat to 6.30pm, Sun 11am-5pm) and a **post office** (Mon-Sat 9am-5.30pm, Sun 11am-3pm), which is in a branch of WH Smith's, and some **ATMs** are all on George St.

Richmond is well connected to the rest of London by **bus**, **underground** (District line) and **train** (South Western Railway; see box pp52-3).

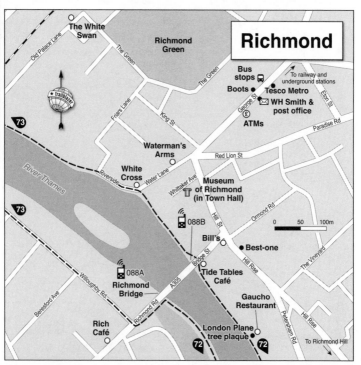

For information about **accommodation** in Richmond; visit 🖳 visitrichmond .co.uk/accommodation.

Where to eat and drink

There are plenty of options here. Neatly housed in one of the brick arches beneath Richmond Bridge, *Tide Tables Café* (☎ 020-8948 8285, 🖳 tidetablescafe.com; Mon-Fri 8.30am-6.30pm, Sat & Sun to 8pm, winter months hours variable; WI-FI; 🐾) has a spacious outdoor space backed by a large bank of wild flowers – it's really quite idyllic. The prices are not as wince-making as some places in Richmond and the food is good, with baked potatoes from £4.50 and hummus on toast £2.50! They also provide plenty of vegetarian/vegan and gluten-free options, and filter coffee comes with a free refill on weekdays.

Dining at *Bill's* (☎ 020-8948 0768, 🖳 bills-website.co.uk; Mon-Sat 8am-11pm, Sun 8am-10.30pm; WI-FI; 1-3 Hill Rise) is another option close to the bridge; the lunch menu includes cod fish-finger sandwiches (£9.95) and chicken burgers (£12.95).

Pub food can be found just past the bridge at the end of Water Lane. Both *Waterman's Arms* (☎ 020-8940 2893, 🖳 rampubcompany.co.uk; food Tue-Sat 11am-9.30pm, Sun noon-7pm; WI-FI; 🐾) and *White Cross* (☎ 020-8940 6844, 🖳 the-whitecrossrichmond.com; food Mon-Sat noon-10pm, Sun to 9pm; WI-FI; 🐾) have decent and imaginative menus; the latter's roasts (£13.50-17) are delicious.

Real-ale fans may wish to continue a little further along the river to *The White Swan* (☎ 020-8940 0959, 🖳 whiteswan richmond.co.uk; food Mon noon-2.30pm & 6.30-9pm, Tue-Fri noon-2.45pm & 6.30-9.30pm, Sat noon-3.45pm & 6.30-9.30pm, Sun 12.30-3.30pm & 6.30-8.30pm; WI-FI; 🐾; Old Palace Lane). As well as serving pints of Doom Bar and Otter Ale, the pub is also renowned for its food; the lunch menu includes sandwiches (£8.95-11.95) which are sure to appease the peckish.

MORTLAKE   [Map 75, p211]

Once one of the many sites where a ferry would cross the Thames, the bridge here (**Chiswick Bridge**) has, since 1845, over-looked the finishing line for The University Boat Race (see box below). Splendidly located to cheer on the bitter boating rivals is *The Ship* (☎ 020-8876 1439, 🖳 greene king-pubs.co.uk; food daily noon-9pm; WI-

R O U T E   G U I D E   A N D   M A P S

❏ The University Boat Race

In 1829 the first-ever Boat Race between Oxford and Cambridge universities was held between Hambleden Lock (Map 49) and Henley Bridge (Map 48), Henley-on-Thames. Organised by two school friends who were studying at the rival universities, this inaugural competition attracted a crowd of 20,000 who witnessed an easy Oxford win. The second race wasn't held until 1836 when the two universities raced between Westminster and Putney. Back then, however, the event was constantly interrupted by commercial traffic and a row broke out over where to hold the race – with Oxford wanting to race at Henley while Cambridge preferred London. In 1839 it was decided definitively that London would host the race, with the route moved to its current 4-mile, 374-yard course between Putney Bridge (Map 77) and Mortlake (Map 75), just shy of Chiswick Bridge, in 1845. And there it has remained ever since, save for the odd exception such as the Second World War when it was moved from London. As of 2018, Cambridge had won 83 times and Oxford 80.

The Boat Race is held every year on a Saturday near Easter. For further information visit 🖳 theboatrace.org.

On the Fulham side of the river after Putney Bridge (see Map 77) look out for the mosaic on the ground saying 'Oxford & Cambridge Boat Race since 1829' along the bottom and round the top 'The world's longest surviving sporting challenge'.

FI; 🐾; 10 Thames Bank). There's a wide-ranging selection of traditional pub grub such lamb shank shepherd's pie with mashed potatoes (£14.99).

Further along the river is **Rick Stein** (☎ 020-8878 9462, 🖥 rickstein.com/eat-with-us/barnes; food daily noon-3pm & 6-10pm; WI-FI; 🐾 outside on terrace; Mortlake High

50–60 MINS TO/FROM SYON HOUSE (MAP 73) — KEW BRIDGE — 35–45 MINS TO/FROM CHISWICK BRIDGE (MAP 75)

BRENTFORD
1 PAPPADUMS RESTAURANT
2 GALATA PERA TURKISH RESTAURANT
3 PREMIER INN - LONDON KEW
4 RIVER CAFÉ
5 McDONALD'S
6 TRAVELODGE LONDON KEW BRIDGE

STRAND ON THE GREEN
7 CAFÉ ROUGE
8 THE BELL & CROWN
9 THE CITY BARGE
10 ANNIE'S CHISWICK
11 THE BULL'S HEAD

MAP 74

PATH ENTERS WATERMAN'S PARK

TAKE RIGHT AFTER VICTORIA STEPS QUAY

KEW BRIDGE RD

KEW BRIDGE RAILWAY STATION

BRENTFORD

PHARMACY COSTCUTTER & ATM

JET GARAGE

A315

STRAND ON THE GREEN

THAMES RD

GROVE PARK RD

BRENTFORD HIGH ST

KEW PALACE (RED BRICK BUILDING)

KEW BRIDGE

089A

PATH FOLLOWS ALONGSIDE STRAND ON THE GREEN

METAL ARTWORK

CAR PARK & ENTRANCE TO KEW GARDENS

KEW RIVERSIDE PARK SNAIL RESERVE

KEW

ROYAL BOTANICAL GARDENS

VICTORIA GATE

KEW GARDENS RAILWAY & TUBE STATION

0   ¼ mile
0   APPROX SCALE   500m

KEW BRIDGE — 25–30 MINS TO/FROM CHISWICK BRIDGE (MAP 75)

ROUTE GUIDE AND MAPS

St), another in the TV chef's chain, with smart fish dishes including an Indonesian seafood curry for £22.95.

Take a slight detour before the railway bridge at Barnes for the local branch of **Sainsbury's** (daily 7am-10pm). Next door, *Orange Pekoe* (☎ 020-8876 6070,

🖳 orangepekoeteas.com; Mon-Fri 7.30am-5pm, Sat & Sun 9am-5pm; WI-FI; 🐾 front area only and on lead; No 3) specialises in brewing **tea** of a superior standard to your average mug of builders. Lunches including salads and sandwiches are available as are cream teas (£8.95).

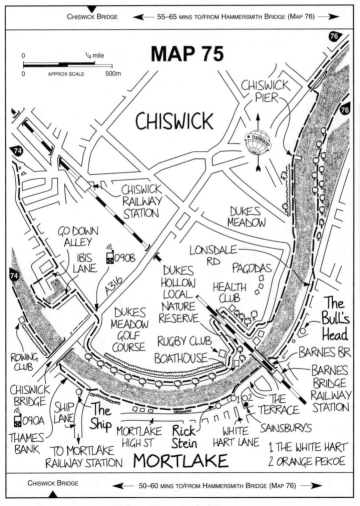

MAP 75

CHISWICK

CHISWICK PIER

★ trailblazer

CHISWICK RAILWAY STATION

DUKES MEADOW

GO DOWN ALLEY

IBIS LANE

090B

LONSDALE RD

PAGODAS

DUKES HOLLOW LOCAL NATURE RESERVE

HEALTH CLUB

A316

DUKES MEADOW GOLF COURSE

RUGBY CLUB

BOATHOUSE

The Bull's Head

BARNES BR

BARNES BRIDGE RAILWAY STATION

ROWING CLUB

CHISWICK BRIDGE

090A

THAMES BANK

TO MORTLAKE RAILWAY STATION

SHIP LANE

The Ship

MORTLAKE HIGH ST

Rick Stein

WHITE HART LANE

THE TERRACE

SAINSBURY'S

1 THE WHITE HART

2 ORANGE PEKOE

MORTLAKE

ROUTE GUIDE AND MAPS

The menus at **The White Hart** (☎ 020-8876 5177, 🖥 whitehartbarnes.co.uk; food Mon-Sat noon-10pm, Sun noon-9pm; WI-FI; 🐕 bar only; The Terrace) for both Canon Bar and the Terrace Kitchen change regularly but include imaginative dishes such as

Wellington venison (£23); the bar menu starts from £13.

The closest **railway stations** are either Mortlake or Barnes Bridge; South Western Railway's services (see box pp52-3) operate to both.

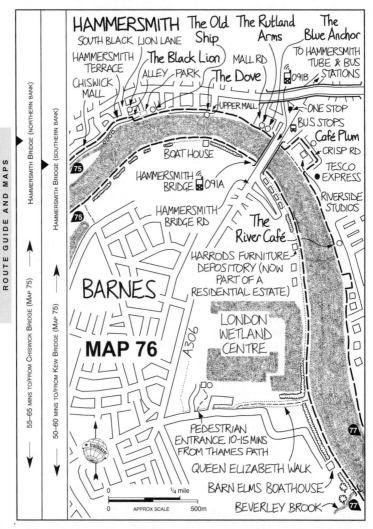

ROUTE GUIDE AND MAPS

HAMMERSMITH BRIDGE (NORTHERN BANK)

HAMMERSMITH BRIDGE (SOUTHERN BANK)

55–65 MINS TO/FROM CHISWICK BRIDGE (MAP 75)

50–60 MINS TO/FROM KEW BRIDGE (MAP 75)

HAMMERSMITH
SOUTH BLACK LION LANE
The Old Ship
The Rutland Arms
The Blue Anchor
HAMMERSMITH TERRACE
The Black Lion
MALL RD
TO HAMMERSMITH TUBE & BUS STATIONS
CHISWICK MALL
ALLEY PARK
The Dove
091B
UPPER MALL
ONE STOP
75
BOAT HOUSE
BUS STOPS
Café Plum
CRISP RD
HAMMERSMITH BRIDGE 091A
TESCO EXPRESS
75
HAMMERSMITH BRIDGE RD
RIVERSIDE STUDIOS
The River Café
HARRODS FURNITURE DEPOSITORY (NOW PART OF A RESIDENTIAL ESTATE)
BARNES
LONDON WETLAND CENTRE
MAP 76
A306
trailblazer
77
PEDESTRIAN ENTRANCE 10-15 MINS FROM THAMES PATH
QUEEN ELIZABETH WALK
BARN ELMS BOATHOUSE
BEVERLEY BROOK
77

0   ¼ mile
0   500m
APPROX SCALE

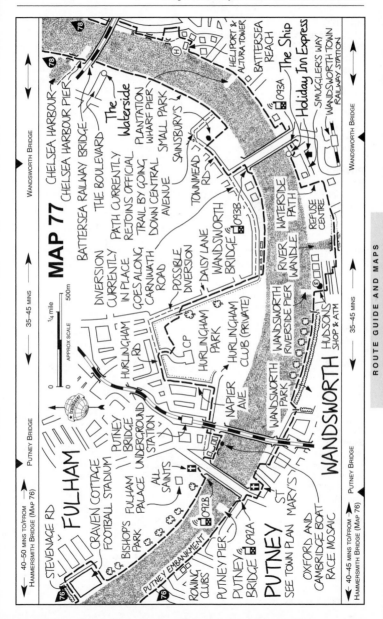

MAP 77

FULHAM

STEVENAGE RD

CRAVEN COTTAGE FOOTBALL STADIUM

BISHOP'S PARK

FULHAM PALACE

ALL SAINTS

PUTNEY BRIDGE UNDERGROUND STATION

PUTNEY

SEE TOWN PLAN

ROWING CLUBS

PUTNEY PIER

PUTNEY BRIDGE

092A

092B

PUTNEY EMBANKMENT

OXFORD AND CAMBRIDGE BOAT RACE MOSAIC

ST MARY'S

WANDSWORTH

NAPIER AVE

HURLINGHAM CLUB (PRIVATE)

HURLINGHAM PARK

CP

HURLINGHAM RD

DIVERSION CURRENTLY IN PLACE

DIVERSION CURRENTLY GOES ALONG CARNWATH ROAD

POSSIBLE DIVERSION

DAISY LANE

WANDSWORTH BRIDGE

093B

PATH CURRENTLY REJOINS OFFICIAL TRAIL BY GOING DOWN CENTRAL AVENUE

TOWNMEAD RD

SAINSBURY'S

SMALL PARK

PLANTATION WHARF PIER

THE BOULEVARD

The Waterside

BATTERSEA RAILWAY BRIDGE

CHELSEA HARBOUR PIER

CHELSEA HARBOUR

78

78

WANDSWORTH BRIDGE

WANDSWORTH BRIDGE

HELIPORT & ALTA TOWER

BATTERSEA REACH

The Ship

Holiday Inn Express

093A

SMUGGLER'S WAY

WANDSWORTH TOWN RAILWAY STATION

REFUSE CENTRE

RIVER WANDLE

WATERSIDE PATH

WANDSWORTH RIVERSIDE PIER

WANDSWORTH PARK

HUDSON'S SHOP & ATM

WANDSWORTH

0   ¼ mile
0   500m
APPROX SCALE

← 40-50 MINS TO/FROM HAMMERSMITH BRIDGE (MAP 76)

← 35-45 MINS →

PUTNEY BRIDGE

← 35-45 MINS →

PUTNEY BRIDGE

← 40-45 MINS TO/FROM HAMMERSMITH BRIDGE (MAP 76)

76A

76

78

BARNES
[Map 75, p211; Map 76, p212]
The Bull's Head (☎ 020-8876 5241, 🖥 the bullsheadbarnes.com; food Mon-Fri 11am-10pm, Sat noon-10pm, Sun to 9pm; WI-FI; 🐾 in bar; 373 Lonsdale Rd) is past Barnes Bridge. The menu changes according to the season but may include fish pie (£14.50). There is live jazz here every night.

Barnes Bridge **railway station** is a stop on South Western Railway's train services to London Waterloo; see box pp52-3.

Birdwatchers, in particular, are likely to want to visit **WWT London Wetland Centre** (Map 76; ☎ 020-8409 4400, 🖥 wwt .org.uk/wetland-centres/london; Mar-end Oct daily 9.30am-5.30pm, rest of year to 4.30pm; £12.72, free for WWT members) has a *café* (Kingfisher Kitchen) serving snacks and hot food. The entry charge is refundable if you eat or drink in the café and stay less than an hour.

PUTNEY
Between Putney and Fulham (see p220) stands the only bridge along the river with a church at both ends: All Saints on the Fulham side of the river and St Mary's on the Putney side. Legend has it that the two churches were built by two giant sisters, who, possessing only one hammer, would hurl it over the river to each other, one bellowing 'Put it nigh!'; the other, 'Heave it full home', so leading to the twin towns' names.

In 1647 **St Mary's Church** hosted the Putney debates between members of Oliver Cromwell's New Model Army, during which the then radical idea of 'one man one vote' was first articulated.

Services
Along Putney High St there is a Boots **pharmacy** (Mon-Fri 9am-7.30pm, Sat 9am-6.30pm, Sun 11am-5pm). For **supermarkets** there's a branch of Waitrose (Mon-Sat 8am-8pm, Sun 11am-5pm) in Putney Exchange Shopping Centre and a Sainsbury's (Mon-Sat 7am-9pm, Sun 11am-5pm) on Werter Rd.

There is a **post office** (Mon-Fri 7am-7pm, Sat 9am-5.30pm) on Upper Richmond Rd; **ATMs** and **banks** are dotted along the High St.

Transport
Putney is connected by **train** (South Western Railway; see box pp52-3) to London Waterloo via **Putney railway station** on the High St. **East Putney underground station**, on Upper Richmond Rd, is on the District line. The **river bus** (see p60) calls at the pier here.

Where to stay
Away from the river is the elegant *Lodge Hotel* (☎ 020-8874 1598, 🖥 thelodgehotel london.com; 5S/50D/2Tr; 🐾; WI-FI; 🐾). Rates vary constantly but you can expect to pay approximately £65pp in summer (sgl/sgl occ from about £90) with breakfast costing an extra £15pp (£12 if booked in advance). To get there follow the High St as

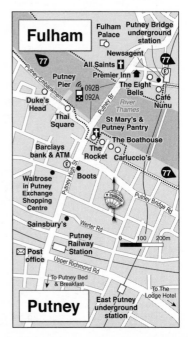

far as Upper Richmond Rd and turn left; the hotel is at Nos 52-54.

Unfortunately, *Putney Bed and Breakfast* (☎ 020-8780 1255, 🖥 www.put neybedandbreakfast.com; 1D private bathroom, 1S/1T share facilities; 🍸; WI-FI) does not accept advance bookings for one-night stays, but if you call in the relevant week it may be possible to stay just one night though a supplement will be charged. Situated close to East Putney underground station, the three rooms (£46-48.50pp, sgl/sgl occ from £67) are worth considering if you are planning to base yourself in one spot whilst walking in London. Following the High St and then Putney Hill away from the river will see you arrive at Lytton Grove on your left; the B&B is at No 11.

If you prefer a hostel the closest option is *YHA London Earl's Court* (see p220); it is a short journey on the underground (District line) from East Putney station.

Where to eat and drink

The riverbank, Putney High St and many of its tributary side streets are lined with high-street chain cafés, pubs and restaurants.

If seeking breakfast or other sustenance, *Putney Pantry* (☎ 020-8789 1137, 🖥 putneypantry.com; Mon-Sat 8.30am-6pm, Sun 11am-6pm; WI-FI; 🐾) is ideal. Part of St Mary's Church, here you'll find scrambled eggs & salmon on toast (£8.50), as well as lunches and cakes/tarts.

There are also several **pubs**. West of the bridge is *Duke's Head* (☎ 020-8788 2552, 🖥 dukesheadputney.com; food Mon-Sat noon-10pm, Sun noon-9pm; WI-FI; 🐾; 8 Lower Richmond Rd). Owned by Young's Brewery, it's a classy establishment with decent food (pan-fried rainbow trout £15). There's also an outdoor seating area, perfect to enjoy a pint at the end of a long day's walk with your goal for the day – Putney Bridge – in your sights.

Past St Mary's Church is *The Rocket* (☎ 020-8780 8970, 🖥 jdwetherspoon.com; food Mon-Sat 8am-11pm, Sun 8am-10.30pm; WI-FI; 🐾 outside on terrace). Wetherspoon's Putney offering, there's a large selection of ales and lagers and the usual lengthy, cheap no-frills menu, this one including an 8oz sirloin & chips for just £11.89. Nearby, *The Boathouse* (☎ 020-8789 0476, 🖥 boathouseputney.co.uk; food summer Mon-Fri 11am-10pm, Sat 9.30am-10pm, Sun 9.30am-9pm; WI-FI; 🐾 in bar; No 32) is rightly proud of its seafood (pan-fried seabass with puy lentils for £16.50).

Should English pub grub be giving you a bellyache Italian-style dishes such as seafood linguine with crab meat, prawns, mussels & clams (£14.50) can be found by the water's edge at *Carluccio's* (☎ 020-8789 0591, 🖥 carluccios.com/restaurants; Mon-Fri 8am-11pm, Sat 9am-11pm, Sun 9am-10.30pm; WI-FI; 🐾 outside), whilst there is a branch of *Thai Square* (☎ 020-8780 1811, 🖥 thaisq.com/restaurants; Mon-Fri noon-3pm & 6-11pm, Sat & Sun noon-11.30pm; WI-FI; 2-4 Lower Richmond Rd) overlooking the river from Putney Embankment. Jungle curry (£12.95) and all things Thai are available.

Kingston to Putney Bridge: northern bank

From **Teddington** (see p216) the route begins with a lengthy suburban road walk, though a brief respite from all this pavement pounding is provided by **Radnor Gardens** (Map 71).

Arriving in **Twickenham** (see p216). the path turns sharply back down to the river and **Eel Pie Island** (Map 72) – on which The Rolling Stones, Pink Floyd and The Who all once rocked. It then rambles on past **Orleans House** and **Marble Hill House** (see box p217); between them, should you wish to cross the bank, is Hammerton's Ferry (🖥 hammertonsferry.com; Mar-Oct daily 10am-6pm, ferry on demand; £1 single). You then pass **Richmond Bridge**.

More road walking brings you to **Isleworth** (see p217) and then the gates of **Syon Park and House** (Map 73; see box p217) before you escape an industrial estate to reach **Thames Lock** on the River Brent. The path then follows an uninspiring route through **Brentford** (see p218; Map 74) to **Kew Bridge** and **Strand on the Green** (see p218), from which more road plodding leads you through **Chiswick** (Map 75) and on to perhaps the most pleasant section of the day, a riverside walk along the bank of **Duke's Meadow**.

Another, final stretch of suburbia before **Hammersmith Bridge** (Map 76) has at least some historic pubs (see Hammersmith, p219) by way of compensation, following which a diversion round **Craven Cottage** – home to Fulham Football Club – leads to a welcome amble through **Bishop's Park** – passing **Fulham Palace** (see box opposite) – to **Putney Bridge** and **Fulham** (see p220).

TEDDINGTON   [Map 70, p205]

Teddington Lock is the final and largest on the Thames (Richmond has a lock but as it is operational at low tide only, Teddington is generally referred to as being the last). In 1940 an enormous flotilla of boats congregated here before setting off to rescue the British army from the beaches of Dunkirk.

Having crossed the lock you'll find *Flying Cloud Café* (daily 9am-5.30pm weather dependent; hot drinks, ice-cream and cakes (£2.30-2.80) are served from an Airstream but there is an area where you can sit and enjoy your refreshment.

Pub food is also available. The chefs at *The Anglers* (☎ 020-8977 7475, ☐ anglers-teddington.co.uk; food Mon-Fri noon-10pm, Sat 10am-10pm, Sun noon-9pm; WI-FI; ✻) offer some fine meals; the menu changes seasonally but may include coconut, chilli & lemongrass steamed mussels with fries (£13).

The Tide End Cottage (☎ 020-8977 7762, ☐ greeneking-pubs.co.uk; food daily noon-9pm; WI-FI; ✻) does a fine line in burgers including a dirty burger (smoked cheese, chilli con carne, roasted red onions, gherkin, mustard mayonnaise & onion rings) for £11.75.

Teddington **railway** station (South Western Railway; see box pp52-3) is a short stroll (¾ mile) from the path. See also p55 and p60 for transport information.

TWICKENHAM
[Map 71, p205; Map 72, p206]

Your time here will probably be brief but there are a few amenities in the vicinity of the Thames Path.

A number of **shops** dot the route through Twickenham, including Riverside Supermarket (Mon-Sat 7.30am-11pm, Sun 8am-11pm), an M&S Simply Food (Mon-Sat 8am-9pm, Sun 9am-8pm) and for a **chemist** there's a Day Lewis (Mon-Fri 9am-6.30pm, Sat 9am-1pm) and a Boots (Mon-Sat 8.30am-6.30pm, Sun 11am-5pm). You'll see several **ATMs** just across the road on King St.

Twickenham has a **railway station** (South Western Railway; see box pp52-3); see also p55 & p60.

Accommodation can be found at *Alexander Pope Hotel* (☎ 020-8892 3050, ☐ alexanderpope.co.uk; 20D/12T; ✻; WI-FI; ✻ bar area; Cross Deep). The tariff varies widely but on average a classic double room including breakfast costs £49.50-84.50pp (sgl occ £89-159); book direct for the best rates. **Food** (Mon-Fri 7-10am & noon-9pm, Sat & Sun 8-10.30am & noon-9pm) is available throughout the day.

As well as the **cafés** in central Twickenham there are three en route. *Radnor Gardens Café* (daily 9am-5pm, though closed if it's raining), deals in baps (bacon and sausage £4.50) and wraps (£5) and *Orleans Café* (summer daily 8.30am-6pm, winter 8.30am-3.30pm) has a selection of sandwiches and hot drinks. The best option for walkers is *Café Sunshine* (☎ 020-8538 9599; Apr-end Oct daily 10am-5pm, rest of year to 4pm, food served 11am-3pm; WI-FI), at the end of Wharf Lane, where there are sandwiches and also jacket potatoes (from £4.50). Two **pubs** overlook the path. Rugby-fan favourite, *The Barmy Arms* (☎ 020-8892 0863, ☐ greeneking-pubs.co.uk; food daily noon-9pm; WI-FI; 🐕 in bar) has an extensive menu of sandwiches, burgers and pub classics but it can be very busy, particularly if there's a game on at the nearby stadium, the home of English rugby.

In stark contrast is the tranquillity offered at *The White Swan* (☎ 020-8744 2951, ☐ whiteswantwickenham.co.uk; food Mon-Fri noon-3pm & 6-9pm, Sat noon-9pm, Sun noon-6pm; WI-FI; 🐕), a

free house with a peaceful beer garden right next to the river. The menu changes regularly but should include a good selection of burgers, salads and main dishes such as halloumi, beetroot & guacamole burger with chips (£11).

By Richmond Bridge [map p208]

Still technically Twickenham but near to the path at the end of Richmond Bridge is *Rich Café* (daily 7am-5pm; WI-FI; 🐕 outside), which sells English breakfasts (£5.50) as well as sandwiches, wraps and crêpes for less than £5.

ISLEWORTH [Map 73, p207]

The Thames Path passes by **two great pubs** on its way through Isleworth. *Town Wharf* (☎ 020-8847 2287; food summer daily noon-9.30pm, winter Mon-Fri noon-3pm & 6-8pm, Sat & Sun noon-6pm; WI-FI; 🐕 in downstairs bar) is your typical Samuel Smith Brewery establishment with no music

but cheap ales and lagers and a varied menu which may include pulled pork sandwiches (from £5.50) and liver & onions (£9.25).

Meanwhile, a little further along the trail, *The London Apprentice* (☎ 020-8560 1915, ☐ greeneking-pubs.co.uk; food daily noon-10pm; WI-FI; 🐕; 62 Church St) offers

ROUTE GUIDE AND MAPS

❏ **Sights between Kingston and Putney Bridge**

● **Orleans House** (Map 72; ☎ 020-8831 6000, ☐ richmond.gov.uk/orleans_house_gallery; Tue-Sun 10am-5pm; free) Now home to an art gallery, in 1815 this 18th-century house was leased by the exiled King of France, Louis Philippe Duc d'Orleans. Though he actually resided here for only two years, it is his name that remains.

● **Marble Hill House** (Map 72; ☎ 020-8892 5115, ☐ english-heritage.org.uk; Apr-Oct Sat & Sun house entrance by guided tour only, at 10.30am, noon, 2.15 & 3.30pm; £7.40, EH members free; park daily 7am-4pm, free) This Palladian Villa was built for the mistress of King George II.

● **Syon Park and House** (Map 73; ☎ 020-8560 0882, ☐ www.syonpark.co.uk; mid Mar to end Oct: house Wed, Thur, Sun and Bank Holidays 11am-5pm; gardens daily 10.30am-5pm; £13, gardens only £8) This, the London home of the Duke of Northumberland, is the last surviving ducal residence in London. The gardens were designed by Capability Brown.

● **Kew Royal Botanic Gardens** (Map 74; ☎ 020-8332 5655, ☐ www.kew.org; open daily from 10am, until: late Mar-end Aug Mon-Thur to 7pm, Fri-Sun to 8pm, rest of year shorter hours; £17.75, or £16 online) The only one of the 'sights' on this stage that's on the river's **southern bank**, the world's most famous botanical gardens are home to a plethora of flora and fauna. The Temperate House, the largest Victorian glasshouse in the world, was reopened in May 2018 after a 5-year restoration project.

● **Fulham Palace** (Map 77; ☐ fulhampalace.org; Bishops Avenue; free) The 'country' residence of the bishops of London from the 11th century until 1973, parts of the Palace can be visited including the museum (summer Sun & Bank Holiday Mon noon-5pm, Mon-Thur 12.30-4.30pm, winter Sun noon-4pm, Mon-Thur 12.30-3.30pm) and *café* (Apr-Oct daily 9.30am-5pm, Nov-Mar daily 10am-4pm) as well as the palace's historic gardens (daily dawn to dusk) to explore.

cashback to ensure you can afford to fill up on falafel burgers (£10.29) and any other items from their extensive menu.

BRENTFORD
[Map 73, p207; Map 74, p210]

Situated at the confluence of the rivers Brent and Thames, Brentford could once boast fords across both waterways and evidence of a Bronze Age trading centre suggests humans settled the area before London itself. It is also one of the sites where Julius Caesar and his army could have traversed the river in AD54; the area also witnessed a Civil War battle between the Royalists and Parliamentarians in 1642. Putting such historical significance to one side, there is no reason to hang around.

If you do choose to linger, however, Brentford has everything a walker needs. Shortly after joining London Rd there is *Glad's Mini-market* (Mon-Sat 6.30am-6.30pm, Sun 6.30am-2pm) with an **ATM** (£1.85). The path also joins Brentford High St opposite a **supermarket**, Morrisons (Mon-Sat 7am-11pm, Sun 10am-4pm). Further along the High St you pass another **shop**, Costcutter (Mon-Sat 7am-10pm, Sun 7.30am-10.30pm) which also has an ATM, and a **pharmacy** (Mon-Fri 9am-5.30pm, Sat 9am-1pm).

Accommodation is available at branches of: *Holiday Inn* (Map 73; London Brentford Lock; ☎ 020-8232 2000, 🖳 hibrentfordlock.co.uk; 84D/49T; ☞; WI-FI); *Premier Inn* (London Kew; ☎ 0871-527 8670, 🖳 premierinn.com; 52 Brentford High St; 42D/99D or T; ☞; WI-FI; Map 74); and *Travelodge* (London Kew Bridge;

☎ 0871-984 6040, 🖳 travelodge.co.uk; 34D/6T/71Tr; ☞; WI-FI; 🐾). Rates for all depend on demand (see pp21-2).

There is a somewhat eclectic mixture of places to eat. On Brentford High St is the friendly, down-to-earth *River Café* (Mon-Sat 6am-4pm) with typical fare such as jacket potatoes (from £3.50) and there is a *McDonald's* (daily 5am-midnight; WI-FI) here too.

Pub food can be found just before the path leaves Brentford High St at *The Six Bells* (Map 73; ☎ 020-8758 1278, 🖳 sixbells-brentford.co.uk; food Tue 7-9.30pm, Wed-Fri noon-3pm & 7-9.30pm, Sat noon-9.30pm, Sun noon-6pm; WI-FI; 🐾 in garden). A Fuller's pub, they offer plenty of real ales and football on the telly.

On the path but away from the main roads are *Galata Pera Turkish Restaurant* (☎ 020-8560 1798, 🖳 galatapera.co.uk; food Mon-Fri 5-11pm, Sat & Sun noon-11pm; WI-FI; 🐾 outside), which dishes up a wide variety of kebabs, steak, seafood, and falafel (£10.80); and the award-winning *Pappadums* (☎ 020-8847 1123, 🖳 pappadums.co.uk; Mon-Fri noon-2.30pm & 5.30-11pm, Sat noon-11pm, Sun noon-10.30pm) where you'll find a fine selection of curries such as chicken tikka (£10.95).

For a **train** the nearest station to the path is Kew Bridge (South Western Railway; see box pp52-3). See also p55 & p60 for transport information for London.

Isleworth is a stop on South Western Railway's **train** services (see box pp52-3) from London Waterloo.

STRAND ON THE GREEN
[Map 74, p210]

This short stretch has a number of fine eateries. There are splendid views over the river from *Café Rouge* (☎ 020-8995 6575, 🖳 caferouge.com/locations/kew-bridge; WI-FI; 85 Strand on the Green). French cuisine is available throughout the day (Mon-Thur 9.30am-10pm, Fri & Sat 9am-11pm, Sun 9.30am-10pm) and the main menu includes steak frites (from £13.50).

As high-end a 'café' as you'll find on the Thames Path, the menu at *Annie's Chiswick* (☎ 020-8994 9080, 🖳 annies restaurant.co.uk; daily 10am-10pm; WI-FI; 162 Thames Rd) is as quirky as the décor and changes regularly but may include spicy paella (£14.95), butternut chickpea dhansak (£13.95) and endless other mouth-watering dishes. Note that the kitchen may be closed Monday to Friday 3-6pm.

The first pub that you come to on Thames Rd is Fuller's *The Bell & Crown* (☎ 020-8994 4164, 🖳 bell-and-crown .co.uk; food Mon-Sat noon-10pm, Sun noon-9pm; WI-FI; 🐾; No 11), a very dog-friendly place where there are some unusual offerings including white Texel lamb faggots with creamed potatoes (£12.50).

Further on, on either side of the railway line, are *The City Barge* (☎ 020-8994 2148, 🖳 citybargechiswick.com; food Mon-Fri noon-10pm, Sat 10am-10.30pm, Sun to 9pm; WI-FI; 🐾 in bar area; No 27), an upmarket establishment with relatively reasonably priced food (mains from £13.50), and *The Bull's Head* (☎ 020-8994 1204, 🖳 chefandbrewer.com; food Mon-Sat noon-10pm, Sun noon-9.30pm; WI-FI; 🐾 bar area; 15 Strand on the Green) at which, as well as six constantly changing real ales, there are also ciders and craft lagers on tap. From the lunch menu (Mon-Sat noon-4pm) you can purchase main meals such as fish & chips, or scampi, for as little as £6.29.

Kew Bridge **railway station** (South Western Railway; see box pp52-3) is the closest for Strand on the Green.

HAMMERSMITH [Map 76, p212]

The first suspension bridge across the Thames was located here but concerns over its ability to hold the increasing weight of traffic led to it being replaced by the current ornate green and gold crossing in 1887.

You'll find a **shop**, One Stop (daily 7am-10pm), by turning left just before the path goes below the bridge. A little further on there's a Tesco Express (daily 7am-11pm), while inside The Rutland Arms (see column opposite) there is an **ATM** (£1.85).

Pubs before Hammersmith Bridge include *The Black Lion* (☎ 020-8748 2639, 🖳 blacklion.london; food Mon-Thur noon-3pm & 6-10pm, Fri & Sat noon-10pm, Sun noon-9pm; WI-FI; 🐾; 2 South Black Lion Lane) and *The Old Ship* (☎ 020-8748 2593, 🖳 oldshiphammersmith.co.uk; food Mon-Fri noon-10pm, Sat & Sun noon-9pm; WI-FI; 🐾; 25 Upper Mall). Both have real ales to indulge in and particularly good food.

As you get closer to the bridge there are **three pubs** brimming with history, character and fine ale. *The Dove* (☎ 020-8748 9474, 🖳 dovehammersmith.co.uk; food Mon-Sat noon-10pm, Sun noon-9pm; WI-FI; 🐾 on lead; 19 Upper Mall) is one of London's most famous drinking haunts. It has the world's smallest bar-room and should you choose to stop for a libation you are in good company: Charles II, Ernest Hemingway and Dylan Thomas have all supped from the pub's taps and it is even claimed that the Scottish poet James Thomson penned *Rule Britannia* whilst watering here. Owned by Fuller's Brewery, The Dove has a menu of tempting options such as sea trout fillet (£22) as well as 12oz Hampshire sirloin on the bone (£25), though some mains cost from £12.

A short way further along the river is *The Rutland Arms* (☎ 020-8748 5586, 🖳 greeneking-pubs.co.uk; food Mon-Fri 11am-10pm, Sat & Sun 10am-10pm; WI-FI; 🐾; 15 Lower Mall). They are very dog friendly, have several guest ales on the go at any one time and serve items such as steak & ale pie (£11.49), or sandwiches and wraps (£5.49-8.99). An outside seating area affords views of the bridge.

Next door is *The Blue Anchor* (☎ 020-8748 5774, 🖳 blueanchorlondon.com; food Mon-Thur noon-3.30pm & 6-9.30pm, Fri & Sat noon-9.30pm, Sat 10am-10.30pm; WI-FI; 🐾; 13 Lower Mall). A popular place with film crews, the pub has featured in a number of television series such as *New Tricks* as well as the film *Sliding Doors*. There's a varied menu which includes sausages & mash (£11.50) but they may also have a superfood salad with squash & beetroot (£10.50).

Along the stretch following the bridge there are two **cafés**. *Café Plum* (☎ 020-8741 5001, 🖳 cafeplum.com/cafe/ hammersmith; Mon-Fri 8am-5pm, Sat & Sun 9am-4pm; 🐾; 17 Crisp Rd) has a reasonably priced menu with a large specials board which may contain such delights as a chicken burrito (£6.10), or risotto carbonara (£6.25); whilst *The River Café* (☎ 020-7386 4200, 🖳 rivercafe.co.uk; Mon-Sat lunch 12.30pm, Sun noon, last sitting at

2.15pm, closes at 5pm; Mon-Sat dinner 7pm with last sitting at 9/9.15pm; WI-FI; Rainville Rd) is *really* a restaurant, and one where it's likely the prices (wild Scottish salmon £40) will put many walkers off. Booking is advisable, though it is not impossible to get a table on the day.

There are two **underground stations** around Hammersmith Broadway: the entrance on Beadon Rd is for the Hammersmith & City and Circle lines; the other, in the centre of the Broadway, is for the District and Piccadilly lines. See also p55 & p60.

FULHAM [map p214]

Putney Bridge, between Fulham and Putney is the only bridge along the river with a church at both ends (see p214). After going under the bridge look out for the mosaic on the ground (Map 77; see box p209).

Putney Bridge **underground station** is on the District line; see p55 and p60.

A **newsagent** (Mon-Sat 6am-9pm, Sun 7am-8pm) and a cluster of **cafés** face the station and there are two free **ATMs** to the left of the entrance to the station.

Nearby is a ***Premier Inn*** (London Putney Bridge; ☎ 020-7471 8318, 🖳 premierinn.com; 151D/30T; ☕; WI-FI; 3 Putney Bridge Approach) where Saver rates (see p21) are from £60.

The Eight Bells (☎ 020-7736 6307; food Mon-Fri noon-2.30pm & 6-9pm, Sat & Sun noon-9pm; WI-FI; 🐕; 89 Fulham High St) serves quality real ales alongside excellent value pub **food** such as steak & ale pie (£7.95).

- For **hostel accommodation** the best place is ***YHA London Earl's Court*** (☎ 0345-371 9114 or ☎ 020-7373 7083, 🖳 yha.org.uk/hostel/london-earls-court; 186 beds, 2, /3-, 4- and 6-bed rooms; some with double bed and a few en suite; WI-FI in communal areas; dorm beds £13-30pp, private/family rooms from £39/35; 38 Bolton Gardens); it is a short journey on the District Line from Putney Bridge underground station. This hostel has 24hr access and laundry/drying and self-catering facilities though a continental breakfast (£4.99) is available.

PUTNEY BRIDGE TO TOWER BRIDGE [MAPS 77-81]

As with yesterday's stage you need to make a decision over which bank to follow. Both sides of the river have plenty to savour; however, the southern bank probably edges it again, primarily due to it encompassing both the pleasant stroll through Battersea Park and also the excitement of London's Southbank area. The views of Westminster and the Tower of London (both on the northern

❑ Diversion and signpost warning

One small word of warning before we continue, however: as you make your way through the centre of the capital you'll no doubt notice that your progress is not as smooth as you may imagine. This is not only due to the traffic, of course, but also because of the lack of signage. Several **signposts** have been taken down, or moved, or actually never existed in the first place – so do keep this book with you and open on the correct map to help you negotiate the many twists and turns of the official path. We should also point out that we can think of no other section of any national trail that is as subject to so many **diversions**, so often, as this section of the Thames Path. This does, of course, reflect the restless, ever-changing nature of the capital, which is part of its charm, but it does mean you have to keep your wits about you to avoid wasting time by wandering down some temporary dead-ends.

bank) are also splendid from the southern side. And, of course, if you wish to visit either of them all you need do is cross over either Westminster or Tower Bridge. Indeed, with the stage being quite short, there's no reason not to cross the river as often as takes your fancy! Before starting off, see box opposite.

Putney Bridge to Tower Bridge: southern bank

Despite being shorter, the **9¼-mile (14.7km, 3½-4¾hrs)** route along the southern bank will undoubtedly take longer because of the mass of tourists on the stretch between Lambeth Bridge and Tower Bridge; there are indeed numerous sights to consider (see box pp232-3). This section used to be somewhat blighted by the laborious road walking necessitated to go around the regeneration work at Battersea Power Station, but thankfully that is no longer necessary.

The stage begins by passing through **Wandsworth** (see below; Map 77) and along **Battersea Reach** to **Albert Bridge** (Map 78), one of the city's finest, from where a peaceful stroll takes you through **Battersea Park**. The official path goes inland here but an infinitely preferable route is to go through the vast construction site around **Battersea Power Station** (see Battersea p223). Having rejoined the official path, look out for the **Father Thames mural**, by Stephen Duncan, on Riverside Walk; the impressive new **US Embassy** provides a backdrop. At the time of writing there was a (temporary?) diversion around **MI6**.

In the **Church of St Mary** (Map 79), next to **Lambeth Palace** there is a Garden Museum; see box pp232-3 for details of both. Continuing on the trail, you come to the busiest section of the entire walk; for the rest of the day you will probably find yourself walking at somebody else's pace as tourists, street entertainers and food stalls abound. This is particularly true around **County Hall** (Map 80), the former offices of the Greater London Council (the GLC), now home to all manner of tourist attractions (such as Sea Life Aquarium, Shrek Adventure & London Dungeon) and several fast-food restaurants. Opposite, for a different view of the river, **The London Eye** (see pp232-3) rises above the chaos. Back on ground level you will soon pass the **Southbank Centre** (Royal Festival Hall and Hayward Gallery), **BFI Southbank**, **National Theatre (NT)** and **Tate Modern** art gallery (see box pp232-3) amongst other tourist attractions en route to what is London's most spectacular – and the river's last great – crossing point: **Tower Bridge** (see p226).

ROUTE GUIDE AND MAPS

WANDSWORTH   [Map 77, p213]

Wandsworth grew around the mouth of the **River Wandle** – London's largest Thames tributary – and is the city's oldest industrial area. Before its closure in 2006 Ram Brewery had been brewing beer here since 1581; the area was also the base of Young's Brewery – whose pubs feature frequently along the river – until they too stopped mass production here in the same year.

Shortly after Wandsworth Park the path turns inland and you will pass Hudson's **shop** (Mon-Fri 6.30am-11pm, Sat & Sun

from 7am) which has a free **ATM**. Nearby is a Sainsbury's Local (daily 7am-11pm).

There is a *Holiday Inn Express* (London Wandsworth; ☎ 020-8877 5950, 🖳 expresswandsworth.co.uk; 74D/74T; WI-FI; B&B from approx £101 per room but the rate varies a lot and it is best to book online in advance) on Smuggler's Way.

There are several places offering food along this stretch, most of them part of some new development or other and most fairly similar, shiny glass-fronted affairs

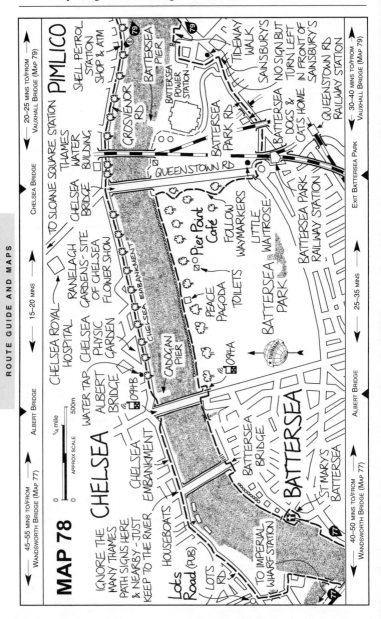

MAP 78

CHELSEA

PIMLICO

BATTERSEA

← 45-55 MINS TO/FROM WANDSWORTH BRIDGE (MAP 77) →

← ALBERT BRIDGE →

← 15-20 MINS →

← CHELSEA BRIDGE →

← 20-25 MINS TO/FROM VAUXHALL BRIDGE (MAP 79) →

← 40-50 MINS TO/FROM WANDSWORTH BRIDGE (MAP 77) →

← ALBERT BRIDGE →

← 25-35 MINS →

← EXIT BATTERSEA PARK →

← 30-40 MINS TO/FROM VAUXHALL BRIDGE (MAP 79) →

IGNORE THE MANY THAMES PATH SIGNS HERE & NEARBY - JUST KEEP TO THE RIVER

0   ¼ mile   500m
APPROX SCALE

Lots Road (PUB)

LOTS RD

TO IMPERIAL WHARF STATION

HOUSEBOATS

CHELSEA EMBANKMENT

WATER TAP

ALBERT BRIDGE

109+B

CADOGAN PIER

109+A

St MARY'S BATTERSEA

BATTERSEA BRIDGE

CHELSEA ROYAL HOSPITAL

RANELAGH GARDENS - SITE OF CHELSEA FLOWER SHOW

CHELSEA PHYSIC GARDEN

CHELSEA EMBANKMENT

PEACE PAGODA

TOILETS

Pier Point Café

FOLLOW WAYMARKERS

BATTERSEA PARK

LITTLE WAITROSE

BATTERSEA PARK RAILWAY STATION

TO SLOANE SQUARE STATION

THAMES WATER BUILDING

CHELSEA BRIDGE

QUEENSTOWN RD

QUEENSTOWN RD

SHELL PETROL STATION SHOP & ATM

CROSVENOR RD

BATTERSEA PIER

BATTERSEA POWER STATION

BATTERSEA PARK RD

BATTERSEA DOGS & CATS HOME

NO SIGN BUT TURN LEFT IN FRONT OF SAINSBURY'S

SAINSBURY'S

TIDEWAY WALK

QUEENSTOWN RD RAILWAY STATION

PIMLICO

79

79

77

77

that lack a bit of character and are often overpriced. For this reason, our favourite option is a more traditional place with a bit of history that lies tucked away just before Wandsworth Bridge. The bar menu at *The Ship* (☎ 020-8870 9667, 💻 theship.co.uk; food Mon-Sat noon-4pm & 6-10pm, Sun noon-8pm; WI-FI; 🐾 in bar; 41 Jews Row) includes a good selection of sandwiches (Mon-Fri £6.50) and daily specials to choose from with real ales to wash it all down. Mains start at £14.20 for the vegetarian option of grilled asparagus with rosemary onion jam, Jersey royal potatoes and a Cornish brie tart with poached duck egg tomato confit.

Wandsworth Town **railway station** is a short walk from the Holiday Inn; services are operated by South Western Railway (see box pp52-3). The **river bus** (see p60) calls at Wandsworth Riverside and Plantation Wharf piers.

BATTERSEA [Map 78; Map 79]

Your walk through Battersea is now much more enjoyable than it used to be. After the **Church of St Mary** – where poet William Blake married in 1782 – you reach the peaceful splendour of **Battersea Park** and then the new psychedelic entrance (under the railway line) to Battersea Power Station. During 2019 the work on the power station itself should be complete; it will open to the public in 2020 and in 2021

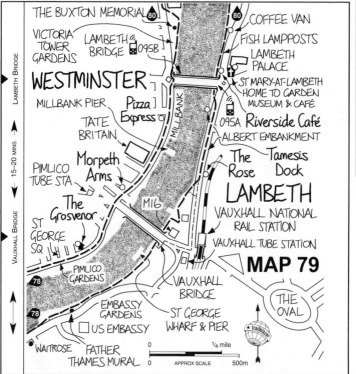

ROUTE GUIDE AND MAPS

Apple will move into its UK campus in the power station.

If you want a **supermarket** to buy your lunch you've got a couple of choices. Soon after rejoining the official path (after passing through the Power Station), the trail ducks left off Battersea Park Rd behind a branch of Sainsbury's (daily 7am-11pm) which has an **ATM**. Further on, as you rejoin Battersea Park Rd, there's a larger Waitrose (Mon-Sat 7.30am-10pm, Sun noon-6pm). If you prefer to follow the official Thames Path route there's a branch of little Waitrose (daily 24hrs) by the corner of Battersea Park, as you cross Queenstown Rd.

For sit-down **food**, in Battersea Park, *Pier Point Café* (daily 9am-6pm; 🐾) sells

coffees (cappuccino £2.50) and snacks. In **Circus West Village** there are a few options with more opening all the time: at the time of writing *Fiume* (🖥 fiume-restaurant.co.uk; food Tue-Sun noon-3pm & 6-9pm), serving Italian food was open but soon there will be branches of The Coffee Works Project, Ben's Canteen, Cinnamon Kitchen and Tonkotsu amongst others.

Between the park and Battersea Dogs' & Cats Home is **Battersea Park Railway Station** with services operated by Southern to London Victoria. Nearby is **Queenstown Road station** with services operated by South Western Railway. See box pp52-3.

Battersea Power Station pier is a stop on the river bus (see p60).

LAMBETH & VAUXHALL
[Map 79, p223]
As you approach Lambeth Bridge **pub food** can be found at *The Rose* (☎ 020-7735 3723, 🖥 therosepublondon.co.uk; daily 11.30am-10.30pm; WI-FI; No 35). One of the better-value eateries on the path in the capital (mains £9.95-14.95), you can peruse Westminster on the northern bank.

Should the idea of a **floating restaurant** entice, hop aboard *Tamesis Dock* (☎ 020-7582 1066, 🖥 tdock.co.uk; food Mon-Fri 11.30am-10pm, Sat & Sun 10.30am-10pm; 🐾; WI-FI). It's moored off Albert Embankment, and the boat's menu includes burgers (£9.95-12.95), good-value mains (£7.95-8.95) and a full English breakfast (£8.95).

In the vicinity of both the bridge and palace (see box pp232-3) are two **cafés**. On the riverbank is *Riverside Café* (Mon-Fri 8am-5 or 6pm, Sat & Sun from 9am; 🐾 outside), with an extensive menu of breakfasts and lunches (12" pizzas from £12.45). Meanwhile, in the **Garden Museum** (see box p232) at St Mary-at-Lambeth Church is a *café* (Mon-Fri 8am-5pm, Sat 9am-3.30pm, Sun 9am-5pm, lunch noon-3pm).

With a peaceful garden to its rear it's possible to be almost oblivious to the fast pace of London that surrounds you. The menu is certainly exotic – indeed, some of it is rather experimental – and may include pig's cheeks & plums for starters (£8), followed by pigeon, beetroot & sheep's yoghurt (£14.50); tea, cakes and the like are available the rest of the day. They may also be open Tuesday & Friday 6-9pm but check this in advance.

Coffee stalls and eateries dot the riverbank almost continually from Lambeth Bridge onwards. Most of the big chains are represented (eg *McDonald's* and *Pret a Manger* in the old County Hall offices near Sea Life London Aquarium) as well as *Giraffe*, *Eat*, *Yo Sushi*, *Wagamama* etc etc etc. In short, there are too many to mention and review in a walking guide such as this, but suffice to say you shouldn't go hungry or thirsty on this stretch of the trail!

Vauxhall has both railway (South Western Railway; see box pp52-3) and tube (Victoria line) services as well as a large bus station with toilets. The **river bus** (see p60) stops at St George Wharf (Vauxhall).

SOUTHWARK
[Map 80]
Between Westminster Bridge and London Bridge are the areas now known as **Southbank** and **Bankside**. Developing

more slowly than its northern twin during the Middle Ages, the area became the haunt of prostitutes and a venue for bear-baiting.

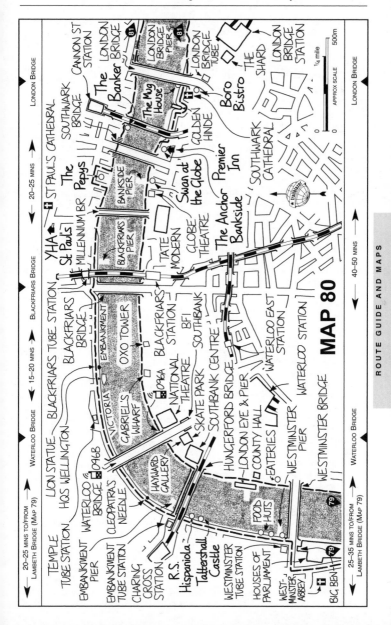

Following a brief time as an industrial area in the 18th century, today it is again one of London's great centres of entertainment (though this time minus the bears).

Situated by Southwark Bridge is a branch of *Premier Inn* (see p21; London Southwark Bankside; ☎ 0871-527 8676, ⌨ premierinn.com; 35D/24D or T; ☞; WI-FI; 34 Park St). Saver rates here are from £60 and room rates can up to £233.

Eateries of every kind line this section of river and unsurprisingly there are several **pubs** worth considering. Amongst the many, for bard-watchers there's *Swan at The Globe* (☎ 020-7928 9444, ⌨ swanlondon.co.uk; bar food all day from 8am, Sat & Sun 10am; restaurant Mon-Sat noon-3pm & 5-10.45pm, Sun 11.30am-10.30pm; WI-FI; 🐾 bar only; 21 New Globe Walk), which as well as fine views of St Paul's Cathedral on the opposite bank also supplies temptingly tasty fare including roast sea trout with summer vegetable ragout (£19.50). During the hours the kitchen is closed they serve afternoon tea (daily noon-3pm; from £28.50); booking is recommended.

The Anchor Bankside (☎ 020-7407 1577, ⌨ greeneking-pubs.co.uk; food Mon-Sat noon-10pm, Sun noon-9pm; WI-FI; 🐾 on covered terrace only; 34 Park St) has a rather macabre past: occupying the site of a Roman grave, it is said to have been built on a bear-baiting venue and allegedly is also where one of the pits where plague victims were buried in 1603. Luckily, there's a reasonably priced and extensive menu (eg burgers £10-99-15.79) as well as views of the river to keep your mind away from such morbid thoughts.

Should eating with a view of the Thames start to feel a little too commonplace, *The Mug House* (☎ 020-7403 8343, ⌨ davy.co.uk/wine-bar/mug-house; food Mon-Sat 10am-10pm; WI-FI) offers the perfect escape. Situated below London Bridge, it's a dimly lit and atmospheric place. Away from the mania of some of the riverside pubs, they serve mains from £12.95 up to £24.95 for a 28-day-aged sirloin steak.

Tucked down the western side of London Bridge is *Boro Bistro* (☎ 020-7378 0788, ⌨ borobistro.co.uk; Mon 1-8.30pm, Tue-Thur noon-3pm, Fri-Sat noon-10.30pm, Sun 1-8.30pm), perhaps best described as a 'French tapas' sort of place with little dishes from £4, including French duck potted meat (£4.50) and artichoke hummus with baguette (£5.50).

While the above two options are very good, if you're looking for food in the region of London Bridge you should really head to **Borough Market** (⌨ boroughmarket.org.uk; Mon-Thur 10am-5pm, Fri to 6pm, Sat 8am-5pm), opposite, where cuisines from all over the world are available. It isn't cheap and it's a bit of a tourist attraction in its own right – but it's a characterful place and the food is, on the whole, great. Note that on Monday and Tuesday some shops/stalls may not be open.

In addition to being sandwiched between two iconic bridges, this stretch of the river is also sandwiched between two of the city's great **railway stations**: London Bridge and Waterloo (as well as Waterloo East) – service providers are South Western Railway, Southern, Southeastern & Thameslink (see box pp52-3).

Both London Bridge and Waterloo **underground stations** are on the Northern and Jubilee lines; Waterloo is also on the Bakerloo line and Southwark is also a stop on the Jubilee line. The **river bus** (see p60) stops at London Eye (Waterloo).

TOWER BRIDGE: southern bank
[Map 81]

[For details about the bridge and services on the northern side of the river see p232] There is a **shop**, Krystals Express (24hrs) and, nearly opposite, a Sainsbury's (Mon-Sat 7am-11pm, Sun 8am-10.30pm).

The nearest **railway station** is London Bridge (see above and box pp52-3).

London Bridge is also on the underground (see above).

There is a branch of *Premier Inn* (see p21; ⌨ premierinn.com) at 159 Tower Bridge Rd (London Tower Bridge Hotel; ☎ 0871-527 8678; 196D or T; ☞; WI-FI); saver rates (see p21) are from £64. **Pubs** line Tower Bridge Rd, amongst them *Draft*

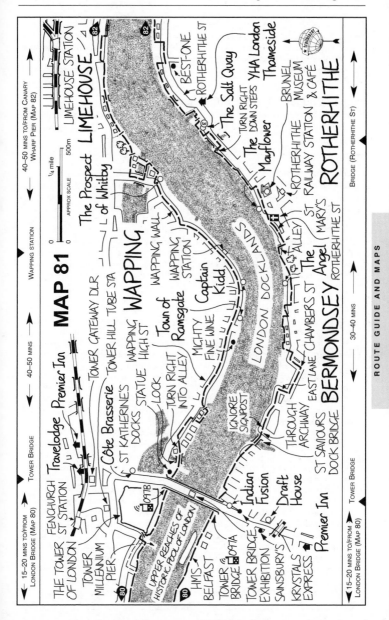

House (☎ 020-7378 9995, 💻 draft
house.co.uk; food Mon-Sat noon-10pm,
Sun noon-9pm; WI-FI; 🐾). The pub boasts
tasty versions of messy fast food such as a
cheeseburger (£8.90) and a 'rib & wing
feast' to share (£20.50).

For Indian food, *Indian Fusion* (☎
020-7403 9242, 💻 theindianfusion.com;
214 Tower Bridge Rd; Mon-Thur noon-
2.30pm & 5.30-11.30pm, Fri 5.30-
11.55pm, Sat & Sun noon-11.55pm; WI-FI)
is tasty.

Putney Bridge to Tower Bridge: northern bank

London's bridges (see box below) now become yardsticks measuring the
progress of your day and this **10-mile (16km, 3¼-4¼hrs)** section features no
fewer than 20.

❏ London's bridges

Until relatively recently it was believed that the **Romans** were the first to build a
bridge across the Thames in London. However, in 2001 the study of a number of
wooden stakes discovered in the riverbed close to Vauxhall Bridge led archaeologists
to conclude that there had once been a walkway across the river that dated back to
the **Bronze Age**. Caesar came and went in 55BC and again the following year, though
he never mentioned a bridge, Bronze Age or otherwise, and he and his troops forded
the river instead. But his Roman compatriots who followed a century later, in AD43,
did eventually build a bridge across the Thames in approximately AD47. This wood-
en bridge traversed the river a little downstream from today's London Bridge and was
built so that the Roman roads of Stane St (from Chichester) and Watling St (from
Kent), which met at the Thames, could connect with the road continuing north-west
across the Midlands. (The Romans did build another bridge across the Thames at
Staines, but these were the only two. Preferring to move troops and goods by fording
the river or ferry, it would appear that they saw bridges as strategic weak links.)

Over the following half century this wooden Roman bridge was replaced with a
more permanent stone edifice; however, following the Roman desertion of the British
Isles, the bridge too disappeared and it is not known what happened to this crossing.

In AD994 the **Vikings** ransacked London. This would lead to the Anglo-Saxons
building *their* first bridge across the river: lying low across the water, it was a defensive barrier as much as a crossing point. Not that this deterred the Vikings. In 1014
King Olaf of Norway simply attached his boats to the bridge with cables, waited for
the tide, and pulled it down.

The **Anglo-Saxons** would build a number of wooden bridges in the vicinity of
London to try to protect both their capital and the populace upstream but they were
forever falling foul of the tides and inadequate construction. Indeed, their London
Bridge was such a frequent victim that the bridge's numerous disasters are believed to
have been the inspiration behind the nursery rhyme *'London Bridge is falling down.'*

So it was left to the **Normans** to place the first lasting structure across the river.
Built with stone, **Old London Bridge** was completed in 1209, having taken 30 years
to construct. Miraculously, considering the lifespan of other London bridges, it lasted six centuries until 1831 when it was replaced with a new bridge – which was in
turn replaced with today's structure in 1973. Boasting 19 small arches, Old London
Bridge acted as a weir when the tide came in and the difference in the height of the
waters on either side of the bridge could be several feet. The bridge was covered in
houses and shops and in winter the water about the bridge – its flow slowed by the
tiny arches – could freeze, leading to what would become known as 'Frost Fairs'
where thousands of people would take to the ice to skate and frolic.

A great deal of the stage is spent walking along embankments, initially passing by such places of interest as **Chelsea Physic Garden** (Map 78) and **Ranelagh Gardens**, the site of Chelsea Flower Show.

There is also the opportunity to visit **Tate Britain** art gallery (Map 79) before you arrive at one of London's most iconic buildings: the Palace of Westminster, home to the United Kingdom's **Houses of Parliament** (Map 80) and commonly referred to as such. Be sure not to allow the palace's splendour to lead you to miss **Westminster Abbey**, its neighbour and namesake. Peering down at the river from the palace's northern end since 1858, the Elizabeth Tower is perhaps the iconic London building, even though few people know

Blocking off the river to all but the smallest craft meant that traders approaching the city from the sea had to moor below the bridge, so creating the **Pool of London** (see box p201 and p236) – the stretch of the Thames immediately downstream of London Bridge. It also meant the area of land directly about the bridge – The City – accumulated massive wealth from this riverine trade.

It was to be five centuries after the construction of Old London Bridge before the London Thames would be traversed again in either wood or stone. The City had a vested interest in keeping their monopoly over the Old London Bridge and any plans for a second bridge were also opposed by the ferrymen and watermen who plied their trade carrying people across the river; another bridge, they predicted, would lead to the demise of their business. But in 1726 King George I finally gave the go-ahead for a new wooden bridge to be built at Fulham. A fair distance from London Bridge, its construction was begrudged by those whose livelihoods it threatened. Opposition was greater still for the next bridge though in 1736 the king once again accepted the case for a new crossing at Westminster and an Act of Parliament granted it the final go-ahead. Opening in 1750, the arrival of **Westminster Bridge** was to be a watershed moment.

With Old London Bridge's monopoly broken the City finally gave up its struggle and began to build more bridges, the first being **Blackfriars** in 1769. The City of London's crossings were free but the idea of building a bridge to the west of the Square Mile and charging a toll attracted much private enterprise. **Chelsea** (1776), **Vauxhall** (1816), **Waterloo** (1817) and **Southwark** (1819) were all originally **toll bridges**. Their charge, however, merely led to congestion at the City of London's bridges – people preferring not to pay a toll if it wasn't necessary. The City's response was to purchase Southwark Bridge in 1866 and remove the charge, so 'freeing' the bridge and relieving congestion at its own bridges. The 'freeing' of a further 11 bridges would occur in 1877 thanks to their purchase by the Metropolitan Board of Works, a body initially formed to construct the city's sewers and a precursor to London's County Council.

No fewer than 30 bridges span the Thames today between Richmond and the Tower of London. The oldest still standing is **Richmond** (1777), the newest the **Millennium Bridge** (2002), joining St Paul's with Tate Modern; while the most regularly crossed by vehicle is **Putney**. Currently, West London has one crossing for every 250,000 residents, whilst East London has one for every 1.7 million.

Plans for a 'Garden Bridge' (a pedestrian bridge) between Southbank and Temple have been shelved but a bridge (or tunnel) beyond the eastern end of the Thames Path at Gallions Reach to replace the Woolwich Ferry is still possible.

that this is the correct name for the bell tower that houses **Big Ben**. However, the bells have been silenced until 2021 whilst restoration work takes place on the whole structure. Statues and monuments – including **Cleopatra's Needle**, which, having stood by the banks of the River Nile for 3000 years, was moved to its current location in 1878 – are passed as you progress towards **Waterloo Bridge** and then **Blackfriars Bridge**.

Even those who opted for the southern bank may want to cross over the **Millennium Bridge** to admire **St Paul's Cathedral**. It's then just a short hop to the site of the capital's oldest river crossing point at **London Bridge**. Your day ends at what was once the city's most feared building and the home of many an infamous inmate: **The Tower of London** (Map 81).

Note that Tower Bridge is the last place you can cross to the southern side of the river on foot if you aren't happy at the thought of walking through the Greenwich Foot Tunnel (see p237).

> For details of the day's numerous tourist attractions mentioned here see the box on pp232-3.

CHELSEA
[Map 77, p213; Map 78, p222]
The Mercian king Offa called a synod (a council) here in the 8th century, though these days you're more likely to hear discussions about football or flowers (see p39 & p232) than debates between Saxon monarchs.

Technically still in Fulham but shortly after Wandsworth Bridge (Map 77) the path passes near a branch of Sainsbury's (daily 7am-11pm), the **supermarket** chain, but for a hot/sit-down meal you may prefer to walk on to *The Waterside* (☎ 020-7371 0802, 🖥 watersideimperialwharf.co.uk; food Mon-Sat 10am-10pm, Sun 11am-9pm; WI-FI; 🐾). A dog-friendly place, the menu includes classic pub meals as well as sourdough pizzas (from £12).

Shortly after passing **Chelsea Harbour** the path joins Lots Rd (Map 78) and its namesake pub, *Lots Road* (☎ 020-7352 6645, 🖥 foodandfuel.co.uk; food Mon-Sat noon-10pm, Sun noon-9pm; WI-FI; 🐾; No 114), where there's a decent menu including chicken, mushroom & spinach pie (£14).

Imperial Wharf railway station (on London Overground & Southern line; see pp52-3) is a short walk from Chelsea Harbour. For **Sloane Square underground station** (Circle/District lines) turn left at Chelsea Bridge and walk along Chelsea Bridge Rd which becomes Lower Sloane St and then reaches Sloane Square.

PIMLICO
[Map 78, p222; Map 79, p223]
As you follow Grosvenor Rd through this small and fashionable area of the City of Westminster there is a Shell petrol station with a **shop** (24hrs) and an **ATM** (£1.85).

A bit further on, *The Grosvenor* (☎ 020-7821 8786; WI-FI; 🐾; No 79) is well worth considering especially if money is tight. It has some remarkably cheap **rooms** (2S/4D shared bathroom; 🛏; £25-35pp, sgl occ room rate) but you do – of course – get

what you pay for. Away from the tourist hordes, it's also a great spot to dine with some fantastic-value meals (**food** daily 11am-9.30pm) with ribeye steak & chips only £10.95. With its nautically themed walls you almost get the sense of being back in a pub on the Upper Thames rather than a bit more than a stone's throw away from the Palace of Westminster.

Pimlico underground station (Victoria line), on Bessborough St, is a short way from Vauxhall Bridge. Victoria station, about 10 minutes' walk along Vauxhall Bridge Rd, has both tube (District, Circle & Victoria lines) and railway services (operated by Southern, box pp52-3). Victoria Coach Station (see p54) is on Buckingham Palace Rd, about 10 minutes from the railway station.

WESTMINSTER
[Map 79, p223; Map 80, p225]

If you feel the need for a meal, just before Tate Britain on Millbank *Morpeth Arms* (☎ 020-7834 6442, 🖳 morpetharms.com; food daily noon-9pm; WI-FI; 🐾 in bar; No 58) is the place for you. One of their burgers (£14) will certainly ensure you're not perusing London's sights with a grumbling stomach.

Also on Millbank is a branch of *Pizza Express* (☎ 020-7976 6214, 🖳 pizza express.com/millbank; Mon-Sat 11.30am-10.30pm, Sun 11.30am-9pm; WI-FI; No 25). Pizzas of all types are available (from £11.95).

Returning to the river and with the Palace of Westminster in your wake, there are several **coffee** and **food stalls** by Westminster Bridge, next to which you'll also find **Westminster underground station** (Circle/District/Jubilee lines).

The option of eating aboard a **floating restaurant** may appeal. Anchored at Hungerford Bridge are both *The Tattershall Castle* (☎ 020-7839 6548, 🖳 thetattershallcastle.co.uk; WI-FI; 🐾 deck only; food daily 11am-10pm), aboard which the bar menu includes a ploughman's platter (£13); and *RS Hispaniola* (☎ 020-7839 3011, 🖳 hispaniola.co.uk; food Mon-Sat noon-9.30pm, Sun to 8.30pm) on which you can dine on dishes such as flat iron steak sandwich, onion jam & chips (£14.50).

CITY OF LONDON   [Map 80, p225]

Finding somewhere to eat could not be easier. Diverting from the path will lead to innumerable pubs, cafés, takeaways and restaurants.

If time allows, heading away from the river at Millennium Bridge to visit **St Paul's Cathedral** (see box pp232-3) is well advised. Near to this iconic landmark is *YHA London St Paul's* (☎ 0345-371 9012, or ☎ 020-7236 4965, 🖳 yha.org.uk/hostel/london-st-pauls; 213 beds: 1-, 2-, 3-, 4-, 5-, 6-, 7-, 8-, 10- & 11-bed rooms, shared facilities but one en suite; (L); WI-FI communal areas; 36 Carter Lane). The hostel has male & female dorms and some rooms have double beds; dorm beds cost from £16pp (private/family rooms from £39/49). The hostel is licensed and meals are available but (unusually) there are no self-catering facilities. However, there are laundry & drying facilities, credit cards are accepted and there is 24hr access.

Charing Cross, Blackfriars and Cannon St **railway stations** (Southeastern & Thameslink; see box pp52-3) can be accessed from this stretch of the river. Charing Cross (Northern & Bakerloo lines) as well as Blackfriars and Cannon St (both Circle & District) are also stops on the **underground**; other convenient tube stations are Embankment (Circle, District & Bakerloo) and Temple (Circle & District). See also p55 and p60 for transport information in London.

Pubs en route include, on either side of Southwark Bridge, *The Pepys* (☎ 020-7489 1871, 🖳 thepepys.co.uk; food Mon-Fri noon-3pm & 6-9.30pm; WI-FI; small 🐾; Stew Lane, off Upper Thames St) a fairly sedate place with pizzas (from £10), grills (from £13), mains (around £15) and weekly specials on the menu; and Fuller's *The Banker* (☎ 020-7283 5206, 🖳 banker-london.co.uk; food Mon noon-8.30pm, Tue-Fri noon-10pm; WI-FI; small 🐾; Cousin Lane). Unlike the profession after which it is named, this place is quite popular, with a menu including sharer boards (from 3pm; £12.50-23.50). Note this pub is only open Monday to Friday.

ROUTE GUIDE AND MAPS

TOWER BRIDGE: northern bank
[Map 81, p227]

[For services on the southern side of the river see p226] The city's most impressive bridge and the only one that can open for shipping, Tower Bridge is one of the river's most recent crossing points. By the 1870s a million people lived east of London Bridge but with no way across the river and congestion rife it was conceded that a new crossing was needed, though one that still allowed large ships through to discharge their cargo at the Pool of London (see box p236). As a result, a part-suspension, part-fixed bridge design was agreed. Built in 1894, its medieval appearance is meant to complement the nearby Tower of London.

Actually on the bridge, **Tower Bridge Exhibition** (☎ 020-7403 3761, 🖳 tower bridge.org.uk; Apr-Sep daily 10am-5.30pm, Oct-Mar 9.30am-5pm; £9.80, £8.70 if booked online) allows you up on to the bridge's walkways and also into its engine rooms.

There are numerous transport options; the closest stations are **Tower Gateway** (DLR line; see box pp52-3) and **Tower Hill** (District/Circle lines) for the **underground**.

Where to stay and eat
There are branches of *Premier Inn* (London City Tower Hill Hotel; ☎ 0871-527 8646, 🖳 premierinn.com; 165D or T; 🖢; WI-FI), at 22-24 Prescot St, and also *Travelodge* (London Central Tower Bridge Hotel; ☎ 0871-984 6388, 🖳 travelodge .co.uk; 184D/6T; 🖢; WI-FI; 🐾), at Goodmans Yard, here; see p21 for rates.

❏ SIGHTS BETWEEN PUTNEY BRIDGE AND TOWER BRIDGE

Southern bank
● **Lambeth Palace** (Map 79; 🖳 www.archbishopofcanterbury.org/pages/visit-lam beth-palace.html; guided tours £12 plus £2.95 booking fee) The London home of the Archbishop of Canterbury; it isn't generally open to the public other than on a guided tour, see the website for details.
● **Garden Museum** (Map 79; ☎ 020-7401 8865, 🖳 gardenmuseum.org.uk; Sun-Fri 10.30am-5pm, Sat 10.30am-4pm; £10, church tower only £3) This is at St Mary-at-Lambeth Church and it offers welcome respite from the city's streets. Note that the museum is always closed on the first Monday of the month.
● **The London Eye** (Map 80; 🖳 londoneye.com; June-Sep daily 10am-9/9.30/11.30pm, rest of year 10/11am-6/8pm, standard/fast track entry from £24.30/33.30 if booked online, from £27/37 on the day; packages available, see the website) This giant ferris wheel (443ft/135m high) provides great views of London.
● **Tate Modern** (Map 80; ☎ 020-7887 8888, 🖳 tate.org.uk/visit/tate-modern; Sun-Thur 10am-6pm, Fri & Sat 10am-10pm; free except for special exhibitions) An art gallery focusing on contemporary art.

Northern bank
● **Chelsea Physic Garden** (Map 78; ☎ 020-7352 5646, 🖳 chelseaphysic garden.co .uk; Apr-early Nov Mon-Fri, Sun & Bank Holidays 11am-6pm; £10.50; 66 Royal Hospital Rd) Founded in 1673, this is the second oldest botanic garden in England and one of the most important botanical centres in the world. The entrance is on Swan Walk.
● **The Houses of Parliament and Big Ben (The Palace of Westminster)** (Map 80; ☎ 020-7219 4114, 🖳 www.parliament.uk) Home to both the House of Commons and the House of Lords, which together make up the UK's Houses of Parliament, it was originally a medieval palace built in 1097 though a fire destroyed most of the original building in 1834. Today's replacement opened in 1867.

Alternatively there are two **YHA hostels** in the vicinity (see p231 and p238).

There are plentiful **coffee huts** and **chain cafés**, such as *Starbucks* (Mon-Fri 6.30am-9pm, Sat & Sun 7.30am-10pm; Lower Thames St), plying their trade about the Tower of London.

Côte Brasserie (☎ 020-7488 3668, ⌨ cote.co.uk; Mon-Fri 8am-11pm, Sat 9am-11pm, Sun 9am-10.30pm; WI-FI; 1 St Katherine's Way) offers varying breakfast options as well as three-course meals for £14.95 (Mon-Fri noon-7pm).

TOWER BRIDGE TO GREENWICH & THE THAMES BARRIER
[Maps 81-84]

And so, via weir, lock and bridge, on footpath, bridleway and road, you've made it to this your final stage of the Thames Path. Away from the tourists and historic sites, it is a day on which you see another side of the city at **London Docklands** (see box p236). It is also a day when – between the Isle of Dogs and Greenwich – the route from the northern bank burrows beneath the river, courtesy of the Greenwich Foot Tunnel (see p237) and the bifurcated trail becomes one once more, with the trail's official end a mere 4½ miles further on.

While Big Ben is the name often used to refer to Parliament's tower, its actual name is The Elizabeth Tower, Big Ben being the nickname of the tower's bell (its actual title is the Great Bell). Note that The Elizabeth Tower is closed for restoration work which is scheduled to be completed in 2021. However, it is still possible to visit the Houses of Parliament; for details see the website.

● **Westminster Abbey** (Map 80; ☎ 020-7222 5152, ⌨ westminster-abbey.org; May-Sep Mon-Fri 9.30am-3.30pm, Sat 9am-3pm, rest of year Mon-Fri 9.30am-3.30pm, Sat 9am-1pm; £22 or £20 if booked online) Founded in AD960, this is the traditional site for both the coronation and burial of English and British monarchs. Note that the times quoted above are the last entry times and also that the Abbey can be closed at short notice.

● **St Paul's Cathedral** (Map 80; recorded info ☎ 020-7246 8348, general enquiries ☎ 0207 246 8350, ⌨ stpauls.co.uk; Mon-Sat 8.30am-4.30pm; £18, £16 online in advance) Designed by Christopher Wren, the construction of St Paul's Cathedral in the late 17th century was part of London's rebuilding programme following the Great Fire of London in September 1666. Its iconic dome is the subject of many a postcard and, famously, it somehow avoided the German bombs during the Blitz.

● **The Tower of London** (☎ 0844-482 7799, ⌨ hrp.org.uk/TowerOfLondon; Mar-Oct Tue-Sat 9am-5.30pm, Sun & Mon 10am-5.30pm; Nov-Feb same but to 4.30pm; £26.80, or £22.70 if bought online) Royal palace, fortress, prison, place of execution, arsenal, mint and home to the crown jewels, the Tower has served as many things during its 900-plus year history. Begun by William the Conqueror in 1078, it was primarily used as a prison during the 16th and 17th centuries with one of its most famous prisoners being Anne Boleyn.

● **Tate Britain** (Map 79; ☎ 020-7887 8888, ⌨ tate.org.uk/visit/tate-britain, daily 10am-6pm; free except for special exhibitions) An art gallery which focuses on British art from 1500 to the present day.

ROUTE GUIDE AND MAPS

Tower Bridge to Greenwich: northern bank

Just **6¾ miles (11km, 2¼-2¾hrs)** in length, this stage begins by passing **St Katherine's Docks** (Map 81; see box on p236) before following an – at times – awkward route along a mixture of cobbled road and embankment through **Wapping** (see below) and **Limehouse** (below) to **Canary Wharf** (Map 82).

A tour of the housing estates of **Millwall** follows before you arrive, somewhat gratefully, at the base of **Isle of Dogs** (p237; Map 83), from which **Greenwich Foot Tunnel** leads you, not surprisingly, to Greenwich itself, on the southern bank. Note that if you take this route you will have to cross to the southern bank in the Greenwich Foot Tunnel (see p237). For the route description from Greenwich see p241.

WAPPING   [Map 81, p227]

Once pastures and fields, Wapping has changed a lot throughout the centuries. What was once a tenement slum that became depopulated by the rise of the city's 19th-century docks, the area was devastated by the blitz before blossoming, thanks to the post-war closure of the docks, into today's modern area, full of luxury apartment blocks and estate agents.

Along **Wapping High St** you'll find a **shop**, Mighty Fine Wine (daily 7am-11pm), and two historic **pubs**. At *Town of Ramsgate* (☎ 020-7481 8000, 🖳 townof ramsgate.pub; food Mon-Sat noon-4pm, Mon-Thur 5-9pm, Fri & Sat 5-10pm, Sun noon-9pm; WI-FI; 🐾 on ground floor; No 62) there's a fine selection of burgers (£10.95) on the menu whilst at *Captain*

Kidd (☎ 020-7480 5759; food Mon-Sat 12.30-2.45pm, Sun noon-4pm, Mon-Fri 6.30-8.30pm; 🐾; No 108) there's your normal cheap Samuel Smith drinks and meals such as decent Sunday roast for £10.95.

Along **Wapping Wall** and similarly historic, *The Prospect of Whitby* (☎ 020-7481 1095, 🖳 greeneking-pubs.co.uk; food Mon-Sat noon-10.30pm, Sun noon-9.30pm; WI-FI; 🐾 in garden area only; No 57) has a large selection of food including their 'Ultimate Fish & Chips' (£14.99). All three pubs have beer gardens overlooking the river.

Wapping **railway station** (London Overground line; see box pp52-3) is on Wapping High St.

LIMEHOUSE   [Map 82]

Meaning 'place of lime oasts', lime kilns operated here from the 14th century until 1935. Known for shipbuilding in the 18th century and for its opium dens in the 19th, the area long had a seedy reputation. Decimated by the closures of the nearby docks in the 1960s, Limehouse, like Wapping, is now an area dominated by expensive apartments.

On Narrow St there is a **shop**: Riverside Store (daily 7am-9.30pm) which has an **ATM** (£1.65) and also a tremendous **pub**. As brimming in character as they come, *The Grapes* (☎ 020-7987 4396, 🖳 thegrapes.co.uk; food Mon-Fri noon-2.30pm & 6.30-9.30pm, Sat noon-9.30pm, Sun noon-3.30pm; 🐾 downstairs; No 76)

has a traditional Victorian long bar and a terrace hovering over the Thames. Who knows, maybe it was the 'Sir Ian' meaty shepherd's pie (£17.50), or the taste of the light and crispy calamari salad (£8.95) which once compelled Charles Dickens to dance on the tables here?

The Narrow Restaurant (☎ 020-7592 7950, 🖳 gordonramsay.com/thenarrow; food Mon-Sat noon-4.30pm & 4.45-10.30pm, Sun noon-8pm; WI-FI; 🐾; No 44) is foul-mouthed TV chef Gordon Ramsay's contribution to the local cuisine. It's not too extortionate (pan-fried sea bream with mussels for £22) given the fame of the chef (though how often he's actually seen in the kitchen is, of course, a moot point) and if

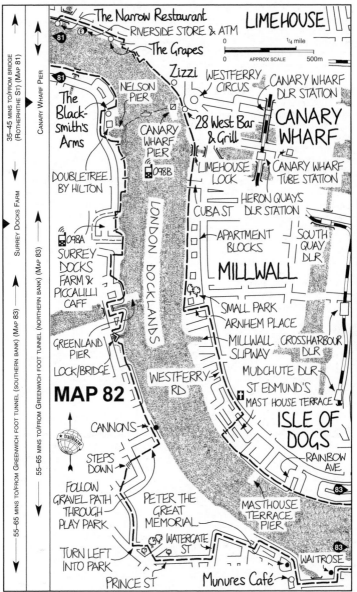

The Narrow Restaurant

RIVERSIDE STORE & ATM

The Grapes

LIMEHOUSE

0 ¼ mile

0 APPROX SCALE 500m

Zizzi

WESTFERRY CIRCUS

CANARY WHARF DLR STATION

NELSON PIER

28 West Bar & Grill

CANARY WHARF

The Black-smith's Arms

CANARY WHARF PIER

LIMEHOUSE LOCK

CANARY WHARF TUBE STATION

098B

DOUBLETREE BY HILTON

HERON QUAYS DLR STATION

CUBA ST

098A

LONDON DOCKLANDS

APARTMENT BLOCKS

SOUTH QUAY DLR

SURREY DOCKS FARM & PICCALILLI CAFF

MILLWALL

SMALL PARK

ARNHEM PLACE

GREENLAND PIER

MILLWALL SLIPWAY

CROSSHARBOUR DLR

LOCK/BRIDGE

WESTFERRY RD

MUDCHUTE DLR

ST EDMUND'S

MAP 82

MAST HOUSE TERRACE

ISLE OF DOGS

CANNONS

RAINBOW AVE

STEPS DOWN

FOLLOW GRAVEL PATH THROUGH PLAY PARK

PETER THE GREAT MEMORIAL

MASTHOUSE TERRACE PIER

TURN LEFT INTO PARK

WATERGATE ST

PRINCE ST

Munures Café

WAITROSE

trailblazer

35–45 MINS TO/FROM BRIDGE (ROTHERHITHE ST) (MAP 81)

CANARY WHARF PIER

SURREY DOCKS FARM

55–65 MINS TO/FROM GREENWICH FOOT TUNNEL (SOUTHERN BANK) (MAP 83)

55–65 MINS TO/FROM GREENWICH FOOT TUNNEL (NORTHERN BANK) (MAP 83)

you fancy an end-of-walk feed-up this wouldn't be a bad choice though booking is advisable, especially if you want a table with a view.

Limehouse DLR station (Map 81) is a short way from the path; services operate to Bank, Tower Gateway and Greenwich. Limehouse railway station is on c2c's line (see box pp52-3) to Shoeburyness from Fenchurch Street station.

CANARY WHARF   [Map 82, p235]

Part of West India Docks – once the busiest in the world – Canary Wharf takes its name from the cargoes of fruit which used to be disembarked here from the Canary Islands and Mediterranean. Following the dock's closure and subsequent regeneration the area has been transformed into London's second business district (after The City) and the site of one of London's most iconic Thames-side scenes, with the office buildings being some of the tallest in Britain.

There are several restaurants opposite Canary Wharf Pier although most are unlikely to appeal to the humble rambler. Of them, 28 West Bar and Grill (☎ 020-3757 6664, 🖳 www.28-west.co.uk; food Sun-Wed noon-9pm, Thur-Sat noon-10pm; WI-FI; 28 Westferry Circus) has some tasty offerings, beginning with a goat's cheese salad for £12.50 and rising to a rump steak for £18.

Italian-lovers may be relieved to see a branch of Zizzi (☎ 020-7512 9257, 🖳 zizzi.co.uk; Mon-Sat 11.30am-11pm, Sun 11.30am-10.30pm; WI-FI; 33 Westferry Circus) which offers their usual large menu including skinny pizzas (from £9.95) – though why you might be concerned about your weight after all the walking you've done is anybody's guess.

Canary Wharf has both a DLR (services operate to Greenwich and Bank; see box pp52-3) and an underground station (Jubilee line). The river bus (see p60) calls at the pier and there is also a service (RB4; daily 3-6/day) across the river, between the pier and Doubletree Docklands Nelson Pier (Map 82).

❏ London Docklands

Between the start and end of the 18th century the number of ships mooring in the Pool of London (see box p210 and box p229) trebled until, by the 19th century, it had become the world's greatest seaport. With the river becoming so heavily congested crime became rife, boats would have to wait for days to disembark their cargo and pollution increased. Something had to be done.

The solution was to carve out huge swathes of land, beginning on the Isle of Dogs, to create what would become known as the London Docklands, the construction of which would irrevocably change the city's landscape once again. The first docks to be constructed were West India Docks (now Canary Wharf), which opened in 1802; when the last, St Katherine's Docks, opened in 1828, it meant that the Docklands had spread all the way back to the City and the Pool of London, where their story begun.

Badly damaged by the Blitz and deemed redundant by the advent of both 'containers' and ever larger ships, which the docks and river could not accommodate, the demise of the docks occurred swiftly in the late 1960s. In 1981 Margaret Thatcher created the London Docklands Development Corporation, which, offering investors the opportunity to develop free of planning controls and commercial rates, proved a remarkable success and led to foreign investment flooding in, so leading to the affluence of much of the old dockland areas which you walk through today.

ISLE OF DOGS   **[Map 83, p239]**

Originally Stepney Marshes, the name 'Isle of Dogs' (actually a peninsula, not an island) possibly derives from the fact that Tudor monarchs kept their hunting hounds here. Decimated by the Blitz and the closures of the docks, the area, as with Millwall before it, doesn't feel as if it's been rewarded with quite the same level of regeneration as its western neighbours which reside closer to the city.

Greenwich (see p238) remains the best option for a range of food on this stage but for those who need a full stomach before

they even contemplate walking beneath the river there is a café as well as a few pubs in the vicinity.

Island Gardens Café (☎ 020-7515 2802; Tue-Sun 10am-6pm; 🐾 outside), by the entrance to the foot tunnel, is somewhat of a surprise; it serves up delicious plates (from £7) of Jamaican food (jerk chicken/curried goat) as well as some standard British food.

Island Gardens **DLR station** has services to Greenwich, Bank (tube) and Stratford (railway) stations; see box pp52-3.

Tower Bridge to Greenwich: southern bank

A mile shorter than its northern-bank counterpart, the **5¾-mile (9.2km, 2-2½hrs)** route along the southern bank begins by following side streets and alleyways through **Bermondsey** (see below) and **Rotherhithe** (p238) before a section of embankment walking eventually leads you to **Surrey Docks Farm** (Map 82; ☎ 020-7231 1010, 🖳 surreydocksfarm.org.uk; daily summer 10am-5pm, winter to 4pm; free but donation requested). If the working farm is open simply pass through but if it happens to be closed follow the diversion signs or consult Map 82.

Following a stint pacing residential streets, fortunately split by the occasional pretty park, a sojourn around some apartment blocks leads you to the southern end of **Greenwich Foot Tunnel** (Map 83; open 24hrs). The tunnel was built to replace an unreliable ferry and enable workers to get to work on the other side of the river; it was opened in 1902.

BERMONDSEY   **[Map 81, p227]**

Appearing in *The Domesday Book* as 'Bermundesy', initially Bermondsey was developed by the monks of the local 11th-century Benedictine Abbey. The 18th century saw the area's growth as a manufacturing centre specialising in tanning and the production of glue; old trades which are still evident in some of the road names – such as Tanner St – today.

By the 19th century the coming of industrialisation and the docks led to the area being one of the worst slums in London; Charles Dickens immortalised the notorious Jacob's Island rookery in *Oliver Twist*, with his character Bill Sikes meeting a true villain's end here.

A 20th-century riverscape of warehouses and wharves was targeted during the Blitz and fell further into decline after the war. As a result, the Bermondsey of today certainly feels far more upmarket than one imagines its predecessors to have been.

The Angel (☎ 020-7394 3214; food Tue-Fri noon-3pm & 6-8.30pm, Sat noon-3pm, & 6-9pm, Sun noon-4pm; 🐾 on ground floor only; 101 Bermondsey Wall East) is a Samuel Smith boozer selling the brewery's typically cheap food and drinks, with pies for about £10.50.

Bermondsey is a stop on the **underground** (Jubilee Line); overground **train** lines go to South Bermondsey (services are operated by Southern; see box pp52-3).

ROUTE GUIDE AND MAPS

ROTHERHITHE
[Map 81, p227; Map 82, p235]

Rotherhithe's main claim to fame is its shipyards and it was from this London suburb that *The Mayflower* set sail for Southampton en route to the New World. The captain of the boat, Christopher Jones, is buried at **St Mary's Church**. Rotherhithe also plays host to Isambard Kingdom Brunel's first engineering feat, a tunnel under the Thames that he began at the age of just 19. Isambard's works are celebrated at **Brunel Museum** (☎ 020-7231 3840, 🖳 brunel-museum.org.uk; daily 10am-5pm, £6; Railway Ave) from which the tunnel can be visited and where there is also a *café* (open same hours).

Towards the eastern end of Rotherhithe St is a Best-one **shop** (daily 7.30am-9pm).

YHA London Thameside (☎ 0845-371 9756, 🖳 yha.org.uk/hostel/london-thameside; 320 beds; 2-, 3-, 4-, 5-, 6- & 10-bed rooms, all en suite; WI-FI communal areas; Ⓛ) is at 20 Salter Rd. Some rooms have double beds and the rooms for 3/5 people have a pull-out bed; dorm beds (male & female) cost from £15pp, private/family rooms are £35-55/29-95. The hostel has 24hr access and there are laundry & drying facilities. Meals are available and the *café* (meals 1-8pm) is open to non residents.

The closest you'll get to *The Mayflower's* historic departure point is actually where the **pub** now stands. Indeed, it claims to be the *oldest* pub actually on the Thames (the Olde Bell at Hurley, see p166,

may be older, but it's a few hundred metres from the river's edge) *The Mayflower* (☎ 020-7237 4088, 🖳 mayflowerpub.co.uk; food Mon-Sat noon-9.30pm, Sun noon-9pm; WI-FI; 🐾 in bar only; 117 Rotherhithe St) has plenty of guest ales; the menu changes seasonally but turn up on a Wednesday and you can enjoy their £15 pie night, including a pint of beer or a glass of wine.

En route along Rotherhithe St, *The Salt Quay* (☎ 020-7394 7108, 🖳 greene king-pubs.co.uk; food Mon-Thur 11am-10pm, Fri-Sun 10am-10pm; WI-FI; 🐾 downstairs only; No 163) has a menu full of pub classics and sandwiches (£5.45-6.45).

Meanwhile, *The Blacksmiths Arms* (Map 82; ☎ 020-7064 4355, 🖳 blacksmiths armsrotherhithe.co.uk; food Mon-Fri noon-4pm & 5-10pm, Sat noon-10pm, Sun noon-9pm; WI-FI; 🐾 in bar and garden; No 257) offers British and Thai fare including Panang Curry (£12.95).

A **café** worth a stop is *Piccalilli Caff* (Map 82; ☎ 020-7237 6892, 🖳 piccalilli caff.com; food Tue-Sun 10am-4pm; WI-FI; 🐾) at **Surrey Docks Farm** (see p231). There are five or six daily specials and a build your own breakfast from £1.50 per item.

Rotherhithe's **railway station** (Map 81; London Overground line, see box pp52-3) is a short walk from the path.

There is a **river bus** service (see p60) between Nelson Dock Pier and Canary Wharf.

GREENWICH   [map p240]

A World Heritage Site, Greenwich's history is a far cry from those of its neighbours on the Thames Path. The site of the 15th-century Palace of Placentia, where both Henry VIII and Elizabeth I were born, is now the **Old Royal Naval College** (☎ 020-8269 4747, 🖳 ornc.org; grounds daily 10am-5pm; free) with the current twin-domed Christopher Wren-designed masterpiece built between 1696 and 1712. Inside you'll find **Greenwich Tourist Information Centre** (☎ 0870-608 2000, 🖳 visitgreen wich.org.uk; daily 10am-5pm), in the

Discover Greenwich Visitor Centre (same hours; free), which has a deluge of maps, pamphlets and guidebooks detailing the town's historic sites and museums, including the Naval College, **National Maritime Museum**, and **Royal Observatory**. Standing at the latter you are at the Prime Meridian of the World: Longitude 0.

For further information on Greenwich's royal museums or visiting the Cutty Sark, consult the website.

Shops include branches of Waitrose (Map 82; Mon-Sat 7am-10pm, Sun

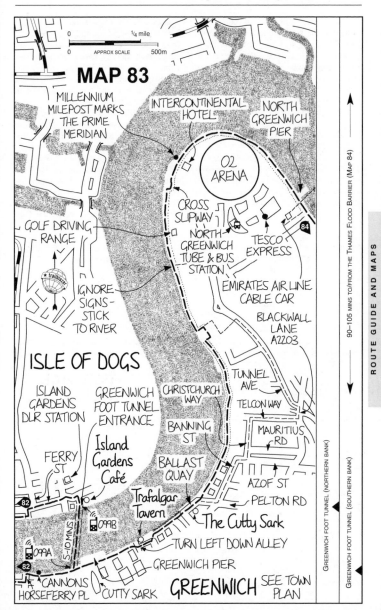

MAP 83

0 ¼ mile
0   500m
APPROX SCALE

MILLENNIUM
MILEPOST MARKS
THE PRIME
MERIDIAN

INTERCONTINENTAL
HOTEL

NORTH
GREENWICH
PIER

O2 ARENA

CROSS
SLIPWAY

NORTH
GREENWICH
TUBE & BUS
STATION

TESCO
EXPRESS

84

GOLF DRIVING
RANGE

trailblazer

IGNORE
SIGNS -
STICK
TO RIVER

EMIRATES AIR LINE
CABLE CAR

BLACKWALL
LANE
A2203

ISLE OF DOGS

TUNNEL
AVE

ISLAND
GARDENS
DLR STATION

GREENWICH
FOOT TUNNEL
ENTRANCE

CHRISTCHURCH
WAY

TELCON WAY

Island
Gardens
Café

BANNING
ST

MAURITIUS
RD

FERRY
ST

BALLAST
QUAY

AZOF ST

82

PELTON RD

099B

Trafalgar
Tavern

The Cutty Sark

5-10 MINS

099A

TURN LEFT DOWN ALLEY

82

GREENWICH PIER

A
HORSEFERRY PL

CANNONS

CUTTY SARK

GREENWICH

SEE TOWN
PLAN

ROUTE GUIDE AND MAPS

90–105 MINS TO/FROM THE THAMES FLOOD BARRIER (MAP 84)

GREENWICH FOOT TUNNEL (NORTHERN BANK)

GREENWICH FOOT TUNNEL (SOUTHERN BANK)

10.30am-5pm; New Capital Quay), an M&S Simply Food (Mon-Sat 8am-10pm, Sun 9am-9pm) and the **chemist** Boots (Mon-Fri 9am-6pm, Sat 9am-7pm, Sun 10am-8pm) near the Cutty Sark. **ATMs** can be found outside Cutty Sark DLR station.

Wandering towards Greenwich you pass *Munures Café* (Map 82; Tue-Thur 8am-6pm, Fri & Sat 8am-8pm, Sun 9am-8pm; WI-FI; 🐾 small dogs; Glaisher St).

Pub food can be found adjacent to the Visitor Centre at *The Old Brewery* (☎ 020-3437 2222, 🖳 oldbrewerygreenwich.com; WI-FI; 🐾; food Mon-Sat 10am-10pm, Sun to 9.30pm), with lovely outside seating and a menu consisting of sandwiches (£5.50-7) and half a dozen mains including a Lancashire hotpot (£14.50) – ideal for a chilly day.

A short way back from the river is *The Gipsy Moth* (☎ 020-8858 0786, 🖳 thegipsy mothgreenwich.co.uk; food daily noon-10pm; WI-FI; 🐾), 60 Greenwich Church St. There's outdoor seating; the menu includes beef & amber ale pie (£13) to chomp on as you watch Greenwich Mean Time go by.

There are also two decent pubs further along the path and away from the tourist masses. *The Trafalgar Tavern* (Map 83; ☎ 020-3887 9886, 🖳 trafalgartavern.co.uk; food Mon-Sat noon-10pm, Sun noon-9pm; WI-FI; 🐾 in bar only; Park Row) has a large menu including Trafalgar whitebait (£7.50), although the whitebait no longer come fresh from the river as they did in days gone by; while *The Cutty Sark* (Map 83; ☎ 020-8858 3146, 🖳 cuttysarkse10.co .uk; food Mon-Sat noon-10pm, Sun noon-9pm; WI-FI; 🐾 in bar; Ballast Quay) also has some fine dishes (mains £12-23.50).

Chicken lovers will find a *Nando's* (☎ 020-8269 1770, 🖳 nandos.co.uk; Sun-Thur 11am-10.30pm, Fri & Sat 11am-11pm; WI-FI) by the entrance to the foot tunnel; while nearby is a **Byron** burger joint (☎ 020-8269 0800, 🖳 byronhamburgers.com; Sun-Thur 11.30am-10pm, Fri & Sat to 10.30pm).

Greenwich has both a **DLR** (Cutty Sark for Maritime Greenwich) and a **railway station** (Southeastern) a little further from the river; for details of services from both see box pp52-3.

The **river bus** (see p60) also stops at the pier here.

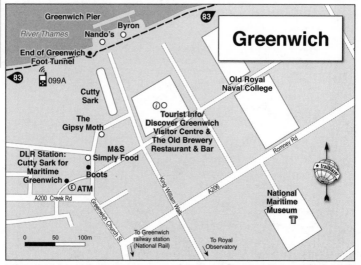

Greenwich to the Thames Barrier [Maps 83-84]

This final stretch of the trail is **4½ miles (7km, 1½-1¾hrs)** and can only be walked on the southern side of the river.

Having passed the impressive **Old Royal Naval College** (Map 83), the Thames Path embarks on one last great meander, passing below wharves and scything through construction sites, past **O2 Arena** – built in 1999 to celebrate the millennium – and beneath **Emirates Airlines Cable Car** (🖥 emiratesairline .co.uk; Apr-end Sep Mon-Fri/Sat/Sun 7/8/9am-11pm, rest of year Mon-Thur/Fri/Sat/Sun 7/7/8/9am-9/11/11/9pm; £4.50, £3.50 with Oyster card/ Travelcard) before sweeping you along to the Thames Barrier and the end of your epic journey. En route you pass **Greenwich Peninsula Ecology Park** (Map 84; 🖥 tcv.org.uk/greenwichpeninsula; Wed-Sun 10am-5pm), a freshwater habitat where wildlife – in what otherwise is a landscape of metal, concrete and stone – somehow thrives. Keeping your eyes riverwards will present some marvellous views back across London as you edge ever closer to the sea. Before too long the **Thames Barrier** (see box below) will heave into view. Once there go up and down some steps to pass through a **tunnel**; the profile of the Path on the wall – from Kemble (105m) to sea level (0m) – is an excellent way to reflect on your journey. On the other side you reach a tidy park with a good viewing spot for the barrier piers and a **Visitor Centre** on its far (eastern) side; your riverside odyssey will be at an end.

One of the barrier piers

> ### ❏ The Thames Barrier
>
> Owing to the rather ominous fact that London – indeed the whole of the south-east of England – has been sinking, over the decades the city has grown ever more vulnerable to those very waters which gave it life: those of the River Thames. The embankments have to some effect held back the river's waters but in the 1950s it was estimated that in order to cope with the ever-rising tides the city's defences would have to be raised by another 6ft. And so plans for some form of barrier began. Work was started on the Thames Barrier in 1974 and completed in 1982, officially opening in 1984.
>
> One of the largest moveable flood barriers in the world, it protects some 125 square kilometres of Central London. First used to fend off a dangerous tide in February 1983, between then and the July of 2014 it had been closed 174 times. Run by the Environment Agency since 1996, it stretches 520 metres across the river and comprises 10 steel gates which can be raised across the river whenever a tidal surge is predicted. When raised, the barrier's main gates are as high as a five-storey building and are as wide as the opening of Tower Bridge.
>
> The barrier is projected to remain effective against rising sea levels until 2030; but the Environment Agency is already in the process of considering new ways in which to keep London safe.
>
> **Thames Barrier Information Centre** (☎ 020-8305 4188, 🖥 gov.uk/the-thames-barrier; Thur-Sun & Bank Hols 10.30/11am-5pm, daily in August; £4) tells its tale.

CHARLTON   **[Map 84]**

Depending on the strength of your liver you will either be relieved or distraught to reach *Anchor and Hope* (☎ 020-8858 0382, 🖥 anchorandhope.co.uk; food Mon-Fri 11am-5.45pm, Sat 11am-4pm, Sun 1-4pm; WI-FI; 🐾 outside), the last pub on the Thames Path. It's a friendly place where locals drink after work, taking advantage of the outdoor seating to stare out over the river. For those who – having walked *almost* 184

miles – are in need of a good meal the pub provides your last Thames-side menu and includes ham, egg & chips (£6.95).

The View Café is part of the Thames Barrier Information Centre (see box p241) and is open the same hours.

Central London is easily accessed from **Charlton Railway Station** (Southeastern; see box pp52-3).

❑ Getting back from the Thames Barrier

Leaving the path and returning to the 'real world' is not as straightforward as you may hope. The pier by the Information Centre is for private boats only so the nearest river bus (see p60) stop is either back at North Greenwich, by Emirates Airline Cable Car, or further along the Thames at Woolwich (Royal Arsenal). The options therefore are to return to either North Greenwich or Charlton, or walk along the extension path (not part of the official Thames Path) to Woolwich, or for those who are particularly keen all the way to Crayford Ness (see 🖥 www.thames-path.org.uk/thames_charlton_cray ford.html).

● **From North Greenwich by river bus, tube or bus** For most of us, the easiest way to get back from the Thames Barrier is to walk for five minutes south (inland) from the barrier and river, passing industrial units and going through a small park, to emerge onto Woolwich Rd (A206) by Royal Greenwich Trust School. Here, having crossed the road, bus Nos 161 and 472 head west towards North Greenwich bus/tube station, from where you can catch a bus, or take a tube (Jubilee line). Better still, walk five minutes back to the river and the Thames Clipper (river bus) pier, where boats will take you back to the centre of the city. Bus Nos 177 and 180 from the same stop head to Greenwich town centre (see p238), where you can also catch a river bus or take Docklands Light Railway to various destinations within the city.

● **From Charlton by train** The easiest way to reach Charlton Railway station (see above) is to walk back to the Anchor & Hope pub and then turn left and walk along Anchor & Hope Lane till you reach the A206. Cross that and keep going south; the station is on the right-hand side a little further along.

● **From Woolwich by river bus, ferry, DLR, train or tube** If a bit more walking appeals (following the Thames Path extension route) it is only just over a mile to Woolwich. At the time of writing a diversion route was in place at the Barrier but by the time you are there you should be able to walk along the riverside all the way. Both Woolwich Foot Tunnel and Woolwich Ferry (Mon-Sat 4-8/hr between 6.10am and 8pm, Sun 4/hr between 11.30am and 7.30pm; free) cross to the northern bank and from there it is easy to reach London City Airport, or take a DLR from King George V station.

If you continue on the southern bank it is not long till you reach Woolwich (Royal Arsenal) pier. Unfortunately, from this during the week river bus services (see p60) depart before 10am and after 6pm only, though at the weekend there is a shuttle service (2/hr) to North Greenwich where you can pick up the main services.

However, Woolwich also provides rail options: Woolwich Arsenal station offers both rail (Southeastern) and DLR services (see box pp52-3 for both). From December 2018 the Crossrail Elizabeth line (Woolwich station) will be open (see box p51).

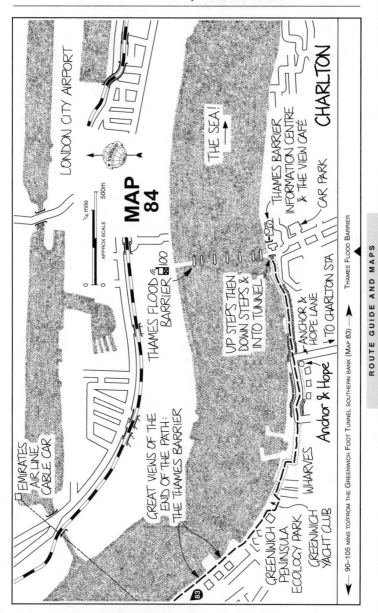

LONDON CITY AIRPORT

MAP 84

★ trailblazer

¼ mile

500m

APPROX SCALE

THE SEA! →

CHARLTON

Thames Barrier
Information Centre
& The View Café

CAR PARK

THAMES FLOOD
BARRIER

UP STEPS THEN
DOWN STEPS &
INTO TUNNEL

ANCHOR & HOPE LANE
→ TO CHARLTON STA

Anchor & Hope

EMIRATES
AIR LINE
CABLE CAR

GREAT VIEWS OF THE
END OF THE PATH:
THE THAMES BARRIER

GREENWICH
PENINSULA
ECOLOGY PARK

GREENWICH
YACHT CLUB

WHARVES

83

← 90–105 MINS TO/FROM THE GREENWICH FOOT TUNNEL SOUTHERN BANK (MAP 83) →   THAMES FLOOD BARRIER ▶

APPENDIX A: TAKING A DOG

TAKING DOGS ALONG THE PATH

Many are the rewards that await those prepared to make the extra effort required to bring their best friend along the trail. You shouldn't underestimate the amount of work involved, though. Indeed, just about every decision you make will be influenced by the fact that you've got a dog: how you plan to travel to the start of the trail, where you're going to stay, how far you're going to walk each day, where you're going to rest and where you're going to eat in the evening etc.

If you're also sure your dog can cope with (and will enjoy) walking 10 miles or more a day for several days in a row, you need to start preparing accordingly. Extra thought also needs to go into your itinerary. The best starting point is to study the village and town facilities table on pp30-5 (and the advice opposite), and plan where to stop and where to buy food.

Looking after your dog

To begin with, you need to make sure that your own dog is fully **inoculated** against the usual doggy illnesses, and also up to date with regard to **worm pills** (eg Drontal) and **flea preventatives** such as Frontline – they are, after all, following in the pawprints of many a dog before them, some of whom may well have left fleas or other parasites on the trail that now lie in wait for their next meal to arrive. **Pet insurance** is also a very good idea; if you've already got insurance, do check that it will cover a trip such as this.

On the subject of looking after your dog's health, perhaps the most important implement you can take with you is the **plastic tick remover**, available from vets for a couple of quid. These removers, while fiddly, help you to remove the tick safely (ie without leaving its head buried under the dog's skin).

Being in unfamiliar territory also makes it more likely that you and your dog could become separated. For this reason, make sure your dog has a **tag with your contact details on it** (a mobile phone number would be best if you are carrying one with you); you could also consider having your dog **microchipped** for further security.

When to keep your dog on a lead

● **When crossing farmland**, particularly in the lambing season (Mar-May) when your dog can scare the sheep, causing them to lose their young. Farmers are allowed by law to shoot at and kill any dogs that they consider are worrying their sheep. During lambing, most farmers would prefer it if you didn't bring your dog at all.

The exception is if your dog is being attacked by cows. Pretty much every year there are deaths in the UK caused by walkers being trampled as they tried to rescue their dogs from the attentions of cattle. The advice in this instance is to let go of the lead, head speedily to a position of safety (usually the other side of the field gate or stile) and, once there, call your dog to you.

● **In the presence of waterfowl** Ducks, swans and geese will not appreciate the approaches of your inquisitive hound.

● **Around ground-nesting birds** It's important to keep your dog under control when crossing an area where certain species of birds nest on the ground.

Most dogs love foraging around in the woods but make sure you have permission to do so; some woods are used as 'nurseries' for game birds and dogs are only allowed through them if they are on a lead.

● **At all locks** There's nearly always a sign at the start and end of every lock telling you to keep your dog on a lead; even if there isn't, assume you have to – it's only sensible.

What to pack
You've probably already got a good idea of what to bring to keep your dog alive and happy, but the following is a checklist:

- **Food/water bowl** Foldable cloth bowls are popular with walkers, being both light and taking up little room in the rucksack. You can also get a water-bottle-and-bowl combination, where the bottle folds into a 'trough' from which the dog can drink.
- **Lead and collar** An extendable one is probably preferable for this sort of trip. Make sure both lead and collar are in good condition – you don't want either to snap on the trail, or you may end up carrying your dog through sheep fields until a replacement can be found.
- **Medication** You'll know if you need to bring any lotions or potions.
- **Tick remover** See opposite
- **Bedding** A simple blanket may suffice, or you can opt for something more elaborate if you aren't carrying your own luggage.
- **Poo bags** Essential.
- **Hygiene wipes** For cleaning your dog after it's rolled in stuff.
- **A favourite toy** Helps prevent your dog from pining for the entire walk.
- **Food/water** Remember to bring treats as well as regular food to keep up the mutt's morale. That said, if your dog is anything like mine the chances are they'll spend most of the walk dining on rabbit droppings and sheep poo anyway.
- **Corkscrew stake** Available from camping or pet shops, this will help you to keep your dog secure in one place while you set up camp/doze.
- **Raingear** It can rain!
- **Old towels** For drying your dog.

How to pack
When it comes to packing, I always leave an exterior pocket of my rucksack empty so I can put used poo bags in there (for deposit at the first bin I come to). I always like to keep all the dog's kit together and separate from the other luggage (usually inside a plastic bag inside my rucksack). I have also seen several dogs sporting their own 'doggy rucksack', so they can carry their own food, water, poo etc – which certainly reduces the burden on their owner!

Cleaning up after your dog
It is extremely important that dog owners behave in a responsible way when walking the path. Dog excrement should be cleaned up. In towns, villages and fields where animals graze or which will be cut for silage, hay etc, you need to pick up and bag the excrement. If you're walking somewhere uncultivated and remote then it's probably preferable for both you and the environment if you adopt the 'stick and flick' approach, grabbing hold of a nearby stick to flick the poo well away from the trail and the footwear of other walkers.

Staying and eating with your dog
In this guide the symbol 🐾 denotes where a hotel, pub or B&B welcomes dogs. However, this **always needs to be arranged in advance** and some places may charge extra (£2-20). Also many places have only one or two rooms suitable for people with dogs.

Hostels (both YHA and independent) do not permit them unless they are an assistance (guide) dog. Most campsites happily allow dogs through their gates but will have some restrictions in place, such as they must stay on a lead. When phoning to book a campsite, it's worth mentioning that you're walking with a dog as many will wish to check your pooch before allowing access.

When it comes to **eating**, most landlords allow dogs in at least a section of their pubs, though few restaurants do. Make sure you always ask first and ensure your dog doesn't run around the pub but is secured to your table or a radiator.

Henry Stedman

APPENDIX B: GPS WAYPOINTS

MAP	WAYPOINT	OS GRID REF	DESCRIPTION
1	001	N51 41.673 W2 01.783	Thames Head (source of the River Thames)
1	002	N51 40.806 W2 00.903	Cross A429
2	003	N51 40.587 W1 59.723	T-junction at Ewen
3	004	N51 39.099 W1 58.477	Join road at Somerford Keynes
4	005	N51 38.817 W1 56.167	Ashford Keynes
5	006	N51 38.352 W1 54.844	Car park at Waterhay
6	007	N51 39.096 W1 52.525	Cross bridge by North Meadow NNR
7	008	N51 38.656 W1 51.291	Cricklade High St
8	009	N51 38.656 W1 49.345	Bridge crossing river
9	010	N51 39.657 W1 47.479	The Red Lion, Castle Eaton
10	011	N51 39.753 W1 44.921	Join road by Hannington Bridge
11	012	N51 40.642 W1 42.594	Footbridge
12	013	N51 41.041 W1 42.269	Inglesham
12	014	N51 41.535 W1 41.571	Halfpenny Bridge
13	015	N51 40.895 W1 40.119	Buscot Lock
14	016	N51 41.261 W1 38.127	Turning to Kelmscott
15	017	N51 41.612 W1 35.324	Radcot Bridge
16	018	N51 41.910 W1 32.038	Bridge at Rushey Lock
17	019	N51 42.100 W1 31.040	Tadpole Bridge
17	020	N51 41.705 W1 29.342	Tenfoot Bridge
18	021	N51 42.414 W1 27.871	Shifford Lock
19	022	N51 42.613 W1 25.033	Bridge in Newbridge
20	023	N51 42.972 W1 22.633	Northmoor Lock
21	024	N51 44.103 W1 22.331	The Ferryman Inn
22	025	N51 45.619 W1 21.858	Pinkhill Lock
22	026	N51 46.459 W1 21.539	Swinford Toll Bridge
23	027	N51 47.346 W1 18.441	Kings Lock
24	028	N51 46.766 W1 17.996	Godstow Bridge
24	029	N51 46.010 W1 17.189	Turning to The Perch
25	030	N51 45.159 W1 16.334	Osney Bridge
26	031	N51 44.753 W1 15.384	Folly Bridge
26	032	N51 44.144 W1 14.543	Cross under B4495
27	033	N51 42.484 W1 13.982	Sandford Lock
28	034	N51 41.118 W1 13.324	Turning to Lower Radley and Radley
29	035	N51 40.294 W1 16.260	Abingdon Lock
29	036	N51 40.098 W1 16.726	Abingdon Bridge
30	037	N51 39.045 W1 15.961	Culham Bridge
31	038	N51 38.904 W1 12.663	Clifton Lock
32	039	N51 39.280 W1 12.659	Join road to cross bridge at Clifton Hampden
33	040	N51 38.304 W1 10.747	Day's Lock
33	041	N51 38.085 W1 09.988	Turning to Dorchester-on-Thames
34	042	N51 38.082 W1 08.901	Path joins A4074
34	043	N51 37.514 W1 08.360	Turn off road before Shillingford Bridge
35	044	N51 37.008 W1 06.969	Benson Lock
35	045	N51 36.058 W1 07.271	Cross Wallingford High St

MAP	WAYPOINT	OS GRID REF	DESCRIPTION
36	046	N51 35.229 W1 07.464	A4130 (bridge over Thames)
37	047	N51 33.519 W1 08.588	Footbridge under two viaducts
37	048	N51 32.873 W1 08.888	Turning off A329
38	049	N51 31.381 W1 08.675	Bridge at Streatley
39	050	N51 30.132 W1 06.369	Path leaves river
40	051	N51 29.205 W1 05.129	Whitchurch Bridge (toll bridge)
41	052	N51 29.200 W1 02.412	Mapledurham Lock
42	053	N51 28.171 W0 59.766	Reading Thames-side Promenade starts
43	054	N51 27.930 W0 58.653	Caversham Bridge
44	055	N51 28.030 W0 55.730	Footpath enters trees
45	056	N51 28.528 W0 54.810	Sonning Bridge
46	057	N51 30.702 W0 52.947	Path leaves road
47	058	N51 31.646 W0 53.082	Start of long bridge
48	059	N51 32.253 W0 54.048	Henley Bridge
49	060	N51 33.607 W0 52.416	Hambleden Lock
50	061	N51 33.074 W0 52.214	The Flower Pot Inn
51	062	N51 33.043 W0 48.662	Hurley Lock
52	063	N51 34.052 W0 46.407	Marlow Bridge
53	064	N51 34.527 W0 42.823	Cross river by railway bridge
54	065	N51 33.602 W0 42.425	Cookham High St
54	066	N51 33.009 W0 41.530	Little bridge by fence
55	067	N51 31.449 W0 42.219	Maidenhead Bridge
56	068	N51 30.442 W0 41.158	M4 crosses river
57	069	N51 29.940 W0 40.830	Gap in hedge by start of Dorney Lake
58	070	N51 29.391 W0 38.834	St Mary Magdalene church, Boveney
59	071	N51 29.151 W0 36.497	Windsor Bridge
59	072	N51 29.273 W0 35.493	The Victoria Bridge
60	073	N51 28.278 W0 35.012	Albert Bridge
61	074	N51 26.942 W0 34.019	National Trust Tea Rooms & toilet, Runnymede
62	075	N51 26.240 W0 32.124	Path goes under M25
62	076	N51 26.012 W0 30.996	Staines Bridge
63	077	N51 24.880 W0 29.977	Penton Hook Lock
64	078	N51 23.337 W0 29.154	Chertsey Bridge
65	079	N51 22.964 W0 27.427	Shepperton to Weybridge Ferry
65	080	N51 23.024 W0 26.179	Walton Bridge
66	081	N51 24.297 W0 24.380	Sunbury Lock
67	082	N51 24.514 W0 21.192	Thyme by the River Café
68	083	N51 24.209 W0 20.567	Hampton Court Bridge
69	084	N51 24.668 W0 18.475	Kingston Bridge
71	085	N51 25.854 W0 19.292	Bridge by Teddington Lock

Southern bank

MAP	WAYPOINT	OS GRID REF	DESCRIPTION
71	086a	N51 26.288 W0 19.729	Bridge at Ham Lands Nature Reserve
72	087a	N51 27.085 W0 18.158	Buccleuch Gardens
73	088a	N51 27.456 W0 18.376	Richmond Bridge
74	089a	N51 29.187 W0 17.261	Kew Bridge
75	090a	N51 28.358 W0 16.241	Chiswick Bridge
76	091a	N51 29.268 W0 13.867	Hammersmith Bridge
77	092a	N51 27.964 W0 12.851	Putney Bridge
77	093a	N51 27.829 W0 11.231	Wandsworth Bridge

MAP	WAYPOINT	OS GRID REF	DESCRIPTION
Southern bank *(continued)*			
78	094a	N51 28.880 W0 09.995	Gate by Albert Bridge
79	095a	N51 29.643 W0 07.265	Lambeth Bridge
80	096a	N51 30.432 W0 06.969	Waterloo Bridge
81	097a	N51 30.260 W0 04.587	Tower Bridge
82	098a	N51 29.963 W0 01.954	Surrey Docks Farm
83	099a	N51 28.992 W0 00.607	Greenwich Foot Tunnel
Northern bank			
71	086b	N51 26.374 W0 19.953	Enter Radnor Gardens
72	087b	N51 26.735 W0 19.763	Wharf Lane meets river
73	088b	N51 27.395 W0 18.504	Richmond Bridge
74	089b	N51 29.264 W0 17.263	Kew Bridge
75	090b	N51 28.482 W0 16.041	Cross A316 near Chiswick Bridge
76	091b	N51 29.364 W0 13.779	Hammersmith Bridge
77	092b	N51 28.088 W0 12.743	Putney Bridge
77	093b	N51 27.947 W0 11.325	Wandsworth Bridge
78	094b	N51 28.991 W0 10.040	Albert Bridge
79	095b	N51 29.680 W0 07.486	Lambeth Bridge
80	096b	N51 30.582 W0 07.092	Waterloo Bridge
81	097b	N51 30.397 W0 04.462	Tower Bridge
82	098b	N51 30.345 W0 01.703	Canary Wharf pier
83	099b	N51 29.207 W0 00.561	Greenwich Foot Tunnel
Southern bank			
84	100	N51 29.690 E0 02.221	Thames Barrier

APPENDIX C: MAP KEY

Map key

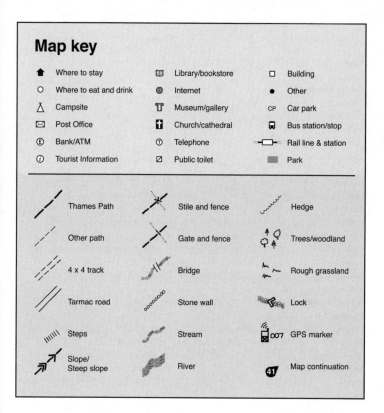

♠	Where to stay	📖	Library/bookstore	☐	Building
○	Where to eat and drink	@	Internet	●	Other
Λ	Campsite	⊤	Museum/gallery	CP	Car park
⊠	Post Office	✝	Church/cathedral	🚌	Bus station/stop
£	Bank/ATM	☏	Telephone		Rail line & station
ⓘ	Tourist Information	☑	Public toilet		Park

Thames Path

Other path

4 x 4 track

Tarmac road

Steps

Slope/ Steep slope

Stile and fence

Gate and fence

Bridge

Stone wall

Stream

River

Hedge

Trees/woodland

Rough grassland

Lock

007 GPS marker

41 Map continuation

APPENDIX D – DISTANCE CHARTS

	Kemble	Ewen	Ashton Keynes	Cricklade	Lechlade	Radcot	Newbridge	Bablock Hythe	Eynsham Lock	Oxford	Sandford-on-Thames	Abingdon	Culham	Clifton Hampden	Shillingford	Benson	Wallingford
Kemble	0																
Ewen	2.7																
Ashton Keynes	7	4.2															
Cricklade	12.2	9.5	5.2														
Lechlade	23.2	20.5	16.2	11													
Radcot	30	27.2	23	17.7	6.7												
Newbridge	40	37.2	33	27.7	16.7	10											
Bablock Hythe	44	41.2	37	31.7	20.7	14	4										
Eynsham Lock	47.5	44.7	40.5	35.2	24.2	17.5	7.5	3.5									
Oxford	54	51.2	47	41.7	30.7	24	14	10	6.5								
Sandford-on-T	58.2	55.5	51.2	46	35	28.2	18.2	14.2	10.7	4.2							
Abingdon	63.7	61	56.7	51.5	40.5	33.7	23.7	19.7	16.2	9.7	5.5						
Culham	66	63.2	59	53.7	42.7	36	26	22	18.5	12	7.7	2.2					
Clifton Hampden	69	66.2	62	56.7	45.7	39	29	25	21.5	15	10.7	5.2	3				
Shillingford	74	71.2	67	61.7	50.7	44	34	30	26.5	20	15.7	10.2	8	5			
Benson	76	73.2	69	63.7	52.7	46	36	32	28.5	22	17.7	12.2	10	7	2		
Wallingford	77.2	74.5	70.2	65	54	47.2	37.2	33.2	29.7	23.2	19	13.5	11.2	8.2	3.2	1.2	
Moulsford	81.2	78.2	74.2	69	58	51.2	41.2	37.2	33.7	27.2	23	17.5	15.2	12.2	7.2	5.2	4
Goring & Streatley	84.2	81.5	77.2	72	61	54.2	44.2	40.2	36.7	30.2	26	20.5	18.2	15.2	10.2	8.2	7
Pangbourne	88.2	85.5	81.2	76	65	58.2	48.2	44.2	40.7	34.2	30	24.5	22.2	19.2	14.2	12.2	11
Caversham (Rdng)	95.2	92.5	88.2	83	72	65.2	55.2	51.2	47.7	41.2	37	31.5	29.2	26.2	21.2	19.2	18
Sonning	98.5	95.7	91.5	86.2	75.2	68.5	58.5	54.5	51	44.5	40.2	34.7	32.5	29.5	24.5	22.5	21.2
Lower Shiplake	102	99.2	95	89.7	78.7	72	62	58	54.5	48	43.7	38.2	36	33	28	26	24.7
Henley-on-Thames	104.2	101.5	97.2	92	81	74.2	64.2	60.2	56.7	50.2	46	40.5	38.2	35.2	30.2	28.2	27
Hurley	110.5	107.7	103.5	98.2	87.2	80.5	70.5	66.5	63	56.5	52.2	46.7	44.5	41.5	36.5	34.5	33.2
Marlow	112.7	110	105.7	100.5	89.5	82.7	72.7	68.7	65.2	58.7	54.5	49	46.7	43.7	38.7	36.7	35.5
Bourne End	116	113.2	109	103.7	92.7	86	76	72	68.5	62	57.7	52.2	50	47	42	40	38.7
Cookham	117.2	114.5	110.2	105	94	87.2	77.2	73.2	69.7	63.2	59	53.5	51.2	48.2	43.2	41.2	40
Maidenhead	120.5	117.7	113.5	108.2	97.2	90.5	80.5	76.5	73	66.5	62.2	56.7	54.5	51.5	46.5	44.5	43.2
Eton & Windsor	127	124.2	120	114.7	103.7	97	87	83	79.5	73	68.7	63.2	61	58	53	51	49.7
Datchet	129	126.2	122	116.7	105.7	99	89	85	81.5	75	70.7	65.2	63	60	55	53	51.7
Runnymede	132.5	129.7	125.5	120.2	109.2	102.5	92.5	88.5	85	78.5	74.2	68.7	66.5	63.5	58.5	56.5	55.2
Staines	135.5	132.7	128.5	123.2	112.2	105.5	95.5	91.5	88	81.5	77.2	71.7	69.5	66.5	61.5	59.5	58.2
Chertsey	139	136.2	132	126.7	115.7	109	99	95	91.5	85	80.7	73	70	65	63	61.7	57.7
Shepperton Lock	141	138.2	134	128.7	117.7	111	101	97	93.5	87	82.7	77.2	75	72	67	65	63.7
Walton-on-T*	143	140.2	136	130.7	119.7	113	103	99	95.5	89	84.7	79.2	77	74	69	67	65.7
Hampton Ct/E Mol	147.7	145	140.7	135.5	124.5	117.7	107.7	103.7	100.2	93.7	89.5	84	81.7	78.7	73.7	71.7	70.5
Hamptn W/Kingstn	151	148.2	144	138.7	127.7	121	111	107	103.5	97	92.7	87.2	85	82	77	75	73.7

* Reduce the distance walked from Shepperton Lock to Walton-on-Thames by 0.75 miles if you take the ferry

Thames Path
DISTANCE CHART 1

Kemble to Kingston-upon Thames

miles (approx) – 1 mile = 1.6km

	Moulsford	Goring & Streatley	Pangbourne	Caversham (Reading)	Sonning	Lower Shiplake	Henley-on-Thames	Hurley	Marlow	Bourne End	Cookham	Maidenhead	Eton & Windsor	Datchet	Runnymede	Staines	Chertsey	Shepperton Lock	Walton-on-Thames*	Hampton Court / East Molesey	Hampton Wick / Kingston upon Thames
Goring & Streatley	3																				
Pangbourne	7	4																			
Caversham (Reading)	14	11	7																		
Sonning	17.2	14.2	10.2	3.2																	
Lower Shiplake	20.7	17.7	13.7	6.7	3.5																
Henley-on-Thames	23	20	16	9	5.7	2.2															
Hurley	29.2	26.2	22.2	15.2	12	8.5	6.2														
Marlow	31.5	28.5	24.5	17.5	14.2	10.7	8.5	2.2													
Bourne End	34.7	31.7	27.7	20.7	17.5	14	11.7	5.5	3.2												
Cookham	36	33	29	22	18.7	15.2	13	6.7	4.5	1.2											
Maidenhead	39.2	36.2	32.2	25.2	22	18.5	16.2	10	7.7	4.5	3.2										
Eton & Windsor	45.7	42.7	38.7	31.7	28.5	25	22.7	16.5	14.2	11	9.7	6.5									
Datchet	47.7	44.7	40.7	33.7	30.5	27	24.7	18.5	16.2	13	11.7	8.5	2								
Runnymede	51.2	48.2	44.2	37.2	34	30.5	28.2	22	19.7	16.5	15.2	12	5.5	3.5							
Staines	54.2	51.2	47.2	40.2	37	33.5	31.2	25	22.7	19.5	18.2	15	8.5	6.5	3						
Chertsey	54.7	50.7	43.7	42.7	40.5	37	34.7	28.5	26.2	23	21.7	18.5	12	10	6.5	3.5					
Shepperton Lock	59.7	56.7	52.7	45.7	42.5	39	36.7	30.5	28.2	25	23.7	20.5	14	12	8.5	5.5	2				
Walton-on-Thames*	61.7	58.7	54.7	47.7	44.5	41	38.7	32.5	30.2	27	25.7	22.5	16	14	10.5	7.5	4	2			
Hampton Court / East Molesey	66.5	63.5	59.5	52.5	49.2	45.7	43.5	37.2	35	31.7	30.5	27.2	20.7	18.7	15.2	12.2	8.7	6.7	4.7		
Hampton Wick / Kingston upon Thames	69.7	66.7	62.7	55.7	52.5	49	46.7	40.5	38.2	35	33.7	30.5	24	22	18.5	15.5	12	10	8	3.2	

Thames Path
DISTANCE CHART 2

London – Southern Bank

miles (approx) – 1 mile = 1.6km

	Hampton Wick / Kingston upon Thames	Richmond	Mortlake	Barnes	Putney	Wandsworth	Battersea	Lambeth	Southwark	Tower Bridge: southern bank	Bermondsey	Rotherhithe	Greenwich	Charlton
Hampton W/Kingstn	0													
Richmond	4.7													
Mortlake	9.5	4.7												
Barnes	10.2	5.5	0.7											
Putney	13.5	8.7	4	3.2										
Wandsworth	15	10.2	5.5	4.7	1.5									
Battersea	17.5	12.7	8	7.25	4	2.5								
Lambeth	19.5	16.7	12.5	9.2	6	4.5	2							
Southwark	21.5	18.7	14.5	11.2	8	6.5	4	2						
Tower Bridge	22.7	20	15.7	12.5	9.2	7.7	5.2	3.2	1.25					
Bermondsey	23.7	21	16.7	13.5	10.2	8.7	6.2	4.2	2.2	1				
Rotherhithe	24.7	22	17.7	14.5	11.2	9.7	7.2	5.2	3.2	2	1			
Greenwich	28.5	25.7	21.5	18.2	15	13.5	11	9	7	5.7	4.7	3.7		
Charlton	33	30.2	26	22.7	19.5	18	15.5	13.5	11.5	10.2	9.2	8.2	4.5	

Thames Path
DISTANCE CHART 3

London – Northern Bank

miles (approx) – 1 mile = 1.6km

	Hampton Wick / Kingston upon Thames	Teddington Lock	Twickenham	Isleworth	Brentford	Strand on the Green	Hammersmith	Fulham	Chelsea	Pimlico	Westminster	City of London	Tower Bridge: northern bank	Wapping	Limehouse	Canary Wharf	Isle of Dogs	Charlton*
Hamptn W/K u T	0																	
Teddington Lock	2																	
Twickenham	3.5	1.5																
Isleworth	6.7	4.7	3.2															
Brentford	9	7	5.5	2.2														
Strand on the Gr	10.2	8.2	6.7	3.5	1.2													
Hammersmith	13.5	11.5	10	6.7	4.5	3.2												
Fulham	16.2	13.5	12.7	9.5	7.2	6	2.7											
Chelsea	19.7	17	16.2	13	10.7	9.5	6.2	3.5										
Pimlico	21	18.2	17.5	14.2	12	10.7	7.5	4.7	1.2									
Westminster	23.2	20.5	19.7	16.5	14.2	13	9.7	7	3.5	2.2								
City of London	25.2	22.5	21.7	18.5	16.2	15	11.7	9	5.5	4.2	2							
Tower Bridge	26.2	23.5	22.7	19.5	17.2	16	12.7	10	6.5	5.2	3	1						
Wapping	27.5	24.7	24	20.7	18.5	17.2	14	11.2	7.7	6.5	4.2	2.2	1.2					
Limehouse	28.7	26	25.2	22	19.7	18.5	15.2	12.5	9	7.7	5.5	3.5	2.5	1.2				
Canary Wharf	29.7	27	26.2	23	20.7	19.5	16.2	13.5	10	8.7	6.5	4.5	3.5	2.2	1			
Isle of Dogs	33	30.2	29.5	26.2	24	22.7	19.5	16.7	13.2	12	9.7	7.7	6.7	5.5	4.2	3.2		
Charlton*	37.5	34.7	34	30.7	28.5	27.2	24	21.2	17.7	16.5	14.2	12.2	11.2	10	8.7	7.7	4.5	

* Distance includes walking through the Greenwich Foot Tunnel

INDEX

Page references in **bold** type refer to maps

Abingdon/Abingdon Lock 123, 126, **127**, 128-30, **129**
access rights 71, 73
accidents 76
accommodation 18-22, 78
    see also place name
Airbnb 22
amphibians 68
Appleford **132**
Appleton 110
apps
    flora and fauna 50
    travel 54, 55, 60
Ashton Keynes 81, 82-3, **84**, 86
Aston 164, **165**, 166
ATMs 24, 25, 26

Bablock Hythe 107, **109**, 110
Backpackers' Club 48
Back Water 123, **127**
baggage transfer 25, 78
bank holidays 26
banks & banking 24, 25, 26
Barnes/Barnes Bridge **211**, **212**, 214
Battersea/Battersea Bridge 221, **222**, 223-4
bed and breakfasts (B&Bs) 20-1, 29
beers & breweries 23
Bell Weir Lock 184, 187, **188**
Benson 133, 137, **138**
Bermondsey **227**, 237
Binsey 108, 112, **114**
birds 64-6
Bisham 164, **168**
Blackfriars Bridge **225**, 229
Black Water 123, **127**
blisters 73
Blumenthal, Heston 177
Boat Race, The 38, **161**, 164, **164**, 167, 209
boat services 55
    see also ferries and river bus services
books 46-7, 49-50

boots 40-1
Boulter's Lock 172, 174, **175**
Bourne End 170, **171**, 172
Boveney/Boveney Lock 172, **178**
Bray 176, **176**, 177
breakfasts 22
Brentford **207**, **210**, 218
British Summer Time (BST) 27
Brunel, Isambard Kingdom 142, 174, 238
budgeting 28-9
Buscot/Buscot Lock 95, **98**, 98
business hours 26
bus services 55, **56**, **57**, 58-9
    in London 55, 60
    see also coach services
    and river bus services
butterflies 61-2

camping and campsites 18-19, 29, 31, 33, 35
camping gear 43
camping supplies 24
Canary Wharf **235**, 236
Carfax Conduit Building **125**, 126
cash machines see ATMs
Castle Eaton 88, 90, **91**
Caversham/Caversham Bridge 151-2, **153**, 154, **154**, **155**, 156
cell phones see mobile phones
Charlton 242, **243**
Chelsea/Chelsea Bridge **213**, **222**, 229, 230
Chelsea Flower Show 39, **222**, 229
Chelsea Physic Garden **222**, 229, 232
Chertsey/Chertsey Bridge 184, 190, **191**, 192
Chimney Meadows NNR 70, 98, **103**
Chiswick Bridge **211**

churches 116
    see also place name
Churn, River 79, **87**
City of London **225**, 231
Clifton Cut/Lock 130, **132**
Clifton Hampden 130 133, **133**
Clifton Meadow 63, **133**
clothing 41-2, 76
coach services
    to Britain 50
    within Britain 54
Cock Marsh 170, **171**
compasses 42, 43, 75
conservation 70
Cookham 38, 172, **173**, 174
Cotswold Water Park 81, **84**
Countryside & Rights of Way Act 71, 73
Countryside Code 72
credit cards 24, 26, 43
Cricklade 39, 86, **86**, **87**, 88
Crowmarsh Gifford 133, 137, **138**
Culham Cut/Lock 130, **131**
currency 26

Datchet **179**, 184
Day's Lock 130, 134, **135**
day walks 16, 48
daylight hours 15
debit cards 24, 26, 43
Didcot Power Station 130
difficulty of walk 11
digital mapping 43, 46
direction of walk 38
disabled access 28
distance charts 250-3
diversions, London 220
dogs 21, 28, 72, 244-5
Dorchester-on-Thames 130, 134, **135**, 136
Dorney Lake 172, **177**
Dorney Reach 176
drinking water 24, 73, 75
driving: from Europe 50; within Britain 54-5
Dumsey Meadow **191**, 192
duration of walk 11-12

East Molesey 192, 194, 196, **197**
Eel Pie Island **206**, 215
Egham 184, 187, **188**
emergencies & emergency services 27, 76
emergency signal 76
Environment Agency 10, 18, 48, 70, 97, 193, 241
environmental impact of walkers 69-71
equipment 40-3
erosion 69-70
Eton 172, **179**, 180-1, **181**
Eton College **179**, 180
etymology, Thames 44
European Health Insurance Cards (EHICs) 26-7
evening meals 23-4
events 38-9
Ewen 81, **81**, 82
exchange rates 26
extension path 242
Eynsham/Eynsham Lock 107, 110, **111**, 112

Father Thames *see* Old Father Thames
ferry services
    to Britain 50
    on the Path 192, 196, **197**, **206**, 215, 242
festivals 38-9
field guides 50
first-aid kit 42
fish 68
fish ladders 151
flashlights *see* torches
flash locks 96-7
flights to Britain 50
flooding 76, 204
flora & fauna 50, 61-8, 70
flowers 62-3
food 22-4, 42
food stores 31, 33, 35
    see also place name
footwear 40-1
Fulham **213**, **214**, 220
Fulham Palace **213**, 217

geography of the Thames 45
gloves 41

Godstow Abbey 107, **114**
Godstow Lock 108, **114**
Goring 39, 142, **145**, 146
Goring Gap 45, 142, **145**
GPS & waypoints 17-18, 43, 246-8
Grahame, Kenneth 49, 66, 147, 148, 151
Greenwich 39, 238, **239**, 240, 242
Greenwich Foot Tunnel 230, 234, 237, **239**, 240
Greenwich Mean Time (GMT) 27
guesthouses 20-1, 29
guidebooks 47
guided holidays 25, 27

Hambledon Lock 164, **164**
Ham Lands Nature Reserve 204, **205**
Hammersmith/Hammersmith Bridge **212**, 216, 219-20
Hammerton's Ferry **206**, 215
Hampton Court 192, 194, **198**, 198-9
Hampton Court Palace 198, **198**
    Flower Show 39
Hampton Ferry 196, **197**
Hampton Wick 193, **199**, 200-1
Hardwick Estate 148, 151, **152**
hats 41
hazards 75-6
head of navigation (Thames) 89, **93**
health 73-4
health insurance 26-7
heat exhaustion 74
heatstroke 74
Henley-on-Thames 39, 151, 160, **161**, 162-4, **163**
Henley Royal Regatta 39, 160
history
    bridges in London 228-9
    city of London 200-1
    path 9
    River Thames 45

hostels 19-20, 29, 31, 33, 35
hotels 21-2, 29
Houses of Parliament **225**, 229, 232-3
Hurley/Hurley Lock 164, 166, **167**
hyperthermia 74
hypothermia 74

Iffley Lock **121**, 123
Iffley Meadows Nature Reserve 63, **121**, 123
Inglesham 88, **93**
inns *see* pubs
insects 61
insurance 26-7, pet 244
Isis, river 44
Isle of Dogs 234, **235**, 237
Isleworth **207**, 217-18
itineraries 36-8

Jerome K Jerome 49, 126, 150, 156
John F Kennedy Memorial 186, **187**

Kelmscott 98, **99**, 100
Kemble 79, **80**, 81
Kew/Kew Bridge 204, **210**
Kew Riverside Park Snail Reserve 68, **210**
Kew Royal Botanic Gardens **210**, 217
King's Lock 107, 112, **113**
Kingston Bridge 192-3, **199**
Kingston upon Thames 193, **199**, 201-4, **203**

Laleham 184, **189**, 190
Lambeth/Lambeth Bridge **223**, 224
Lambeth Palace & Garden Museum 221, **223**, 232
Lechlade 38, 44, 88, 90, **93**, **94**, 94-5
length
    of the path 7
    of the river 44
Limehouse **227**, 234, **235**, 236
litter 69, 72

locks 96-7
see also place name
London Bridge **225**, 228, 229, 230
London's boundary 193
London's bridges 228-9
London Docklands 39, **227**, 233, **235**, 236
London Eye 221, **225**, 232
London Stone **188**, 193
Long Distance Walkers' Association 48
Long Wittenham Nature Reserve 134
Lower Shiplake 151, **158**, 159
Lower Wolvercote 112, **114**
luggage transfer 25, 78
lunches 23
Lyd Well **80**, 81

Magna Carta Island/ Monument 186, **187**
Maidenhead 174-6, **175**
mammals 66-8
map keys 249
map scale 77
Mapledurham House 148, 151, **152**
Mapledurham Lock 151, **152**
maps 43, 44-6
Marble Hill House **206**, 215, 217
Marlow 39, 168-70, **168**, **169**
Marsh Lock 151, **159**
meals 22-3
Millennium Bridge **225**, 229, 230
minimum impact walking 6, 69-73
mobile phones 27
Molesey Lock 192, **198**
money 24-5, 43-4
Morris, William 100
Mortlake 209-12, **211**
Moulsford 142, **144**

national holidays 26
National Trails 9, 17, 48

National Trust 26, 70, 100, 170, 186
Natural England 9, 70
nature reserves 70, 82, 98, 123, 134, 204
Newbridge 98, 104, **106**
North Meadow NNR 63, 70, 82, **85**
Northmoor Lock 107, **108**, 110
Nuneham House 123, **125** 126

Old Father Thames 46, 76, 95, 160, 221
Old London Bridge 201, 228, 229
Old Windsor/Old Windsor Lock 184, **185**, 186
online information 48
Orleans House **206**, 215, 217
Osney Bridge/Lock 115, **115**
Oxford 108, 112, 114, 115, **115**, 116-18, **119**, 120, **121**, 122-3
Oxford & Cambridge Boat Race *see* Boat Race
Oyster cards, London 60

Palace of Westminster *see* Houses of Parliament
Pangbourne 142, 147-8, **149**, **150**, 150
Penton Hook Island/Penton Hook Lock 184, **189**
phones *see* mobile phones
pill boxes 95
Pimlico **222**, 230-1
Pinkhill Lock 107, 110, **111**
Pool of London 201, **227**, 229, 232, 236
Port Meadow 108, **114**
Port of London Authority 70
post offices 24-5, 26, 30, 32, 34
pound locks 96-7, 123
public holidays 26
public transport 51-5, **56**, **57**, 58-60, 69
in London 55, 60
pubs 18, 21, 23, 26

Purley-on-Thames 151, **152**
Putney **213**, **214**, 214-15
Putney Bridge **213**, 229

Radcot/Radcot Bridge 98, 100, **101**
Radley 123, **125**, 126
rail services
in London 51, 53, 55, 60
to Britain 50
within Britain 51, 52-3, 54, **56**, **57**
rainfall chart 15
Ramblers 9, 48
rates, accommodation 22
Reading 39, 151-2, **152**, **153** 154, **154**, **155**, 156
recommended reading 46-7, 49-50
reptiles 68
restaurants 22-3
RHS flower shows
Chelsea 39
Hampton Court Palace 39
Richmond 193, 204, **206**, **207**, 208-9, **208**
Richmond Bridge **207**, **208**, 217, 229
Richmond Lock **207**
Ridgeway, The 142, **143**
right to roam 71, 73
river bus services, London 60
River Thames Society 9, 48
Rotherhithe **227**, 237, 238
route finding 17-18
rucksacks 40
Runnymede 184, 186-7, **187**
Rushey Lock **102**, 104

safety 74-6
Sandford 'Lasher' weir 123, **124**, 126
Sandford Lock 123, **124**
Sandford-on-Thames **124**, 125
school holidays 26
seasons 12-15
self-catering supplies 24
self-guided holidays 25-8
Shepard, EH 148, 151

Shepperton/Shepperton
  Lock 192, 194, **195**
Shepperton to Weybridge
  ferry 192, **195**
Shifford 98
Shifford Lock 104, **105**
Shillingford 130, 136-7,
  136
Shiplake **158**, 159
  see also Lower Shiplake
shops 26
signposts 17, 220
Sinodun Hills 130, 134, **135**
Sites of Special Scientific
  Interest (SSSIs) 70, 170,
  192
smoking 27
Somerford Keynes 81, 82,
  83
Sonning 151, **157**, 157-9
source of the River
  Thames 79, **80**
Southbank Centre 221, **225**
Southwark 224, **225**, 226
Southwark Bridge **225**, 229
Spencer, Stanley 46, 174
St John's Lock 46, 76, **93**,
  95, 98, 100
St Mary/Virgin Mary
  churches 116
St Paul's Cathedral 90,
  225, 231, 233
Staines 184, **188**, **189**, 190
Standlake **106**, 107
Strand on the Green **210**,
  218-19
Streatley 39, 142, **145**, 146
sunburn 74
Sunbury Lock 192, **196**
swan upping 39
Swift Ditch 123, **127**
swimming 75
Swinford Toll Bridge 107,
  111
Syon Park & House 204,
  207, 215, 217

Tadpole Bridge **103**, 104
Taplow **175**
Tate Britain 46, 174, **223**,
  229, 233
Tate Modern 221, **225**, 232

Teddington 193, **205**, 215,
  216
Teddington Lock 44, 204,
  205, 216
telephones *see* mobile
  phones
temperature chart 15
Temple Island 160, 164, **164**
Temple Lock 164, **167**
Thames Barrier 241, 242,
  243
Thames, The
  facts & figures 44-5
  festival 39
  head of navigation 89, **93**
  literature 47
  music 46
  painting 46
  poetry 47
  sculpture 46
  source 79, **80**
  tidal 204, **205**
Thames Head 79, **80**
Thames Lock **207**, 216
Thames-Severn Canal 89,
  90, **93**
Tilehurst 151, **153**
toiletries 42
toilets 71
toll booths/bridges 90, **93**,
  107, **111**, 147, **149**, 229
torches 42, 76
tourist information centres
  (TICs) 30, 32, 34, 48
Tower Bridge 221, **227**, 230
  northern bank 232-3
  southern bank 226, 228
Tower of London **227**,
  230, 233
town facilities 30-5
trail maps 77-8
trains *see* rail services
Transport for London (TfL)
  60
travel insurance 26-7
trees 63-4, 208
Trewsbury Mead 79, **80**, 90
Turner, JMW 46, 174, 204
Twickenham **206**, 215,
  216-17
Twickenham Bridge **207**
Upper Inglesham 88

Vauxhall/Vauxhall Bridge
  223, 224, 229
viaducts 142, **144**
village facilities 30-5

walkers' organisations 48
walking alone 75
walking companies 25-8
walking poles 42
walking times 77
Wallingford 39, **138**,
  139-41, **140**
Wallingford Castle, site of
  133, **138**, 139
Walton-on-Thames 192,
  194, **195**, **196**
Wandsworth/Wandsworth
  Bridge **213**, 221, 223
Wapping **227**, 234
water, drinking 24, 73
water bottles/pouches 42
Waterloo Bridge **225**, 229
weather 15
weather forecasts 76
weekend walks 16
weights and measures 27
weirs 96, **124**, 126, 151
Westminster **223**, 231
Westminster Abbey **225**,
  229, 233
Westminster Bridge **225**,
  229
whistles 42, 76
Whitchurch-on-Thames
  142, 147, **149**
wi-fi 25
wild camping 19
Wimbledon Lawn Tennis
  Championships 39
Windsor 39, 172, **178**, **179**,
  181-4, **181**
Windsor Castle 170, 181,
  181, 182
Wittenham Clumps 130,
  134, **135**
Woolwich 242
Wytham Woods 107, **113**

Youth Hostels Association
  (YHA) 19

TRAILBLAZER'S LONG-DISTANCE PATH (LDP) WALKING GUIDES

We've applied to destinations which are closer to home Trailblazer's proven formula for publishing definitive practical route guides for adventurous travellers. Britain's network of long-distance trails enables the walker to explore some of the finest landscapes in the country's best walking areas. These are guides that are user-friendly, practical, informative and environmentally sensitive.

'The same attention to detail that distinguishes its other guides has been brought to bear here'.
THE SUNDAY TIMES

● **Unique mapping features** In many walking guidebooks the reader has to read a route description then try to relate it to the map. Our guides are much easier to use because walking directions, tricky junctions, places to stay and eat, points of interest and walking times are all written onto the maps themselves in the places to which they apply. With their uncluttered clarity, these are not general-purpose maps but fully edited maps drawn by walkers for walkers.

● **Largest-scale walking maps** At a scale of just under 1:20,000 (8cm or 3¹/₈ inches to one mile) the maps in these guides are bigger than even the most detailed British walking maps currently available in the shops.

● **Not just a trail guide – includes where to stay, where to eat and public transport** Our guidebooks cover the complete walking experience, not just the route. Accommodation options for all budgets are provided (pubs, hotels, B&Bs, campsites, bunkhouses, hostels) as well as places to eat. Detailed public transport information for all access points to each trail means that there are itineraries for all walkers, for hiking the entire route as well as for day or weekend walks.

● **Includes downloadable GPS waypoints** Marked on our maps and downloadable from the Trailblazer website.

Cleveland Way *Henry Stedman*, 1st edn, ISBN 978-1-905864-91-1, 208pp, 56 maps

Coast to Coast *Henry Stedman*, 8th edn, ISBN 978-1-905864-96-6, 268pp, 110 maps

Cornwall Coast Path (SW Coast Path Pt 2) *Henry Stedman & Joel Newton*, 5th edn, ISBN 978-1-905864-71-3, 352pp, 142 maps

Cotswold Way *Tricia & Bob Hayne*, 3rd edn, ISBN 978-1-905864-70-6, 204pp, 53 maps

Dales Way *Henry Stedman*, 1st edn, ISBN 978-1-905864-78-2, 192pp, 50 maps

Dorset & South Devon (SW Coast Path Pt 3) *Henry Stedman & Joel Newton*, 2nd edn, ISBN 978-1-905864-94-2, 336pp, 88 maps

Exmoor & North Devon (SW Coast Path Pt 1) *Henry Stedman & Joel Newton*, 2nd edn, ISBN 978-1-905864-86-7, 224pp, 68 maps

Great Glen Way *Jim Manthorpe*, 1st edn, ISBN 978-1-905864-80-5, 192pp, 55 maps

Hadrian's Wall Path *Henry Stedman*, 5th edn, ISBN 978-1-905864-85-0, 224pp, 60 maps

Norfolk Coast Path & Peddars Way *Alexander Stewart*, 1st edn, ISBN 978-1-905864-98-0, 224pp, 75 maps,

North Downs Way *Henry Stedman*, 2nd edn, ISBN 978-1-905864-90-4, 240pp, 98 maps

Offa's Dyke Path *Keith Carter*, 4th edn, ISBN 978-1-905864-65-2, 240pp, 98 maps

Pembrokeshire Coast Path *Jim Manthorpe*, 5th edn, ISBN 978-1-905864-84-3, 236pp, 96 maps

Pennine Way *Stuart Greig*, 4th edn, ISBN 978-1-905864-61-4, 272pp, 138 maps

The Ridgeway *Nick Hill*, 4th edn, ISBN 978-1-905864-79-9, 208pp, 53 maps

South Downs Way *Jim Manthorpe*, 6th edn, ISBN 978-1-905864-93-5, 204pp, 60 maps

Thames Path *Joel Newton*, 2nd edn, ISBN 978-1-905864-97-3, 256pp, 99 maps

West Highland Way *Charlie Loram*, 6th edn, ISBN 978-1-905864-76-8, 218pp, 60 maps

'The Trailblazer series stands head, shoulders, waist and ankles above the rest. They are particularly strong on mapping ...'
THE SUNDAY TIMES

TRAILBLAZER

British Walking Guides

SEE OVERLEAF FOR FULL TITLE LIST

Orkney

Thurso

Stornoway ○

Scottish Highlands Hillwalking Guide

Skye

○ Inverness

Great Glen Way

Aberdeen ○

SCOTLAND

Fort William ○

Mull

West Highland Way

Milngavie ○
Glasgow ○

Edinburgh

Berwick upon Tweed

Kirk Yetholm ○

Arran

Pennine Way

. IRELAND

○ **Belfast**

Bowness-on-Solway ○
Carlisle ○

Hadrian's Wall Path

○ Wallsend
Newcastle upon Tyne ○

Coast to Coast

St Bees ○
Bowness-on-Windermere ○

Robin Hood's Bay ○

○ Filey

EP. OF ELAND

Isle of Man

Dales Way

Helmsley ○

Cleveland Way

○ Dublin

○ Ilkley ○ York

Hull ○

Pennine Way

Leeds ○

IRISH SEA

Liverpool ○ Manchester ○ Edale

Norfolk Coast Path & Peddars Way

Anglesey

Prestatyn ○

Lincoln ○

Bangor ○ ○ Crewe

Cromer ○
Norwich ○

ENGLAND

Great Yarmouth

Nottingham ○

Birmingham ○

Knettishall Heath

Offa's Dyke Path

Cambridge ○

Cardigan ○

Cotswold Way

WALES

Chipping Campden ○

The Ridgeway

Amroth ○

Kemble ○

Ivinghoe Beacon ○

Pembrokeshire Coast Path

Chepstow ○

London

Thames Path

Cardiff ○
Bristol ○

Bath ○ Overton Hill ○

Canterbury ○

Exmoor & N Devon Coast Path

Winchester ○ Farnham ○

Dover ○

Minehead ○

Salisbury ○

North Downs Way

Bude ○

Portsmouth ○

Brighton ○

Eastbourne ○

Cornwall Coast Path

Exeter ○

Poole ○

South Downs Way

Plymouth ○

Isle of Wight

Dorset & S Devon Coast Path

es of
cilly

| 0 | 50 | 100km |
| 0 | 25 | 50 miles |

TRAILBLAZER TITLE LIST

Adventure Cycle-Touring Handbook
Adventure Motorcycling Handbook
Australia by Rail
Cleveland Way (British Walking Guide)
Coast to Coast (British Walking Guide)
Cornwall Coast Path (British Walking Guide)
Cotswold Way (British Walking Guide)
The Cyclist's Anthology
Dales Way (British Walking Guide)
Dorset & Sth Devon Coast Path (British Walking Gde)
Exmoor & Nth Devon Coast Path (British Walking Gde)
Great Glen Way (British Walking Guide)
Hadrian's Wall Path (British Walking Guide)
Himalaya by Bike – a route and planning guide
Inca Trail, Cusco & Machu Picchu
Japan by Rail
Kilimanjaro – the trekking guide (includes Mt Meru)
Madeira Walks – 37 selected day walks
Moroccan Atlas – The Trekking Guide
Morocco Overland (4WD/motorcycle/mountainbike)
Nepal Trekking & The Great Himalaya Trail
New Zealand – The Great Walks
North Downs Way (British Walking Guide)
Offa's Dyke Path (British Walking Guide)
Overlanders' Handbook – worldwide driving guide
Peddars Way & Norfolk Coast Path (British Walking Gde)
Pembrokeshire Coast Path (British Walking Guide)
Pennine Way (British Walking Guide)
Peru's Cordilleras Blanca & Huayhuash – Hiking/Biking
The Railway Anthology
The Ridgeway (British Walking Guide)
Sahara Overland – a route and planning guide
Scottish Highlands – Hillwalking Guide
Siberian BAM Guide – rail, rivers & road
The Silk Roads – a route and planning guide
Sinai – the trekking guide
South Downs Way (British Walking Guide)
Thames Path (British Walking Guide)
Tour du Mont Blanc
Trans-Canada Rail Guide
Trans-Siberian Handbook
Trekking in the Everest Region
The Walker's Anthology
The Walker's Anthology – further tales
The Walker's Haute Route – Mont Blanc to Matterhorn
West Highland Way (British Walking Guide)

For more information about Trailblazer and our
expanding range of guides, for guidebook updates or
for credit card mail order sales visit our website:

www.trailblazer-guides.com

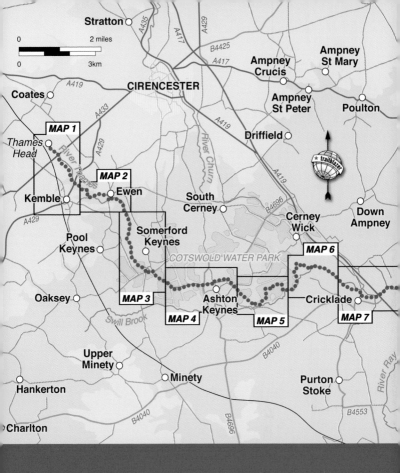

Stratton

2 miles
3km

CIRENCESTER

Ampney Crucis
Ampney St Mary

Coates

MAP 1

Thames Head

Ampney St Peter
Poulton

Kemble

MAP 2   Ewen

Driffield

Pool Keynes

Somerford Keynes

South Cerney

Cerney Wick

Down Ampney

COTSWOLD WATER PARK

MAP 6

Oaksey

MAP 3

Ashton Keynes

Cricklade

MAP 4   *MAP 5*   *MAP 7*

Upper Minety

Minety

Purton Stoke

Hankerton

Charlton

Thames Head

Cricklade

Thames Barrier

Maps 1-7
Thames Head to Cricklade
12¼ miles/19.7km – 4¼-5hrs
NOTE: Add 20-30% to these times to allow for stops

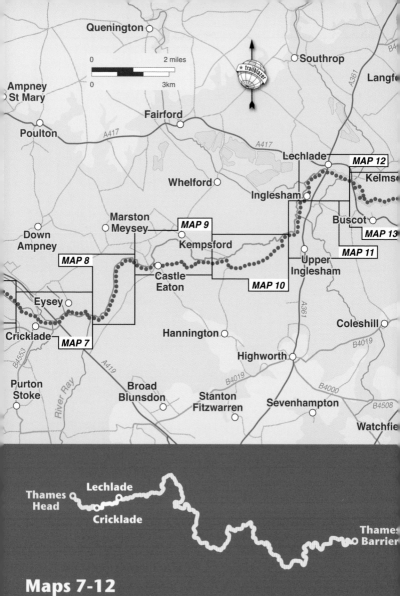

Maps 7-12
Cricklade to Lechlade
11 miles/17.7km — 3¾-4¾hrs
NOTE: Add 20-30% to these times to allow for stops

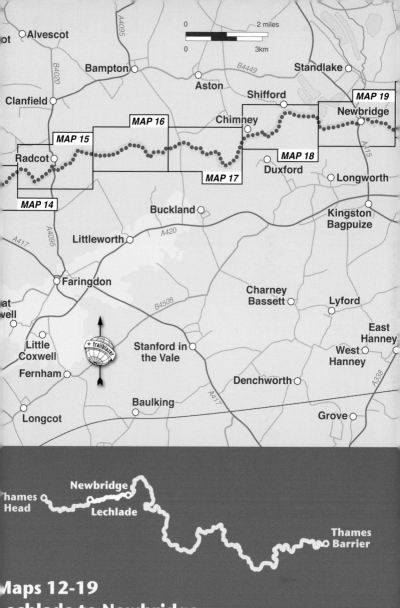

Maps 12-19
Lechlade to Newbridge

6¾ miles/26.7km – 5-6½hrs

NOTE: Add 20-30% to these times to allow for stops

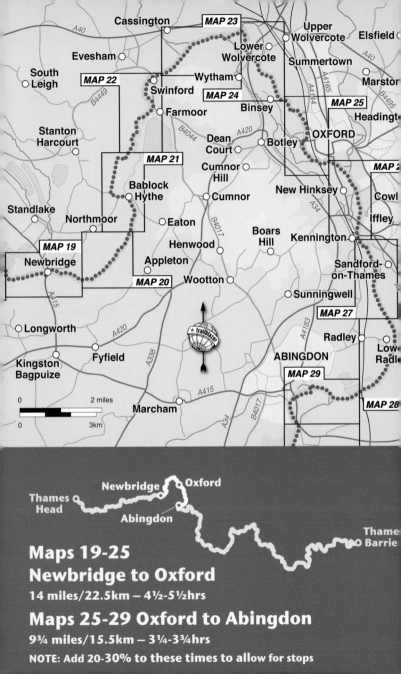

MAP 23

Cassington

Upper
Wolvercote   Elsfield

A40

Evesham

South
Leigh

MAP 22

Lower
Wolvercote

Summertown

Marsto

Wytham

A4165

B4449

Swinford

MAP 24

MAP 25

Stanton
Harcourt

Farmoor

Binsey

Headingt

B4044

Dean
Court

A420

Botley

OXFORD

A414

MAP 21

Cumnor
Hill

MAP 2

Bablock
Hythe

Cumnor

New Hinksey

Cowl

Standlake

Northmoor

Eaton

B4017

A34

Iffley

Henwood

Boars
Hill

Kennington

MAP 19

Appleton

Sandford-
on-Thames

Newbridge

MAP 20

Wootton

A415

Sunningwell

Longworth

A420

MAP 27

A4183

Radley

Low
Radl

A338

Fyfield

ABINGDON

Kingston
Bagpuize

MAP 29

MAP 28

A415

2 miles

Marcham

A34

B4017

0
3km

Newbridge   Oxford

Thames
Head

Abingdon

Thame
Barrie

Maps 19-25
Newbridge to Oxford
14 miles/22.5km – 4½-5½hrs

Maps 25-29 Oxford to Abingdon
9¾ miles/15.5km – 3¼-3¾hrs

NOTE: Add 20-30% to these times to allow for stops

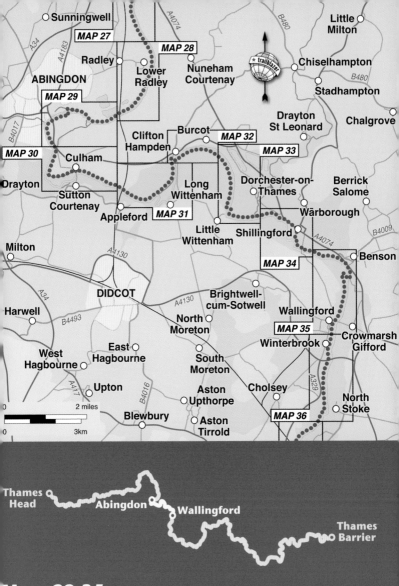

Thames
Head

Abingdon

Wallingford

Thames
Barrier

Maps 29-35
Abingdon to Wallingford
13½ miles/22km – 4½-5½hrs
NOTE: Add 20-30% to these times to allow for stops

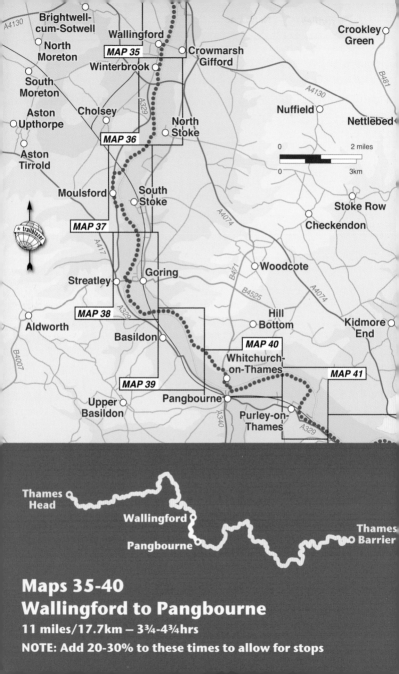

A4130

Brightwell-
cum-Sotwell

North
Moreton

Wallingford

MAP 35

Crowmarsh
Gifford

Winterbrook

South
Moreton

Cholsey

A329

North
Stoke

Crookley
Green

B481

Aston
Upthorpe

MAP 36

Nuffield

Nettlebed

Aston
Tirrold

Moulsford

South
Stoke

A4074

Stoke Row

MAP 37

A417

Checkendon

Streatley

Goring

B471

Woodcote

MAP 38

A329

Aldworth

Basildon

B4525

A4074

Hill
Bottom

Kidmore
End

B4007

MAP 39

Upper
Basildon

MAP 40

Whitchurch-
on-Thames

Pangbourne

A340

MAP 41

Purley-on-
Thames

A329

0   2 miles

0   3km

Thames
Head

Wallingford

Pangbourne

Thames
Barrier

Maps 35-40
Wallingford to Pangbourne
11 miles/17.7km — 3¾-4¾hrs
NOTE: Add 20-30% to these times to allow for stops

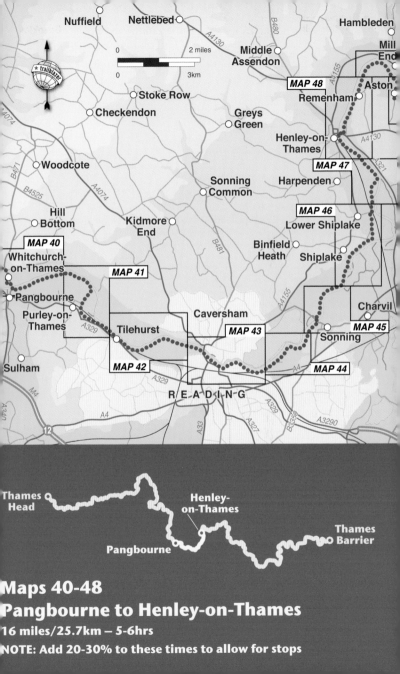

Nuffield
Nettlebed
Hambleden
Mill End
Middle Assenden
MAP 48
Aston
Remenham
Stoke Row
Greys Green
Checkendon
Henley-on-Thames
MAP 47
Woodcote
Sonning Common
Harpenden
MAP 46
Hill Bottom
Kidmore End
Lower Shiplake
Binfield Heath
Shiplake
MAP 40
Whitchurch-on-Thames
Charvil
MAP 45
Pangbourne
MAP 41
Purley-on-Thames
Tilehurst
Caversham
MAP 43
Sulham
Sonning
MAP 42
MAP 44
R E A D I N G
12

Thames Head

Henley-on-Thames

Pangbourne

Thames Barrier

Maps 40-48
Pangbourne to Henley-on-Thames
16 miles/25.7km – 5-6hrs
NOTE: Add 20-30% to these times to allow for stops

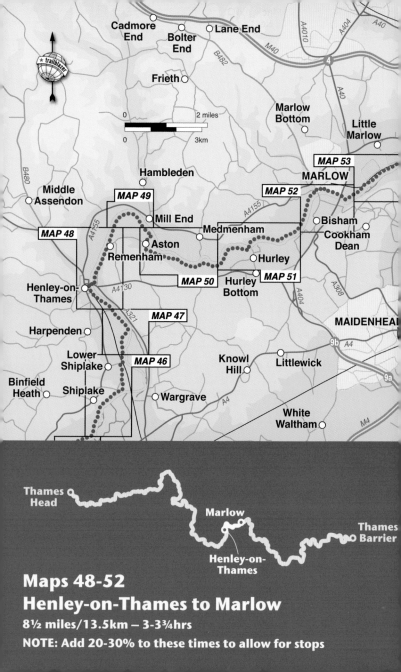

Maps 48-52
Henley-on-Thames to Marlow
8½ miles/13.5km – 3-3¾hrs
NOTE: Add 20-30% to these times to allow for stops

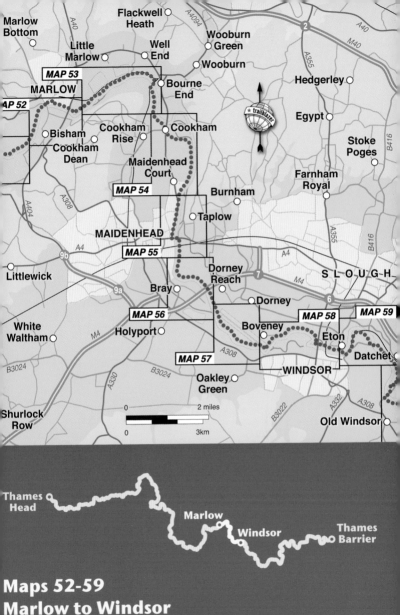

Maps 52-59
Marlow to Windsor
14¼ miles/22.7km – 5-6hrs
NOTE: Add 20-30% to these times to allow for stops

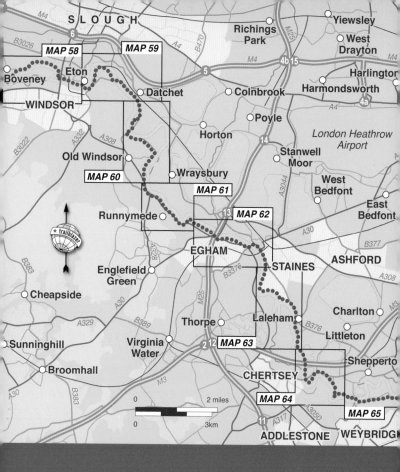

SLOUGH

MAP 58
MAP 59

Richings Park

Yiewsley

West Drayton

Boveney
Eton
WINDSOR
Datchet
Colnbrook
Harmondsworth
Harlington

Poyle

Old Windsor
Horton

London Heathrow Airport

MAP 60
Wraysbury
Stanwell Moor

West Bedfont

East Bedfont

Runnymede
MAP 61
MAP 62
13

trailblazer

EGHAM
STAINES
ASHFORD

Englefield Green

Cheapside

Thorpe
Laleham
Charlton
Littleton

Sunninghill

Virginia Water
MAP 63
Shepperton

Broomhall
CHERTSEY
MAP 64

0   2 miles
0   3km

MAP 65
11
ADDLESTONE
WEYBRIDGE

Thames Head

Windsor

Thames Barrier

Chertsey Bridge

Maps 59-64
Windsor to Chertsey Bridge
12 miles/19.5km – 4-5¼hrs
NOTE: Add 20-30% to these times to allow for stops

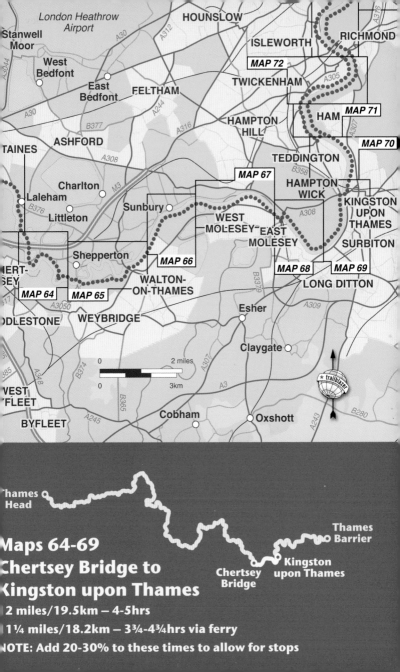

London Heathrow Airport

Stanwell Moor

West Bedfont

East Bedfont

FELTHAM

HOUNSLOW

ISLEWORTH

RICHMOND

MAP 72

TWICKENHAM

HAMPTON HILL

HAM

MAP 71

MAP 70

ASHFORD

TAINES

Charlton

Laleham

Littleton

Sunbury

MAP 67

TEDDINGTON

HAMPTON WICK

KINGSTON UPON THAMES

WEST MOLESEY

EAST MOLESEY

SURBITON

Shepperton

MAP 66

MAP 68

MAP 69

HERT-SEY

MAP 64

MAP 65

WALTON-ON-THAMES

LONG DITTON

DDLESTONE

WEYBRIDGE

Esher

VEST FLEET

BYFLEET

Cobham

Oxshott

Claygate

trailblazer

0 — 2 miles

0 — 3km

Thames Head

Thames Barrier

Maps 64-69
Chertsey Bridge to
Kingston upon Thames

Chertsey Bridge

Kingston upon Thames

2 miles/19.5km – 4-5hrs

1¼ miles/18.2km – 3¾-4¾hrs via ferry

NOTE: Add 20-30% to these times to allow for stops

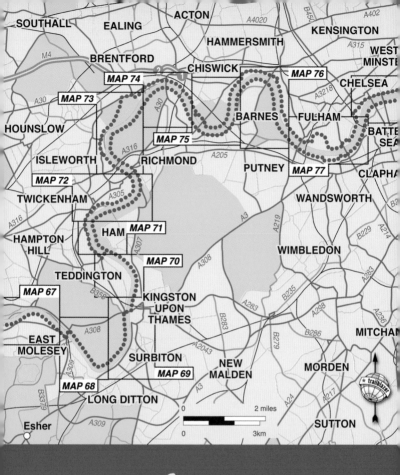

Maps 69-77
Kingston upon Thames
to Putney Bridge

16¼ miles/26km – 5¾-7hrs via northern bank

13½ miles/21.7km – 4½-5¼hrs via southern bank

NOTE: Add 20-30% to these times to allow for stops

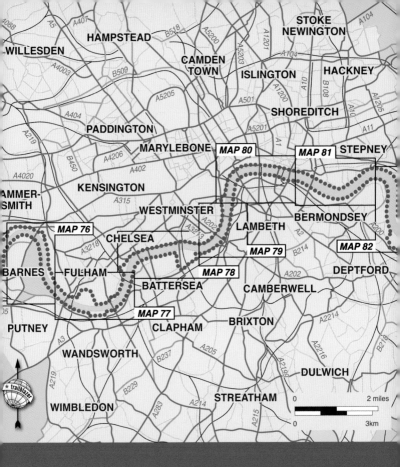

Maps 77-81
Putney Bridge to Tower Bridge
10 miles/16km – 3¼-4¼hrs via northern bank
9¼ miles/14.7km – 3½-4¾hrs via southern bank
NOTE: Add 20-30% to these times to allow for stops

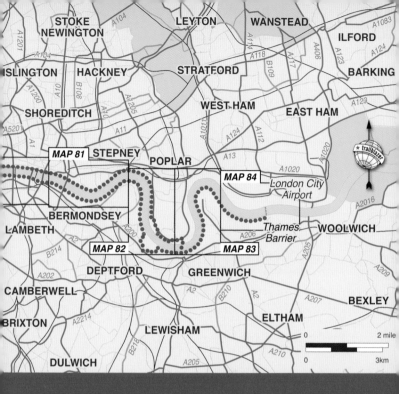

Maps 81-84
Tower Bridge to G̶̶̶̶̶̶̶̶̶

6¾ miles/11km – 2¼-2¾hrs via northern bank

5¾ miles/9.2km – 2-2½hrs via southern bank

Greenwich to the Thames Barrier

4½ miles/7km – 1½-1¾hrs

NOTE: Add 20-30% to these times to allow for stops

JAN 0 8 '19

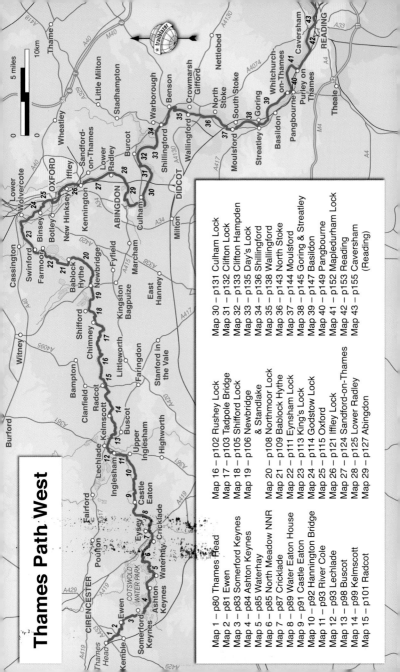

Thames Path West

Map 1 – p80 Thames Head
Map 2 – p81 Ewen
Map 3 – p83 Somerford Keynes
Map 4 – p84 Ashton Keynes
Map 5 – p85 Waterhay
Map 6 – p85 North Meadow NNR
Map 7 – p87 Cricklade
Map 8 – p89 Water Eaton House
Map 9 – p91 Castle Eaton
Map 10 – p92 Hannington Bridge
Map 11 – p93 River Cole
Map 12 – p93 Lechlade
Map 13 – p98 Buscot
Map 14 – p99 Kelmscott
Map 15 – p101 Radcot

Map 16 – p102 Rushey Lock
Map 17 – p103 Tadpole Bridge
Map 18 – p105 Shifford Lock
Map 19 – p106 Newbridge
         & Standlake
Map 20 – p108 Northmoor Lock
Map 21 – p109 Bablock Hythe
Map 22 – p111 Eynsham Lock
Map 23 – p113 King's Lock
Map 24 – p114 Godstow Lock
Map 25 – p115 Oxford
Map 26 – p121 Iffley Lock
Map 27 – p124 Sandford-on-Thames
Map 28 – p125 Lower Radley
Map 29 – p127 Abingdon

Map 30 – p131 Culham Lock
Map 31 – p132 Clifton Lock
Map 32 – p133 Clifton Hampden
Map 33 – p135 Day's Lock
Map 34 – p136 Shillingford
Map 35 – p138 Wallingford
Map 36 – p143 North Stoke
Map 37 – p144 Moulsford
Map 38 – p145 Goring & Streatley
Map 39 – p147 Basildon
Map 40 – p149 Pangbourne
Map 41 – p152 Mapledurham Lock
Map 42 – p153 Reading
Map 43 – p155 Caversham
         (Reading)

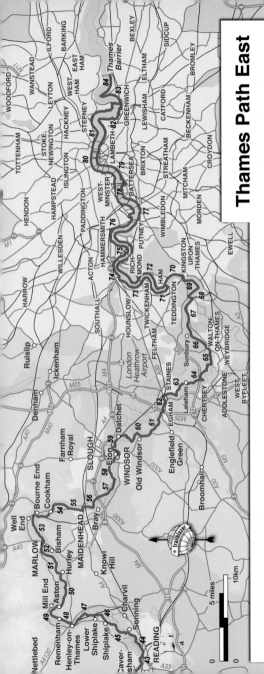

Thames Path East

Map 43 – p155 Caversham
Map 44 – p156 Reading Boat Club
Map 45 – p157 Sonning
Map 46 – p158 Lower Shiplake
Map 47 – p159 Marsh Lock
Map 48 – p161 Henley-on-Thames
Map 49 – p164 Temple Island
Map 50 – p165 Aston
Map 51 – p167 Hurley
Map 52 – p168 Marlow
Map 53 – p171 Bourne End

Map 54 – p173 Cookham
Map 55 – p175 Maidenhead
Map 56 – p176 Bray Lock
Map 57 – p177 Dorney Lake
Map 58 – p178 Boveney
Map 59 – p179 Eton & Windsor
Map 60 – p185 Old Windsor
Map 61 – p187 Runnymede
Map 62 – p188 Egham
Map 63 – p189 Staines
Map 64 – p191 Chertsey

Map 65 – p195 Shepperton Lock
Map 66 – p196 Walton-on-Thames
Map 67 – p197 West & East Molesey
Map 68 – p198 Hampton Court Palace
Map 69 – p199 Kingston upon Thames
Map 70 – p205 Teddington
Map 71 – p205 Ham
Map 72 – p206 Twickenham
Map 73 – p207 Richmond
Map 74 – p210 Brentford & Kew

Map 75 – p211 Chiswick Bridge
Map 76 – p213 Hammersmith Bridge
Map 77 – p213 Putney & Fulham
Map 78 – p222 Chelsea Bridge
Map 79 – p223 Vauxhall Bridge
Map 80 – p225 Southwark
Map 81 – p227 Tower Bridge
Map 82 – p235 Canary Wharf
Map 83 – p239 Greenwich Foot Tunnel
Map 84 – p243 Thames Barrier